D1378308

WOULD YOU LIKE TO KNOW SOMETHING ABOUT ISLAM?

THE TIME IS RIPE

MOHAMMAD MASOOD AHMED

CRESCENT BOOKS INC.

Published by

CRESCENT BOOKS INC.
NEW YORK, USA

Copyright © Mohammad Masood Ahmed, 2011

To reach the author and for general inquiries, please contact:

Crescent Books Inc.
P.O. Box 786
Wingdale, NY 12594-1435
www.crescent-books.com
info@crescent-books.com

Cover & book designed by MANSOOR AHMED

PRINTED IN THE UNITED STATES OF AMERICA

10 9 8 7 6 5 4 3 2 1

First Edition

ISBN 978-0-9836003-1-2 (Hardback)
ISBN 978-0-9836003-2-9 (Paperback)

With the Grace of Allah ﷻ, I dedicate this work to
every seeker of truth who found [it]
and acquired ultimate success;

To my mother, who showed me how to crawl and
take the first steps of my life;

And to my teachers and mentors who taught me how
to distinguish between right and wrong, just and
unjust, who defined the value of knowledge and the
consequences of ignorance, and filled my heart with
love for all, and much more.

—◆ ✕ ◆—

May Allah ﷻ bless their souls and elevate
their status in the Hereafter.

Acknowledgments

RATEFULNESS IS A VIRTUE, and in Islam, being grateful is a religious obligation on Muslims. Muslims are to thank the Lord for His bounties verbally and physically, and to thank people for their help and favors. The Prophet Muhammad ﷺ once said, "Anyone who is not grateful to people can never be grateful to Allah ﷻ."

I cannot thank the Lord Almighty enough for His bounties and blessings, the beloved Prophet Muhammad ﷺ for his sacrifices and hard work for Islam, and the righteous scholars of Islam who preserved and propagated it. I am deeply indebted to all my teachers and mentors, specifically Chaudhry Mohammad Iqbal Hameed Suharwardy, Shah Ahmad Noorani Siddiqui, Dr. Professor Muhammad Mas'ud Ahmed (may Allah ﷻ bless their souls and elevate their status), and to Shaykh-ul-Hadith Allama Mohammad Nasrullah Khan, Mufti Mohammad Athar Naeemi, Mohammad Ibrahim (Bholey Baba), and Shaykh-ul-Islam, Syed Mohammad Madni Ashrafi Jilani (may Allah ﷻ grant them all a long life).

I am also indebted to my wife Rukhsana for her lifelong companionship, and to my brothers and sisters, their spouses and my nieces and nephews for their moral and financial support throughout, especially to Fareed for his hard work.

This book could not have taken its current shape without the untiring efforts of my son Mansoor and my younger brother Waseem, who edited, typed, and designed it many times over. I am grateful to Mufti and Imam Fakhruddin Alvi, who provided many religious references and advice, and to Mohamed Iqbal, Imtiaz Ameen, Sharif Patel, and Afroz Ashrafi of the UK for their suggestions and comments. Much financial and moral support came from Imam Alvi, Aijaz, Ghazala, Nuzhat, Fareed, Tahmina, Hina, Iqbal, and Maqsood in publishing this book.

To avoid injustice, it is incumbent upon me to thank all those who have helped me in my religious endeavors, including Syed Riaz Ali, Masroor Ali Qureshi, Saiyed Shokat Ali, Sabbir Ismail Patel, and Mufti Mohammad Ayyoub Ashrafi.

A special thanks goes to Dr. Jerald F. Dirks for his sincere editing and input, who although he humbly considers himself a devoted student, he is certainly a renowned scholar of Islam, a man of great insight and dedication, and the author of several remarkable books. I also thank him for writing the Foreword.

Of course, in reality it is Allah ﷻ Who guides, helps, and sustains but does so through people and other means. Certainly, the knowledge and experience I have gained from living in America for the last 30 years has taught me a lot, and for this I am grateful as well.

I finally pray for each and everyone who contributed in this effort in any capacity. May Allah ﷻ bless them all.

Benediction

Allah's ﷻ Name I begin with, Who created the Heavens and the Earth and everything in it, from Whom we all came and to Whom we must return. I thank Him for His divine help and guidance, through which I am able to embark on this great task of providing knowledge and guidance to my fellow man. I pray to the Lord for His blessings on us all, to assist us in seeking the Truth and acquiring 'ultimate success.' (Ameen!)

27th night of Blessed Ramadan, 1430
September 16th, 2009

Contents

About the Title

*D*URING THESE TIMES, when people desire to know every-thing about Islam and Muslims, and many already know a lot, either through the news, electronic media, books or what have you, my asking the question "Would you like to know something about Islam" may offend some. One may feel either that I am ignorant of the fact that people already know so much about Islam or that I truly believe the majority is uninformed or misinformed about it.

By this title, I am *actually* asking, "Would you like to know something *real* about Islam?" It is my understanding that most people do not know anything *real* about Islam. If my understanding is correct, how can I ask people to know 'everything' about the *real* Islam, when, as per my understanding, they do not know 'anything' about it?

Islam is an ocean of knowledge; no matter how much is extracted from it, a lot more is still there to be explored. Thus, at this pre-liminary stage, I can only ask the reader to know 'something' about Islam. Rest assured, you will realize by the time you finish reading this book that even this 'something' is 'a lot' with which to begin. Moreover, readers will come to acknowledge that their prior under-standing of Islam was incomplete or incorrect had they not learned something *real* about Islam.

Among other things, the title of this book also reflects my sincere intent to invite you to study Islam, rather than to impose on you its beliefs.

Since new and controversial issues are emerging almost daily, the sooner we find solutions to current problems, the faster we will achieve worldwide stability, global peace, and security. Certainly, time is of the essence. Wasting time in fruitless efforts will only widen the gap and create more division among the world's communities. A proper understanding of Islam, among other things, is the essential ingredient that will put us many steps forward in achieving the desired goals. Thus, 'the time is ripe' to understand Islam now.

Humbly, I hope to enable you to have a better understanding of Islam and, as a result, its followers.

In support of my argument that the majority of people are uninformed about Islam, the following is the conclusion of surveys undertaken by the Pew Research Center over the course of nine years:

> As in previous Pew Research surveys, most Americans say they know little about the Muslim religion. Currently, 55% say they do not know very much (30%) or know nothing at all (25%) about the Muslim religion and its practices; 35% say they know some about the religion while just 9% say they know a great deal. These numbers are largely unchanged from 2007.

How Much Do You Know about Muslim Religion?

	Nov 2001 %	March 2002 %	July 2003 %	July 2005 %	Aug 2007 %	Aug 2010 %
A great deal	6	5	4	5	7	9
Some	32	29	27	28	34	35
Not very much	37	37	39	36	33	30
Nothing at all	24	28	29	30	25	25
Don't know	1	1	1	1	1	*
	100	100	100	100	100	100

PEW RESEARCH CENTER August 19-22, 2010.
Figures may not add to 100% because of rounding.

Foreword

T BETWEEN 1.5 AND 1.8 BILLION adherents, Islam is the second largest religion in the world and the fastest growing religion in both Europe and North America. Current estimates indicate that 02% of the population of Canada is Muslim and that 01-03% of the population of the United States is Muslim. The percentage of Muslims in the population is even greater for many European countries. For example, Albania's population is 70% Muslim, Austria 04%, Bosnia and Herzegovina 40%, Bulgaria 12%, Cyprus 18%, Denmark 02%, France 05-10%, Georgia 10%, Germany 04%, Greece 10%, Liechtenstein 05%, Macedonia 17%, Netherlands 06%, Russia 10-15%, Switzerland 04%, and the United Kingdom 03%.

Despite the impressive numbers cited above, non-Muslims in Europe and North America frequently have very little knowledge about Islam. Far more disturbing, however, is the fact that what these non-Muslims think they know about Islam is frequently nothing more than distortion or complete fabrication. The following examples should serve to illustrate this point.

In the months and years post September 11, 2001, numerous mass distributed e-mails have claimed that Qur'an 9:11—note that it is 9:11—talks about the destruction of tall buildings and the subsequent wrath of the eagle. Those e-mails go to great length to equate 9:11 with September 11th and the eagle with the United States. There's just one thing wrong with this e-mail, i.e., Qur'an 9:11 mentions neither tall buildings nor an eagle. In fact, the alleged verse can be found nowhere in the Qur'an. The entire e-mail is a complete fabrication.

Another mass distributed e-mail claimed that while the Bible frequently refers to God as love, nowhere in the Qur'an is Allah ﷻ

described as love. In reality, one of the 99 names or attributes of Allah ﷻ that is mentioned in the Qur'an is Al-Wadud, which means "The Loving." This e-mail's claim was once again a complete prevarication, one with the apparent aim of seeking to mislead non-Muslims into believing that Allah ﷻ is somehow other than God.

As a third example, consider statements made by Pat Robertson on the 700 Club in the first third of 2011. According to Rev. Robertson, *halāl* meat (i.e., meat slaughtered according to Islamic rules and regulations, which stipulate that Allah's ﷻ name be said over the animal, that the animal's throat be slit, and that the animal be bled out) supports terrorism. In making his totally fictitious argument, Rev. Robertson went so far as to claim that *halāl* slaughtering was nothing like kosher slaughtering and that *halāl* slaughtering houses are where Muslims take their cows, sheep, and pigs to be slaughtered for meat. In point of fact, *halāl* slaughtering is almost identical to kosher slaughtering. Further, Muslims, like Orthodox Jews, are prohibited from eating pork and do not raise pigs; there is no such thing as *halāl* pork! How an ordained minister could be so far off from the truth when it comes to a religion other than his is bewildering to say the least.

The above examples illustrate the truth of Mark Twain's famous maxim: "It ain't what you don't know that gets you into trouble. It's what you know for sure that just ain't so."

In the present book, Mohammad Masood Ahmed confronts "what you know for sure that just ain't so" about Islam, and he fills in the gaps in "what you don't know" about Islam. His book is far more than merely a brief introduction to Islam; it is a massive work from a devout, lifelong Muslim. It is a book that is written with a deep and abiding love for Islam. May Allah ﷻ reward him for his time and effort.

Jerald F. Dirks, M.Div., Psy.D.
Ramadhan, 2011

Introduction

𝒪N THIS DAY AND AGE when information about practically everything is readily accessible, for one to not have the real knowledge of Islam is a deficiency. Islam has existed for more than 14 centuries, and it is the religion of about 1.6 billion people, making every fourth citizen of the world a Muslim. Therefore, to be well informed, one must know at least something about Islam.

Additionally, many recent events have created the need to acquire knowledge of Islam and to understand and analyze its philosophy. A proper understanding of Islam will help to formulate responses for future scenarios, both domestically and internationally.

Such events have also brought about many conflicting opinions about Islam and Muslims. Some people think that Islam is directly responsible for those events, while others blame Muslims. Moreover, there are other varying and incorrect opinions. In my view, these assumptions are based on incomplete information and knowledge, and it is unjust to formulate an opinion about Islam without having sufficient knowledge of it.

One of the major events of our time was the tragedy of September 11, 2001—a display of the worst form of human nature, out of which evolved the great need to understand Islam and its principles more than ever before.

The incident of 9/11 is the single most horrific tragedy in modern history, and it has brought about unprecedented changes in thoughts and attitudes, in policy-making and its implementation, in achieving global security, and in countering the threat to international peace. Many people, especially in the West, were first introduced to such terms as Islam, Muslims, Qur'an, jihad, fundamentalism, terrorism, and suicide bombing as a result of 9/11. Those who already knew about Islam and Muslims became confused because of the new and distorted interpretations attached to these terms. The emergence of this entirely new and changed environment made almost everyone at least somewhat angry, but mostly there was insecurity on both sides of the aisle. As a result, for some time, peace has been disturbed throughout the world.

As the clouds of smoke drifted away and the shock waves began to fade, and as people struggled to return to normalcy—though it would never be the same because of the long-lasting memories of that event—the need to understand the true message of Islam and the behavior and beliefs of Muslims became widespread. This demand could not be overlooked, and bridging the gap between Muslims and non-Muslims became vital.

Many people became interested in learning about Islam and Muslims, either out of curiosity, a genuine desire to learn the truth, or the wish to expand their knowledge and information base. Thousands of articles and books were written, countless discussions took place, colleges began to offer courses on Islam, websites appeared, friends and foe alike became active in this process, and a completely new field became open for exploration and interrogation.

For quite some time, I had thought about writing a book on Islam, but the events of 9/11 completely changed the direction of my thinking, and the task of writing such a book became difficult. Prior to that, I could choose any direction and style in which to present the message of Islam, but now I had to answer specific questions, clarify conceptions and misconceptions, address just and unjust objections, and present a clear picture of what Islam and Muslims are all about. I decided to wait and see, and I hoped that someone more educated, knowledgeable, and experienced might produce something better to meet this requirement of the time.

Anyone writing about Islam can take one of two approaches to explain it and get it across. One approach is simply to put down facts about Islam and Muslims and leave readers to understand it according to their own judgment. The second approach is not only to give facts but to explain the true wisdom and philosophy behind Islamic teachings and practices. I have chosen the latter approach because I believe that people do not just wish to be informed of such facts but, at this point in time, want to know the inner meanings and purposes of Islam.

There is no doubt that many informative books and articles have been published on different aspects of Islam ever since the need to learn about them became a necessity, but not one single book satisfied my desire for a simple and thorough presentation of Islam: the way of life of about one-fourth of the world's population. Some books were written on specific topics and did not present a complete picture of Islam, while others were written exclusively for a highly educated audience and were quite useless to the general populace. Many questions remained unanswered or were answered unsatisfactorily. The fact is that clouds of confusion continued to linger while seekers of truth and knowledge were still digging harder and deeper by themselves, without any proper direction or course of action.

Finally, I took this task on my own shoulders and heartily embarked on this project to fulfill this great need and responsibility. I have to admit that I am not an experienced writer, nor do I possess mastery over the English language. However, I am confident that, with my pure intentions, I can get the message across and produce a somewhat thorough book on Islam, in simple and easy-to-read English, which even a layman can understand. I hope that other more knowledgeable

XX

and experienced writers will follow my lead in producing similar literature to create a better understanding of Islam.

I will try to answer the questions raised, remove misunderstandings, clarify objections, and bridge the gap between Muslims and non-Muslims at every level of our society, in order to achieve increased understanding, peace, happiness and prosperity for all. I have included much more than simply those issues that people are asking about these days, hoping to present a complete and clear picture of Islam that will enhance their knowledge. Furthermore, my intention in writing this book is not in any way to convert anyone to Islam or to impose my feelings and/or beliefs. In this regard, I am a firm believer in the freedom of religion and in people's right to choose.

Thus, this book is simply a step towards achieving the purposes mentioned above. The purity of my intention and commitment in this book requires me to present Islam and its teachings truthfully and as they are, plainly and simply, and to project them to the best of my knowledge, understanding, and belief. Therefore, in the beginning, the reader may not like some concepts and practices of Islam, while many other aspects may seem too good to be true. Certainly, in the end, a clear picture will come to light. For all errors and mistakes, I seek forgiveness from my audience and from the Lord of us all.

I do not know how successfully I present Islam, but one thing is certain, i.e., that I do not assign anyone to Hell or secure for anyone a place in Heaven. This is a matter of what people choose and what the Lord grants them. I kindly request the reader not to blame Islam if its qualities/teachings are not reflected in a Muslim whom they may have come to know. Islam invites *all* into its realm of peace but only obligates *its* followers to bring its teachings and commandments into practice. Its benefits and rewards—given here and in the Hereafter—are for those who believe in and practice it, and punishments are set aside only for those who deny truth after it has become clearly available to them.

I did not gather and compile Islamic knowledge in any clever way, but only honestly conveyed Islam to give people a chance to know what they, perhaps, are missing from their lives. I did not rearrange or manipulate Islam in any way to make it look any better; however, I did simplify it for better understanding. I did not hide any fact, because I firmly believe that truth cannot be hidden. I did not criticize anyone or attack any religion/ideology/system, but I simply explained clear facts about Islam. I did not have any hidden agenda or purpose that may cause any harm to anyone. However, I have tried my best to get my point across, hoping that the Almighty may accept it as a token of gratitude for the bounties He has bestowed upon me. I hope readers, too, will benefit greatly from this book.

Entering into the fold of Islam out of one's own choice and knowing about Islam and the way of life it promotes and offers are two separate issues. Just knowing about Islam does not compel anyone to accept it and become a Muslim. If the advantages and benefits of acquiring knowledge of Islam are fully established, then one will not say "No" when asked, "Would you like to know something about Islam?"

Some unfamiliar terms and names are used throughout the book and may be confusing to the reader. As such, I list the most commonly used terms in the beginning in order that readers may become acquainted with them, and others are listed at the end of the book.

It is to be noted at this point that I am obligated to add proper salutations whenever I mention holy personalities. Since I cannot ignore these salutations and my non-Muslim readers are not obligated to recite them, I have included them in Arabic, in small calligraphic form. In doing so, I have fulfilled my religious duty of including these salutations, while enabling the reader to avoid them and to continue reading fluently. Since the salutations are not in English, they are easy to ignore.

To prove my arguments and the deep wisdom of Islam that has brought positive changes to peoples' lives, I have avoided stories and real-life examples to keep the book in its current size. Examples and true accounts do help in understanding the matter presented, but I am certain that a majority of readers will easily understand Islam and its deep philosophies as I have intelligibly put together.

Finally, yet importantly, the reader will notice that I have not used any references in support of my arguments, nor have I criticized any literature on the subject of Islam or any other religion. I strongly believe that common sense and absolute truths do not require any reference or support to establish their validity. The truth speaks for itself and stands alone. Whenever I refer to the holy Qur'an, sacred *ahadīth*, or authentic sayings of Islam's holy personalities and others, I have referenced them. Much of my knowledge comes from authentic Islamic literature in Urdu, most of which has not been translated into the English language.

If you feel that you already have your reasons to know Islam and do not want to know my reasons for writing this book, you may choose to skip the next two sections, although I would prefer that you read through them. Having said the above, I sincerely present to you the teachings of Islam as I understand them. I hope you enjoy every bit of this book.

Selected Key Terms

Allah ‏الله‏ ﷻ – the proper and personal name of the Almighty Lord, the Creator and the Master

Deen – religion, the way of life prescribed by Allah ﷻ

Hadīth (pl. *Ahadīth*) – a saying of the holy Prophet Muhammad ﷺ

Halāl – that which is permitted in Islam

Harām – that which is prohibited in Islam

Iblīs – proper name of Shaytān (Satan), the devil; the open enemy of man as informed to us by Allah ﷻ

Iman – unshakeable faith; belief in the Oneness of Allah ﷻ and in Muhammad ﷺ as the Prophet of Allah

Islam – lit. means "submission;" to surrender oneself to Allah ﷻ

Jihad – struggle in the way of Allah ﷻ and for the sake of Allah ﷻ alone

Kufr – infidelity; heresy; Allah ﷻ abhors this act of man

Madinah al-Munawwarah – the second holiest city of Islam and the resting place of the Prophet Muhammad ﷺ

Makkah – the holiest city of Islam located in present-day Saudi Arabia

Masjid (pl. *Masajid*) – place of worship for Muslims; Allah's ﷻ house

Muhammad ‏محمد‏ ﷺ – the last Messenger and Prophet of Allah ﷻ to humankind; the name Muhammad literally means, "One who is overwhelmingly praised"

Muslim – "one who submits his/her will to the will of Allah ﷻ"; a follower of Islam

Qur'an – the final book of divine guidance and direction for mankind revealed to Prophet Muhammad ﷺ by Allah ﷻ; *only* the text in the Arabic language is the Qur'an, not its translation/interpretation

__Ruh__ – soul; spirit; Allah's ﷻ divine command, energy, power

__Sahaba (pl. As-hāb)__ – the holy and noble companions of the Prophet Muhammad ﷺ

__Sharia'__ – Islamic jurisprudence; law

__Shirk__ – to associate partner(s) with Allah ﷻ; the most heinous sin and an unforgiveable sin in Islam

__Sunnah__ – tradition of the holy Prophet Muhammad ﷺ

__Tawhīd__ – the Oneness of Allah ﷻ

__Ummah__ – believers of Islam; the worldwide community of Muslims

ﷻ – A calligraphic style of *"subhanahu wata'ala"* meaning "Glorified and exaled is He;" to be written/recited only with Allah's ﷻ name

ﷺ – A calligraphic style of *"sallalahu alaihay wassalam"* meaning "Allah's peace and blessings be upon him;" to be written/recited only with the name of the Prophet Muhammad ﷺ

السلام‎ – A calligraphic style of *"alayhis-salām"* meaning "Peace be upon him;" to be written/recited only with the names of holy prophets and angels

عليها السلام – A calligraphic style of *"alayhas-salām"* meaning "Peace be upon her;" to be written/recited with the names of holy female personalities in Islam

رضي الله عنه – A calligraphic style of *"radhi allahu anho"* meaning "May Allah ﷻ be pleased with him"; to be written/recited with the names of holy male personalities in Islam, who are not prophets

Reasons for Writing This Book

*U*SUALLY WHEN PEOPLE SEE A BOOK ON RELIGION, they tend to think that it was written to attract people towards the religious philosophy/ideology discussed in it. In many cases, the author does hope to attract the audience to the philosophy being presented. I, at the outset, clearly state that my intent in writing this book is explicitly not to convert anyone to Islam. If you are attracted to Islam, it may be because of the truthfulness of the facts presented here; hence, no special credit should go to me. However, if you are not, then it is your understanding of and decision about the same facts. Those who are curious to know why I wrote this book should refer to the following reasons:

   I. To express gratitude by spreading the knowledge of Islam

   II. To show my love for all people

   III. To clear up misconceptions and misunderstandings about Islam

   IV. To fulfill people's desire/need for Islamic knowledge

   V. To enhance the knowledge of Islam

   VI. To bridge the gap between Muslims and non-Muslims

I. To express gratitude by spreading the knowledge of Islam

I consider myself fortunate to have been born into a Muslim family and to have initially learned about Islam from the lap of my parents, and later from my grandparents and my surroundings. I did not have to make any special effort to learn the religion and its teachings. Secondly, I am thankful to the Lord who brought me to America and the West, where I learned what I would probably never have had a chance to learn in my native country, Pakistan.

I also consider myself a blessed Muslim who was granted, among other qualities, the ability to understand the inner wisdom of Islam and to be in the spiritual company of many saintly personalities. Therefore, I am hopeful of acquiring ultimate success for myself.

If I were just to say for all these blessings and bounties, "O Lord! I am thankful for everything You have given me," would it be sufficient thanks? I think not. To *truly* thank the Lord, I must first become a true Muslim as per the teachings of Islam and not a hypocrite. Secondly, I must convey the message of Islam to others. To fulfill this latter part of my religious duty, I must provide information about Islam objectively and to the best of my knowledge and ability, and I must be an example of the best moral character. With this, my duty is fulfilled. What people choose thereafter ought to be based on their free will. Only the Lord shows guidance and enlightens hearts, but because He always rewards peoples' good intentions, I intend to spread the knowledge of Islam.

II. To show my love for all people

There are many types of relationships that exist amongst people: parent-child, husband-wife, siblings, other relatives, friendships, colleagues and co-workers, employer and employee, tenant and landlord, government and its people, etc. Among other things, we know that if relationships are based on love, they become strong and everlasting. Love brings progress, happiness, prosperity, and greatly improved life for all.

I contend that it is possible to love all; however, the kind of love varies in each case. When we truly love, most often we are loved in return; thus, the reservoir of love never goes dry because it is continuously replenished. Therefore, it is not difficult to have love for all.

In this regard, simply repeating the words "I love you" is insufficient. A solid proof of some experience or of a future expectation must accompany that claim of love. When you truly love someone, you not only say or wish it, but you are also willing to contribute whatever is necessary towards the success of that person. You are ready to sacrifice your time, energy, wealth, and anything else that is needed.

I am not only thankful to the Lord for His bounties, as I mentioned earlier, I also have the love for the Lord in my heart. I like to thank, worship, and serve Him with that love. This relationship based on true love requires me to love His creations, (i.e., it requires me to love my fellow human beings). It means that I must wish for their success and do everything possible for them to achieve it.

I believe, success in the Hereafter, which I refer to as 'ultimate success,' is greater and more important than every other type of success. Therefore, I seek 'ultimate success' for everyone and take steps accordingly, showing that I truly love all people.

There are many good-hearted people out there, and I cannot withhold the knowledge of Islam from them. I have nothing of this world to share with my fellow citizens, except for the true knowledge of Islam, which I share through this book. I hope this brings abundant benefits to the reader and ultimate success to the fortunate ones. I wish everyone good luck!

III. To clear up misconceptions and misunderstandings about Islam

The third most important reason for writing this book is to clarify misconceptions and misunderstandings about Islam. I firmly believe that Islam and its principles are based on divine truth and that it is the ultimate way of life through which people can acquire success in this world and in the Hereafter. It is incumbent upon me as a loyal follower of Islam, like many other Muslims, to defend my religion. For whatever reason(s), many misconceptions and misunderstandings about Islam have emerged and are causing great harm everywhere.

Since no man invented Islam, we cannot give credit to anyone for it. However, Prophet Muhammad ﷺ deserves much praise and credit for undergoing so much physical pain, for laboring so hard, with utmost sincerity, to preach the message revealed to him by Allah ﷻ, and for being the physical example for us of how to be a Muslim, through first applying that divine message in his own life. His life-long achievements and sincere dedication to save humanity from the torment of this world and of the Hereafter, and his overwhelming success in his prophetic obligation, mean that every misunderstanding and misconception about Islam deserves to be corrected and removed. This duty lies with every single follower of Islam, including myself. Thus, I try my best to fulfill this responsibility, so help me Lord.

IV. To fulfill people's desire/need for Islamic knowledge

As noted earlier, many people, either out of curiosity, to increase their knowledge base, or because of a genuine desire to know the truth, have become interested in learning about Islam. Therefore, it would be unfair to them if information about Islam was not readily available. Further, such information must be made available to them in a form that satisfies their desire for complete and accurate Islamic knowledge. It must not create more confusion, questions, or the need to search further for truth. Who else is more obligated to provide that information and knowledge than knowledgeable Muslims? I desired to have that privilege for myself.

In the past decades, many people have embraced Islam, and the number is continuously increasing, contributing to making Islam the fastest growing religion in the world. Among these converts to Islam, many studied Islam extensively to their full satisfaction before embracing it, but some, excited by a few good things, hurriedly embraced

Islam. This latter group now desires to learn about Islam in detail, either for their own sake, to explain Islam to others, or perhaps to justify making such an important decision. This is yet another purpose of the book.

It has also come to my attention that some newcomers to Islam had sour experiences because they entered with inaccurate expectations that did not come true or because of the misbehavior of some fellow Muslims. Instead of blaming Muslims, they place the blame on Islam and turn away from it without giving themselves a chance to know more about it. I hope they will feel differently after acquiring the true knowledge of Islam through this book, and I am confident that their perception will change. Moreover, some among them are seeking more reasons to stick to Islam. In this regard, I feel obligated to provide them with help through this book.

I believe that people should not make important decisions, such as embracing a new faith, without first having complete information or being fully satisfied. If, for example, someone has decided to embrace Islam with incomplete information, then I advise him or her to stick to Islam and acquire more knowledge about it. I hope that this book also does a great service with regard to this issue.

V. To enhance the knowledge of Islam

Generally, when people desire to learn about Islam, they turn to the translations of the holy Qur'an. This is one reason why there was a shortage of translated copies of the Qur'an post-9/11. However, in my humble opinion, at a preliminary stage, not everyone can learn a whole lot from translations of the holy Qur'an. Translations are merely renditions of the Arabic text into another language and sometimes do not answer many of the frequently asked questions.

It is truly difficult for anyone to study the entire Qur'an to find answers to a few of their questions. When embarking on a mission to explore Islam, I suggest that referring to translations of the holy Qur'an not be the first step. After familiarizing oneself with the teachings and practices of Islam, such as presented in this book, understanding the message of the holy Qur'an through translations will become easier. This does not mean that one should not possess a copy of the translation of the holy Qur'an in his or her respective language. By this suggestion, I intend to make gathering and acquiring the information easier. Thus, this book provides the elementary knowledge that will help in understanding the holy Qur'an in-depth. Nonetheless, I personally admire those motivated and dedicated individuals who refer to the holy Qur'an and its translations and learn what they want to.

VI. To bridge the gap between Muslims and non-Muslims

In America and throughout the world, extensive work is underway to bridge the gap and to achieve a better understanding between Muslims and non-Muslims. This book is my addition to this noble cause and my contribution to the effort.

I am confident that as people gain a sufficient knowledge base of Islam and Muslims, greater understanding will develop, peace and happiness will prevail, and the social and cultural gap between Muslims and non-Muslims will be bridged. If this comes about, then the purpose of this book will be achieved. I leave it to my readers to decide how successful I am in presenting the matter to achieve the desired goals, and I look forward to their response.

Reasons for Reading This Book

WHEN WE ARE EXTENSIVELY BUSY in coping with our lives, our priorities vary according to our situations. We are forced to handle things at hand first, and then those that affect us in the short-run. Thus, for the time being, we avoid thinking of long-term or of otherworldly matters. As a result, reading about religions draws much less interest than many other pursuits. This is especially true when learning about a religion other than one's own.

In addition, some might say, "OK, you told us your reasons for writing this book; now tell us why we should read it." In response, I list the following reasons for reading this book.

   I. To contribute towards achieving global peace and security

   II. To maintain a healthy and progressive society

   III. To obtain answers to specific questions

   IV. To fulfill personal, private, or business needs

   V. To find solutions to personal problems

   VI. To consider the 'Big Ifs'

I. To contribute towards achieving global peace and security

We have recently witnessed a worldwide desire for and optimism with regard to change. Sincere individuals and institutions are now seeking new directions and different strategies to achieve peace, prosperity, and global security. This desire and hope for change played a crucial role in the 2008 presidential elections in the United States of America, as people from all walks of life and diverse backgrounds came closer to each other to express their support for this change. This show of unity was unprecedented, and it was for a single purpose: to bring about change, nationally and internationally.

Almost every citizen of the world looks towards the leading countries on the international arena, mainly the United States, because of their desire to move ahead in the right direction, coupled with an enthusiasm to bring real and everlasting peace, by removing unnecessary differences, and through worldwide cooperation. Since this has become a worldwide need and a great responsibility, no single country/nation is capable of fulfilling it on its own. All countries must come together to fulfill this great responsibility; however, the big players will have to play the leading roles.

In this modern age, the world has become so close-knit that if anyone or any force pulls even one thread, the entire web is affected and may lose its present shape or place. To secure the entire web, not only do great countries have to bring about change within their own boundaries, they have to think and plan beyond it. Otherwise, any entity can pull a thread from anywhere in the world and may destroy the entire web. If this happens, whether one is a great or not so great nation, one will feel the jolt or at least its shockwaves.

We truly do need the type of courage, will, and resolve to bring everlasting change, as reflected in the 2008 U.S. presidential elections.

Not only I, but almost everyone in the world, admired the sentiments of bringing change. I firmly believe that if all positive forces join together, they can truly bring about change. "Yes, We Can," and "Yes, we should." Great nations such as the United States are equipped with the necessary tools and can achieve this great goal through collaborating with other nations. Simultaneously, I fear that if this chance is lost or if the enthusiasm to bring change fades, we might not get another opportunity, and the dream of achieving international peace and prosperity may never come true. For the greater good, we should give all, whatever we have and whatever we can!

Many factors need to be considered or reconsidered in a different light to succeed in this goal. One necessary factor is unity among all people, Muslim and non-Muslim, especially in those Western countries with considerable Muslim populations. To achieve this unity, we have to bridge the gap between Muslims and non-Muslims, so that all can stand on one platform and work hand-in-hand to bring change. Initially, this will require an understanding of Islam by everyone, from the top to the bottom, from policymakers to their supporters, from elected officials to their constituents.

Certainly, Muslims, both individually and collectively, have to work extensively on their own and in cooperation with non-Muslims to achieve this goal. Muslims must eliminate all misconceptions and misunderstandings about Islam and themselves. They must not collaborate with anyone who attempts to increase the already widened gap between Muslims and non-Muslims. Furthermore, Muslims, domestically and internationally, must progress with wisdom, utmost care, and sincere intent to forge peace and happiness. They must lend a generous hand for the greater good of mankind and to show the hospitality, tolerance, generosity, and true character of Islam.

Moreover, a genuine desire, a balanced strategy, and the proper use of resources are a few of the key elements required from both sides to achieve this goal. To fulfill the responsibility on my part, I present this book as a small contribution and gesture to assist in this effort. Now it is your turn. Read the book and learn something about Islam.

II. To maintain a healthy and progressive society

Not all people are involved in the policymaking process or are able to affect it considerably, but everyone can certainly be somewhat effective in forming a healthy and progressive society around them. Where Muslims and non-Muslims live side-by-side, an understanding of Islam, and consequently of Muslims, will help bring peace and prosperity at all levels. Islam and a true Muslim are one and the same, because a true Muslim reflects the message of Islam. As such, in order to understand Muslims, in my opinion the best way is to first understand Islam and the way of life it presents.

Generally, to formulate assessments, to understand and predict behavior, and to better interact with someone, it is necessary to know his or her personality and beliefs. It is also a fact that if a society desires to be healthy and progressive, there must be a certain level of psychological understanding among its members. For example, if Muslims, on the one hand, continue to conceive of America or the West as enemies of Islam, and subsequently of Muslims, and if, on the other hand, Americans and Europeans remain skeptical of Muslims and consider them as enemies and enemies of their system, then it will not be easy for them to interact freely. Therefore, a visible or hidden, physical and/or mental distance will be ever-present. Consequently, the growth of society will definitely be negatively affected, especially where Muslims and non-Muslims live together in large numbers.

An understanding of each other's culture, customs, beliefs, norms, and other aspects helps people to interact closely and freely, thereby resulting in widespread cooperation to bring peace, happiness, and prosperity for all. Since its inception, Islam has molded the lives of its followers in such a unique way that one cannot have a true understanding of a Muslim and/or his or her lifestyle without knowing Islam.

III. To obtain answers to specific questions

Many questions about Islam have surfaced because of current affairs, personal interaction, and/or witnessing the religious activities of Muslims. Such common questions include, but are not limited to the following. What is the true phenomenon behind jihad? Does Islam support or encourage terrorism? Do Islamic teachings result in extremism? What are women's rights in Islam? Why are men allowed to have more than one wife at a time? What are the justifications for capital punishment in Islam? Is there a separation of church and state in Islam? Is democracy compatible with Islam? What is the extent to which advancements in science and technology are allowed? What are the definitions of life, liberty, and the pursuit of happiness in Islam? What is the role of marriage, family, education, clergy, etc.? What is meant by the rule of law in Islam? Are there any freedoms of speech, religion, choice, etc. in Islam? In addition, there are many other similar questions.

It is easy simply to list answers to the questions above, but what benefit is there in knowing answers that will generate even more questions and confusion. I contend that without keeping the entire structure of Islam in mind, one cannot correctly analyze or truly understand its different aspects. Furthermore, to comprehend the true philosophy behind each aspect, it is important to understand the fundamental beliefs and the message underlined. Without that, the purpose(s) of a given idea, duty, or practice cannot be completely and accurately understood.

IV. To fulfill personal, private, or business needs

It is worthwhile to acquire knowledge of Islam, the way of life of approximately 1.6 billion people, even if one does not have specific questions about it. It will be amazing to know why and how Islam is the fastest growing religion in the world, especially in the West. The population of Muslims is rapidly increasing in major cities across America, Canada, Europe, and other parts of the world. Beautiful and unique houses of worship, called *Masjid* (pl. *Masajid*), are being built, and many religious activities take place, about which all informed people should have some basic knowledge.

For example, it is interesting to know the concept of the month of Ramadhan and the daily fasting that takes place in it. How do Muslims take time out to pray five times a day, and how and why do they pray? Why must Muslims eat *halāl* and abstain from pork? Why are they prohibited from consuming alcoholic beverages? Why do they cover their heads and wear *hijāb?* These are all interesting subjects, and knowing about them will surely enhance your knowledge about Islam and Muslims.

Many non-Muslims have Muslim colleagues and friends in school. Instructors are teaching an increased number of Muslim students, and many pupils are coming across Muslim teachers. Doctors are treating Muslim patients, and hospitals have an increasing number of Muslim doctors. Businesspeople and trade centers are becoming increasingly involved with Muslim clients, investors, and consumers. Politicians, in many places, cannot ignore the presence of their Muslim constituents, either for votes or for support. Whatever the situation may be, it is certainly beneficial to know about Islam and its followers.

Many Muslims have emigrated from their native countries and settled in the West and other places. The first generation of Muslims may or may not go back to their native countries, but certainly their subsequent generations will remain where they are born. They are respected citizens and nationals of their respective countries, to which their parents and/or grandparents once immigrated, and they are not moving out any time soon.

If someone has never come across a Muslim, eventually for one reason or another, he or she will. Therefore, to create everlasting impressions, and to build good relationships, friendships, partnerships, etc., it will surely be a plus to know about their religion.

It has also come to my attention that intimate relationships are taking place between Muslims and non-Muslims. Thus, to proceed to build a solid relationship, knowing about Islam will benefit both partners. Even for this private reason, it is advantageous to know at least *something* about Islam. After all, history is witness that for love, kings have even abdicated their thrones.

Anyway, in my view, either for personal, private, or business reasons, it is advantageous to know about Islam. I am confident that you will be glad to have learned *something* about Islam—there is nothing for you to lose by it.

V. To find possible solutions to personal problems through Islam

No honest person can claim to be living a completely trouble-free life and to have no problems at all. The truth of the matter is that everyone has at least one or several problems in his or her life. There

are some problems that people cannot even discuss with others
because they cannot be expressed in words or
because they may simply not know how to share
them. Sometimes, others cannot easily observe
these problems, no matter how close the
relationship is.

Some are
returning to their
previous religious
beliefs, while
others are looking
elsewhere.

Whether people share them or not, the reality is that concerned
individuals are always in search of remedies to their problems. If in
search of such remedies, concerned individuals turn to modern-day
sources of science, technology, and material wealth, they will fail to
find appropriate solutions because many of those problems are, in fact,
the creation of modern times, technology, and thinking. Therefore,
one should not look for remedies in them, and search somewhere else.

In this regard, I suggest people turn to religion in search of
remedies to their social, moral, and spiritual issues. Actually and in
fact, this is taking place as we speak: many are turning to religion,
willingly or unwillingly. Some are returning to their previous religious
beliefs, while others are looking elsewhere.

I request these sincere seekers to look into Islam and to pay close
attention to determine if Islam contains solutions to their problems. I
am confident that they will find the Islamic message interesting and
may even locate firm footings upon which they can easily build a
foundation to acquire success. After all, one does not have to be a
Muslim to eat *halāl*. Anyway, this is another important reason to
study Islam, i.e., the hope of finding solutions to one's problems.

VI. To consider the 'Big Ifs'

I do not want to leave out this important reason to study Islam.
However, in doing so, let me re-emphasize that I am not trying to

convince my readers to convert to Islam. I simply intend to put the facts on paper.

Who are we? Where did we come from? Where are we headed? What is the purpose of our life on earth? Almost every single person asks these and similar types of questions. Whether or not we find answers to them or are even satisfied with our findings, we cannot deny the fact that we have been born into this world. Therefore, we have to live our life, and, of course, one day we will die.

Now, it is all up to us to choose how we spend our time on earth. Do we want to be successful in all endeavors and live a healthy life? Do we want to be peaceful and in equilibrium with nature? Do we want to live a fear-free and fulfilling life? Answers to these types of questions and what we choose to want in this life shape our behavior.

Now I present some 'Big If' questions, the answers to which will clarify and explain how to proceed in this life and make the best of it. What will happen *if* there is life after death? What will happen *if* there is a Day of Judgment? What will happen *if* we realize on the Day of Judgment that our life on earth was to prepare for a successful and trouble-free life in the Hereafter? What *if* we find out that our life was for a higher purpose, to which we did not pay any attention? What *if* we will have to admit that Allah ﷻ had sent us complete guidance for our salvation, but we failed to accept and abide by His commandments? What *if* on that Day, we acknowledge that we really are among the ultimate losers?

I contend that now is the time to think and pay attention. Despite differing claims about what the ultimate truth is and how to achieve ultimate success, for the sake of the 'Big Ifs', we must think now, gather information now, acquire knowledge now, and make the right decision now. What will happen *if* we become ultimate losers just because we ignored this important matter, wasted our time, and did not pay attention to the higher purpose of life on earth?

We alone will bear the consequences for our choices; therefore, whatever path we choose for success, we must choose wisely and make our decision only after obtaining complete information and knowledge. I will not mind even if you reject Islam because of *your understanding* of it. However, I humbly request you not to reject Islam without first knowing about it. This will require an unbiased study of Islam, a commitment to learn the truth, and a genuine desire for ultimate success. Here, my obligation is only to put all the facts regarding Islam on paper, plainly and simply.

Testing the Veracity of a Religion/Ideology

I HOPE THE REASONS FOR WRITING AND READING this book, as noted in the previous pages, have stirred interest in reading further and have increased the desire to know something about Islam. The question of Islam's veracity may have preceded the interest and desire added by the previous two sections. Therefore, before addressing facts about Islam, if readers are given the necessary tools to analyze Islamic teachings critically, they will be better equipped to uncover Islam's righteousness. As a result, they will have a better understanding of Islam.

Every religion claims to be the truth and insists that salvation can only be achieved through it. Every ideology claims to have solutions to the problems of humanity. Islam also makes the same claim. Indeed, how can a religion or an ideology exist without making these and other similar claims? Since all religions and ideologies differ from each other so much, it becomes difficult to decide which one leads to the right path, to salvation, and to ultimate success.

To prove Islam's righteousness that ensures humankind's ultimate success—if I refer to its holy book, the Qur'an, it will have no meaning for those who do not believe it to be the holy book revealed by the Creator. Thus, I will put forth conditions through which one can critically analyze the veracity of a religion/ideology to see what the real position of Islam is under every given condition.

To understand the truthfulness of a religion or a uniform code of life, and to see if it ensures success in this life and in the Hereafter, one must test it against the following principles:

I. Carefully examine if that code of life is fit for human nature.

II. Who is the founder, advocate, or author of the system, by which people are to live?

III. Does the moral character and qualities of the advocate/lawgiver of that religion/ideology fit the proposed system/constitution?

IV. Does the founder/prophet claim that the set of rules presented is universal and valid for all times and conditions?

V. If it is claimed that that ideology/religion is otherworldly and revealed by the Supreme Being, then see if it could have been forged by the human mind.

I. Carefully examine if that code of life is fit for human nature

Does that code of life demand or direct its followers to do something of which they are naturally incapable? Under normal circumstances, can people draw benefits and create positive differences from it? Is it applicable to the majority, and can it bring considerable change in/to its constituents or to society at large? Does it demand too much, which may be unreasonable, or bestow too little, which may not justify the balance between what it offers and demands? Does it bring inner peace and fulfillment? Does it encompass all aspects of human life, or does it leave its followers in a vacuum and a state of vagueness?

Moreover, does it fulfill humankind's natural desire to connect with the Supreme Being? If these conditions cannot be met, then that religion/ideology/code of life does not pass the test. In fact, it will prove to be disastrous to the lives of its followers and will certainly be void of any success, let alone ultimate success.

II. Who is the founder, advocate, or author of the system by which people are to live?

Is the ideological or religious system manufactured or organized by someone whose intellect, authority, and prudence are questionable, whose observations and empirical justifications are inconsistent, whose desires, wants, and objectives change with the passage of time, whose principles are unconventional, whose personal/hidden agenda misleads, or whose credibility is not reliable? If any of the above is the case, then the code of life and set of rules laid down by that individual cannot be comprehensive or be entitled 'righteous,' and that code will definitely not bring success.

III. Does the moral character and qualities of the advocate/law-giver of that religion/ideology fit the proposed system/constitution?

Is he a materialist, or does he seek to acquire power, prestige, and/or material pleasures? If the answer is yes, then that individual is clearly taking advantage of people and of their need to bring some sort of comfort and meaning to their lives. If so, then the ideology presented will certainly fail to bring everlasting success.

IV. Does the founder/prophet claim that the set of rules presented are universal and valid for all times and conditions?

If there is such a claim, then one must examine the validity of that claim. If there is no such claim or if it is found to be invalid for certain times and conditions, then that proposed ideology does not pass the test. It will need to be constantly amended according to ever-changing needs and times. Therefore, it is an inefficient medium for achieving permanent/ultimate success.

V. If it is claimed that that ideology/religion is otherworldly and revealed by the Supreme Being, then see if it could have been forged by the human mind.

Can the imagination of an intellectual or philosopher reach the wisdom of that proposition and what it purports to achieve for humanity? If not, only then can one be sure that it originated from the higher authority, known as the Lord and the Creator. In addition, one has to know for certain that the pleasure of the Supreme Being is guaranteed through it and by observing the rules presented in it, so that ultimate success can be achieved.

By keeping these criteria and methods in mind, I request the readers to analyze the message of Islam critically and determine its concrete relevance to humanity. I am confident that they will certainly arrive at positive conclusions about Islam. From time to time, I myself will dig into more detail and test Islam against these criteria to show clearly where Islam stands as a religion.

WOULD YOU LIKE TO KNOW SOMETHING ABOUT ISLAM?

THE TIME IS RIPE

CHAPTER 1

Islam
AN OVERVIEW

*I*SLAM IS THE NAME OF THE COMPLETE WAY OF LIFE revealed and prescribed by the Lord of this universe for human beings, "the Best among His creatures."

> Without a doubt, the *deen* in the sight of
> Allah is Islam only. • [Qur'an: 3:19]

Islam is not just a religion; it is also a complete way of life that covers both religious aspects and all other matters commonly considered to be secular. In fact, for Islam, no part of life is secular; it regulates every aspect of human life. In short, it encompasses and provides guidance for all matters, material and immaterial.

Since the Supreme Being created the universe and everything in it, including humans, He also established every law governing their natural activities. Creation itself was incapable of formulating laws to govern complete well-being and to fulfill its intended purpose. Therefore, the All-Knowing, All-Powerful, the Almighty Allah ﷻ established every law to govern His creations, according to their needs.

The *Deen-e-Islam* (Islamic way of life), guides people to live a successful life on earth and prepares them for success in the Hereafter. The perfection of Islam is such that complete guidance is made available to acquire success in this world and ultimate success in the

Hereafter. Whether we choose to earn the pleasure of the Master, and consequently achieve ultimate success and eternal happiness, or mistakenly or intentionally choose otherwise, becoming the ultimate loser by earning His wrath, the choice is ours [Qur'an 17:84].

Islam guides us to the right path and warns us against deviating from it. It fully explains the right path, describes how to walk on it properly, mentions the rewards for doing so, and designates Heaven as the final destination for its true followers. Islam instructs us on how to secure ourselves from harm's way, from deviating, from misguidance, from falling into the trap of our base self, from becoming a slave of this world, from the treachery of Shaytān (Satan), and from becoming a permanent resident of Hell by earning the Lord's wrath.

In Islam, there is no reason to worry or be confused as to what one should do regarding any matter; everything has been explained. We just have to learn and follow. In doing so, the utilization of every human faculty is permissible in order to choose wisely. Islam encourages reasoning and constructive criticism—if the intent is to strengthen one's belief in it [Qur'an 6:75-79]. Since it is our decision that brings success or failure in this world and in the Hereafter, we should explore deeply and with sincerity.

Does Islam really provide a complete way of life and answer every question of humanity? In response, I will explain what Islam is and explore every nook and cranny that falls within the subject matter of this book.

Islam is a heavenly religion, revealed by the Lord to humankind through His chosen individuals, i.e., the prophets.

- It is monotheistic (the belief in one Creator, the Lord of us all)
- It is the complete guide and a comprehensive manual containing everything we need to know about human life and its purpose

- It is not simply limited to a place of worship; rather, it regulates the entire life of its followers beyond the place of worship
- It is a complete set of codes governing every faculty of human life, and it does not leave aside even the smallest detail that should concern us
- It affects our personal lives and our most private moments
- It provides guidance at both the micro and macro levels and facilitates workable agendas for both national and international relations

Islam is completely in-sync with human nature, because the Creator of both is one and the same.

- It lays down fundamental principles to establish relationships between individuals and among nations
- It provides rules for social, economic, and political needs
- It establishes what is right and what is wrong
- It differentiates between good and bad deeds
- It shows the way to success and protects against failure
- It mentions the past and highlights the future
- It gives glad tidings of reward and threats of punishment

Islam is aware of the problems man encounters in life and provides practical solutions. It takes into consideration all aspects of human life and provides guidance accordingly. Islam is completely in-sync with human nature because the Creator of both is one and the same. Who else can know better than our Lord, Who prepared the message that so perfectly fits our nature?

Our physical and mental state is not an enigma to Islam, and thus the duties prescribed and demands put forth are just and practical. Man's weaknesses are not foreign to Islam; flexibilities in Islam are designed in light of our shortcomings. Therefore, similar to an inventor of a machine who is familiar with its every component, our Lord knows us well and provides for our needs and capabilities according to His limitless knowledge.

Islam is not a force that repels people from itself; instead, it attracts them. Islam wants people to build meaningful, strong, and everlasting relationships with each other. It intends to strengthen the human community through a variety of interrelationships held together for the sake of pleasing the Almighty [Qur'an 41:34]. Such relationships are at the core of the human society that Islam intends to build. Islam promotes human-to-human interaction based on equality, dignity, love and mutual respect [Qur'an 49:10-12]. It does not advocate individualistic or selfish attitudes. Mutual care and cooperation are the foundation on which Islam wants people to erect their structure of life. Love, sacrifice, favor, tolerance, forgiveness, respect, patience, perseverance, piety, morality, chastity, modesty, sincerity, honesty, humility, purity of intent, promoting equality, respecting privacy, maintaining dignity, enforcing justice – these are among the essential ingredients of the Islamic faith that assist its followers in fulfilling their duties towards man and the Almighty. All of these qualities lead to amicable inter-action and prevent individualism and selfishness, thereby allowing the human community to progress towards its intended purpose.

The core of the Islamic model for humanity consists of physical and everlasting relationships among different segments of society, and it is based on the common goal of acquiring the pleasure of the Lord and recognition of His Lordship. Hence, Islam gathers people on an equal footing, for one purpose and towards one objective: providing solid foundation for unity and cooperation to achieve ultimate success in the Hereafter. At the same time, it discourages individualistic attitudes that are usually for monetary success and disapproves of merely pursuing temporary material pleasures. Seeking the pleasure of the Almighty is always the priority in Islam and the utmost concern of its devout followers.

Islam suppresses that part of human nature that harms oneself and others, creates disturbance in society, destroys peace, inflicts injuries, brings injustice, violates human rights, forms social classes, establishes hierarchies, abuses power, enjoins hypocrisy, diminishes values, spreads individualism, promotes selfishness, overlooks responsibilities, ignores duties, gives rise to carelessness, and brings all sorts of suffering on society and humanity. Whenever people fail to suppress this part of human nature, they turn into heartless beasts causing great harm to fellow humans. Islam never wants people to degrade themselves and fall from the higher state that Allah ﷻ granted them—the "Best of all Creatures."

Recognizing the inherently harmful aspects of human nature, Islam provides the necessary tools and guidance to suppress and control it. Those who succeed in suppressing the harmful aspects of human nature will maintain their higher state, eventually acquiring the pleasure of the Almighty and, subsequently, eternal life in Heaven.

Through its sacred revelations and heavenly laws, Islam explains its protection of people from the time they are in the embryonic state to their final moments in this world, and even beyond that. It makes it incumbent upon individuals and societies to implement those heavenly laws that guarantee protection to all, regardless of wealth, status, gender, ethnicity, or any other aspect of their identity.

To ensure enforcement of heavenly laws and for justice to prevail, Islam provides severe but appropriate punishments for all crimes, hidden or open, and deals rigorously, but equitably with criminals who usurp their victim's rights and freedoms. Islam inherently recognizes that without the protection of law and the enforcement of relevant punishments, through due process, peace and order cannot prevail [Qur'an 24:2]. Therefore, Islam provides an outline for a justice system by which people can acquire justice, live in peace, and pursue their greater purpose of life. Moreover, Islam places great responsibility on the government, as well as on every citizen, to provide security and protection. Islam states clearly that no one is above the law.

There are no contradictions or clashes within the rules set forth in Islam. No one is permitted, nor is there ever a need, to violate any

No matter how 'great' the good may seem, violation of any Islamic rule is not permissible. principle, however minute it may be, in order to implement or enforce any other rule. No matter how 'great' the good may seem, violation of any Islamic rule is not permissible. Lack of knowledge is not an excuse, especially when rights are violated and harm is done to others. In such cases, proper punishment must be enforced, and just compensations must be awarded to the victim.

In Islam, a believer is never alone. Islam understands that loneliness is one of the causes of many setbacks in life. Thus, Islam promotes family ties, builds caring friendships, admires strong relationships, and demands constant contact among people. Moreover, by having strong connection and nearness to the Lord, through remembering Him continuously, one never feels lonely and always enjoys His company [Qur'an 50:16]. Through this affinity with the Lord, one always feels someone to be within oneself, with whom one can communicate and consult. This accompaniment brings true and unique satisfaction and happiness. Without that 'someone' within, one may feel lonely even in a crowd of millions.

At this point, I believe I have sufficiently provided an overview of Islam and, to summarize and to put the matter briefly, I would say that by being a complete system of worship, Islam simultaneously promotes human values, protects human rights, admires social work, and allows scientific and technological advances for the betterment of society.

Having briefly stated this, I will further explore each of the above-mentioned and other topics in detail. With the arguments presented, one will also be able to know whether there is complete happiness in this world. Does Islam promise complete happiness? Is there complete peace? Does Islam teach us how to acquire complete peace? Can one acquire a state of contentment? If yes, then how?

CHAPTER 2

What is Islam?

*B*EFORE PROCEEDING, make note that in order for one to truly understand any ideology, religion, or system, it is necessary for one to study it with impartiality, as much as humanly possible. As such, the reader needs to proceed through this book with an open mind and heart. Most ideologies and religions possess or claim to possess the key to humanity's good, but simultaneously they all have specific differences that may seem to be minor but that are concretely fundamental to each philosophy. A biased study can overlook those very basic differences. However, if one properly understands those very basic differences, one can envision the entire philosophy and its purpose and can distinguish it from others.

THE PHILOSOPHY OF ISLAM

*T*HE ENTIRE UNIVERSE AND EVERYTHING IN IT, including us, are created by the Supreme Being, our Lord, Allah Almighty ﷻ. He is the sole Owner and the sole Innovator of everything. He created us to worship Him. Our stay in this world is temporary. Each one of us lives here for a limited time and then passes on to the other world.

One day, the universe will be folded up and the Day of Judgment will arise. Everyone will be handed a 'Register of Deeds,' containing whatever was earned in this temporary life. Based on our performance here, we will earn either *Jannah* (Heaven) or *Jahannum* (Hell). Those who will have acquired 'ultimate success' and earned the pleasure of Allah ﷻ, will be sent to Heaven to live there eternally and to enjoy its endless bounties. Those who did not earn the pleasure of Allah ﷻ and instead earned His wrath will be punished in Hell and will be the 'ultimate loser.'

> *This is the only chance; use it or lose it. It is a one-way ticket, and there is no coming back.*

Allah ﷻ gave people free will to choose right from wrong. Human beings are not animals or angels, neither of which have free will. Allah granted man the power through which he can exceed angels or degrade himself to be even lower than animals. Allah ﷻ bestowed man with free will to test him and to see how he fares in this life [Qur'an 67:2].

If man chooses wisely and uses his faculties to do what is right, he can maintain the higher status granted to him as the 'best of all creatures.' If he does not choose wisely, ignores the inner voice, does not follow the commandments to do good, falls from the original divinely granted status, and degrades himself, he will be unsuccessful and will have earned the displeasure of Allah ﷻ. Any misuse of the fine human qualities and the bounties of Allah ﷻ will make him the ultimate loser. No one will be given a second chance to return to Earth and do good [Qur'an 23:99-100]. This is the only chance; use it or lose it. It is a one-way ticket, and there is no coming back.

Allah ﷻ not only granted and bestowed upon man qualities and capabilities to do what is good and to refrain from what is bad, He has also clearly shown man both good and bad, as well as what pleases and displeases Him. Allah ﷻ equipped man with the necessary tools, such as intellect, sense, instinct, and so on, and provided the necessary knowledge for him to achieve the purpose of his creation.

Allah's chosen beings, commonly known as prophets and messengers, revealed and delivered that knowledge in its entirety and set the standards to be emulated for us to acquire ultimate success. No more

excuses remain, and there can be no more justification for being ignorant. Now, there is no way out. Even though this
may sound imposing and scary, and many people
may not want to hear it, I cannot prevent myself
from speaking the truth as presented by Islam.
This is a clear warning for myself, for every
Muslim, and for every other human being.

*Allah 🕮 and His
prophets have
nothing to lose. We
are the ones at risk
of failing because
we are the only
ones being tested.*

The choices are very clear. Either save ourselves from the hellfire
by choosing to follow the message of the prophets or be responsible
for our fate in Hell. It is all up to us. Punishments are more painful
when guilt is realized. Thus, the guilt of wasting time is to be avoided
at all costs so that choosing wisely, exploring the truth, and following
the right path will become apparent. Allah 🕮 and His prophets have
nothing to lose. We are the ones at risk of failing because we are the
only ones being tested.

One of the most essential aspects of Islam is *Iman bil ghaib* (belief
in the unseen). The 'unseen' includes, but is not limited to:
- The existence of the Supreme Being
- The angelic beings
- The process of creation
- The existence of the soul, after being created and before
  being sent into this world [Qur'an 7:172]
- The state of existence after death (*A'lam-e-Barzakh*) [Qur'an 23:100]
- Resurrection and accountability on Judgment Day
- Eternal life in Heaven or Hell
- Many other truths, purposely kept hidden [Qur'an 16:8]

Evidently, these and other hidden truths were necessary to test
people's faith. If any one of these hidden truths was made obvious,
there would be no need for beliefs and faith. People would have automatically accepted the truth, and the purpose of earthly life would be
pointless. The whole point is to recognize the existence of the Lord,

to believe in Him as our Lord and Creator, to follow His message and abide by His rules.

Even though some Islamic beliefs and teachings are based on the unseen truths that are not visible, they can be seen or felt through positive reasoning and rational thinking. The followers of Islam are required to have firm and unshakeable belief in the unseen without questioning it. However, believing in the unseen after positive reasoning, concentrated thinking, and deep exploration bears the same reward as having faith in them without questioning it. Allah ﷻ states:

> Certainly, the creation of heavens and earth, and the alternation of night and day, and the sailing of ships on sea carrying that which benefits people, and that which is sent by Allah from the sky: water, through which the earth is given life after its death, and scattered animals of all kinds on [it], and the differing movements of winds, and the clouds bound in between the sky and earth—in all of this, indeed, are signs for those people who utilize intellect. • [Qur'an 2:164]

Clearly, Islam invites everyone to pay attention, explore, analyze, and collaborate to reach the truth and become successful. Islam is the truth and nothing but the truth; however, to seek inner wisdom and to strengthen faith, contemplating is always welcomed and rewarded. Those who intend to study Islam to find fault in it, or who are weak in their faith after recognizing Islam's authenticity and divinity, do not do themselves a favor, and they displease the Almighty.

Judgment Day and the concept of accountability are central to Islam because most beliefs and practices are relevant to them. The fear of accountability and of bearing the consequences for failure on Judgment Day leads to lawfulness, the exercise of morality, and the utilization of good manners.

Since Allah ﷻ is All-Knowledgeable and nothing is or could be hidden from Him, the fact that He is always watching us prevents a true servant of Allah ﷻ from all kinds of wrongdoings, the visible and the hidden. Even when one thinks no one is watching, Allah ﷻ is ever watchful of one's deeds, which are always recorded by angels.

In this life, it is possible to avoid indictment and punishment due to loopholes in man-made laws, the inherent weaknesses of those laws, personal cleverness, and the lack of evidence or eyewitnesses, but it is certain that no one can escape from Allah ﷻ on Judgment Day. Thus, it is impossible for anyone to avoid eventual accountability for even the slightest action. Moreover, accountability is the foundation that differentiates between other creatures and humans.

COULD A MAN INVENT ISLAM?

*H*AVING READ SO FAR, the thought that Islam was probably invented by an intelligent person may cross the mind of an objective reader. With regard to that thought, I believe that after developing a true understanding of Islamic teachings and after considering all aspects of Islam, an objective reader can decide what the answer is to this question. The following arguments will assist in reaching a decision.

When studying Islam closely, one discovers that it covers a wide array of physical and metaphysical subjects concerning human life on earth and that it provides guidance for every situation, time, and era. Islam's universality covers all aspects of human necessities, even those of which man cannot conceive.

How could a man, about fifteen hundred years ago, formulate a comprehensive way of life that encompasses human beings' every need for all times to come? How could he ensure that his teachings would remain valid for all times and situations, even until the Day of Judgment? How could he have predicted the future with such precision? How could he have developed such a system of life that would survive for centuries and not even be altered slightly? How could he leave such an indelible mark on history that would be so vivid and valid, even after centuries have passed?

He would have to be superhuman or to have received direct inspiration from a supernatural source. However, history is a witness that he was a man; therefore, he could not have invented such a perfect system of life. This perfection must definitely have come from somewhere else, and where else could it be but from the Lord. Only the Lord, the Almighty, knows all the weaknesses and needs of His creation and could prescribe such a unique and transcendent system, valid for all times and for all places.

Even if a single claim of the holy Prophet of Islam and the holy Qur'an could be disproved, the entire structure of Islam would crumble.

Islam is so confident about its teachings, it claims that no one can change, replace, or add anything to it to make it anymore perfect or to lose/disprove its perfection. This centuries-old claim is still open for challenge. Islam claims to be the perfect way of life, and this claim is certainly valid. Even to this day, researchers successfully find whatever they are searching for. If one cannot locate something in Islam in the first instance, all one has to do is dig a bit deeper, and one will certainly come across it. Islam contains the knowledge of everything and fulfills every human need.

All of Islam's challenges, claims, and qualities are clear proof of its absolute truthfulness. If it were an innovation of any individual, he would never make the claim of infallibility. Therefore, the Architect of Islam must have been certain that no one could meet its challenges or counter its claims. If the architect were a human, he could not be definitely certain about his innovated system. If even a single claim of the holy Prophet of Islam 🕌 and the holy Qur'an could be disproved, the entire structure of Islam would crumble. This has not happened so far and, as claimed, will never happen because this holy system is not an innovation of a human being [Qur'an 4:82].

Inspired by the initial divine revelations and commandments, and as commanded by Allah 🕌, Muhammad 🕌 began to preach the message of Islam. At first, those who had complete confidence in him embraced Islam because of his personal qualities of trustworthiness and compassion. As more and more people witnessed his moral character and the powerful message of Islam that he preached, the circle of Islam began to increase.

If he were the architect of Islam, as claimed by some, then upon gaining so much success, why did he call people to the Lord and not to himself? Why did he not claim this religion to be something of his own making? He did not do so because it was not his invention. It is, in fact, the continuation of the guidance that previous prophets of Allah 🕌 brought to humankind. This divine guidance was merely perfected with the 'final revelations' to Prophet Muhammad 🕌.

In the pages ahead, we will learn in detail that for either a Muslim by birth or anyone who newly embraces Islam, it is necessary to certify one's faith in Islam, not only verbally, but by believing in it from the heart as well. As such, let us suppose for the sake of argument that the inventor of Islam were a human being. If so, he could not possibly read the hearts of people to tell if someone had certified his or her faith from the heart. Why would he even bother to require this kind of certification, which he himself cannot prove or disprove? Clearly, this goes against logic. His main concern would be to increase the number of his followers in order to achieve his purpose, whatever it may be. However, if he was truly conveying the Lord's message and fulfilling his duties to connect the creation to the Creator, he would put forth all the requirements that make that connection possible and that are required by the Creator Himself.

The declaration of faith (verbally) fulfills the requirement of entering into Islam and becoming a member of the Muslim community and brotherhood. Certifying it from the heart is directly related to being accepted by the Lord and to achieving ultimate success. The Prophet 🕌 was required to secure both, declaration and certification. Had he invented Islam, one declaration would suffice. This is another proof that Islam is not a human invention.

In my view, this much is sufficient, but readers will continue to come across more evidence that will enable them to conclude that Islam is not a human invention. Keeping Islam's divinity in mind, I hope the reader can attain a true understanding of it.

NO QUESTION IS UNANSWERED IN ISLAM

*W*HEN WE COMPARE OUR PHYSICAL EXISTENCE with other incredible creations only to find that we are nothing but a tiny particle in the universe, we begin to ask countless questions. Who are we? From where did we come? To where are we headed? What is the purpose of all the things out there? If there is life after death, how is it? If there are Heaven and Hell, what do they look like, and where are they? How are we to believe in the existence of God, Lord, Creator or Allah 🕌? What does He look like? Why can we not see Him? Who are the chosen prophets? Which prophets were real, and how can we believe in them? Is there a book or a set of rules revealed by the Lord, or are all such books merely a creation of the human mind? Who is right, and who is wrong? How can we achieve peace, happiness, prosperity, and so forth? What is good or bad, who decides that, and how can we be sure of it? How is it possible that when we die and turn to dust we become alive again? Is there a spiritual world? Are the body and soul two different things? Everyone asks such questions; some ponder deeply for answers, and others just scratch the surface.

If these and many other questions are not answered to our satisfaction, or if we fail to comprehend the answers or simply abandon the inner voice of curiosity, true satisfaction and peace of heart, mind, and soul cannot be attained. Even if we attain material success at some point in our life, we are not completely satisfied. We continue to feel an emptiness, and thoughts of failure overshadow our conscience. In this vast universe, we tend to lose purpose, sense of placement, and the taste for life until we find answers to these and many other questions that linger in our curious minds.

If an ideology or a religion does not provide complete, satisfactory, and rational answers, or if the answers provided are no longer relevant, then, in my view, that ideology/religion is incomplete. Since Islam claims that it is the complete way of life, then it must provide answers to all questions one can raise. After reading this book, I am confident that the reader will come to believe that Islam has answers to all questions and that nothing remains unanswered.

Allah ﷻ created and revealed to us the system that explains how we should live and prepare to acquire the ultimate success. Besides Him, no one else could have developed this required system, because He is our Lord and knows best our needs and desires, abilities and shortcomings, psychology, and so on. Allah ﷻ is our true Lord and does not want us to go astray; therefore, He has beforehand included answers to every possible question and completed the *deen* of Islam. Thus, there is no mystery in Islam.

However, to obtain answers for complicated questions, the following are some prerequisites: sincere desire, thirst for true knowledge, and a heartfelt wish to search for the truth. Also, bear in mind that this world is Allah's creation and governed by His principles and that we are merely His creation and do not possess unlimited knowledge and power. Even though Allah ﷻ has revealed the complete message, we may not instantly comprehend it and may require deeper knowledge and wisdom. The more knowledgeable we become, the more we understand the word and commandments of Allah ﷻ. I firmly believe that if we continuously strive for answers, we will get them eventually.

ISLAM IS FIT FOR HUMAN NATURE

*I*T IS FIRST NECESSARY TO DEFINE HUMAN NATURE and then proceed to establish its relationship to Islam. Human nature is the collection of inherent qualities and habits that are common to all

We are not merely robots like angels, and we certainly are much better than animals. Neither did we evolve from animals, nor are we as subtle as angels.

people (i.e., the innate qualities and habits humans possess is their nature). For example, we work, eat, drink, sleep, have other physical and intimate needs and desires, have emotions, socialize, fight, and seek power, authority and fame, etc. All of these are but a few examples of human nature.

Human beings are comprised of a spirit and a physical structure, i.e., the soul and body. Therefore, we have both spiritual and physical needs. We are not angels or beasts. According to Islam, it is a great mistake to consider humans mere 'brutes' and to exclude the spiritual aspect of our being. Similarly, it would be a mistake to consider ourselves like or greater than angels and completely disregard the biological and animalistic aspects of our being. We are not merely robots like angels, and we certainly are much better than animals. Neither did we evolve from animals, nor are we as subtle as angels.

We have freedom to choose and power to know good and bad, right and wrong, and impiety and piety. Angels and animals do not have the freedom of choice, nor do they have anything to choose. For example, if a lion desires to have a vegetarian dish, its wish cannot come true. Similarly, if a deer craves for a steak, its wish cannot come true either. In fact, lion and deer cannot even wish for vegetarian and non-vegetarian dishes.

In the same manner, Allah ﷻ did not grant angels the freedom of choice. They are merely robot-like and do as they are programmed. Consequently, they are not rewarded or punished for their behavior.

In contrast, Allah ﷻ granted humans the freedom of choice, and they have a lot from which to choose, so they can use this privilege. For example, they can choose to eat whatever they wish, vegetarian or non-vegetarian, healthy or unhealthy, expensive or inexpensive. In the end, only they will bear the consequences for what they choose.

For any system, ideology, or religion to be fit for human nature, it must comprehensively consider every inherent quality and habit of humans and must provide proper guidance to assist people in reaching their goal of life. If it repels or completely suppresses any inherent quality and habit, and/or if it leaves any one of them out or provides no guidance, then that system, ideology, or religion is not fit for humans and is incomplete and deficient.

> *Islam does not repel, suppress completely, or ignore any part of human nature; instead, it teaches its followers how to control and shape their nature appropriately.*

It is unlikely that a follower of one religion will seek part of another religion to fill a void in his own. If this occurs, then how can one know to which religion this follower really belongs? Where does his loyalty lie? Which religion or system does he call his own? Meanwhile, he is forced to follow parts of other religion(s) because his own religion lacks a necessary aspect. Naturally, humans embrace and follow what is or seems to be most complete, beneficial, and convenient. Thus, in the presence of an absolute system of life, an incomplete system is doomed to fail.

Islam does not repel, completely suppress, or ignore any part of human nature; instead, it teaches its followers how to control and shape their nature appropriately. Wherever there is a slight chance of misusing natural qualities and habits by humans, Islam steps in and changes the course of human nature towards the legitimate purpose. The principles and teachings of Islam do not collide with human nature. They remain side by side with humans, gradually changing humans' course of action so that they can easily adapt and learn to walk confidently on the righteous path. Islam accompanies its followers until they acquire the ultimate success of the Hereafter.

A religion or any secular system of life that attempts to stop any natural behavior of man meets with devastating blows and eventually finds itself without any following. For example, to completely stop the natural flow of a river and save a city from floodwaters is nearly impossible, but, even if achieved temporarily, it may create bigger problems later on. Instead, changing its course, though it requires hard work, eventually solves the problem. If the course of floodwaters is diverted from a city to dry land, it will bring many benefits. The city will be saved from flooding, and the water will simultaneously irrigate dry land, making it arable.

If we seal the cap of a kettle on a burning stove, with the built-up pressure the kettle is bound to burst. Similarly, if an ideology/religion suppresses, ignores, or sacrifices the natural desires and needs of people, even in the name of any greater good, then people cannot function properly, and the outcome will be devastating. As noted earlier, human beings are not like angels, and thus no action should be taken to turn them into angels. Let them be human, and prescribe a system that keeps them 'human' and simultaneously keeps them from falling to the level of animals or even worse. This is exactly what Islam does.

Islam is not against people's natural urge to acquire wealth, but it demands that they earn it through the legitimate means that it establishes and regulates. Islam is not against spending money, but it encourages its followers to spend it for righteous purposes such as, for example, helping the needy. According to Islam, using your wealth and resources for the betterment of the less fortunate or to solve the problems of your community will not reduce your wealth; instead, Allah ﷻ, Who gave you wealth in the first place, certainly has the ability to replenish and increase it. Islam does not forcefully take peoples' wealth against their will, even for the greater good of others. It promises great rewards to people who willingly and with the intent to please Allah 🕮 spend their money for humanitarian purposes.

Islam is not against eating delicious foods, but it teaches that a half-empty stomach is healthier than a stomach stuffed with food. Staying relatively hungry allows one to be thankful to the Lord for His bounties and to be mindful of those starving around the world. Islam is not against wearing lavish clothes, but it rewards simplicity; being simple urges the inner soul and conscience to be less attracted to this material world and more attracted to our higher purpose.

Islam says eat whatever you like, but make sure it is *halāl*, and drink as much as you like, but refrain from *harām* drinks. Sleep as much as necessary, but perform your daily prayers before and after you sleep. Stay up as much as you need to, but be mindful of your health. Love your family and friends to the full extent, but do not forget your Lord and your obligations to Him. Worship your Lord as much as you want to, in order to get closer to Him, but not at the expense of your family, which needs your time and attention. Overall, keep everything in balance, be moderate, and do not become extremists of any sort.

Use time and energy wisely in helping others, and take as much burden as you can bear; correcting the world is not your problem, but it is your continuous duty to correct yourself first. Be flexible and easy on yourself and on others. Teach, but do not impose.

Islam requires its followers to do only what is humanly possible and provides guidance for every situation and according to everyone's capacity. In essence, it is the way of life in strict accordance with human nature. Therefore, on Judgment Day, Allah 🕮 will question and hold everyone accountable according to his or her capability, knowledge, and performance, in order that justice prevails.

The Islamic system of life intends for people to uphold their human status, become devout followers, avoid falling below the status of animals, and surpass angelic qualities. To ensure the fulfillment of this goal, Islam lays down principles that are fit for human nature and easy to follow.

MEANING OF THE NAME 'ISLAM'

*M*OST OFTEN, THE NAME OF AN OBJECT represents its qualities. Choosing a name is an important and creative process, and many times the success or failure of a product or a business entity depends on it. When naming, people try to choose a name that truly represents the object's quality and/or its use. The more comprehensive the name of a product, service, system, ideology or what have you, the faster it is publicized. Sometimes, individuals or companies seek the services of professionals when choosing names. The more expertise is utilized, the better chances for a befitting name.

Islam is the name given to the most complete way of life on Earth for human beings. No man chose this name; the Lord, the Almighty Allah ﷻ, chose it Himself. Now, since the Creator, the All-Knower, chose it Himself, it must mean a lot. It must completely explain Islam as the system of life and refer to its qualities, and the name must be befitting of what it actually claims to be. If we can comprehend the various meanings of the word Islam, we can easily understand the meaning and purpose of the Islamic system, ideology, definition of worship, inner philosophy, and the complete way of life it represents. Only then can we recognize that only the Lord Himself could reveal such a befitting name.

It is pronounced, 'Islam' not 'Izlam.' The 's' in Islam does not sound like the 's' in 'is' but as in 'school' and 'bus.' In Arabic, the root word for Islam is *'salam'* سلم which means 'peace' سِلم. For one to have a complete idea, it is interesting to note the various meanings of the root word 'salam,' when used differently—(سَلَّمَ — سَلِمَ — سَلَمَ — سَلَّمَ — سَلَمَ — سُلِّمَ) prior to explaining the meaning of the word Islam.

Generally, 'salam' is defined as peace, and its derivatives can mean the following: to escape (danger); to be safe, secure; to be sound, intact, unimpaired, or unharmed; to be free (from fault), faultless, or flawless, to hand over; to turn over; to turn in; to submit; to save, rescue, or deliver; to protect, preserve, safeguard, or keep (from harm, injury); to accept or approve of; to give consent or agree; and to acknowledge, allow, or concede. If we select any one of the numerous meanings of 'salam' and relate it to what is inherent in Islam, we see direct parallels.

'Islam' is concurrent with its innermost meaning: peace. Since 'salam' means peace, someone can ask if Islam, as a religion, really brings peace. We will consider this question in the following section, *Different Categories of Peace.*

Islam is also defined as peace, treaty, truce, concord, protection, quarter, safety, security, immunity, mercy, and grace. It also means obedience, reverence, worship, homage, and much more. In a religious context, Islam technically means to establish the *deen* exclusively for Allah ﷻ, i.e., to resign to the will of Allah ﷻ, the submission of one's will to the will of Allah ﷻ, complete submission from the deepest part of one's heart, and paying homage to Allah ﷻ.

Moreover, Islam is the way of life prescribed by Allah ﷻ, beginning with the teachings of the first man and prophet, Adam ﷺ and concluding with the teachings of Allah's ﷻ final and most beloved prophet, Muhammad ﷺ of Arabia, the son of Abdullah.

Most frequently, people refer to Islam as peace and nothing but peace. Some people do not fully understand the association of 'Islam' with 'peace'. They ask if Islam is the peace that is the antonym of 'war' or if it refers to other types of peace.

Upon embracing Islam, an individual enters into a state of total protection. Islam is like a divine umbrella. When held onto tightly, it provides a shade of mercy and brings forth every kind of peace: peace of the heart, mind, soul and body; peace in the family, society, and world; peace from all harm; and peace in the Hereafter. Every kind of peace is attainable under the umbrella of Islam. I am not implying that one cannot find many of these kinds of peace elsewhere; however, I am saying that one cannot find *all* of these necessary types of peace under one roof, unless that roof is Islam.

What I have discussed so far certainly reflects that Islam, through its various definitions, is the befitting name of the complete way of life, of which no man could have conceived. Further explanations will prove this point and make the matter clearer.

DIFFERENT CATEGORIES OF PEACE

PEACE OF HEART

*B*ELIEVERS IN ISLAM BUILD A STRONG connection to the Creator; therefore, they find inner peace that is not attainable through any other means. A believer perpetually acquires peace of heart through performing the activities of worship, continuously remembering Allah ﷻ, and refraining from committing sins.

PEACE OF MIND

A BELIEVER ACQUIRES PEACE OF MIND when he is fully content and recognizes that he is doing everything in his ability to be successful in this world, leaving the rest to the will of Allah ﷻ. When he receives something, he is thankful to the Lord; when at a loss, he recognizes that the Lord has the power to give, as well as to take away. A true believer who has strong faith is at peace within himself, because Islam commands him to use his faculties wisely and to execute actions with his full capabilities, leaving the outcome to the will of Allah 🕌. Upon the positive result of his actions, he is grateful to the Lord, and upon negative result, he is patient and accepts it to be the Lord's will.

PEACE OF THE SOUL

*P*EACE OF THE SOUL IS THE MOST IMPORTANT kind of peace. It is a peace that is deep in the inner self, deep within the heart of hearts. In comparison to the peace of body, heart, and mind that is acquired through simpler means, peace of the soul, unquestionably more precious, cannot be acquired easily. Acquiring peace of the soul requires knowledge of the sacred and knowledge of who one is. What is the purpose of one's life? What is one's final destination? The Islamic answers to these questions bring true peace to the soul.

> *Peace of the heart and mind is essential for people to be active and full of life, but peace of the soul is certainly more precious because it brings ultimate satisfaction.*

Money and other worldly possessions bring a certain amount of peace to the heart and mind, but when one lies lonely in bed, gazing with a deep sigh at the ceiling or at the sky with millions of sparkling stars, one inquires into questions such as those noted above. The soul of man continues to search for answers, but the conclusion is usually incomplete and unsatisfactory.

Islam, on the other hand, guides humanity from the beginning of their journey, through this transitory life, and to the final destination in the Hereafter. It provides comprehensive answers for their curiosity to be at peace, by which they peacefully work towards ultimate success. Peace of the heart and mind is essential for people to be active and full of life, but peace of the soul is certainly more precious because it brings ultimate satisfaction.

PEACE WITHIN A FAMILY

A FAMILY UNIT IS THE MOST IMPORTANT PART of human life. A family is the place where each member finds refuge, support, and inspiration to live and work. If family life is disturbed, its members feel unprotected, each other's support diminishes, a deep emptiness sets in, and overall life gradually begins to disintegrate. Love, peace, and tranquility are the most important ingredients to having a happy and prosperous family life. Sometimes even wealth, success, and fame fail to bring joy, and the true taste of living together is not achieved. Even though some may not admit that life becomes miserable without a family, the fact is that life does become a miserable human failure without a family. This becomes obvious when loneliness begins to bring unbearable sufferings.

In Islam, each member of a family is bound to each other to achieve the pleasure of the Lord and to perform his or her fair share of the duties prescribed by Islam. By fulfilling these great tasks, each member of the family unit maintains and enjoys peace, happiness, and prosperity. To bring peace in the family, Islam fully explains every duty and right of a husband to his wife and vice versa, of parents to their children and vice versa, and so on. Any violation of Islamic rules, regulations, and obligations by any member brings forth tragedy to the family, and every violator will be held accountable on Judgment Day.

In a family unit, it is not a choice, but rather it is incumbent upon a husband to support and fulfill every justifiable and basic need of his wife. They both have to be loyal and faithful to each other and must safeguard their chastity to maintain each other's right and trust. One of the main duties of parents is to provide their children with a solid Islamic education and to train them to become good, practicing Muslims. Similarly, children have equal, if not greater, duties to their parents, which, if neglected, earn the irreversible wrath of the Lord, unless forgiven by the parents. For example, even a simple smile from children on seeing their parents brings countless blessings from the Lord. When each member fulfills his or her duties, the entire family is strengthened and solidified, and

When each family, the building blocks of a society, is peaceful, the entire society becomes full of peace.

peace, happiness, and prosperity prevail in the family. When each family, the building blocks of a society, is peaceful, the entire society becomes full of peace.

PEACE IN SOCIETY

*I*N ADDITION TO PEACE IN THE FAMILY, through Islamic brotherhood, equality, justice, system of punishments, social welfare system, acts of direct and indirect worship, and the concept of accountability on Judgment Day, a society achieves complete and everlasting peace. If Muslims do not implement Islamic principles in their society to establish the divine rule of law, Islam should not be blamed for crime, disturbance, chaos, lack of peace and prosperity, and unhappiness.

If Muslims do not implement Islamic principles in their society to establish divine rule of law, Islam should not be blamed for crime, disturbance, chaos, lack of peace and prosperity, and unhappiness.

The one who claims to be Muslim and fails to apply Islamic principles to his or her life or to the society at large is at fault, not Islam. It is a matter of fact that those societies that implement such Islamic principles in their system enjoy the fruits of it. Those who abuse and exploit Islam to achieve personal agendas are the actual losers, not Islam or the way of life it prescribes. History is witness that not too long ago, faithful Muslims enjoyed an era of peace and prosperity as they truthfully practiced Islam. Even to this day, wherever faithful Muslims practice Islam, they are enjoying the fruits of it.

PEACE IN THE WORLD

*B*Y ACHIEVING PEACE IN A MUSLIM FAMILY and society through Islamic principles, global peace can easily be achieved. Suffice it to say that Islam contains principles that, if fully and universally applied, result in national and international peace and prosperity. Having true knowledge of Islamic principles and having the sincerity of everyone, both Muslim and non-Muslim, are some of the prerequisites for world peace.

After all, we are the creation of one single Lord, He is the One Who prescribed and extended to us all the system of life (Islam) that is so perfectly fit for our nature and purpose. Why should we not benefit from it for the greater good of ourselves and simultaneously achieve worldwide peace?

CHAPTER 3

History of Islam

HE HISTORY OF ISLAM is as old as the history of humankind. Since Islam claims to be the most appropriate form
of guidance, the complete way of life, fit for human nature,
and valid for all times, it must be as old as humankind. Many people
believe that Islam came about in the sixth century C.E. If this were the
case, then how can Islam claim to be the guidance for the first human
to the last one? As I proceed further, this question will be answered.

According to a *Hadīth-e-Qudsi* (sacred *hadīth* that have a particularly important status because the message is from Allah ﷻ, while
the wording is that of the Prophet Muhammad ﷺ),

I was a hidden treasure, (I) willed to be known; therefore, I
created everything. [Shamaa'il Tirmidhi]

'Everything' means the entire universe and everything in it,
including human beings. Among all other creatures, Allah ﷻ granted
humans the status of 'Best of All Creatures.'

The first human being the Lord Almighty created was Adam ﷺ.
Adam ﷺ and his progeny were to become His vicegerents on the
Earth. Initially, Heaven became the abode for Adam ﷺ; however,
Adam soon began to feel lonely. Allah ﷻ then created Hawwa عليها السلام,
commonly known as Eve, the first woman and the second human
being. Amazingly, she was created from the left rib of Adam ﷺ;

Allah ﷻ does whatever He wills because He is the All-Powerful. Allah ﷻ created Adam ﷺ without parents; Hawwa ﷺ was born without a female (mother); Isa ﷺ, known as Jesus, was born without a male (father). All of the above are clear signs of His power.

Adam and Hawwa lived in Heaven, and Allah ﷻ permitted them to eat from wherever they wished, except from the tree prohibited to them. Iblīs/Shaytān (Satan) deceived them into eating from that prohibited tree. This did not amount to 'original sin,' a concept widely promoted in Western Christianity, but it was an innocent mistake. Because of this mistake, they could no longer live in Heaven. Allah ﷻ explains:

> Then Satan caused the two to slip and got them out of the place where they lived, and We said, "Get down, you will be enemies to one another, and now in the Earth shall be your dwelling and provision for an appointed term." • [Qur'an 2:36]

Upon their exit from Heaven, Allah ﷻ further said:

> …get down from here, all of you! Then, if there comes to you from Me 'guidance,' whosoever follows My guidance shall have nothing to fear, nor shall they grieve. • And those who disbelieve and shall deny Our signs—they are to be the inmates of Hell, and therein they shall abide forever. • [Qur'an 2:38-39]

Adam ﷺ and Hawwa ﷺ, the first couple and parents to all the people to come, were lost on Earth and separated from each other for a very long time. They were truly ashamed of their mistake in Heaven, for not abiding by the commandment of the Lord. Adam ﷺ felt guilty and wept profusely, asking for forgiveness. Thereafter, Allah ﷻ forgave him, and Adam ﷺ and Hawwa ﷺ found each other and continued to live together. Gradually, the population of the world increased, and guidance began to come, as Allah ﷻ had stated on their departure from Heaven.

As the population grew widespread and men learned the ways to live life on Earth, laws were needed to establish societies and solve basic problems. An ideology was needed to satisfy humanity's natural curiosities about their existence and to fulfill their natural desire to worship. To fulfill this need, the Almighty revealed His guidance periodically, according to the need of the times and the level of peoples' understanding, through His chosen individuals, known as prophets. From the outset, that very guidance was Islam, and all of the prophets, including those people who chose to believe in them, were Muslims. With the teachings of the last Prophet Muhammad ﷺ, the guidance was completed and perfected. Allah ﷻ officially chose Islam as the *deen* and on its completion stated:

> This day, I have perfected for you your religion and have completed My favor to you, and I have approved Islam as the religion for you. • [Quran 5:3]

Some may ask, if these teachings were perfected in the form of Islam through Muhammad ﷺ, what were the teachings of the previous prophets called? They were Islam, but in its incomplete form. Every prophet's *deen* (religion) was Islam; however, their *sharia* (the rules and commandments appropriate for their time, place, and need as revealed to them in their respective books) varied. [Qur'an 5:48] The major *sharias* came to be known as Judaism and Christianity. In Islam, the followers of those *sharias* are referred to as *Ahle Kitāb* (People of the Book).

Since the Creator and the One Who completed His guidance is One and the same, how could His message vary among the prophets when they were all sent by Him and towards the same creation? The basic beliefs—such as the belief in Allah ﷻ, His prophets, the unseen, refraining from *shirk* and idolatry, worshiping Allah ﷻ, life in the Hereafter, the Day of Judgment, and belief in Heaven and Hell—were all the same as they are in Islam today. Every Muslim must declare that,

> ...we believe in Allah and what has been sent down to us and that which was sent down to Ibrahim (Abraham) and Ismail and Is-

hāq (Isaac) and Yaqūb (Jacob) and their offspring and what was given to Musa (Moses) and Isa (Jesus) and the other prophets from their Lord. We make no distinction between any of them, in the matter of faith and to Allah have we surrendered ourselves. • [Qur'an 3:84]

Furthermore, Allah ﷻ reveals:

And whosoever seeks a religion other than Islam, it shall certainly not be accepted of him; and in the Hereafter, he shall be of the losers. • [Qur'an 3:85]

Allah ﷻ continued to send prophets, one after another, to all nations, giving them a fair chance to accept and believe. Written and/or oral guidance was revealed to almost all of them: some followed the message of their prophets, and some ignored it; some even killed their prophets, while some followed for a short period and then forgot the true teachings; and some completely altered the guidance after their prophets passed away. All hopes of those who continuously disregarded the sacred guidance and transgressed, mocked, and disrespected the prophets were dismissed, whereupon Allah ﷻ sent His wrath. The following verses of the holy Qur'an explain this further.

Surely, Allah chose Adam and Nuh (Noah) and the progeny of Ibrahim (Abraham) and the progeny of Imran (Amran) above all people of the world... • [Qur'an 3:33]

And indeed We raised in every community a prophet to instruct them... • [Qur'an 16:36]

And We did not send any prophet but (to preach) in the language of his own people in order that he might explain to them in clear terms (the commandments of Allah)... • [Qur'an 14:4]

And mankind was but a single community (in the beginning), then they began to differ among themselves... • [Qur'an 10:19]

And surely We sent Nuh (Noah) to his people, and he said, "O, my people! Worship Allah, you have no god for yourselves besides Him"... • [Qur'an 23:23]

The nation of Nuh ﷺ, about him, said:

He is not but a mad man... • [Qur'an 23:25]

Nuh الْعَلَيْهِ requested help from Allah سُبْحَانَهُ and said:

He said, "O Lord! Help me, for they have denied me." • [Qur'an 23:26]

Allah سُبْحَانَهُ informed Nuh الْعَلَيْهِ about the great flood and said:

Then we revealed to him, "Build an Ark before Our sight and by Our command"... • [Qur'an 23:27]

And recall when his Lord said to him: "(O Abraham) Surrender!" He submitted: "I surrender myself to the Lord and Cherisher of all the worlds." • And Ibrahim (Abraham) enjoined upon his sons and so did Yaqūb (Jacob), saying: "O my sons! Verily Allah has chosen for you this religion, so die not except as Muslims." • [Qur'an 2:131-132]

And (remember) when Ibrahim (Abraham) was tested by his Lord with regard to His certain commands, which he fulfilled in all entirety. Allah said: "Verily, I am going to appoint you leader for all mankind"... • [Qur'an 2:124]

Surely! Ibrahim (Abraham) was a model of perfection, obedient to Allah and devoted exclusively to the truth. And he was not at all of the polytheists. • [Qur'an 16:120]

And as to Lut (Lot), We gave him authority and knowledge, and We delivered him from the town whose people committed foul deeds. And surely they were a people most wicked and disobedient. •
[Qur'an 21:74]

The People of Lut (Lot) denied the prophets. • [Qur'an 26:160]

...We made subservient to Dawūd (David) the mountains and the birds, so they all celebrated Our praise with him... • [Qur'an 21:79]

And to Sulayman (Solomon), We made subservient the violent wind—that it blew at his bidding to the land that We had blessed... • [Qur'an 21:81]

Then we kept sending our prophets, one after the other... •
[Qur'an 23:44]

Then we sent Musa (Moses) and his brother Harun (Aaron), with Our signs and a clear authority to Pharaoh and his courtiers, but they also became proud and stiff necked, and surely they were a headstrong and insolent people. So they said, "Shall we believe these two humans who are like us, while their people are our worshiping slaves." So they denied both of them; they then were destroyed. And surely, We gave Musa (Moses) the Book that they might be guided aright. • [Qur'an 23:45-49]

We made the son of Maryam and his mother (Maryam) a sign (of Our might) and settled them both on an elevated ground fit for abode with meadows and running springs in sight. • [Qur'an 23:50]

And how many towns have We destroyed when they boasted of their prosperity. So these are their houses that have not been inhabited, after them, but a little; and (in the end) We alone are inheritor. • [Qur'an 28:59]

...so travel on the earth and see with your own eyes how exemplary was the end of those who denied the prophets. • [Qur'an 16:36]

Thus, all divine prophets, succeeding each other, delivered the guidance efficiently, but many prophets' respective nations never fully submitted, and only some were somewhat successful. However, eventually, their nations went astray and their teachings were corrupted. Then came the time when the Final Prophet, the 'Seal of the Prophethood', was born in Makkah, Arabia, roughly six centuries after the holy Prophet Isa (Jesus) ﷺ. Since no prophet was to come after Muhammad ﷺ, Allah ﷻ completed His guidance and made arrangements to safeguard it from human hands, as it had become mankind's habit to distort heavenly guidance. At this point, I can say, with certitude, that Prophet Muhammad ﷺ is the perfection of all previous prophets, that the holy Qur'an is the perfection of all previous scriptures, and that Islam is the perfection of all previous beliefs, as preached by the authentic prophets of Allah ﷻ.

The final guidance was conveyed to humanity through the Final Prophet, Muhammad ﷺ, and complete success in its implementation was achieved during his lifetime. Tens of thousands of Arabs and non-Arabs embraced Islam and were ready to take it across the globe and safeguard it at every cost. Within a short period, the world was not only introduced to Islam, but much of it came under its influence. The guidance, religion, and complete way of life—beginning with the first human being, Adam ﷷ, and completed with the teachings of the Final Prophet, Muhammad ﷺ—have been embraced by billions of people. Currently, it is estimated that every fourth person in the world is a Muslim. Moreover, Islam is still the fastest growing religion. The history of Islam is lengthy, and only a compacted version is possible here.

All of the prophets from Adam ﷷ, the first man and the first human being to Nuh ﷷ, from Ibrahim (Abraham) ﷷ to Is-haq (Isaac) ﷷ to Yaqub (Jacob) ﷷ to Yusuf (Joseph) ﷷ, from Musa (Moses) ﷷ to Isa (Jesus) ﷷ, from Ismail (Ishmael) ﷷ to Muhammad ﷺ, and those mentioned or not mentioned in the divinely revealed books: Taurat (Torah), Zaboor (Psalms), Injeel (Gospel), and the holy Qur'an, brought the same message, i.e., Islam.

> He has decreed for you the religion which He had enjoined on Nuh, and which We have revealed to you, and which We enjoined on Ibrahim and Musa and Isa saying: "Establish this very religion and be not divided therein"... • [Qur'an 42:13]

> O (Our) prophets! Eat of the pure things, and do good deeds. Verily, I am the Knower of what you do. And assuredly, this religion of yours is but one religion, and I am Lord and Cherisher of you all, so you should fear Me and Me alone. • [Qur'an 23:51-52]

> ...follow the faith of your father Ibrahim. He (Allah), it is Who has named you Muslim before, and in this Qur'an as well your name is the same... • [Qur'an 22:78]

> (Look!) Ibrahim was not a Jew or a Christian, but he was an upright Muslim aloof from all falsehood, nor was he of the polytheists. Surely, the nearest of mankind to Ibrahim are those who followed him and this Prophet and the believers. And Allah is the patron of the believers. • [Qur'an 3:67-68]

They said: "What! When we are dead and become dust and bones, shall we then really be raised up again?" • [Qur'an 23:82]

According to the teachings of Islam, Judaism and Christianity in their original form were valid only for their time and until the divine way of life, i.e., Islam, was completed and per-fected. The central teaching of every prophet was about *tawhīd* (Oneness of Allah ﷻ). All their other teachings, e.g., laws of life and belief in the Hereafter, surrounded this fundamental belief and were later either incorporated into, modified by, or repealed by Islam. [Qur'an 2:154]

Islam makes belief in previous prophets and their books one of its necessary tenets because they too were sent by Allah ﷻ and were part of His guidance.

Since then, every previous *sharia* and revealed book has been rendered null and void. Salvation is now possible only through Islam. To this effect, Allah ﷻ reveals in the holy Qur'an:

And whosoever seeks a religion other than Islam, it shall certainly not be accepted of him; and in the Hereafter, he shall be of the losers. • [Qur'an 3:85]

If Islam were a different religion and/or if it were invented by Muhammad ﷺ in the sixth century C.E., it would have been unnecessary to recognize any prophet, let alone all of them, before Muhammad ﷺ and any other book before the holy Qur'an. In fact, Islam makes belief in previous prophets and their books one of its necessary tenets because they too were sent by Allah ﷻ and were part of His guidance. Since they are a part of Islam, Muslims must recognize them and their authentic teachings.

…each one believes in all sincerity in Allah and His angels and His books and His prophets (and they proclaim), "We discriminate not against any of His prophets"… • [Qur'an 2:285]

The laws and commandments brought by the previous prophets were either erased from human history or were corrupted with human intervention. A new set of divine laws and ordinances was needed to replace those that had been tampered with. Therefore,

Allah 🕌 finally and once and for all completed His guidance through the teachings of Prophet Muhammad 🕌 and the holy Qur'an. Allah 🕌 formally and officially approved Islam, and from now on salvation can only be achieved through Islam.

The 'guidance' and teachings had to be completed and perfected with Muhammad 🕌 because no other prophet was to come after him. The need for heavenly guidance was now fulfilled; Allah 🕌 assured the safeguarding of the holy Qur'an from human hands. Now, even the last soul that will come into this world can be guided through it and can prepare for ultimate success.

The holy Qur'an is the final set of commandments from the Almighty and contains the complete way of life. From the day of its first revelation to the day it was completed, Allah 🕌 has protected and preserved the holy Qur'an in its original form. Not even a single vowel or letter has been omitted, added, or changed since its revelation some fifteen centuries ago. This is so and will continue to be until the end of time because the Lord has taken the responsibility of its preservation upon Himself. Allah 🕌 reveals:

> Verily, it is We Who have revealed this discourse (Qur'an), and verily We are its Guardian. • [Qur'an 15:9]

The ordeal that began after Prophet Muhammad 🕌 declared his prophethood in Makkah, Arabia, when the first verse of the holy Qur'an was revealed to him by Allah 🕌 through the Archangel Jibra'il (Gabriel) 🕊, and he 🕌 was commanded to spread the message of Islam, is a subject that requires a separate book.

During the twenty-three years before the divine mission was completed, how much sacrifice was exacted from Prophet Muhammad 🕌 and his companions! How they were persecuted, exiled and boycotted. How much resistance, difficulty, and suffering they endured at the hands of the Quraysh, the Arab tribe living in Makkah. How many battles they had to fight to survive, incurring injury and death.

What price they paid to safeguard their newly acquired faith. How Muhammad ﷺ managed to deliver the guidance to his followers and to lead them in the right direction, keep them united and steadfast, and practically implement Allah's ﷻ guidance by forming treaties and alliances with other tribes, training his companions to take Islam across the globe, and successfully fulfilling all of his obligations. These are all aspects of Islamic history that require lengthy discussions, but as much as I want to discuss these topics, they are not the actual purpose of this book.

The true followers of Islam, the companions of the Prophet ﷺ and others thereafter, carried the message to every corner of the globe. The message of Islam, coupled with the character of its followers, amazed everyone who witnessed it. They had never seen such a complete, simple, and encompassing belief system combined with the humbleness, sincerity, and truthfulness of its loyal followers. Many naturally became attracted to Islam and embraced it. Within a short period, Islam grew rapidly throughout the world and brought people of diverse backgrounds under one umbrella.

It is quite astonishing to know that today, even when so many people are misinformed about Islam, either because of negative campaigning by some, the misbehavior of some Muslims, or other reasons, Islam remains the fastest growing religion in the world. I am hopeful that on finishing this book, the reader will satisfy his or her curiosity as to why Islam continues to grow with such speed.

Some important facts about the history of Islam from the time of Prophet Muhammad ﷺ are mentioned below to increase the reader's knowledge.

Prophet Muhammad ﷺ was born in 571 C.E. in Makkah, Arabia. His father's name was Abdullah, and his mother was Amina. His father passed away before his birth, and his mother passed away when he was six years old. His grandfather then became his caretaker.

Upon his grandfather's death, when he was about eight years old, his uncle Abu Talib lovingly cared for him for a long time. His genealogy is traced back to Prophet Ismail صلى الله عليه, the first son of Prophet Ibrahim (Abraham) عليه السلام. There are no other prophets amongst the descendents of Ismail عليه السلام except Prophet Muhammad ﷺ, while many great and distinguished prophets descended from Prophet Is-haq (Isaac) عليه السلام, the second son of Ibrahim عليه السلام.

Prophet Muhammad's uncle, Abu Talib, witnessing special qualities and characteristics in him, took extra care in his upbringing. He never left him home alone, even when going away on business trips. His uncle never forced him to worship idols, even though the majority of Arabs were idolaters. Just within the confines of the Ka'ba in Makkah, three hundred and sixty different idols were stored and worshiped. Prophet Muhammad ﷺ never went near idols to worship them, even in his childhood. He truly hated idol-worship.

Having acquired experience in trade in the company of his uncle and after a few business trips abroad, Muhammad ﷺ earned respect for his unparalleled honesty and integrity, as well as for his extra-ordinary demeanor. Makkans, witnessing his high moral character, awarded him the title of 'Sādiq' (truthful) and 'Ameen' (trustworthy). On one occasion, he took abroad a merchant caravan of a wealthy Makkan lady, Khadija رضى الله عنها, and earned extraordinary profits for her goods. Upon hearing of his honesty, ethics, and the entire account of his trip from her slave who accompanied Prophet Muhammad ﷺ, she sent him a marriage proposal.

Through arrangements made by his uncle, Abu Talib, he was married at the age of twenty-five to the Honorable Khadija رضى الله عنها, who was forty years old and a widow. Contrary to the belief of many, he did not marry her for any selfish reasons or utilize her wealth to achieve his goals. Moreover, her wealth was not a factor in declaring his prophethood, which came fifteen years later, when he was forty years old. Nevertheless, it did allow him much free time to meditate and remain secluded in a cave on a nearby mountaintop. His wife was always supportive of him and stood by him all the time. When Muhammad ﷺ declared his prophethood, she, with full confidence, became the first person and woman to recognize him as the Prophet of Allah, and she wholeheartedly embraced Islam.

While he was meditating in the cave known as Hira, Allah revealed the first few verses of the holy Qur'an through the Archangel Jibra'īl عليه السلام. In those verses, Prophet Muhammad ﷺ was commanded to:

> Recite! In the name of your Lord, Who created all. • Created man from the clot of congealed blood. • Recite! And your Lord is the Most Bountiful. • Who taught writing by the pen. • Taught man what he knew not… • [Qur'an 96:1-5]

Later, Allah ﷻ commanded Muhammad ﷺ to begin calling people to Islam, and Allah promised to protect him and to make him succeed in his mission. Although he faced resistance from the same people who called him *Sādiq* and *Ameen*, he continued to convey the message as revealed to him by Allah ﷻ with confidence, dedication, and commitment. Muhammad ﷺ called upon his people to recognize the Oneness of Allah and to give up the centuries' old worship of idols.

To the tribe of Quraysh, idol worship was not only a ritual, but it was also a profitable business opportunity, as they earned much income from pilgrims coming to Makkah to worship idols and to buy and sell goods. Thus, the need to resist the Prophet and his teachings was obvious.

Initially, only a handful of people joined him, but with steadfastness and determination he continued to preach even under the harshest conditions. Prophet Muhammad ﷺ, his extended family (some of whom had not yet embraced Islam), and the new Muslims were subject to economic and social boycott and were forced to leave their homes for a nearby valley, Shaib abi-Talib. They lived there for three years under severe circumstances; however, this did not weaken their resolve. The economic and trade sanctions against them were lifted when termites chewed up the document of sanctions drawn up by the Quraysh. This event brought shame to the Quraysh, for misbehaving with their own community members.

Meanwhile, the Muslim community slowly increased and strengthened, even as the resistance and savagery of the non-believers became widespread. Those believers who could not persist were ordered by the Prophet ﷺ to migrate to Abyssinia (contemporary Ethiopia). Muslims met with favorable conditions there and earned the favor and compassion of the Christian King Al Najashi, who on learning about Islam and its Prophet, recognized the divinity of Islam, as Allah ﷻ had revealed it previously to Prophet Isa (Jesus) عليه السلام.

The Muslims who remained in Makkah continued to suffer pain and hardship at the hands of the disbelievers. Soon after, a year of grief came upon the Prophet ﷺ, as two of his great supporters and family members, his wife Khadija رضي الله عنها and his uncle Abu Talib passed away, making his task harder. Now, his life was in greater danger from the Makkan chiefs, because they had feared and respected Abu Talib. Upon his death, all the Makkan chiefs united to prevent the Prophet ﷺ from continuing with his mission, even if they had to take his life.

It was within this period of grief and hardship that the Prophet ﷺ was summoned to meet Allah ﷻ in the heavens. The journey, known as *Isra wal Mi'rāj,* took place within a very short period of the night. In the company of the Angel Jibra'il عليه السلام, he first visited Masjid-e-Aqsa in Baitul Muqaddas (Jerusalem) and then ascended to the heavens. Among other things, the purposes of this miraculous journey were to bring him relief, uplift his morale, strengthen his resolve, show him the heavens, and make him an eyewitness to Allah's signs and majesty, and give him the honor of meeting Allah ﷻ in person, which was not given to any other prophet. There, he was assured of his prophetic success and was given the gift of *salāh* (the five daily prayers of worship), which every adult Muslim is obliged to practice.

Resisting the abuse and persecution of the Quraysh had now become unbearable, and thus the Prophet permitted more of his followers to migrate to Madinah, a city some four hundred kilometers northeast of Makkah, where he would join them in the near future when commanded by Allah ﷻ. Muslims making their way safely out of Makkah angered the disbelievers who then increased their persecution. The Makkan chiefs unanimously decided to attack the Prophet ﷺ in his sleep, but Allah ﷻ informed the Prophet ﷺ and granted him permission to migrate. The Prophet ﷺ left for Madinah, leaving his cousin, Ali ﷜, who would later become his son-in-law, in charge of his affairs and directed him to sleep in his place that night and then to join him in Madinah at a later time.

He traveled with the Honorable Abu-Bakr Siddīq ﷜, his closest companion and the first adult male to embrace Islam. The Makkans followed after them but could not reach them. After travelling for about five hundred kilometers in the excruciating desert heat for fifteen days, they safely arrived in Madinah, where many anxiously awaited him. Out of their respect and honor for him, he was greeted with a grand celebration. This *Hijra* (migration of the Prophet ﷺ) marked the beginning of the Islamic lunar calendar and the second phase of Islam.

In Madinah, the Prophet ﷺ established a common brotherhood among the believers: between the Ansār, the Muslim residents of Madinah, and the Muhajireen, the migrant Muslims. He drew up treaties with local tribes and with the followers of the Jewish faith to coexist in peace and harmony, with toleration and understanding. With a sigh of relief, he established the Muslim community on the solid foundations of Islam, according to the continuous revelations from Allah ﷻ. The Muslim community grew and prospered due to the hard labor of the migrants and with the unprecedented cooperation and show of selflessness of their Ansār brethren. The holy Prophet ﷺ established a *masjid* in Madinah to be the center for this newly formed nation of believers.

On the other hand, the Makkans were in despair at having failed to destroy a handful of poor and disadvantaged people, but, unbeknownst to them, Muslims were truly blessed by the Almighty, Who allowed them to succeed, become strong, sustain themselves, and disseminate Islam throughout Arabia. The Makkans ran amok and looted the belongings and properties the emigrants left behind. They conspired with the local tribes of Madinah to weaken the Muslims. They sought alliances to wage war against Islam and Muslims. Although the Muslims had left the city of Makkah, the Makkans never let the Muslims live in peace in Madinah, and they never left the Muslims alone to practice their religion.

After almost fifteen years of suffering persecution at the hands of the Quraysh, Allah ﷻ finally granted Muslims permission to defend themselves and fight back against their enemies. Many small and full-scale battles were fought where Muslims, though outnumbered, were overall victorious. At this point, both parties were ready to sign a peace treaty and agreed to ten years of peace. This period of peace gave Muslims a chance to focus on other matters, such as strengthening themselves to deal with other tribes and powers in Arabia and to take Islam beyond the Arabian borders.

The relative peace allowed Muhammad ﷺ to send letters via emissaries inviting the Roman, Persian, and other emperors to adopt Islam [Appendix III]. He was also able to deal extensively with the hidden mischief of the hypocrites living among the Muslims. As Islam continued to grow and gain strength, every existing empire became aware of it. Moreover, the revelations of the holy Qur'an accelerated. Uniform codes of conduct, family life, personal and public affairs, economy and social welfare, civil and criminal justice, and conducting war and establishing peace were revealed to Muslims. Simultaneously, the Prophet ﷺ appropriately implemented divine laws among the Muslim community of Madinah and throughout the nearby lands.

When the Makkans and their allies breached the Treaty of Hudaibiya, the Muslims prepared to march towards Makkah. They then conquered Makkah without spilling a drop of blood. Muhammad 🕌 became a conqueror, but being a prophet of mercy, he forgave all Makkans, even his staunchest enemies. He issued a general amnesty and pardoned everyone, whether they embraced Islam or not. Allah's 🕌 promise to His Prophet 🕌 and the Muslims came true. They entered Makkah as victors, when just ten years before they had been forced to leave their homes, belongings, and everything they had in order to find refuge so they could uphold their beliefs and for the love of their Prophet 🕌.

Muhammad 🕌 showed unequivocal generosity that has yet to be duplicated. As a result, tens of thousands embraced Islam without any swords raised, without fear of death, without any killings, and without any compulsion. Those who were willing to give up anything to destroy Islam now became its defenders and joined other Muslims in spreading the message of Islam from Makkah and Madinah to every corner of the world.

The Prophet 🕌 returned to Madinah to remain there for the rest of his life among those who once did him great favors, the Anṣār. Soon thereafter, the holy Qur'an was completed when at the Last Sermon, on the occasion of Hajj, Allah 🕌 revealed to Muhammad 🕌 that,

> …this day, I have perfected for you your religion and have completed My favor to you and I have approved Islam as the religion for you… • [Qur'an 5:3]

The Prophet passed away at the age of 63, leaving the responsibility of taking Islam to every corner of the world to his Companions and to subsequent generations of Muslims. Abu-Bakr Siddīq 🕌 became the first *khalīfa* (caliph) of the Muslim *ummah* (community). The holy Qur'an and the holy *sunnah* (the way of the Prophet 🕌) became the beacon of light for the Muslim ummah. Centuries later, Islam still shines brightly, spreading its rays of guidance to enlighten those who come in its way.

CHAPTER 4

Allah ﷻ
THE LORD ALMIGHTY

WHO IS ALLAH ﷻ?

'Allah' ﷻ is the proper and personal name of the Almighty, the Lord and Creator, Who created the universe and everything in it, including us human beings. The Lord, the Almighty, was not named 'Allah' ﷻ by any human being or by any Muslim. He introduced Himself to us by this name, 'Allah' ﷻ. The first verse of the holy Qur'an and the first Cardinal Article of Faith testify to this.

بِسْمِ اللهِ الرَّحْمٰنِ الرَّحِيْمِ

BISMILLA HIR-RAHMA NIR-RAHIM

In the name of Allah, the Most Compassionate, the Most Merciful

Note: Muslims recite this whenever they begin to do anything and everything. They invoke the name 'Allah' ﷻ to include His blessing, mercy, and assistance with what they undertake, whether it is major or minor; thereby, avoiding the interference of Satan and his evildoings. This bears witness that 'Allah' ﷻ is His proper name.

ٱلْحَمْدُ لِلّٰهِ رَبِّ الْعَلَمِينَ

AL-HAMDU-LILLAHI RABBIL-ALAMIN

All praise is due to Allah, the Lord of the Worlds

Note: This is the first verse of the first *surah* (chapter) namely *Surah-e-Fatiha* (The Opening Chapter), with which the holy Qur'an begins. Here, the Almighty introduces Himself to us as 'Allah' ﷻ.

لَا اِلَهَ اِلَّا اللّٰهُ مُحَمَّدٌ رَسُوْلُ اللّٰهِ

LÂ ILÂHA ILLALLÂHU, MUHAMMADUR RASÛLULLÂH

"[There is] no deity but Allah, Muhammad is the Prophet of Allah"

Note: To remain faithful (Muslim) or to enter into Islam, one must verbally declare this *kalimah* (declaration) of faith, certify it by heart, and have unshakeable belief in its truthfulness.

Countless other verses show that 'Allah' ﷻ is His proper name as He Himself revealed it to us. Allah ﷻ also revealed that He has many attributes or qualities, which are known as the 99 Beautiful Names of Allah ﷻ. We should call Him either by His proper name 'Allah' ﷻ or by any of His attributive names. Since 'Allah' ﷻ is the name of His personal being and comprises all the meanings of His attributes, it is preferable to call Him 'Allah' ﷻ. Simply uttering 'Allah' ﷻ brings many blessings and brings you closer to Him.

Allah ﷻ revealed to Prophet Muhammad ﷺ, "I was a hidden treasure and willed to be manifest, so I created what I created" [Shamaa'il Tirmidhi]. He alone created everything and everyone. To begin the process of creation, Allah ﷻ first created the *nur* (light) of Muhammad from within His *nur* [Al Mawahibu'l-Ladunniyah]. Allah ﷻ created angels from that *nur* as well. The jinns were created from fire, and Shaytān belongs to this category. Allah ﷻ created man from earthly soil, and science confirms that the elements found in the human body are also found in earth.

Unlike the birth of other humans, the creation of Adam, Hawwa and of Isa (Jesus) السلام عليه, as explained before, are all signs of Allah's تعالى power of creation. Allah تعالى blessed Maryam (Mary) السلام عليها and miraculously bestowed on her a son, Prophet Isa (Jesus) السلام عليه without a father. This miraculous birth does not make Isa السلام عليه His son, nor does it make Allah تعالى his father. Allah تعالى is *Wahid* (single and alone), and everything else is His creation that serves Him, surrenders to Him, and worships Him.

Allah تعالى is free from parents and did not choose to have children. He has no partner who shares His being or His power. Allah تعالى is alone; He is One. Never did He beget, nor was He begotten. None is like Him, and He is not like anyone or anything. No one is equal to Him. No one interferes with Him or with His works. He does whatever He wills. His plans and words are unchangeable. No one questions Him, and He is not answerable to anyone. Allah تعالى gives life and causes death at its fixed moment. Allah تعالى causes clouds to release water, wherever and whenever He wills. Allah تعالى merges the day into night and from the night brings out day. He set in motion celestial bodies that constantly travel on their fixed path for a fixed period.

He is the All-Knower. Not a single leaf falls on the ground that escapes His knowledge. He knows the needs of His creatures very well. He provides for all and nourishes all, and no being is left out from His provisions, no matter where they are, whether that is beneath the earth, deep in the seas, high above the skies, or in places we cannot even imagine. Besides humans and jinns, none of His creations have free will. They all submit to Him; they all worship Him (in their own ways) and are busy in His remembrance.

Only humans and jinns are given the unique 'power of choice' to choose between the righteous path and the deviant one. Allah تعالى is merciful and does not take vengeance for His personal sake, but only to make right or for the sake of justice. Allah ﷻ does not destroy any nation until He brings upon them His divine message and warnings and gives them ample time to follow and submit. No creature is able to see Him; yet, He sees all. Humans are not given the power to see Him or the intelligence to conceive of Him, except through his divine message and guidance. What has been said above is but a summary of His introduction of Himself. To develop a better understanding, I quote the following from the holy Qur'an regarding Allah's ﷻ being:

> Say you (O My Prophet!), "He is Allah, the One," Allah, the Independent (but) on Whom all depend. He did not beget, nor was He begotten—Nor is there anyone equal to Him." [Qur'an 112:1-4]

The following is a *tafsir* (explanation) of a very famous verse, called *Aayat-ul-Kursi* (*aayat* – verse, *kursi* – throne). The words in parentheses and boldface are translations of the Qur'anic Arabic embedded within this unique explanation.

AAYAT-UL-KURSI [Qur'an 2:255]

(**Allah**) Almighty is Self-Existing, Self-Sustaining. He has existed for eternity, is the embodiment of all and every outstanding quality, is free of all blemishes, alone is worthy of worship and (**none**) is (**worthy of worship except Him**) who has always remained (**alive by Himself**), is not in need of or reliant on anyone and will remain alive and in existence forever.

He will never experience death and is Self-Sufficient and is (**for everyone**), for the entire universe (**the Sustainer**) and He alone is responsible for the universes' affairs. And (**He does not feel drowsy**) which is the precursor to sleep because He never experiences tiredness or drowsiness, and therefore is also free from inactiveness which is a result of being tired or drowsy.

(**And**) similarly (**nor**) does He (**sleep**) because while asleep the nerves of the mind are relaxed after which knowledge and comprehension are rendered ineffective and become suspended, and the alertness and intelligence of sense become diminished. And it is clear that for Allah Almighty these characteristics are impossible because He is the Inventor of this great universe and is responsible for maintaining its affairs at every moment and every second, as there are changes happening at all times, that are occurring under His attention and with His knowledge. He is aware at all times of all things in their condition and is neither unaware nor asleep.

(It is His and belongs to Him all that which is in the skies and on the Earth); all the creation in the skies and on Earth are His subjects and His property, and everything is submissive to His power and wish. (And who is it that intercedes) for anyone (in His court except by His order). Allah Almighty's greatness, high rank, and majestic attributes mean that without His permission no one can intercede in His presence.

Allah Almighty (is aware) of (everything that is in) the past of those who live in the skies and on Earth and that which (has gone before), that is, all that which has occurred in the world's affairs, (and) knows (everything that is to come) in the future. Therefore, Allah Almighty is aware of both their past and future, (and) those of this universe (cannot encircle) or enclose (anything) that is (in His knowledge) and which He is aware of (except by His own will). In summary, leave alone the knowledge of the entire universe, a tiny iota of Allah Almighty's vast knowledge is too difficult for a human to comprehend. Creatures only have the knowledge that is given to them by Him.

(Permission has been given by His throne), that is, His knowledge...or His greatness...or His power and ownership...or by His magnificent, powerful, everlasting, and immense creations that are below His kingdom but above the skies and is known as His throne; or whose reality no one except Allah Almighty is aware of, whether in (the skies or on Earth). In other words, His knowledge, His magnificence, power, and wisdom or His beautiful, gracious, and magnificent creations who have encircled the skies and the Earth and whose compound has within it the skies and Earth, and which (He finds no difficulty keeping watch on both). Watching over the well-being of the Earth and skies does not tire Allah Almighty, but in fact this caring is simple and very easy for Him. He is the Sustainer and Caretaker of all things, He does what He wills, His intention is firm, and that which He intends, He definitely makes it happen.

And why should not this be so because He is dominant and overpowering over all things, and **(He is)** above all matters **(mighty and superior)**, magnificent, and exalted in His recognition, and this one revealed verse known and recognized as Aayat-ul-Kursi is more elevated and greater than any other verse of the Qur'an.

In the following verse, Allah ﷻ describes Himself through a metaphor of blessed light.

Allah is the light of the heavens and the Earth. The likeness of His light is as a niche wherein is a lamp; that lamp is in (a chandelier of) glass; the chandelier is as a star glittering like a pearl, lit from a blessed olive tree, neither eastern nor western, whose oil is most luminous, even though no fire touches it. (This) is all light upon light! Allah guides unto His light whom He wills... • [Qur'an 24:35]

He is Allah, besides Whom there is none to be worshiped, Knower of everything hidden and open. It is He—the Most Compassionate, the Most Merciful. He is Allah—besides Whom there is none to be worshiped, the Sovereign of all, the Most Holy, the Bestower of peace, the Giver of security, the Guardian over all, the Esteemed One, the Mender of broken hearts, the Exalted in might. Glory be to Allah, He is far above what they associate with Him. He is Allah, the Creator of all, the Maker of all, the Fashioner of all. His are the most Beautiful Names. Whatever is in the heavens and the earth glorifies Him, and it is He, the All-Powerful, the All-Wise. • [Qur'an 59:22-24]

TAWHĪD: THE ONENESS OF ALLAH ﷻ

*T*HE BELIEF IN THE 'ONENESS OF ALLAH ﷻ' IS CENTRAL to Islam, and all other beliefs revolve around [it]. However, it is not simply a matter of belief, but of firm conviction. Even though Allah ﷻ is hidden and invisible to the naked eye, He is clearly visible to positive reasoning and common sense. Wherever we look and explore, we find a unified system and an immaculate work of definite calculations and precise movements. Allah's art of creation cannot be the work of more than one Lord, more than one Supreme Being. He has to be one; otherwise, there would bound to be a clash in the universal systems. There could not be natural symmetry, balance, and the existing fundamental similarities among creatures if there were more than one creator. Even human nature would have been divided and be concretely different in its most fundamental aspects, but since this is not the case, it shows that the Creator is one. If there were more than one god, various creatures, systems of life, and the very nature of humans would not only be very different, it would be impossible to coexist for even a moment.

The more they try to disprove His existence, the more they end up confirming it.

That is why all religions throughout human history, in one form or another, teach of one Supreme Being, one great God, even when some of them believe in lesser gods and goddesses. Experience shows that even people who claim to believe in no god, deep down in their hearts, believe that this phenomenal universe must be the work of a Supreme Being.

Every field of science seems to accept that this universe and everything in it are a creation of some supreme and powerful being, and the results of their research point in this same direction, i.e., there is a supreme being. Some, intentionally or unintentionally, in their attempt to disprove the existence of a supreme being, ironically end up proving its existence or at least fail to deny its existence concretely. The more they try to disprove His existence, the more they end up confirming it.

Humans are naturally connected to the Creator. Hence, no matter how much they have forgotten Him, they still call on Him, especially when in need of help and when no else can help. They submit to Him whenever their power and intelligence fail and return to Him when there is no other place to go and no one else for whom to look or to whom to turn. This and many other experiences of daily life truly indicate that a mighty Lord exists and that He is one and cannot be more than one. Every divine revelation professes this unity, as do all of our natural faculties.

It is not just a matter of belief; it is a matter of fact that when we willfully and verbally declare the 'Oneness of Allah' ﷻ and recognize/certify it by heart, we declare the truth and prepare to enter into Islam and return "home." In Islam, *tawhīd* (the Oneness of Allah ﷻ) is the center of the Islamic belief system. The opposite of *tawhīd* is *shirk*. *Shirk* is not a forgivable sin, but it is forgiven only if Allah's Oneness is embraced, along with the rest of Islam in its entirety. The heavenly guidance from Allah ﷻ that no one should commit *shirk* is clear, complete, and convincing. Thus, according to Islam, there is no other place for a *mushrik* (one who commits *shirk*), but eternal Hell.

The concept of *tawhīd* is that Allah ﷻ is one and has no partners. *Shirk* is to associate an idol or human with Allah's being and to relate someone or something with Allah as His partner, parent, son or daughter, to consider someone equal in power and in attributes or to believe someone has the personal power or ability to interfere or intercede in Allah's will or in His work.

The main purpose of every prophet from Adam ﷺ to Muhammad ﷺ, the Final Prophet, including but not limited to Nuh (Noah) ﷺ, Ibrahim (Abraham) ﷺ, Dawūd (David) ﷺ, Saleh ﷺ, Musa (Moses) ﷺ, and Isa (Jesus) ﷺ, was to prevent their people from committing *shirk* (polytheism). They called upon their people to declare the *tawhīd* (Oneness of Allah ﷻ), to condemn *shirk* and to abandon the worship of anything else besides Allah ﷻ. In light of the prophets' sacrifices, hard work, proselytizing under adverse conditions, and teaching people about Allah ﷻ and His Oneness, every punishment from the Lord is justified for those who continued to commit *shirk*. Even today, this is a matter of real concern and man must refrain from *shirk*, if he does not want to become the ultimate loser.

> *Prophets, angels, saints, and others are to be loved, honored, respected, and remembered, but not worshiped. Worship is due exclusively for Allah ﷻ.*

The clear, divine revelations about the One-ness of the Lord and those revelations denying the existence of any other god clearly conclude that none is worthy of worship besides Allah ﷻ, the Omniscient and Omnipotent Lord. To wor-ship anyone besides Allah ﷻ is another form of *shirk*. Muslims do not worship any prophet or associate prophets in Allah's worship in any way. Although the prophets are all chosen men, some are closer to Allah ﷻ than others, and Prophet Muhammad ﷺ is the most beloved. Prophets, angels, saints, and others are to be loved, honored, respected, and remembered, but not worshiped. Worship is due exclusively for Allah ﷻ.

Islam, as taught by the beloved Prophet Muhammad ﷺ, sums up the description of the Almighty. Allah ﷻ is the Lord, the Creator, the Omnipotent, the Omniscient, the Omnipresent, the Sustainer, and providence is only from Him. Only Allah ﷻ is Eternal. He gives life and takes it away, forgives sins and punishes wrongdoers; He is All-Knowing, and nothing is hidden from Him. Therefore, Allah ﷻ is the only one worthy of worship.

ALLAH ﷻ LOVES HIS CREATION

ALLAH ﷻ CREATED EVERYTHING IN THE BEST MANNER and according to its purpose. Each creature lives by natural rules and plays specific roles set forth by Allah ﷻ. As such, He provided creatures with everything necessary to fulfill their purpose. Since human beings have a higher purpose, He endowed them with free will, intelligence, morality, common sense, etc., and He created them in His own image. To be created in His image does not mean that

He looks like man, but that humans have been endowed with His qualities in accordance with their capacity and ability [Qur'an 30:30] . No other creature has been bestowed with this honor. How can all this be devoid of 'love'?

We apparently love what we make with our own hands, even though we are not creators of anything. We simply put together what is provided to us as raw material by Him. Since we love what we make, He must love us more, because He made us the best among His creatures. How is it possible for us to achieve the purpose of our life without His caring and love?

In the very beginning of the holy Qur'an, Allah ﷻ reveals Himself as *Ar-Rahman* 'the Most Compassionate' and *Ar-Rahim* 'the Most Merciful.' How can He be compassionate and merciful without love? He could have chosen His other attributes at this place to introduce Himself, but He chose *Ar-Rahmān* and *Ar-Rahīm* precisely to show His love and mercy.

Since we are His creatures, however much love we need from Him comes unconditionally. We do not have to do anything special to receive this love; everyone gets it equally. When we require more love and compassion from Him, we have to go out of our way and beseech His mercy, and then work hard and strive to become eligible for it. Certainly, our Lord is full of love for His creations. Besides being Beneficent, Compassionate, Merciful, He is *Al-Wadud*, The Most-Loving. Many other attributes of our Almighty Lord also reflect His love for us.

He knew definitely that in this world we would commit sins, therefore, in the holy Qur'an He says:

> And ask for forgiveness from your Lord; then bow down towards Him; without a doubt my Lord is truly Forgiving and profoundly Loving. • [Qur'an 11:90]

When He warns us, it is to our own benefit. When He mentions His absolute power and comprehensive majesty, He simultaneously reveals Himself to profoundly love all of His creatures. Although He has power to do anything He wills, He prefers to love us. He reveals in the Qur'an:

> Without a doubt your Lord's hold is quite severe. Without a doubt, He creates the first time and He is to do it the second time around. And He is All-Forgiving and Most-Loving, the owner of the magnificent Throne; the Doer of whatever He wills. • [Qur'an 85:12-16]

The Qur'an also tells us that Allah ﷻ loves:

- Those who do good [Qur'an 2:195 & 3:148],
- The repentant and the pure [Qur'an 2:222],
- Those who are mindful (of Him) [Qur'an 3:76],
- Those who love Him and follow Prophet Muhammad [Qur'an 3:31],
- Those who are good [Qur'an 3:134; 5:13; 5:93],
- Those who patiently persevere [Qur'an 3:146],
- Those who trust in Him [Qur'an 3:159],
- Fair judges [Qur'an 5:42],
- Those who are mindful (of their obligations) [Qur'an 9:4 & 9:7],
- Those who make themselves pure [Qur'an 9:108],
- Those who believe and do what is morally right [Qur'an 19:96],
- Those who are evenhanded [Qur'an 49:9],
- The tolerant [Qur'an 60:8], and
- Those who fight in His cause in tight formations [Qur'an 61:4].

In addition to these Qur'anic testimonials to Allah's ﷻ love for us, numerous sayings of Prophet Muhammad ﷺ bear witness that Allah ﷻ loves us.

> The Prophet of Allah said: "Allah, the Blessed and exalted, said: 'My love is obliged for those who love each other in Me, and those who sit with each other in Me, and those who visit each other in Me, and those who give to each other generously in Me."
>
> [Al-Muwatta of Imam Malik, *hadith* #15.51]

> The Prophet said that Allah Himself said, "My servant draws closer to Me through the religious duties I placed upon him. My servant then continues to draw closer to Me with voluntary (good actions) until I love him. When I love him, I become his ears that

he uses to hear, his eyes that he uses to see, his hand that he uses to hold and his foot that he uses for walking. If he then asks Me for anything, I would surely grant it to him, and when he asks for My protection, I will surely give it to him…" [Hadith-e-Qudsi]

Still further, Prophet Muhammad ﷺ informed us that Allah ﷻ loves those who practice abstinence in the world and those who are Allah-conscious, free from want, and hidden from the view of people.

A man came and said: "O Prophet of Allah, direct me to a deed for which I shall be loved by Allah and by people when I have done it." He replied: "If you practice abstinence in the world, Allah will love you, and if you abstain from people's possessions, people will love you." [Al-Tirmidhi, *hadīth* #1350; also transmitted by Ibn Majah]

Allah's Prophet said: "Allah loves the servant who is Allah-conscious and is free from want and is hidden (from the view of people)." [Muslim, *hadīth* #1384]

The message of Allah's ﷻ love that is to be found in Islam, both in the Qur'an and in the sayings of Prophet Muhammad ﷺ, is clear and unmistakable. Allah ﷻ is The Loving, full of loving tenderness. He is The Most Compassionate, enveloping us in a womb-like protection and throwing out to us a rope of salvation whenever we start to stray. He is The Most Merciful, full of mercy to the believers, merciful to all people, and His mercy extends over all things.

On the Day of Resurrection, His mercy to His servants will be 99 times that of all the mercy that all of creation has ever shown to each other. He is also The Forgiving, and He loves to forgive us and will continue to forgive us as long as we ask for forgiveness and repent sincerely. He is ever ready to run towards us if we will just take a few steps towards Him. This is the Islamic concept of Allah.

Allah ﷻ naturally endowed us with common sense and other qualities to find, connect, and relate to Him and to worship Him. It would be quite difficult had He not done that for us. He helped us and saved us from the hassle and pain of trying to discover Him ourselves. This is another sign of His love for us.

Allah 🕮 sent prophets, one after another, to rightly guide and teach us how to work towards achieving ultimate success. He revealed a complete system of life through divine books, so we can know what is good and bad for us in this life and in the Hereafter. He equipped us with every faculty necessary to explore, know, and utilize His bounties in order to be thankful to Him and to achieve the purpose of this life.

He created love and affection in us so that, for example, parents can raise their children, children can care for their parents, husbands and wives can live happy, peaceful and productive lives, and other happy relationships could be established.

Nothing could be possible without His love. Now, that love requires us to understand our Master, to know Him, to properly follow His guidance, to recognize His being, to worship Him properly for His pleasure, and to thank Him for what He has granted us and what He ultimately wishes to give us: success in the Hereafter.

Where else do we find a Lord Who rewards us for treating ourselves well? Before requiring us to fulfill our obligations to Him, He directs us to fulfill our duties to each other. When true believers fulfill their duties to other human beings for His pleasure, He considers it worship of Himself and fully rewards them, too. Even the activities that are part of direct worship bring unlimited benefits to the worshiper and not to Allah 🕮. Where else do we find such a Lord? Nowhere, but He Himself is the One and Only.

The 'lords,' 'masters,' and 'bosses' of this world demand personal service and favors before doing favors for us, but not the Lord of all lords. He is there to give and does not take anything in return for Himself. That Lord is Compassionate, Merciful, and Just. Islam requires its followers to invite others to Allah 🕮 and to His way. It wants people to recognize that fact, so they too can become His true servants and work their way to success, the ultimate success.

Since it is human nature to attempt to perceive the Supreme Being, people ask numerous questions regarding His form and being. The following should give a well-rounded idea and understanding of Allah ﷻ, the Almighty Lord.

Q&A ABOUT ALLAH ﷻ

1. WHAT IS THE GENDER OF ALLAH ﷻ?

Gender is for creatures, not for the Creator. Allah ﷻ is free from any gender category or other classification. He is not like us or like any of His creations. Allah ﷻ is not male or female. He is the Supreme Being, above and beyond any gender categories. When we use a pronoun in place of Allah ﷻ, we use a masculine pronoun not to show that he is male, but as He Himself used it in the divinely revealed books.

2. DOES ALLAH ﷻ KNOW OUR ACTIONS BEFORE OR AFTER THEY OCCUR?

One of Allah's ﷻ attributes is the All-Knower. He knows whatever is taking place and whatever will take place in the future, including our actions and our intentions. His infinite knowledge covers everything from the beginning to the end, and even that which is certainly beyond our conception.

3. CAN WE SEE ALLAH ﷻ?

We are not given the power to see Him. If we could see Him, everyone would have automatically believed in His existence, and the whole purpose of having faith would have been invalidated. On the Day of Judgment, only the 'Successful Ones' will be able to see the

Lord, and it will be a great disappointment and unimaginably painful for the faithless, the losers, not to be able to see Him, even on that day. So close, yet so far!

4. HOW DO WE KNOW IF HE IS PLEASED WITH ANY OF OUR ACTIONS?

When we perform an action, a good deed, with the pure intent of pleasing Him and as per His instructions, we should have unshakeable belief that Allah ﷻ is pleased with our action. The true satisfaction of heart and mind and an unexplainable contentment and joy felt within the soul indicate acceptance of that good deed and that it has earned the pleasure of Allah ﷻ. For example, a simple smile on our parents' face, a thumbs-up gesture from our coach, or a handshake with our boss is a sign of contentment and joyful victory. An indication of Allah's ﷻ acceptance of our good deeds is felt within our soul and shows up brightly on our faces.

5. WHAT DIFFERENCE DOES THE BELIEF IN THE 'ONENESS OF ALLAH' ﷻ MAKE IN MUSLIMS?

Belief in the Oneness of Allah ﷻ causes undivided attention towards the Supreme Being when: submitting to His will, performing the acts of direct worship, following His commands, maintaining a spiritual connection, and being fearful and being accountable. This belief clears away confusion and satisfies the soul. It assures us that there is only one place from where we can find help, justice, and the fulfillment of our desires. It provides strength, confidence, a sense of belonging, peace of heart, mind and soul, hope, dignity, and unshakeable belief.

Since Allah ﷻ is One, His message and guidance must also be one. The way of life prescribed by Him is also one. The unity of

Allah ﷻ brings unity to all, and the powerful energy that radiates is immense. The Unity of Allah is perfection, and anyone who comes close to this perfection finds absolute satisfaction.

6. WHY DOES ALLAH ﷻ NOT HAVE CHILDREN?

The short and simple answer is that Allah ﷻ does not need children, but this short and simple answer may not be satisfactory to all, so I will elaborate further.

Having children is naturally a sign of weakness and ultimate recognition that a father/mother will eventually die and children will take over. A human father is naturally weak and eventually requires the help of a child to remain strong. A child fulfills the needs of his father who may suffer from many inherent deficiencies, or if a father is rich he needs a child to inherit his wealth and prolong his name or business. All these are signs of weaknesses.

However, Allah ﷻ is not weak, and He thus does not need children. All of His attributes are clear proof to that effect. According to the biological process of reproduction, a male requires a female to have children. Allah ﷻ has never taken a female companion; therefore, He does not have children.

CHAPTER 5

The Need and Role
of Prophets

*A*S WE LEARNED EARLIER, ALLAH 🕮 willed to be known; therefore, He created everything for Him to be known. A creature, later to be called human, was a part of His will from the beginning and a part of the process of creation. It was also included in His will that humans be given a fixed time to live on earth and be granted free will and the power to choose. They are taught right from wrong and tested to see if they follow Allah's 🕮 will or their own will. Then, finally, on the basis of the results of their actions, they will be given permanent life in Heaven or Hell. All of this was included in His will from the moment "Allah willed to be known" and thereafter began to create according to His will.

Only Allah 🕮 knows how many millions of years later the time arrived to create Adam 🕮, the first human. Soon thereafter, it became necessary to send him and his wife Hawwa عليهاالسلام to Earth. Eventually, the need arose to teach and guide humans, so they could distinguish right from wrong and choose to be successful; the process of teaching and guiding people had to be undertaken. Thus, those who had been chosen by Allah ﷻ to fulfill this great task of teaching, preaching, and guiding humankind are the messengers and prophets of Allah ﷻ. These people are among the best of humankind.

At the time the father of us all, Adam عليه السلام, was created, every human soul that had to come to life on earth was also created. Allah ﷻ assembled every soul and asked, "Am I not your Lord?" All replied, "Why not." Allah ﷻ had knowledge that they would soon forget this covenant upon reaching earth [Qur'an 7:172]. Therefore, arrangements were made to teach, preach, guide, and remind people about the 'Great Gathering' to take place in the end, where undoubtedly everyone will witness or at least feel His presence and be held accountable for their actions.

> There is no coming back; it is either now or never.

However, had we remembered our reply to "Am I not your Lord?" we would be much better off. Had we remembered, how could we have done so much wrong in this life? How could we have gone astray? How could we now have denied the existence of Allah ﷻ? How could we now have committed the sin of *kufr* (infidelity) and *shirk* (polytheism), and disobeyed His commandments? Had we remembered Allah ﷻ all along, why would we be tested? Had we remembered this, we would never have deviated from the righteous path, and acquiring success would not have been a problem. Hence, there would have been no need for prophets to teach, preach, and guide us, because we would know and remember Allah ﷻ, the Almighty, our Lord.

As we came to live on earth and grew, we forgot the covenant we made with Allah ﷻ [Qur'an 9:67]. However, as soon as we depart from this life, we will come to realize it. Remembering our prior covenant with Allah ﷻ at the time of our departure from this life cannot bring us back to the beginning to fulfill our covenant. There is no coming back; it is either now or never.

The essence of Islam is to believe in the unseen/metaphysical/ spiritual, which is invisible to the naked eye, but visible to positive reasoning. To believe in the unseen/hidden, it is necessary to receive Allah's ﷻ assistance, guidance, signs, and symbols that are evidence of His existence. We also need them to satisfy our curiosity and to provide answers to all of our questions, so we can confidently believe in the unseen. Each one of us, by ourselves, is unable to receive that guidance directly from Allah ﷻ, because if such were the case, nothing would remain unseen or hidden.

Therefore, there was a need for someone to: receive guidance from Allah ﷻ and convey it to us, learn from Allah ﷻ and teach us, store Allah's ﷻ energy and energize our soul, and be enlightened by Allah's ﷻ radiance and lift us from the darkness of ignorance and bring us into the light of knowledge. These beings were to be trusted beyond any doubt, to be worthy and capable of this great deed, to relate to us and to the Lord Almighty at the same time, to remind us of our purpose and our destination, and to show us how to follow in their footsteps in a practical manner.

Who can these exalted beings be? Could they be any other than those chosen by our Lord? No. Then, they are quite obviously His prophets and messengers. They came and fulfilled their duties with utmost diligence, selflessness, and steadfastness. Now, it is all up to us, because this lifetime is our only chance; we must use it or lose it.

Adam ﷺ was the first prophet. Right from the beginning, he had to be the first one to teach the message of Allah ﷻ to his children. Later, other prophets came to every nation, one after another, to guide them and deliver the message of Allah ﷻ. Finally, from among them, the last one was Prophet Muhammad ﷺ.

All prophets were human beings, but chosen ones, exalted among the people. They had to come from among humankind because if it were otherwise, they could not relate to us, and we could not follow them. It would have become easy for us to deny them and their teachings, simply because we could say to Allah ﷻ, "O Lord! How could we replicate their life, their sacrifices and their trials and tribulations, when we are just humans and they are different from us?"

> And if We had made the prophet an angel, even then We
> would have made them (in the form of) a man, and thus We would
> have confused them in a matter wherein they are now confused. •
> [Qur'an 6:9]

This is why the All-Knowing Allah ﷻ chose His prophets from among humans, so people can follow their example and emulate their lives. It was also necessary to give the prophets the power of miracles, so people who chose to believe in the prophets could have unshakeable faith in them, and those who chose to deny them would have no excuse on Judgment Day by saying that they could not verify them to be Allah's ﷻ prophets. Certainly, through prophets, Allah ﷻ completely conveyed His guidance to humanity. It is now our choice to be righteous or to be evil, to be successful or to fail, and to live the eternal life in Heaven or in Hell. The burden to choose and act falls on us individually. No one else benefits or loses by what we choose for ourselves. Islam teaches us to choose wisely and for our own good.

Allah ﷻ sent prophets from among their own people. They called their nations towards one Lord and explained to them the purpose of life on Earth. They taught them how to live and worship Allah ﷻ, how to fulfill their duties to Allah ﷻ and to their fellow humans. The prophets delivered to humanity whatever they were assigned and were required to do.

Allah ﷻ required people, as a prerequisite, to have faith in His prophets and recognize them as beloved beings of Allah [Qur'an 4:80 & 2:253]. Not a single prophet demanded anything in return from his people for the favor of conveying Allah's ﷻ guidance to them. The prophets did not seek monetary benefit, power, or adulation; instead, they sacrificed their time and energy, endured pain and suffering, and were humiliated to save their people from evildoings, grave sins, *shirk,* and being disobedient to Allah ﷻ.

As one prophet passed away, Allah ﷻ would send another one. According to a saying of the Prophet Muhammad ﷺ, Allah ﷻ sent about 124,000 prophets. During their lifetime, the prophets and their followers suffered greatly at the hands of disbelievers, who many times forced them to leave their homeland or even killed them. However difficult the environment became, the prophets remained steadfast and never gave in or disavowed their divine obligations.

As prophets passed away, their teachings were corrupted and in many cases purposely changed to legitimize the rule of the elites over the less fortunate. The true believers always remained steadfast to the teachings of their respective prophet, and Allah ﷻ brought countless rewards and blessings upon those steadfast believers. In contrast, Allah's ﷻ wrath destroyed those who disobeyed prophets, so that future generations and other nations would learn of their fate and avoid following their example. Whether or not people followed past prophets, Allah ﷻ completed His guidance to humanity through His Final Prophet ﷺ.

His Final Prophet ﷺ completed the divine guidance. He was to be successful and fulfill his duties, and his nation would completely surrender to the will of Allah ﷻ. His teachings would last forever. His people, language, holy book (Qur'an), teachings/practices and sacred words would be preserved forever and would become the beacon of light and guidance for all humanity until the end of time. He is no other than Muhammad ﷺ, whose book is the Qur'an, whose teachings are Islam, and whose followers are Muslim. He testified to past prophets, recognized the authenticity of their revealed scriptures, eradicated *shirk*, and now forever rules over the hearts of his followers, leader of all prophets.

Islam recognizes every prophet. In fact, denying or disrespecting any one of them is un-Islamic, because they are all Allah's prophets. All are dear to Muslims. Some among them are Adam الْعَلَيْهِ, Idrees الْعَلَيْهِ (possibly the same as Enoch), Nuh (Noah) الْعَلَيْهِ, Hud الْعَلَيْهِ, Saleh الْعَلَيْهِ, Ibrahim (Abraham) الْعَلَيْهِ, Isma'il (Ishmael) الْعَلَيْهِ, Is-haaq (Isaac) الْعَلَيْهِ, Yaqoob (Jacob) الْعَلَيْهِ, Yusuf (Joseph) الْعَلَيْهِ, Ayyoub (Job) الْعَلَيْهِ, Shu'aib الْعَلَيْهِ, Musa (Moses) الْعَلَيْهِ, Harun (Aaron) الْعَلَيْهِ, Lut (Lot) الْعَلَيْهِ, Yunus (Jonah) الْعَلَيْهِ, Al-Ya'sa (Elisha) الْعَلَيْهِ, Zulkifl (Ezekiel) الْعَلَيْهِ, Dawūd (David) الْعَلَيْهِ, Sulayman (Solomon) الْعَلَيْهِ, Ilyas (Elijah) الْعَلَيْهِ, Zakaria (Zachariah) الْعَلَيْهِ, Yahya (John the Baptist) الْعَلَيْهِ, Isa (Jesus) الْعَلَيْهِ, and the 'Seal of the Prophethood,' Muhammad ﷺ. They are to be honored, loved, remembered, and respected to the extent that, when saying or writing their names, Muslims must attach proper attributes and salutations next to their names, such as shown above.

The prophets' main purpose was not to teach us what we could learn on our own, but what we could never comprehend by ourselves. When our intellect fails, the prophets' teachings take charge. When our reasoning comes to a dead end, the prophets' wisdom opens new dimensions for us to proceed forward. When our faculties fail, their teachings rescue us from the darkness of failure. Whenever we are in need of a model or an ideal, the best resource is Allah's ﷻ prophets, who are the best models and icons of wisdom.

The holy prophets came to connect us to the Creator, since we could not do it on the basis of our limited intellect. They came to tell us who the Lord is, since we could not fully know by ourselves. They came to teach us how to please the Lord because we could not find this out without the Lord telling us through them. They came to show us how to worship the Lord because we could not develop the system of worship by which the Lord could truly be pleased. They came to declare the Oneness of the Lord and stop us from committing *shirk* because we could not have come to believe in one Lord by ourselves. The prophets came to warn us about the Day of Judgment and the trials of that Day because by the time we would have figured it out on our own, it might have been too late for us.

The prophets informed us about *halāl* and *harām* (permitted and forbidden), good and bad, virtues and sins, benefits and harm, rights and duties; and all other prescriptions and proscriptions. On our own, we would have reversed the entire system of life, misunderstood the whole idea of existence, misused the bounties of Allah ﷻ, increased our spiritual diseases, put in place improper justice systems, and failed to achieve the ultimate success of the Hereafter. We needed help from the Lord, which came through His prophets.

The prophets did not come to teach us how to build skyscrapers, but to find peace and prosperity within simplicity. They did not come to show us techniques on becoming millionaires, but how to love our fellow human beings and share our wealth. They did not come to teach us how to make airplanes, but to uplift the suffering humanity. They did not come to give us ideas on how to explore outer space, but how to explore our inner self and discover Allah's ﷻ great workmanship.

None of what we could have learned, invented, explored, designed, manufactured, thought of, formulated, and discovered by ourselves was on the agenda of any prophet. Eventually, we would naturally do these things as the need arose, and human history is witness that we did.

Rather, the prophets informed us well in advance of whatever we were incapable of finding out on our own. They fulfilled their duty of guiding people, and they are not responsible for anything beyond that. They will not be questioned for our wrongdoings, bear the burden of our mistakes, and suffer for our *kufr* (infidelity), *shirk* (polytheism), and deviation from the righteous path. They are already the chosen ones, the rewarded ones, and the blessed ones. They have done their job well and have nothing to lose.

CHAPTER 6

The Sources of Islamic Knowledge

HERE ARE TWO PRIMARY SOURCES of Islamic knowledge: the holy Qur'an and the *sunnah* of the Prophet Muhammad ﷺ, i.e. what he said and did. The secondary sources of knowledge are *ijma, qiyās,* and *ijtihād,* all of which are explained towards the end of this chapter, must find their basis in the Qur'an and *sunnah* and must not reject or contradict the Qur'an and *sunnah*. These secondary sources were initially derived by and from the noble companions of the Prophet ﷺ, and Islamic scholars and jurists thereafter.

THE TWO PRIMARY SOURCES

THE HOLY QUR'AN IS THE LIVING WORD OF ALLAH of which every letter of every verse was revealed to Prophet Muhammad ﷺ through Archangel Jibra'il (Gabriel) عَلَيْهِ السَّلَام. Many verses of the holy Qur'an are clear and to the point, and the message, rules, and regulations contained in them can be easily understood. At the same time, the Qur'an contains many verses with terms that can have multiple meanings, and some terms can never truly be interpreted to show their real meaning. A consensus has been reached among exegetes to leave them as is to avoid controversies over their definitions. However, if it becomes necessary to explain what they may mean, they should be interpreted in such a way that their definition does not contradict other verses of the holy Qur'an. In any case, the safer route is to leave their underlying meaning to the Revealer Himself.

To truly comprehend the divine message in the holy Qur'an and to see its commandments in practice, we need to focus on the life of the holy Prophet ﷺ. If we ignore the ideal example of the Prophet and his explanation of the holy Qur'an, interpret the holy Qur'an as per our own initiative, and set our own precedents, we will certainly be misguided. As such, Muslims rely upon the *sunnah*, which is what Prophet Muhammad ﷺ said and did. To determine the *sunnah*, Muslims turn to reports by the Prophet's ﷺ companions as to what the *sunnah* was. The reports are known as the *ahadith* (sing. *hadith*). Thus, the *ahadith* and *sunnah* are the second primary source of Islamic knowledge.

THE HOLY QUR'AN

AT THE AGE OF FORTY, MUHAMMAD ﷺ received the first verses of the holy Qur'an from Allah ﷻ. Allah ﷻ later commanded him to proclaim prophethood and to begin calling people to the One God, Allah ﷻ. For the next twenty-three years, Allah ﷻ sent revelations to the holy Prophet Muhammad ﷺ as they were needed. After the entire Qur'an was revealed to the Prophet ﷺ and had been well preserved, he passed away at the age of sixty-three.

Every word with its proper pronunciation was revealed by Allah ﷻ to Prophet Muhammad ﷺ, who after receiving it, memorized it almost instantly through the grace of Allah ﷻ. The Prophet ﷺ immediately communicated every word and message of the holy Qur'an to his companions. Those who were literate among them wrote it down and some memorized it. Since the revelations came as they were needed, the Prophet ﷺ, according to Allah's direction, instructed and designated seventeen of his companions to compile them. Even though its chapters and verses were revealed in a different order, the Qur'an was compiled according to the way it is written in the *Lauh-e-Mehfûz* (Sacred Tablet in the Heavens), of which the holy Qur'an is a small portion. The holy Qur'an has 114 chapters consisting of about 6,600 verses. Not only the text, but also the way it was written and pronounced is preserved in its original form since its inception.

The third caliph, Uthman ﷺ compiled a complete copy of the holy Qur'an *(Mas-hafe Uthmāni)* on papyrus fourteen hundred years ago, and it is currently available for public viewing at the Topkapi Museum in Istanbul, Turkey. Moreover, not only is the Qur'an preserved in book form, but millions of Muslims have also memorized the entire Qur'an, word for word. Preservation through memorization has continued from the days of its first revelation and will continue until the last day. If every written copy of the holy Qur'an were destroyed (may Allah ﷻ forbid), which is highly unlikely, no force or individual can erase it from the hearts of millions of *Huffaz-e-Kirām,* the honorable Muslim adults and children who have memorized it.

A miracle of the holy Qur'an is that Allah ﷻ made it easy to be memorized by anyone who intends to do so. [Qur'an 54:17] In the Muslim *ummah* (community), millions memorize the entire Qur'an in Arabic, some as early as ten years of age, regardless of their mother tongue. This is one of the great miracles of the holy Qur'an and the best way to preserve and safeguard it. No other book on the face of this earth, heavenly or not, can match this divine quality or duplicate this miracle of its followers' and their affection for the Qur'an.

Allah revealed the holy Qur'an in Arabic, the language of the holy Prophet ﷺ and of the Arabs. Previous holy books were not protected from human interference, and the language in which they existed became obsolete. Those books only exist in much later manuscripts by which one cannot verify the authenticity of their contents. However, the holy Qur'an is protected and remains in its original form, and Arabic is well preserved and widely spoken throughout the world.

Almost every single Muslim, regardless of his or her mother tongue, learns to recite the holy Qur'an in Arabic from childhood. During *salāh* (daily prayers), the Qur'an must be recited in Arabic. To understand the meanings of the Qur'anic verses, translations are available in almost every language. However, it is preferred that one know the Qur'anic Arabic in order to concentrate on and grasp the wisdom of the holy Qur'an, and it is very beneficial and rewarding to do so.

Arabic is a complex language. A slight error in pronunciation and/or misplacement of the diacritical marks can change the meaning of a word. When used in different contexts, Arabic words can have different meanings, and in just a few words one can say and mean a lot.

Allah ﷻ reveals in the holy Qur'an that it contains the knowledge of everything we need to know to reach our ultimate goal. To reveal the holy Qur'an, Allah ﷻ chose the Arabic language, because it is inherently unique and has the capacity to hold such an ocean of knowledge in a compacted form. No other language could have encompassed the Qur'an's vast knowledge and wisdom. This may be the reason why it was revealed in Arabic. As human faculties progress, especially in the fields of science and technology, new and amazing information and miraculous knowledge from the holy Qur'an are continuously unfolding, proving its universality, the divinity of Allah's book and His choice of the Arabic language.

The literal meaning of the word Qur'an is 'read a lot.' This also explains why the Qur'an is the most read book in the world. Tens of millions of Muslims recite the holy Qur'an five times a day in *salāh* and many millions recite a considerable portion of it on a daily basis. The holy Qur'an is continuously recited throughout the world in millions of *masajid* (mosques), especially in the two holiest places of Islam (Makkah and Madinah). It is recited in thousands of holy shrines and in Islamic educational institutions. Ever since its inception, this practice has been ongoing and continuous. When a Muslim passes away, friends and family members recite the holy Qur'an abundantly and convey its earned blessings to the deceased. In the holy month of Ramadhān, the ninth month of the Islamic calendar and the month of fasting, almost every single Muslim recites the entire Qur'an at least once, and some do it many times more.

People who constantly read the holy Qur'an feel an indescribable pleasure, peace, and contentment, making them want to read more and more. No other book has drawn so much attention, and the privilege given to the holy Qur'an is unique. The name Qur'an says it all. Such a befitting name could not be chosen by any man, but only by its own Author, the All-Knowledgeable Allah سبحانه وتعالى. The proof of its holiness is within it, and man's natural attraction to it shows that the Maker of both humanity and the Qur'an is One. Let alone recitation and contemplation, just touching the holy Qur'an with clean hands brings many blessings.

The holy Qur'an is a miracle. Miracles become possible only through supernatural qualities. Allah سبحانه وتعالى, the All-Powerful, gives the power of miracles to His prophets to prove their claim of prophethood. Allah سبحانه وتعالى revealed the holy Qur'an to Prophet Muhammad ﷺ. It is, therefore, his miracle, and no man can ever produce a chapter or even a verse of its kind, thereby proving that it is the book of Allah سبحانه وتعالى.

To defeat and overcome the disbelievers, Allah سبحانه وتعالى granted miracles to almost every prophet. The kinds of miracles shown by prophets were the kind needed in their specific times. Ibrahim (Abraham) عليه السلام, Musa (Moses) عليه السلام, Isa (Jesus) عليه السلام, and other prophets were given various miracles to make people believe in their prophethood.

The time of Muhammad ﷺ was the time of literary excellence and eloquence in the Arabic language. To prove his prophethood, among other miracles, a miracle full of eloquence and linguistic qualities was needed. The revelation of the holy Qur'an fulfilled the need for that miracle and miraculously provided everlasting guidance to mankind. It was revealed orally to Prophet Muhammad ﷺ, who had not acquired any education from any person, nor did he read or write.

The holy Qur'an was written as it was being revealed, in the order established by the Prophet ﷺ and as instructed to him by Allah ﷻ. It was later compiled in the same order in the form of a book, shortly after the Prophet's ﷺ passing. Then again, within a matter of years, during the leadership of the third righteous *khalīfa* (caliph), Uthman ﷺ, more copies from that original were drafted and sent to different parts of the Islamic world to be copied as needed. To make it easy for non Arabic-speaking Muslims to read the Qur'an precisely and to pronounce each word without error, diacritical marks were placed within the Qur'anic text.

Those well versed in the Arabic language were spellbound upon hearing the unique coherence, style and prose of the holy Qur'an. The holy Qur'an's compilation, coherence, relevance, rhetoric, eloquence, perfect order, and arrangement of words, phrases, and inner meanings were completely unique to the contemporary Arab style of prose and poetry. The orators and masters of linguistics were awestruck by the miraculous Qur'an.

The way the holy Qur'an laid down the authentic stories of the previous nations, especially of *bani Israīl* (nation of Israel) and the past prophets, amazed even the scholars of *Ahle Kitāb* (primarily Jews and Christians). They themselves did not know for certain the true accounts of those authentic narratives and held varying views about them. Moreover, future events revealed in the holy Qur'an happened as predicted, proving it to be a miracle and the book of Allah ﷻ. It is not possible for a man to compile such creativity, rarity of words and meanings, and hundreds of other qualities with such precision.

Throughout the history of Islam, Muslim scholars have dedicated their entire lives with love and affection, without intending to earn fame or money, but only to serve the holy Qur'an in every way possible. Thousands of translations came to the fore and guided Muslims throughout the ages by explaining the teachings of the holy Qur'an.

Many people have served the holy Qur'an in unique ways. Some translated it into poetic form, and others inscribed it in gold letterings. Some carved it on gold plates, and some inscribed it on huge parchments, making it the largest and heaviest edition. Some wrote it so minutely that it became the smallest, legible version. Some became experts in Qur'anic calligraphy, developing thousands of different designs. Muslims created and perfected the art of recitation of the holy Qur'an. In summation, Muslims have served and continuously serve the book of Allah 🕮 in every way possible to gain the pleasure of Allah 🕮. No other book besides the holy Qur'an can claim such a unique love and affection from its followers.

The Qur'an is unlike any other book. It is the word of Allah 🕮 and must be respected in every possible way. There are uniform rules and regulations about its safekeeping, transportation, and even how it should be placed on a shelf. Its utmost care and protection bring many spiritual benefits, and even a slight gesture of care pleases Allah 🕮. Even the thought of disposing it with everyday garbage or intentionally placing it on walkways or on the floor earns Allah's wrath, and there are grave consequences for doing so. Old and worn-out copies of the Qur'an and any of its verses, no matter what material it is written on should be recycled with other holy material, buried in the ground or submerged in a body of water, i.e., pond, river, or ocean. It must not be taken into bathrooms, placed under beds, or put close to any filth. Muslims must be in the state of *tahāra* (purity) before touching the holy Qur'an. In any case, great care must be utilized when handling holy verses of the Qur'an, and any and all disrespect must be avoided.

Compared to other books, whether sacred or secular the holy Qur'an surpasses every book in every respect. It is the most published, decorated, read, researched, and analyzed book in the world. To this day, new knowledge and wisdom are being extracted from it, and its mysteries are being disclosed as the science of every field progresses and makes new discoveries. Science brings to light what the Qur'an informed us of some 1,400 years ago. Numerous examples of this fact can be found.

THE CONTENTS OF THE HOLY QUR'AN

As per the holy Qur'an, Allah ﷻ states:

...and We have sent down to you this book explaining in detail everything... • [Qur'an 16:89]

And there is not a grain in the dark recesses of the earth, nor anything wet or dry, but it is written in the Luminous Book. • [Qur'an 6:59]

Allah ﷻ reveals Himself in the holy Qur'an and tells us how and why He created the universe and, most importantly, human beings. [Qur'an 41:9-12 & 51:56] The Qur'an underlines the main purpose of our earthly life, i.e., how and why we will pass on to the Hereafter and what are the next and final phases of human life. It guides us in how to live life successfully on Earth and teaches us how to achieve ultimate success in the Hereafter. It tells us how to obtain the pleasure of Allah. It informs us of our inner and external enemies, about our physical and spiritual aspects, and about the positive forces that assist us and the negative forces that oppose us in life.

The Qur'an establishes rules and regulations for every human affair, from the most personal and private to those that affect society as a whole. It explains forms of direct and indirect worship. It discloses to us what Allah ﷻ likes and dislikes. It describes reward and punishment for good and bad behavior. It reminds us how previous nations disobeyed Allah's ﷻ prophets and earned His wrath. It recounts how the prophets struggled to deliver Allah's ﷻ message to humanity. It discusses human nature and the nature of everything, the creation process, the powers of the Almighty, the relationship of the Creator to His creations and every bit of matter that is required for man's journey through this temporal state to the state of eternity.

On the one hand, the Qur'an is divine guidance for believers and remains with them all the way to their final destination. On the other hand, the Qur'an is a guide for all other people whom it informs, but then does *not* remain with them all the way. Taking one to his destination and simply giving him directions are two different things. Islam is the complete way of life, and all relevant information, knowledge, wisdom, and guidance are revealed in the holy Qur'an.

Here, I include the translation of the opening chapter of the holy Qur'an, which in a few short verses is believed to contain the entire message of the Qur'an [Tibrani]. Many scholars have written volumes to explain this preamble to the holy Qur'an.

In the name of Allah, the Most Compassionate, the Most Merciful

All praise is due to Allah indeed • Sustainer of all the worlds • the Most Compassionate, the Most Merciful • Master of the Day of Judgment. • You alone we worship, and You alone we ask for help. • Walk us on the straight path, • the path of those upon whom You (have given) blessed favors, • not of those who were put under wrath, nor of those who are astray. • [Qur'an 1:1-7] *(Ameen!)*

WHAT DOES THE HOLY QUR'AN SAY ABOUT ITSELF?

*O*N SEVERAL PLACES, THE QUR'AN testifies to its own authenticity and absolute divinity. The following verses illustrate this fact.

That book in which there is no doubt of any kind; it is guidance for the fearful ones. • [Qur'an 2:2]

And this is a book We have sent down, a blessed one, confirming those that were before it... • [Qur'an 6:92]

Announce that "If all people and jinns united on that to bring the like of the Qur'an, they cannot bring one like it, even if they become each other's back support." • And without a doubt, We clearly explained to people every thing in the Qur'an in many ways; yet many of them, indeed, rejected (it) ungratefully. • [Qur'an 17:88-89]

And We sent the Qur'an bit by bit, so you can read it to people little by little, and We revealed it slowly and slowly. • [Qur'an 17:106]

Had We sent this Qur'an on a mountain, certainly, you would see it humbled, split asunder in the fear of Allah... • [Qur'an 59:21]

It is but a glorious Qur'an, • in the Sacred Tablet • [Qur'an 85:21-22]

And if you are in any doubt about what We have sent upon Our exclusive being (Muhammad), then bring just one chapter like it and call your own helps besides Allah, if you are truthful. • But if you cannot do it—and certainly, you will not be able to do it—so fear the fire, whose fuel is people and stone idols, prepared specifically for disbelievers. • [Qur'an 2:23-24]

And this is not a Qur'an produced by anyone, besides Allah... •
[Qur'an 10:37]

And without a doubt, We have explained for people in this Qur'an in every way so they may embrace guidance. • [Qur'an 39:27]

Those who rejected guidance when it came to them (are going to lose), and this certainly is a dignified Book • falsehood cannot come from before it nor from behind it—sent from the All-Wise, the All-Praiseworthy. • [Qur'an 41:41-42]

"Do they not use intellect in (evaluating) the Qur'an?" Had it been from other than Allah, they would have found much contradictions in it. • [Qur'an 4:82]

INTERPRETING THE HOLY QUR'AN

*M*OST PEOPLE WHO ARE INTERESTED IN LEARNING about Islam, turn to the holy Qur'an. Perhaps this is because of its accessibility, because they do not know of any other book that may fulfill their need to know about Islam, or maybe because they just prefer the holy Qur'an. Since the holy Qur'an is in Arabic, and not everyone knows Arabic, people choose a translation in the language with which they are most familiar. At this point, it is important to note the difference between a translation and an interpretation of the holy Qur'an.

To translate simply means to convert one language into another, and to interpret means to explain in terms in which the matter can easily be understood. The holy Qur'an is the Word of Allah ﷻ in the Arabic language therefore, a true translation is not possible. Now, if someone insists on taking a literal meaning of every word of the holy Qur'an, it will create confusion and the intended message of the holy Qur'an will not be understood. To understand the underlying meanings of the Qur'anic text, we need the help of a legitimate interpretation; a translation does not suffice.

The proper Arabic term for the 'explanation of the holy Qur'an' is *tafsīr*. Anyone who genuinely desires to study the holy Qur'an must resort to its *tafsīr*. It is also important to note that not everyone is qualified to do the *tafsīr* of the holy Qur'an, even if one is an expert in the Arabic language. An unqualified or a less qualified person who writes *tafsīr* only interprets what he understands and does not bring forth the actual or closest meaning; therefore, he should never be entrusted with the work of *tafsīr*.

Many unqualified people have attempted to explain the holy Qur'an according to their poor judgment and have thereby caused great harm to the religion and divided the Muslim *ummah* (community) into many factions. Presently, many individuals and groups refer to a literal meaning of the Qur'anic text and its interpretations to promote their personal/political agendas in Muslim and non-Muslim communities. I fear that if this practice continues, it will bring forth irreparable damage to peace and harmony.

Thus, before forming opinions or making decisions about the holy Qur'an or any of its verses, a thorough study of a legitimate explanation is necessary. Only a *tafsīr* written by a qualified *mufassir* (one who does *tafsīr*) sufficiently explains the actual meaning of the Qur'anic text.

As stated earlier, the holy Qur'an is an ocean of knowledge and wisdom, and it is full of guidance. Therefore, new information from it will continue to surface according to the needs of the time until the Day of Judgment. The process of this flow of knowledge will be ongoing, as it has been, through proper *tafsīr* of the holy Qur'an. Every unqualified interpretation only brings harm and causes misunderstandings about Islam, the Prophet of Islam ﷺ, and about the Qur'an itself.

There are established guidelines to translate/interpret the holy Qur'an and set requirements for an individual to become a certified *mufassir*. Allah ﷻ revealed the holy Qur'an to the sacred heart of the Prophet Muhammad ﷺ and made it compulsory for him to teach Allah's ﷻ word to his companions and, subsequently, to all of humanity. Allah ﷻ verifies this in the holy Qur'an:

> Undoubtedly, Allah conferred a great favor on Muslims when He raised a prophet from among them, who recites to them the revelations of Allah and purifies them and instructs them in the Qur'an and Sunnah, whereas before, they were in manifest error. • [Qur'an 3:164]

Prophet Muhammad ﷺ fulfilled this duty. He taught the Qur'an, in its entirety, to his companions in the best manner possible. Therefore, he became the first *Mufassir-e-Qur'an* (authorized commentator on the Qur'an) and, at the same time, he established rules to undertake further work of *tafsīr*. Why would he not be the first *mufassir*, since the Qur'an was revealed and well taught to him by Allah Himself [Qur'an 55:2] and why would he not establish rules to further the work of *tafsīr* through his sayings that safeguard the final book and guidance of Allah ﷻ? If anyone deviates from the Prophet's ﷺ way and attempts to write *tafsīr* through his own judgment, opinions, and explanations of choice or convenience, he will not only become a sinner, but the proper message of the holy Qur'an will never be understood that way. In this regard, a *hadīth* states that if anyone misquotes the Prophet ﷺ intentionally, he secures a place in *Jahannum* (Hell) for himself [Bukhari and Muslim].

Some basic requirements for becoming a certified scholar of *tafsir* are listed below. Only once someone has mastered these skills and fields of knowledge can he begin the arduous process of explanation. Can you imagine what would become of a philosopher's thesis or arguments if "Joe the Plumber" were to break it down and explain its meaning? Similarly, what would happen to the living word of Allah ﷻ if an unqualified person attempts to define it?

A person must be an expert in the following areas before undertaking the task of Qur'anic *tafsīr*: [al-Itqān]

1) He must first be a righteous believer
2) Knowledge of the Arabic lexicon and etymology (derivation)
3) Knowledge of Arabic syntax (grammar)
4) Knowledge of Arabic morphology (internal construction of words)
5) Knowledge of Arabic rhetoric, eloquence, and manners of oration
6) Knowledge of Qur'anic recitation
7) Knowledge of the principles of Islam (dogmas, axioms)
8) Knowledge of the principles of Islamic *fiqh* (jurisprudence)
9) Knowledge of *fiqh* (jurisprudence – to interpret laws)
10) Knowledge of the reason for revelation of a specific verse (to know proper context; *Makki, Madni, Muhkam* and *Mutashabih*)
11) Knowledge of those verses (that annul other verses or are annulled)
12) Knowledge of principles of *hadīth*
13) Knowledge of *hadīth* (at least those related to tafsir of a verse)
14) Knowledge of history (of past prophets, nations, and peoples)

15) Knowledge of Arab culture (prevailing norms and practices)

16) *Ilm-e-Ladunni* – divine knowledge bestowed by Allah ﷻ; usually granted to only a select few

17) Knowledge of the fundamentals of Islam (beliefs)

18) To some, the main ingredient is the love of Allah ﷻ, His Prophet ﷺ, the holy Qur'an, and the propagation of Islam – this love brings the light necessary to acquire and spread the knowledge of Qur'an

19) *Ikhlās* – Purity of intent – through which Allah's ﷻ help is granted

Even with these qualifications, one must embark on this task with utmost care, common sense, foresight, and complete knowledge and command of the language in which he attempts to write *tafsīr*. Attempting to guide just a few at the inadvertent cost of misguiding many, through unqualified work of *tafsīr*, is disastrous and unacceptable. Anyone insisting on doing *tafsīr* without fulfilling these core prerequisites is not serious in serving the Qur'an and Islam and is in clear violation of the rules of Allah ﷻ and of the Prophet ﷺ. Thus, before choosing a translation/interpretation/explanation of the holy Qur'an, it is important to verify the author's qualifications, and not to accept a *tafsīr* just because it is widely available, commonly referred to, or free-of-charge.

The holy Qur'an is the word of Allah ﷻ, and Muhammad ﷺ, is the complete reflection of the message of the holy Qur'an. Thus, The Prophet's *sunnah* (sayings and actions) became the second main source of Islamic knowledge.

SUNNAH OF THE HOLY PROPHET ﷺ

*T*HE COLLECTED ACTIONS AND practices of Prophet Muhammad ﷺ are called his *sunnah,* and Muslims are required to follow them. The *sunnah* is also used to explain Qur'anic verses and the message and the guidance of Allah ﷻ. Whatever he said or did became his *hadīth (pl. ahadīth)*. Furthermore, whatever actions taken or performed by his companions that the Prophet ﷺ took notice of or was informed of and did not overrule or object to were also included in his *sunnah*.

During the holy Qur'an's revelation, the common practice of Muslims was to memorize it; nevertheless, many companions were assigned to transcribe in written form. In the early days, the Prophet ﷺ prohibited the writing of his words (*ahadīth*), except for the revealed verses of the Qur'an. Later, when the difference between the Qur'anic text and *ahadīth* was fully established and understood by the noble companions, the Prophet ﷺ permitted the writing of *ahadīth* separately from the holy Qur'an.

Let me digress a bit at this point and indicate that the holy Qur'an is the word of Allah ﷻ. If it were not Allah's ﷻ word and were put together by Muhammad ﷺ himself, then why was the distinction between the Qur'an and the *hadīth* necessary? If both originated from the same source, contained the teachings of the same person, and were unconditionally accepted by the companions of the Prophet ﷺ, then this distinction would be unnecessary. The separation of the *ahadīth* from the Qur'an clearly shows that the Qur'an is the word of Allah ﷻ as revealed to Prophet Muhammad ﷺ through Angel Jibra'īl (Gabriel) عليه السلام and that the Qur'an was not written by Prophet Muhammad ﷺ.

It is well-recorded history, supported by authentic proofs and conveyed through reliable sources, that some companions continuously wrote down *ahadīth* of the Prophet ﷺ in his lifetime with his permission and separately from the holy Qur'an. The Islamic nation was emerging; therefore, everyone close to the Prophet ﷺ kept himself busy doing essential work. After the Prophet's ﷺ passing, the emergence of the new Islamic nation, stretching from East to West, occupied almost every companion in such activities as governmental affairs, teaching and preaching Islam, and solving issues related to the responsibilities of defending Islam. Under these circumstances, only the compilation of the holy Qur'an into one volume could be achieved, and up to that point, no considerable need arose to compile the *ahadith* collectively.

As time progressed, and due to the publicizing of false *ahadith*, the Prophet's companions and the rightly guided scholars after them, began to compile the *ahadith* in various orders and categorical sequences. They developed rigorous methods to verify the authenticity of narrations and to test and establish the credibility of the narrator in order to avoid preserving false sayings. With such a standard in place and with the application of other stringent procedures, individually and collectively, formally and informally, scholars compiled a treasury of *ahadith*. A new field of knowledge and many subfields related to it evolved, in which thousands of researchers became extensively engaged from the latter part of the first century of Islam and continuing until this task was completed and brought in order.

This topic itself requires a separate book to be fully explained. It is sufficient to say that due to extensive efforts of the companions and later scholars, a huge treasury of authentic *ahadith* was compiled and published. Now, anyone interested in Islamic knowledge can refer to this treasury of *ahadith* and know anything and everything contained therein. Most verses of the holy Qur'an could now be understood through relevant *ahadith* of the Prophet ﷺ. Because of these efforts, many great works on *ahadith* became available in which every *hadith* was placed into relevant categories/subjects.

The famous authentic books of *ahadith* are referred to as *Al-Sihah al-Sittah* ("The Authentic Six"), which includes Sahih Bukhari, Sahih Muslim, Sunan an-Nasa'i, Sunan Abu Dawood, Jami Al-Tirmidhi and Sunan ibn Majah. They have been translated from Arabic into all major languages, and their *shuruh* (explanations/commentaries) are available worldwide. Besides Prophet Muhammad 🕌, no other personality can be accounted for in such detail; his every action and saying is well-preserved. His *ahadith* are the second primary source of Islamic knowledge.

The companions and religious scholars who came immediately after them, not only transmitted the *ahadith* in their most authentic version, but they also gave explanations and defined them and their historical context, i.e., what the occasion, circumstance, and purpose were when the Prophet 🕌 said it or executed an act. Many books of *ahadith*, along with their explanations and with explanations of those explanations to clarify them further, have been written to enhance the Islamic knowledge.

Allah 🕌 makes it incumbent upon Muslims to follow the *sunnah* (sayings and actions) of Prophet Muhammad 🕌 in addition to the teachings of the holy Qur'an. Allah 🕌 states:

> And obey Allah and His Prophet in order that you may be shown mercy. • [Qur'an 3:132]

Allah 🕌 further states:

> Surely, you have an excellent example for your guidance in (the life of) the Prophet of Allah... • [Qur'an 33:21]

As stated earlier, the *sunnah* of Prophet Muhammad 🕌 is the second of the two primary sources of knowledge. If we are unable to locate or understand anything from the Qur'an, we have to consult the *sunnah* of the Prophet 🕌. For example, the holy Qur'an obligates Muslims to establish *salāh* (daily prayers of worship), but it does not explain how to do it. It is only in the *sunnah* that Muslims can find how to perform *salāh*. Thus, we find in the *sunnah* how to perform correctly and practically our religious duties. According to a *hadith*:

Ibn Abbas ﷺ narrated that the Prophet ﷺ in his Last Sermon said, "I leave two things among you. If you strongly hold onto them, you will not go astray. One is the book of Allah (Qur'an), and the other is the sunnah of the Prophet of Allah. [Al-Mustadrak]

This shows the importance of *sunnah/ahadīth* for Muslims. The knowledge contained in them is essential to understand and apply the message of the holy Qur'an. Leaving aside the *sunnah* will make an understanding of Islam incomplete and will result in the holy Qur'an being misunderstood or misinterpreted.

Upon sending the honorable companion Muaz ﷺ to Yemen to resolve a matter of distributing alms to the poor, the Prophet ﷺ asked him, "O Muaz, by what rule will you act?" The companion replied, "By the law of the Qur'an." The Prophet ﷺ said, "If you find no direction therein?" He replied, "Then I will act according to the *sunnah* of the Prophet." The Prophet ﷺ said, "What if you do not find it there?" to which he replied, "Then I will make *ijtihad* and act on that." Approving of his response, the Prophet ﷺ bade him farewell and, raising his hands, said, "Praise be to Allah, Who guides His Prophet in what He pleases." The Prophet's ﷺ approval of the companions' *ijtihad* (use of best judgment based on Qur'an and *sunnah*) set a precedent and became a permissible way to make decisions. According to the Qur'anic injunctions, whatever Allah's Prophet ﷺ approves of becomes legitimate and is made into law, and whatever he disapproves of becomes prohibited and is made unlawful.

IJMA, QIYĀS, AND IJTIHĀD

*T*HE ACT OF DEDUCING AND FORMULATING INJUNCTIONS based on the Qur'an and *sunnah* is called *ijtihād* (the use of personal judgment) and *qiyās* (logical deduction by way of analogy). The one who does *ijtihad* is called a *mujtahid* (pl. *mujtahidūn*). *Ijma* is the majority consent of the *mujtahidūn*. These three standards interchangeably are considered the secondary sources of Islamic knowledge.

Whenever learned scholars of Islam are unable to locate specific religious injunctions because the holy Qur'an and *sunnah* are silent and do not clearly define a course of action, they have been permitted to exercise their judgment and formulate a course of action for new circumstances/issues. The verdict of a *mujtahid* is widely accepted because it is deduced from the primary sources. If any individual or collective judgment contradicts the Qur'an and *sunnah*, it is unacceptable, no matter how sound or appropriate it may seem.

After the passing of the Prophet 🖌, *ijtihad* and *qiyās* became a normal practice of his companions as new issues surfaced. The first and second generations of scholars after the companions were also authentic *mujtahidun* because they came immediately after and were direct descendents and students of the companions who learned Islam directly from the Prophet 🖌.

The notable Imam Abu Hanīfa strongly supported *qiyās* to deduce judgments as new and unusual needs and circumstances arose. Since these needs will continue to come about, the use of *qiyās* can be utilized. For example, a Muslim wants to know whether a kidney transplant is allowed in Islam or wants to obtain a *fatwa* (religious edict) from a *mufti* (Muslim jurist) on what Islam says about selling beer. It is a religious duty of a *mufti* to issue a *fatwa* on the basis of Islamic *sharia* law and properly guide the inquirer. In Islam, no human being has authority to insert ideas into Islam. Thus, the original message and guidance of Allah 🖌 remain preserved.

Some of the initial qualities required for a *mujtahid* to serve Islam are piety, religious and spiritual knowledge, inner wisdom, compassion and affection for the Prophet 🖌, *ikhlās* (purity), dedication, and determination. At this point, it is fair to say that since these authentic saintly and selfless beings who served Islam have now become scarce, it is necessary to keep *ijtihad* off-limits to incapable Muslims in order to preserve and maintain the validity of the authentic teachings of Islam.

The holy Qur'an, the Prophet's ﷺ *sunnah*, *ijma*, and *qiyās* cover every aspect of human life. Nothing is left out for Muslims to search anywhere else for religious and ethical answers. A well-regulated system and knowledge base to legislate laws have been established by the historical *mujtahidūn*. Every Muslim scholar of law must refer to these when making new laws for the ever-changing needs of the Muslim society.

CHAPTER 7

The Purpose of
Human Life

*I*T IS COMMONLY KNOWN that human life is a precious gift. It is not just life, but specifically human life that is precious. What is so special about human life that makes it precious, and why not the life of animals? Like animals, we are born, and we eat and build shelters with a few differences here and there. We work to bring food and other necessities, and animals look for their food and needs as well. They fulfill their sexual needs, and we do the same. They protect and defend themselves and watch and safeguard their territories just as we do. They care for their offspring and get old, sick, injured, and die, and all these things happen to us, too. What then is so special about human life, why is it precious?

If I were to give you a ten-ton rock as a gift to be placed in your already rocky backyard, would you call it a precious gift? Normally, it would not even be called a gift, let alone a precious one, because there is no purpose attached to it. Since there is no purpose to it, it has no value, and as a result it is not precious. Whereas, if I were to give you a diamond ring or a Rolex watch, you would certainly say it was a precious gift. The purpose of the diamond ring and the Rolex watch is what makes them valuable and worthy to be called precious. These items will certainly be of use to your life, and they will beautify your appearance, increase your wealth, reflect your personality, and so on.

Now we know that *the purpose of something* is what makes it valuable and precious—the greater the purpose, the more the value and preciousness. Furthermore, purposes and their values vary according to each person's taste, choice, and use. One must know the purpose of anything before attaching any value to it. Therefore, it is the *purpose of human life* that makes it a valuable and precious gift from our Lord. If our purpose is the same as that of animals, then their life should be equally valuable and precious as ours.

Human life is more valuable than any other life and is correctly called precious because there is *a greater purpose* attached to it. Islam teaches us that Allah ﷻ created the universe to serve man and created man to serve Allah ﷻ. Man has every animal quality and habit, but the difference is that man is granted *a special purpose* in life, which is to worship and please Allah ﷻ. To fulfill this special purpose, humans must first control and suppress those animalistic qualities that hinder them from their purpose, and they must simultaneously develop, purify, and promote those qualities that assist them. At this point, man truly becomes worthy of his status as the best of all creatures, and only then does his life become precious. How we choose to live this life determines what our end will be in the Hereafter.

Allah ﷻ states in the holy Qur'an:

> And I did not create jinn and men, but to worship Me. • [51:56]

> Surely We have created man in the best mold (form). • [95:4]

> (I swear) By time! Verily man is necessarily in loss – except those who believe and do good deeds, and enjoin one another to accept the truth and to be patient. • [103:1-3]

The Lord created us in the best manner possible and equipped us with every quality necessary to live as humans and prepare ourselves for the success of the Hereafter. Whoever fulfills this greatest purpose of life—to worship the Lord as He taught us—will become the guided and successful one; otherwise, he will be a loser. The choice is ours.

FROM MAN TO MACHINE

*F*ORGETTING THE GREATER PURPOSE for which he was created has led man to think of this world as his permanent abode. In making arrangements to live in this supposedly permanent home, man has become a machine, and he does not control his life anymore.

> *The earth and everything else was created to serve him, instead of enslaving them, he became their slave.*

Willingly or unwillingly, intentionally or not, he has become a slave, either of society or of his self-created artificial life. Competing for success, wealth, luxuries of life, fame, and other material desires has turned him into a machine, by which he has lost the inherent and necessary charm of real life. In fact, the earth and everything else were created to serve him, but instead of enslaving them, he became their slave. He was supposed to use them to fulfill his divine purpose; yet, he gave himself into their service and became a subordinate. This servitude caused him to ask, "Why this?" and "Why that?" when he should have been looking into himself and asking "Why me?" and "What for?" Instead of appreciating the perfection of Allah's creativity and invoking His good name, he forgot his *main purpose* and lost himself to the temporary charm of this deceptive world.

Those who are lost in this world have become like machines that do not observe or think, have a heart, or worry about accountability for their actions. Machines are not mindful of their "death" or ponder what will happen to them thereafter. They do not need to ask about their creator, their purpose, or what will happen to them in the end (when they are junked or wrecked). Humans, however, should inquire into these realities.

Considering the same example from a different angle shows that machines, which are the creation of man, never deviate from their purpose. They follow the orders of their owner and, even without having a mind of their own, function properly and perform tasks according to the intent of their inventor/purpose. Humans, on the other hand, even after becoming like machines, do not completely perform like them. This is, of course, because humans still have free will. Even though they can think, observe, ponder, and have a mind of their own, they fail to function properly, deviate from their course, and do not act according to the orders of their Creator and Master.

Man's fall from humanity to barbarism is a global phenomenon and is not limited to any one specific area or society. Even most animals do not kill their own kind, but people through unjustifiable reasons and purposes, individually and collectively, in one way or another, kill other humans ruthlessly and without any remorse. In one place, there are kings who use toilets forged in gold; yet, there are people elsewhere who barely have enough to cover their basic needs. In some places, so much food is thrown in the garbage and wasted through other means that, if it were saved, it could easily feed millions of people who are starving elsewhere.

Forget about other creatures; look what man has himself become! Even among millions, he is alone. Regardless of different relationships and friendships, he is lonely. True friendships no longer exist, and he therefore had to replace them with artificial ones to pass the time. Sometimes, even with abundant wealth, he seems needy because he cannot buy those things that he truly needs, such as love and affection. Even those nearest to him, such as his spouse and children, seem to be after his money and wealth and have no regard for his life and hard work. We are such intelligent beings, but we seem to be fooling ourselves. Fooling others is a day-to-day business for some, but the fool of all fools is the one who fools himself.

Even after all the scientific and technological advancements in every aspect of human life, we fail to recognize our true status in this universe. Even with our immense power, we fail to rule over hearts and are unable to solve our own problems. This condition seems to be worsening day by day. Even with all the luxuries in the world, man is not at peace and is often fearful.

Mankind has walked on the moon and has gone far out into the universe, something that no other creature can even imagine doing. In my opinion, and forgive me for saying this, he has not even learned how to properly live on Earth, in his own habitat. Had he found a living being on the moon and had it asked, "Have you even learned to live properly on Earth that you dare to intrude on the space of others?" what response would he have?

We have all the right to explore whatever we like and need and to know the purpose of everything, but we should know *our own purpose* first. To ask "why this" and "why that" is justifiable only once we have found out "why me" and "what for."

Instead of utilizing our faculties and applying the knowledge to determine our proper status in the universe, our purpose, and our destination, we went astray and became busy in denying basic truths. Such truths indicate that there is a purpose to human life and that there is a destination to which we all are headed.

Some think that death is the end of life, but in fact it is just a mode of transportation for the soul to get to the other world. Through death, the soul and the body are temporarily separated until the Day of Judgment when everyone will be resurrected. On that Day, souls will rejoin their bodies and will be held accountable for their actions. Divine justice will be served, and everyone will be held accountable for every iota of injustice that he may have brought upon himself or others. After all, human beings are not machines that are free from accountability. They are animate beings who have been created for a specific purpose. Whether humans choose through free will to fulfill their specific purpose or do otherwise dictates whether Allah ﷻ will reward or punish them in the Hereafter.

It is impossible for people to acquire success by going against the forces of nature. The will of Allah ﷻ, through these forces of nature, will always prevail. Why? Because He is the Creator of these forces. This is His world and His universe; people do not have any overriding authority over His plans. They may devise plans to shape the world in unique ways and take actions accordingly, but they end up causing more problems and more unrest. The duty of every human being is to follow His commands and apply the rules set forth by Him.

People should not interfere with the forces of nature, and they should let the physical world be as it is. Their duty is to learn about their obligations and figure out what role they have to play. A study of Islam will clearly show what people's roles are as human beings and how they can avoid a head-on collision with the will of Allah ﷻ, both individually and collectively. Islam also clearly states the answers to such questions as: What are people's limits? How much must they submit their will to the will of Allah ﷻ? How much choice do they have? How much freedom do they require? What is the result of their choice if they do not choose wisely? What are the outcomes of the extra freedoms they sometimes demand and/or acquire? A true understanding of Islam helps in molding the decision-making process and in wisely choosing the steps to be taken, individually and collectively, to bring peace, prosperity, and happiness for all.

CHAPTER 8

Worship and Its Broader Meaning in Islam

UMANS ARE CREATED WITH AN INNATE DESIRE to worship, making them naturally inclined to seek a higher authority whom they can worship. This built-in desire and natural urge to worship a higher authority require them to inquire into and know who that being could be or actually is. Whichever higher authority people, individually or collectively, settle on to worship naturally brings some sort of mental and/or physical satisfaction, and it somewhat fulfills that inherent desire. However, we keep ourselves busy in fulfilling other personal needs and wants and often suppress that innate desire to worship. In our search, we often fall short of seeking and understanding who this higher being is or should be and how we can truly worship to fulfill this inner desire.

We not only seek to satisfy this need of worshiping, but through it seek the pleasure of that higher being and try to build a connection to acquire protection, assistance, favor, and security. Without being certain who this higher being is from whom we can draw these blessings, our worship will be misguided, fruitless, and unproductive, and will not bring any satisfaction to us. Therefore, we must, first and foremost, know who that higher being is.

Through the passage of time and as the human intellect progressed, people came to realize and believe that there is one single Being, Who is the Creator, the All Controlling, the Almighty, the All-Powerful. Our knowledge, understanding and common sense have brought us to the conclusion that there can only be, and in fact there is, one Supreme Being.

Whether we are religious or not, we believe that there is an Almighty Lord, Whom some call God and some call Allah ﷻ. Religion strengthens our belief in Him and gives direction, a path to reach Him. Muslims believe in one Lord Allah ﷻ, and others call Him by other names. Whatever the case may be, since we have come to believe in one Lord, then the questions that follow are—how are we to worship Him, fulfill our innate desire, and acquire His pleasure? Who decides what the process of worship should be? How can we strengthen our relationship with Him?

In all honesty, if we do not know what pleases them and what may upset them, it is difficult to strengthen relationships even with our own friends, families, and colleagues. Similarly, if we do not know what pleases Allah/God, then how can we go about pleasing Him and refraining from displeasing Him? Thus, to assure the pleasure of others, it is a prerequisite to find out, know, and be certain about their likes and dislikes before assuming anything on our own.

Every religion has some sort of religious practices and rituals for its followers, through which they can satisfy their inner desire and build connections to the one true Lord. It sets rules, times, and holy places for its followers who gradually become attuned to its way and purpose. Some find satisfaction through it and continue their practices. Others do not and thus feel no reason to continue practicing.

Today, most religions have become limited to rituals and are confined to places of worship. Many see religion as just a part of life, like any other, that barely governs over any facet of their secular lives. Its followers simply live their lives according to the prevailing norms of society and believe religion has no say in them. This may either be because the religion does not provide guidelines for secular matters or because the followers are not fully aware of its teachings. Another reason may be that they simply do not want religion to interfere in their secular lives (outside the place of worship).

> *Islam provides for and governs the entire life of its followers, from the cradle to the grave and, spiritually speaking, from the womb to the tomb, and even beyond.*

For them, their religion plays a minimal role in their lives and is usually set aside for special occasions or holy days. Thus, the line drawn between the religious and the secular becomes quite distinctive.

However, Islam is the complete way of life. It provides guidance for every facet of life and is not and cannot be limited to a place of worship. It does not let its followers wander outside its system or place of worship. Islam provides for and governs the entire life of its followers, from the cradle to the grave and, spiritually speaking, from the womb to the tomb, and even beyond. This is why Islam is not just a religion, but a *deen* (complete way of life) prescribed by Allah. Worship in Islam is not limited to a *masjid* (place of worship) or set aside for special times, days, or occasions. Rather, worship in Islam plays a greater role in the life of a Muslim and has a broader meaning.

Since Islamic acts and everything included in the entire process of worship are not man made, but revealed and prescribed by the Almighty Himself, they provide complete fulfillment and satisfaction to our natural desires. When Muslims abide by every commandment and fulfill every obligation, they acquire complete peace, harmony, and fulfillment. They successfully build a strong connection to Allah ﷻ. By this, Muslims do not try to please the Lord through their own way and understanding, but through divine rules set forth by the Almighty Himself. Thus, they acquire Allah's ﷻ pleasure, a contented life in this world, and finally ultimate success in the Hereafter.

Every rule and activity in Islam are interconnected to the 'actual purpose of human life,' which is to seek Allah's pleasure and to prepare for the life in the Hereafter. In Islam, worship and what it entails encompass the entire idea of human life. Whether an act is religious or secular, obligatory or voluntary, directly related to the Lord or to His creatures, a physical act or just a mental thought, a moral act or a matter of business— whatever Muslims do with the pure intent to seek Allah's ﷻ pleasure becomes worship. The actions of Muslims who mean well and intend to do good turn into constant worship, and they receive reward from Allah ﷻ for everything they do.

Islam turns man's every action into an act of worship when it is performed in accordance with Islam.

As mentioned earlier, Allah ﷻ reveals in the holy Qur'an:

> And I did not create jinn and man, but to worship Me. • [51:56]

This holy verse reveals that the purpose of our lives is to worship Allah ﷻ. If worship, as commonly understood, were limited to the confines of a place of worship, would we all just be able to sit there our entire lives and worship because it is *the* purpose of life? Who would do all the other necessary chores of our lives? Clearly, Allah ﷻ must have meant worship of Him to have a broader meaning so that we could simultaneously carry on other necessary activities and acquire Allah's ﷻ pleasure through them. This is precisely the broader meaning of worship in Islam, for which Allah ﷻ created us. Islam turns man's every action into an act of worship when it is performed in accordance with Islam.

Humans are called *abd* in the Qur'an, and Allah ﷻ is our *Ma'bood*. *'Abd* means slave, and *Ma'bood* means that Which this *'abd* worships. Thus, the relationship of man to Allah ﷻ is like the relationship between a slave and master. Upon recognizing Allah as our Master, we must keep this relationship in good standing and never cross over its boundaries or break it in any way. It is imperative to establish this relationship of *'abd* and *Ma'bood* and to embrace the fact that Allah is our Master and we are His slaves. By fulfilling every duty set forth by Him, we keep this relationship in good standing. Through love, loyalty, and performing other good deeds in addition to the required obligations, we strengthen our relationship to Him.

We must prove our relationship to Him by defeating every force of evil within *(nafs,* i.e., one's base self, and *Satan)* and outside (the material world) us, especially when our faith is put to the test. We must never cross the limits of this relationship by violating His commandments, breaching the contract of *'abd* and *Ma'bood,* overlooking the duties set forth by Him, abrogating the rights of or inflicting pain on others, stepping out of the boundaries clearly defined by Him, neglecting the rules of conduct set forth by the holy Prophet ﷺ, or through any other way.

In short, every mental and/or physical effort we make to remain within the limits of this relationship of *'abd* and *Ma'bood,* Islam considers and rewards as part of worshiping Allah ﷻ. Fulfilling the rights of Allah ﷻ and the rights of our fellow human beings are all part of the broader concept and meaning of worship in Islam. Allah ﷻ considers every human action as worshiping Him if it is executed with the intent of pleasing Him, whether it is an act of direct worship or executed for His creatures. Where else do we find such a generous and gracious Lord? Allah ﷻ accepts our positive interactions and the good we do to others as being worship of Him and rewards us for them. Even those acts of direct worship that we do for Him that fulfill His rights do not bring any benefit to Him; rather, they benefit our own self, body, mind, and soul. He rewards us for those acts just because we followed His commandments with the intent to please Him and for maintaining the relationship between *'abd* and *Ma'bood*.

Islam places two types of duties on its followers so they may fulfill the greater purpose for which they were created. Muslims are to fulfill *Huqūq-ul-Allah* (the rights of Allah ﷾) and *Huqūq-ul-Ibād* (the rights of people). They must perform every duty before they can hope to acquire the pleasure of Allah ﷾ and ultimate success. Fulfilling these rights and performing all related duties becomes, therefore, the 'broader meaning of worship' in Islam.

RIGHTS AND DUTIES

*I*SLAM DOES NOT EMPHASIZE DEMANDING RIGHTS any more than it demands and prepares its adherents to fulfill their duties. There is much difference in the outcomes for demanding rights and the demand for performing duties. The demand to perform duties creates a different kind of society, where its social and moral outlook and the mentality of citizens are uniquely different.

By instilling the sense of fulfilling duties, Islam intends to make its followers sincere and responsible. In contrast, the sense of coveting rights may make people demanding and perhaps even dissatisfied. Islam promotes the ideas of fulfilling duties first and to be content and patient. Only secondarily does Islam allow individuals to press for rights, especially if and when they are purposely denied. This does not mean that people should become cowards and never ask for their rights. In fact, this only means that Islam emphasizes the fulfillment of duties more than it does the demand for rights. Certainly, as people fulfill their duties to others, everyone receives what is theirs rightfully. Nevertheless, Islam provides all means to claim one's rights and to struggle against oppressors and their oppression.

When every member of a Muslim society voluntarily and willingly fulfills his or her duty to Allah ﷻ and to others, the government will play only a limited role in that society. However, if rights are fulfilled only through continuous demand, then the government must become a comprehensive overseer and make sure people's rights are being respected. In Islam, voluntarily fulfilling the rights of others with the intent to please Allah ﷻ turns every act into a good deed, whereas fulfilling other peoples' rights unwillingly does not bear the quality of fruit designated for the successful ones. Therefore, Islam emphasizes fulfilling duties more than demanding rights.

One may feel and become lonely even among a crowd of millions. Law is cold, and love is warm. Relationships based on love are everlasting and abundantly fruitful.

Islam wants its followers to be ever mindful of Judgment Day, when Allah will deliver His justice according to individuals' performance. The more willingly and humbly we perform our duties, the more love and harmony develop in society, and the more peace and happiness prevail. In contrast, constantly and selfishly demanding rights, even lawfully, gradually makes people arrogant, unhappy, and self-centered, thereby distancing themselves from others and increasing the likelihood of being lonely and depressed. Thus, one may feel and become lonely even among a crowd of millions. Law is cold, and love is warm. Relationships based on love are everlasting and abundantly fruitful.

Everyone is supposed to fulfill prescribed duties on the basis of their individual circumstances, capacity, and capability. On Judgment Day, Allah ﷻ will hold an individual accountable according to his or her capabilities. No one will answer for others or be responsible for them, unless their responsibilities overlapped. The Qur'an reveals:

Allah does not burden any soul with more than it can bear... • [2:286]

RIGHTS OF ALLAH ﷻ

*T*HE RIGHTS OF ALLAH ﷻ INCLUDE, but are not limited to, the following. We must:

- Have unshakeable faith, recognize *tawhīd* (the Oneness of Allah ﷻ), and never commit *shirk* (polytheism)
- Recognize Allah ﷻ as the Lord and recognize all of His attributes
- Worship no one but Allah ﷻ
- Submit our will to the will of Allah ﷻ
- Engage in constant remembrance of Allah ﷻ
- Fear Allah's ﷻ wrath
- Glorify Allah's ﷻ majesty and sublimity
- Invoke Allah ﷻ in our supplications
- Never call upon anyone besides Allah ﷻ to seek repentance

Worshiping Allah ﷻ means paying utmost homage to Him, expressing the deepest humility and gratitude to Him, completely submitting to Him, bowing down to Him in recognition of His greatness and glory, continuously remembering Him, and following His commandments. We must take every step towards acquiring His pleasure, especially through spending our wealth, time, and energy. In this process of worship, some practices are made obligatory/compulsory—such as, for example, the five pillars of Islam—and others are categorized as desirable and voluntary. These duties must be performed on a daily, weekly, monthly, and yearly basis or once in a lifetime, as prescribed.

Some of these duties require physical acts, some require spending of money, and some require both (explained in Chapter 9). A follower can perform these duties individually and/or collectively, privately and/or publicly, in a *masjid* (mosque) or outside of it. Islam clearly outlines rewards for performing these duties and punishments for not fulfilling them. Let me remind you that these actions and fulfillment of duties do not bring any benefit to Allah ﷻ, but to the worshiper. Punctually following His rules brings success both here and in the Hereafter.

RIGHTS OF PEOPLE

*T*HE SECOND DUTY IS TO FULFILL THE RIGHTS OF PEOPLE. In the Qur'an and *sunnah*, Muslims are warned repeatedly that they will earn the wrath of Allah for violating the rights of others. [Bukhari] On the Day of Judgment, Allah ﷻ will not forgive these violations; instead, the violators will first have to seek forgiveness from their victims in order to receive Allah's pardon [Bukhari]. In many cases, violators will have to forfeit their good deeds to their victims, resulting in depletion of good deeds from their roster [Bukhari]. They may have many good deeds, but because of not fulfilling or abrogating the rights of others, they may end up in Hell, until their punishment is complete.

These days, when no one lets anyone go free, how can one expect that anybody will let anyone go free at that crucial juncture?

In the court of Allah ﷻ, victims will have the authority to forgive their oppressor and may choose not to take any good deeds as compensation from them. On Judgment Day, when everyone will be looking for salvation and be in need of good deeds, only some will be generous enough to forgive those who inflicted pain on them for nothing in return. These days, when no one lets anyone go free, how can one expect that anybody will let anyone go free at that crucial juncture?

In many cases, Allah may forgive the shortcomings and deficiencies in our duties to Him and may forgive our sins, except the sins of *kufr* (infidelity) and *shirk* (polytheism). The main purpose of Judgment Day is to bring justice to the oppressed who suffered at the hands of others and to punish the criminals, sinners, and violators. The obligation of fulfilling the rights of people has priority over many matters and is central to the Islamic philosophy of the broader meaning of worship.

People to whom duties must be fulfilled include parents, spouses, children, siblings, paternal/maternal relatives, neighbors, wayfarers, distant relatives, friends and co-workers, employers and employees, dependents, especially those whose needs you can fulfill, people entrusted to you, orphans, widows, the elderly and disabled, refugees, the poverty-stricken, the sick, and non-Muslims living under Islamic governments. Islam even obligates Muslims to fulfill the rights of animals.

It is said that, "Heaven is at a mother's feet." Thus, by serving her fully, Muslims can earn Heaven easily. A mother deserves her children's love, respect, care, and assistance because she bore them, endured labor pains, sacrificed many nights of her sleep to keep them warm and well, and much more.

Allah's pleasure is assured when Muslims serve their fathers well. Fathers work selflessly to raise their children, earn lawful wages, and toil hard to train their children in the best manner and to be fit for society. Thus, the success of children depends on their father's hard work and sacrifice. According to the Prophet ﷺ, when a father gets two of his daughters married, he is rewarded with Paradise. [Mishkat]

Parents are promised an exalted status in Heaven if they raise their children to be true and sincere Muslims and properly equip them with the necessary tools to be protected from Hellfire. Allah directly commands in the holy Qur'an:

> O you who believe! Guard yourselves and your families against the fire, the fuel of which are men and stones... • [66:6]

Moreover, a loyal and sincere wife who performs her duties to her husband is guaranteed Paradise. A husband is granted abundant rewards for being trustworthy and just to his wife and for caring for her and fulfilling her needs. A husband and a wife are made for each other, and they must fulfill each other's rights.

The wrath of Allah 🕮 is removed from those who give to people in need for the sake of pleasing Allah 🕮, and these givers are blessed. Great are the rewards for those Muslims who fulfill their duties to others without discriminating and without selfish reasons. No single deed, however insignificant, will go unaccounted [Qur'an 99:7-8].

From performing daily prayers to offering a glass of water to the thirsty, from erecting a *masjid* (mosque) to feeding the hungry, from leading a country with honesty and justice to providing shelter to orphans, from giving millions in charity to the charity of just a smile, all are part of the broader concept of worship in Islam. Where else can we find such a Lord Who guides peoples' interactions with each other and rewards them as being worship of Him? Nowhere! Allah 🕮 is the Lord of us all, the Most Compassionate, the Most Merciful.

SPIRITUALITY IN ISLAM

*H*UMAN BEINGS CONSIST OF BODY AND SOUL. The soul alone cannot be referred to as human, and the body without the soul is a dead body that has a place not on earth, but rather beneath it. Islam provides for both, the body and soul. Its teachings fulfill the requirements of the body and teach us how to uplift spiritually. For example, food nourishes the body, and constant and unceasing remembrance of Allah 🕮 nourishes the soul.

As per the principles of Islamic spirituality, the soul, while living in the body, tries to acquire nearness to Allah 🕮. The aim of Islamic spirituality is to seek complete purification of the soul and of the inner self and to try to submerge with the Supreme Source [Kashful Mahjoob]. However, in no way is the seeker permitted to leave the bondage of this life and the duties attached to it, until death comes to the body.

In other words, the seekers of spirituality—sages, saints, and mystics—live in this world but do not let the world live in them. Their famous sayings and teachings are true reflections of Islamic spirituality. For example, they say, "Let the boat be on the water, and let not water be in the boat," and "Let the heart live in the world, and let not the world live in the heart." During their lives, they keep their hearts empty of worldly desires and purify themselves to receive divine reflections of the Supreme Being and the light of ultimate truth. They acquire the higher state of nearness to the Almighty and enjoy the true taste of existence and of life.

Islamic spirituality does not permit seekers to renege on worldly obligations, even when they have attained the pleasure of and nearness to Allah ﷻ. They just have to exclude this world from their heart and keep Allah's ﷻ remembrance in their hearts, while living among people and performing all the duties of this life. Islam gives new meaning to monasticism, one with which the world was not previously familiar.

If you decide to live in a cave or on a mountain peak, separating yourself from the world, but are negligent of the Lord, then according to Islam you are not living a monastic life and will not acquire spirituality. On the other hand, if you live in society, take care of your worldly responsibilities, fulfill your duties to others, and are not inattentive to Allah ﷻ, even though you are not physically separate from the world, you are living a monastic life and can acquire spirituality.

Furthermore, the meaning of the monastic life that Islam presents is the most applicable, practical, suitable, and fitting for human nature. By not separating its followers from the physical world, Islam reminds and reiterates that the world is created for humans and that humans are not created for this world, but for Allah ﷻ. They should utilize the world and its bounties as prescribed by Islam and work to attain spirituality. Islam does not allow its followers completely to suppress natural desires and needs for any reason.

To summarize, a human being is the embodiment of both animalistic needs and spiritual qualities. Islam does not advocate for complete suppression of our needs and instincts in order to acquire spiritual uplifting. We must fulfill both needs to obtain the higher and illuminated state for our soul.

FROM WHERE DO TRUE MUSLIMS DRAW ENERGY?

*I*T IS DIFFICULT FOR A PERSON TO LIVE A LIFE OF UTMOST PIETY, refrain from every harmful act, and attain spiritual advancement. In other words, it is hard to swim in water and not get wet, to play with fire and not be burned, and to pass through the filth of this world and come out clean *on the other side*. Repelling worldly desires requires lots of courage and energy, patience to persevere, endurance to remain steadfast, and lots of hard work to maintain piety. The reward for this challenge and spiritual advancement is so fruitful and deeply satisfying and the acquisition of divine energy is so immense that man must do what is necessary to achieve it.

Faithful Muslims remember Allah 🕮 with every beat of their hearts and try to imitate every action of the beloved Prophet Muhammad 🕮. They mold their lives according to Allah's 🕮 will and build their character through continuously replicating the model presented by the Prophet 🕮. Even though they live among people, deep down in their hearts and mental states, they are always present in the company of the Almighty and of His Prophet 🕮. They draw unique pleasure from this spiritual company and acquire the true state of everlasting peace and happiness, which is only felt by them and which cannot be described in words.

Faithful Muslims continuously receive spiritual pleasure and happiness by being in the company of the Lord spiritually and by living among people physically. They are not affected by the pain or oppression inflicted upon them. They are full of energy and are always willing to do whatever is necessary to maintain this spiritual state and strong connection with their Master. They sacrifice their wants and do not wish for any worldly material that may affect this state. They punctually fulfill every duty and do not do anything that may displease Allah ﷻ, nor do they disobey Him in any way. They never deviate from the straight path and never become hypocrites. Most importantly, out of humility, they never disclose their elevated state of spirituality.

By truly following the Qur'an and *sunnah*, they prove that they have attained the purpose for which they were created, thus becoming the embodiment of the broader meaning of worship. At such a purified state, they are the only people living the true life on Earth, while others just exist.

Please note that I just spoke of those *mominīn* (the faithful ones) who truly comprehend the broader meaning of worship in Islam and have applied it to their lives. I am not talking about the saints of Islam, whose state of being is so much more exalted, as are their achievements, pleasures, happiness, and rewards. Certainly, their duties and obligations are far greater as well.

CHAPTER 9

Obligatory Acts in Islam

*I*N THE PREVIOUS CHAPTER, we learned the broader meaning of worship in Islam, which is that Muslims must fulfill their duties to Allah ﷻ and to people. Therefore, we now need to know what those obligations under these two categories are. A detailed discussion of these obligations is not necessary, but the following overview will bring about a greater understanding of Islam and of Muslims.

Initially, upon embracing Islam, Muslims declare verbally and recognize from the heart, "There is no god but Allah, Muhammad is the Prophet of Allah." Through this declaration, they enter into a contract with the Lord. They recognize Allah ﷻ as the Lord, the entire concept of *tawhīd* (the Oneness of Allah ﷻ), Muhammad ﷺ as the Prophet of Allah and as the Seal of Prophethood (which is to say that no other prophet of Allah ﷻ will come after him), and that the holy Qur'an is the final word of Allah ﷻ. Through this contract, Muslims completely submit their will to the will of Allah ﷻ, guarantee that they are not going to disobey Him or insert their own ideas in any way into religious matters, and will follow His commandments.

If Muslims do not totally surrender, then they have not entered into Islam completely. If this is the case, then what can they be considered? Who can tell, and what should one call them: half in, half out; head in, body out; sneaking into Islam; fooling themselves or others or trying to "fool" Allah ﷻ; or just hypocritically entering Islam? Regarding this, Allah ﷻ demands in the holy Qur'an:

> O faithful believers! Enter into Islam with complete submission and do not follow in the footsteps of Shaytān; undoubtedly, he is for you a manifest enemy. • [2:208]

Simply writing one's initials is not sufficient; one's complete signature must appear on a contract for it to be valid and enforceable. Upon signing a contract voluntarily and willfully, it is presumed that it will be followed and any breach thereof is dealt with in full force as underlined in the contract. Mistakes here and there may be forgiven, but violations must be cured through appropriate measures. However, completely disregarding a contract renders it null and void, and no benefit can be claimed by the party at fault.

Recently, I have come across terms such as "practicing" and "non-practicing" being used to explain how religious a person is. Even some Muslims are noticed uttering, "We are non-practicing Muslims." Also, it is becoming common for some Muslims to ask each other, "Are you a practicing Muslim?" or "Are you a non-practicing Muslim?" or "Are you a not-so practicing Muslim?" Remarks such as "I am not *that* kind of a Muslim" or "Oh, you are *that* kind of a Muslim" have become common. Whatever the reply is, it is said boldly, without any remorse and sometimes with pride.

Let me state very clearly that, Islamically speaking, there are no such terms as a "non-practicing Muslim" or a "not-so practicing Muslim." One is either Muslim or not; there is nothing in between. However, there are other terms for willful violators in Islam, such as *fājir* (sinner), *fāsiq* (transgressor), *munāfiq* (hypocrite), and *murtad* (apostate). Allah ﷻ categorized people in the Qur'an Himself and revealed:

And some from the general populace say, "We people have come to believe in Allah and the Last Day," whereas they are not from the believers. They intend to deceive Allah and Muslims, but they do not deceive but themselves and are unaware of it. In their hearts is a disease, so Allah lets them progress in the disease, and for them is a painful torment for they used to lie. • [2:8-10]

By intentionally and willfully declaring the following Cardinal Article of Faith, one becomes a Muslim:

I have faith in **Allah**; His **angels**, His **holy books**, His **prophets**, the **Day of Judgment**, (the fact that both) **good and bad comes from Allah**, and in the **resurrection** (after death).

I have discussed in detail about **Allah** ﷻ in Chapter 4.

Angels are Allah's ﷻ creatures who were created from *nur* (light) and do not have a *nafs* (base self). They neither disobey Allah ﷻ nor deviate from their purpose of serving Him. Their purpose in the kingdom of Allah ﷻ is fixed, and they perform accordingly. Their nourishment is the remembrance of Allah ﷻ. They do not procreate. It is required for Muslims to have faith in their existence. The most important and exalted angels are Jibrail (Gabriel) ﷺ, Mekail (Michael) ﷺ, Izrail ﷺ, and Israfil ﷺ.

Having faith in the **holy books** means that Muslims must believe that the Taurat (Torah), Zabūr (Psalms), Injīl (gospel) and the holy Qur'an were revealed by Allah ﷻ to His prophets and were not written by men. According to Islam, the Taurat, Zabūr, and Injīl do not exist in their original form and are no longer valid. Now, only the holy Qur'an remains valid as the guidance from Allah ﷻ for all times to come. The holy Qur'an was discussed briefly in Chapter 6.

To have faith in Allah's ﷻ **prophets** means to recognize all of them as chosen men who were sent to guide humankind. As per Islam, Muslims cannot disbelieve in even one of them. They must believe and respect all of them, from Adam ﷺ to Isa (Jesus) ﷺ

and of course Muhammad ﷺ, the Final Prophet and Seal of Prophethood. Muslims must attach proper salutations whenever saying or writing their names, in order to pay utmost respect to them, and must have affection in their hearts for them. I discussed the need for and role of prophets in Chapter 5.

Believing in the **Day of Judgment** is central to Islam. The matter of accountability, fear of punishment, and expectation of reward, all provide impetus to follow the commandments of Allah ﷻ in this life. Believing in the Day of Judgment and everything that will happen in it brings unique and worthwhile changes to a person's behavior. (See the next chapter for more details)

Believing that **good and bad comes from Allah** ﷻ means that He is All-Powerful, Almighty, and All-Knowing; nobody else brings good to us besides Him, and nobody else can bring misfortune but Him. When good comes to us, it is because of His kindness, blessing, and pleasure. When we suffer from misfortune and come across any pain, although it comes from Him, it is because of our own fault, bad deeds, misbehavior, crimes, and sins, for which we must pay. In one sense, it is better to receive pain and punishment for unforgiven sins here in this life because punishments and sufferings of this life are only temporary, while the punishment, excruciating pain, and sufferings of the Hereafter are eternal.

The belief that all good and bad comes from Allah ﷻ does not mean that Allah ﷻ has already decided to inflict pain on some and bring pleasure to others. It only means that both good and bad come from Allah ﷻ. Allah ﷻ is just and never does any injustice.

Having faith in the **resurrection** means believing in life after death. Certainly, without coming back to life, Judgment Day and the concept of accountability to establish punishment or reward are not possible. Thus, Muslims must concurrently believe in life after death.

Every now and then, we see dead bodies, either of our own loved ones, friends, and colleagues or of others. In one way or another, when dead bodies are disposed of, it is certainly difficult to understand and believe how a dead body, after it has been buried for so long and turned into dust, ashes, or mixed into earthly soil,

For Allah ﷻ it is not at all difficult to give life again as He gave it the first time. He can and will give life for a second time.

can be brought back to life. It is easy to believe that death is some permanent reality, but the fact is that this death is temporary, just like this life of ours on Earth.

Allah ﷻ clarifies in the holy Qur'an that:

> Everyone will be tasting death and will be fully given their due only on the Day of Judgment. Whosoever is saved from Hell and is admitted into Heaven certainly becomes successful. And this earthly life is nothing but a deceptive earning. • [3:185]

In this sacred verse, only the "tasting" of death is mentioned, and just the "taste" of it does not make it permanent. For Allah ﷻ, it is not at all difficult to give life again as He gave it the first time. He can and will give life for the second time. This is a matter of belief. However, if this process were easily conceivable, believing in it would have been easy as well, and then there would be no reward for having faith in it.

The Declaration of Faith brings an individual into the fold of Islam. Thereafter, the entire worshiping process begins. The whole business of rights and duties and the contract between man and Allah ﷻ become effective immediately. Among the duties to Allah ﷻ, the first and foremost obligation of an adult Muslim is to perform the daily *salāh* (the prayers of worship offered five times a day), the second is to observe ***saum*** (fasting during the month of Ramadhan), the third is to give ***zakāh*** (obligatory charity), and the fourth is the performance of **Hajj**. These are called the five pillars of Islam, with the **Declaration of Faith** being the first.

Salāh is to be performed five times a day, at prescribed times; it is an obligation of every adult Muslim, as long as he or she remains sane. Adulthood starts at different ages for boys and girls. Boys must start performing their *salāh* from the age of twelve and girls from approximately the age of nine. *Salāh* should not be missed intentionally, and if missed by chance its *qaza* (substitute *salāh*) must be performed as soon as possible. It is important to perform each *salāh* at its due time. The *Fajr Salāh* is before daybreak, *Zuhar Salāh* is at midday, *Asr Salāh* is in the afternoon, *Maghrib Salāh* is immediately after sunset, and the fifth and final obligatory *salāh* is *Isha*, which is to be performed in the night, about two hours after sunset.

On the Day of Judgment, the first question asked of Muslims will be about the establishment of *salāh*. According to Prophet Muhammad ﷺ, "*Salāh* distinguishes a believer from a non-believer; it is the shield (that saves Muslims from sin), the key to Heaven, and the pinnacle point at which a slave meets his Master, Allah ﷻ" [Bukhari and Muslim]. Rain or shine, Muslims must perform their *salāh*.

Salāh entails physical activity as well as spiritual nourishment. Establishing it not only fulfills a Muslim's obligation to Allah ﷻ, it also brings inner pleasure and many blessings from Him. During *salāh*, the act of prostration is the closest point to Allah ﷻ and shows utmost humility, which is one of the core purposes of *salāh*. Furthermore, nearness to Allah ﷻ, peace of heart and mind, uplifting of the soul, steadfastness in faith, security from sins, purification of the body, heart, and mind, and many other physical and spiritual benefits are but a few of the bounties of establishing *salāh*.

Hundreds of millions of Muslim men and women perform *salāh* every day without any problem, hardship, or disruption in their daily routines of life. Those who intentionally miss *salāh* are not credible

Muslims, regardless of how scholarly, pious, elevated, or spiritual they may seem. According to Islamic *sharia* (law), such Muslims are categorized as *fāsiq* (violator) [Bukhari and Muslim]. They have no right to teach or preach Islam and should never be considered an authority on Islam. How can those who do not first properly learn or practice themselves teach or preach to others?

To observe *saum* means to fast in Ramadhan, the ninth month of the Islamic lunar calendar. Ramadhan is an important and blessed month in which there is a night called *Lailatul-Qadr* (Night of Power). It is widely believed to be the twenty-seventh night of Ramadhan, and it was in this night that Allah ﷻ began to reveal the holy Qur'an to Prophet Muhammad ﷺ. The reward for praying throughout this night is equivalent to the rewards for praying for a thousand months.

While fasting, Muslims do not eat, drink, inhale other than air, or consume any substance from dawn to dusk. They break their fasts at sunset. The sick and wayfarers are excused from fasting, but they must make up for the days missed, whenever their condition allows them to do so. Those who are weak and cannot fast should feed one hungry person at least two full meals for every day of fasting that they miss. Intentionally not observing or violating the rules of *saum* displeases Allah ﷻ.

According to a *Hadith-e-Qudsi*, Allah ﷻ stated, "I Myself am the reward for *saum*." Clearly, this is a great blessing that Allah Himself ﷻ becomes its reward. This means that He is very much pleased that the observer has refrained from eating and drinking for His sake and has resisted the pain of hunger all day long just to receive His pleasure and to abide by His rules and commandments. Almost every single adult Muslim throughout the world observes *saum* in the holy month of Ramadhan. Allah ﷻ reveals:

> O faithful believers! Obligatory upon you is fasting, as it was made obligatory upon those before you, that you may now become pious. • [Qur'an 2:183]

This verse also informs us that fasting was made obligatory in one form or another, upon earlier nations. According to this verse, the main purpose of fasting is to achieve piety. It is not simply to refrain from food for a certain period and then eat uncontrollably. During fasts, it is necessary to be extra cautious about refraining from sinful acts and to perform acts of worship and other good deeds as much as possible in order to receive abundant blessings. This month is basically the training period for Muslims to achieve piety and to learn how to remain pious throughout the year. If Muslims do not become pious and simply alter their schedules of food intake during Ramadhan, then they have neglected its entire purpose. The training of Ramadhan is lost if throughout the year Muslims do not act as they are supposed to.

Unfortunately, an increasing number of Muslims are celebrating the end of Ramadhan in an un-Islamic fashion that clearly indicates that they did not learn anything during the holy month and did not acquire any level of piety. Islam does not allow celebrating in such a way that violates its basic teachings and that clearly defeats its intended purpose. The blessings and goodness of Ramadhan will stay with those who perform their best during it. As for those who ignore Allah's commandments or indiscriminately violate them, one can only pray for them to be guided before their time is up.

During fasting, aside from recognizing the pain of starvation, Muslims come to appreciate the value of food and physically feel the pain of poor people who normally never have enough to eat. As humans, we should never take for granted the abundance of food, and we should always be mindful of the less fortunate. The more aware we become of other people's pains through experiencing the same, the more caring we will be. The more caring we become, the more we will share the bounties of Allah ﷻ with others. The more we share, the more love there will be in human society, ultimately resulting in real peace and happiness. The means to obtain real peace and harmony are there; we just have to reach out to them.

In the month of Ramadhan, Allah ﷻ is more forgiving and kind. He readily forgives anyone who earnestly repents. He abundantly blesses those who seek His blessings. The rewards of a good deed performed in the month of Ramadhan are multiplied seventy times and in some cases seven hundred times. Throughout the world, Muslims try to reap more reward in Ramadhan by praying abundantly, reciting the holy Qur'an, spending money for the needy, feeding the hungry, and enjoying every single moment of Ramadhan in the true Islamic spirit. Many Muslims even burst into tears when this blessed month comes to end because they fear they may not live to see it the following year. These genuine believers acquire blessings, achieve piety, complete training, and remain faithful throughout the year. Of course, they will also receive the "Reward of Allah ﷻ Himself" on Judgment Day.

Among the other duties of Muslims is to give *zakāh* (the Islamic obligatory charity) on their wealth. The rule is that anyone in possession of a certain amount of wealth for a full year is obligated to give 2.5% of its total value as *zakāh*. In the holy Qur'an, Allah ﷻ clearly outlines the eight eligible recipients of *zakāh*:

> Charity is (for) the poor and the needy and those employed to collect it and those whose hearts are to be consoled and to emancipate a slave and those in debt and in the way of Allah and the needy wayfarers. These allocations are from Allah and Allah is All-Knowledgeable and All-Wise. • [9:60]

This monetary form of duty is incumbent on all able Muslims, in order that Muslims in need can be helped. Since this is a duty of the relatively rich, the rights of those in need are easily and automatically fulfilled. Through the proper distribution of *zakāh*, an entire society can progress easily and prosper. Giving *zakāh* purifies one's wealth.

When Muslims give *zakāh* willfully, their hearts are cleansed of the love of this material world because the intent is to please Allah ﷻ. This proves that they truly believe in Allah ﷻ and in their accountability on Judgment Day. Not only does giving *zakāh* help fellow Muslims, it is a form of worship as well. The Prophet ﷺ stated:

> Those Muslims who properly give *zakāh*, never lose their honestly earned wealth; in fact, it is secured and can never be destroyed because Allah protects it. [Abu Dawūd]

The institution of *zakāh* has many inner and spiritual benefits. One of the explicit benefits is that it creates the perfect foundation for a sound economic system. *Zakāh* benefits every member of a society and leads to relative economic equality. It can be given directly to deserving Muslims (from the categories quoted above) or entrusted to an Islamic government or to any other designated trustee for its proper distribution. Certainly, individual Muslims who personally give *zakāh* fairly and equitably, reap more reward and satisfaction [Muslim].

So far, we have learned about the Islamic acts of worship of daily *salāh* and fasting, which are of physical nature, and of *zakāh*, which has a monetary aspect to it. Now we come to the obligation that comprises both physical and monetary aspects—the Hajj.

Hajj is the sacred pilgrimage to Makkah and is obligatory once in a lifetime for Muslims who have the physical and monetary means to do so, provided the route of their travel is peaceful enough to make the journey. Moreover, pilgrims must leave behind enough money and provisions for their family for whom they are legally responsible. Anyone who is financially able but physically incapable of making the trip can choose another Muslim to fulfill this obligation on his or her behalf and expense. A Muslim woman can only travel to Hajj while accompanied by her husband or a *mahram,* a man whom she cannot legally marry (e.g., father, son, brother...) [Bukhari].

Hajj takes place in *Zul-Hijjah* (the twelfth and last month of the Islamic calendar). Nowadays, about three million Muslims perform Hajj, and this number increases each year. The experience of Hajj is so unique and full of blessings, spirituality, and inner satisfaction that it cannot be described in words. Pilgrims never wish to leave these holy places; however, they do so with a strong desire to return once again. A Muslim who performs Hajj becomes pure, like a newborn child who has no sins.

Only Muslims are permitted to enter the confines of the holy cities of Makkah and Madinah. Upon watching the Hajj pilgrimage through media broadcasts, even non-Muslims witness its uniqueness that reflects the simplicity of Islamic principles and the equality and unity of Muslims.

Aside from the *faraidh* (obligatory acts) that are to be practiced by all Muslims—jihad, acquisition of the knowledge of *fiqh* (Islamic jurisprudence), joining funeral processions of Muslims, and *a'tikāf* (worshiping in seclusion in the last ten days of Ramadhan) are obligatory acts the performance of which by only a few relieves the rest of the Muslim community from fulfilling them. However, if no one performs these obligations, then the entire community becomes sinful. These obligations are known as *Fardh-e-Kifayah.* There is great reward for those who take on the responsibility of fulfilling them and for relieving their community. Besides the *faraidh*, there are many other acts classified in this way:

- *Wajib* – obligatory, slightly distinguished from *fardh*, which are more obligatory
- *Sunnah* – tradition of the Prophet
- *Mustahab* – recommended
- *Nafil* – supererogatory (more than what is required)
- *Mubah* – neither prohibited nor obligatory
- *Makruh* – unbecoming/disgusting (not unlawful, but disapproved of)
- *Harām* – prohibited (abstaining is obligatory)

After performing the obligatory acts, Muslims who engage in *nafil* acts become closer to Allah ﷻ and receive abundant blessings. They, as a result, are endowed with wisdom and spirituality. Throughout the holy Qur'an and *ahadīth*, Muslims are commanded to practice other good deeds as well; some of which are presented below.

O faithful believers! Enter into Islam completely… • [2:208]

O faithful believers! Spend in the way of Allah out of what He has provided for you… • [2:254]

O faithful believers! Do not waste your charities by boasting (about) favors and by inflicting pain, like those who spend their wealth to show off to others… • [2:264]

O faithful believers! Give from the pure wealth you have earned and that which We took out for you from the Earth, and do not intend to give from what is worthless, which if given to you, you would not accept… • [2:267]

O faithful believers! Fear Allah as He ought to be feared, and do not die except in a state that you people are Muslim. • And strongly grasp the rope of Allah all together, and be not divided… • [3:102-103]

O those who brought faith! Do not consume one another's wealth unlawfully… • [4:29]

O those who brought faith! Stand firmly for justice while testifying, for the sake of Allah, even if it be against yourselves or your parents and immediate relatives... • [4:135]

O those who brought faith! Fulfill your covenants... • [5:1]

O those who brought faith! Stand firmly as witnesses of justice for the sake of Allah. And let not the enmity of a nation excite you to forego justice, so do justice... • [5:8]

O those who brought faith! Whoever among you becomes an apostate in the *deen* (religion), so Allah shall soon bring forth a people making them His beloved, and they too shall love Allah... • [5:54]

O faithful believers! Do not take (as friends) those who have made your religion a mockery... • [5:57]

O those who brought faith! Alcohol and gambling and idols and divining are in fact impure works of Satan, so protect (yourself) from them, to acquire success... • [5:90]

Those who brought faith and did not mix their faith with evil, for them is peace, and they are the rightly guided... • [6:82]

(O Prophet) say that shameless acts have been forbidden by our Lord, those that are visible and hidden, and sins and unjust oppression... • [7:33]

O those who brought faith! Fear Allah, and be with the truthful ones. • [9:119]

O faithful believers! Do not attach (yourselves) to the feet of Satan, and he who attaches to the feet of Satan, so undoubtedly he (Satan) commands (them to do) shamelessness and evildoings... •
[24:21]

O Muslims! Do not go into houses other than your own houses, unless you have asked for permission and greeted the residents with *salām* (greeting of "peace"). This is better for you, if you think. • [24:27]

O faithful believers! Remember Allah with much remembrance. • And glorify Him, morning and evening. • [33:41-42]

O faithful believers! Fear Allah, and speak the most righteous speech. • [33:70]

O faithful believers! If some transgressor brings to you any news, verify it thoroughly, so that you inflict hardship upon any people unknowingly and are left regretful for what you have done. • [49:6]

O faithful believers! Men may not make fun of other men; it is highly possible that they are better than those who make fun. And women may not make fun of women; it is highly possible that they are better than those who make fun... • [49:11]

O faithful believers! Do not be too suspicious, certainly some suspicions are sinful, and do not seek fault, and do not backbite one another. Would any of you like to eat the flesh of your dead brother?... • [49:12]

O faithful believers! Keep fearing Allah, and everyone should look at what they sent forth for tomorrow... • [59:18]

O faithful believers! Why do you say that which you do not do yourself? • It is extremely unpleasant to Allah that you say what you do not do yourself. • [61:2-3]

O faithful believers! Let not your wealth and your children keep you from the remembrance of Allah. And those who do so, they are the losers. • [63:9]

O faithful believers! Save yourselves and your families from that fire, the fuel of which are men and stones... • [66:6]

O faithful believers! Repent while facing Allah, a solid repentance. It may be that your Lord will eliminate your sins and admit you into the Gardens... • [66:8]

Last, but not least:

And those who brought faith and did good deeds—We do not even give a command except for what is bearable—these are people of Paradise wherein they shall eternally live. • [7:42]

WHAT DOES ISLAM WANT MUSLIMS TO BECOME?

*A*LLAH ﷻ CROWNED HUMANS AS THE "Best of all Creatures." He wants us to become worthy of this status. He provided the necessary tools and knowledge in the form of a manual called the holy Qur'an and through the perfect embodiment of it, i.e., the Prophet 🕌, so we can easily achieve our goal. Allah 🕌 did His part, and now if we choose to enter into the "contract" and submit our will to the will of Allah 🕌, we must do our part.

Allah 🕌, wants a believer to carve out the sculpture of a *momin* (believer) from the chunk of meat called 'human.' When a human successfully carves himself into a true believer, he achieves the true purpose of life, and only then is he worthy of being called the "Best of all Creatures." He finally becomes a reflection of Allah's image, in which he was created. Allah 🕌 has provided the necessary tools and knowledge, just as a sculptor is required to have the proper tools and knowledge in order to carve out a beautiful sculpture from a chunk of stone or wood. Moreover, the believer does not have to begin the carving process from scratch; a complete model and example in the form of Prophet Muhammad's 🕌 life is already present, thus making his job easy.

By believing in the **Oneness of Allah** 🕌, a Muslim saves himself from divergent thoughts and begins to focus on the ultimate reality. His concentration becomes fixated and begins to revolve around the one and fixed center. Through performing daily *salāh*, he equips himself with humility, meekness, and modesty. Through **fasting**, he becomes content with his life, grateful for Allah's 🕌 bounties, mindful of the less fortunate, and caring and sharing towards everyone. He learns to control his desires, strengthen his body, and nourish his soul. He lives a monastic life without ever leaving the state of society. He builds resistance and endurance and becomes able to live under harsh circumstances.

Through giving *zakāh*, he purifies his heart from the love of material wealth. He prevents himself from becoming greedy and from miserliness. He frees himself from the enslavement of this world and strengthens his belief in the fact that actual wealth is the rewards of the Hereafter. By performing **Hajj**, he realizes that he is no different from others and that his money and he himself are for Allah's ﷻ sake. He aims for Allah's ﷻ nearness and pleasure. He genuinely pursues ultimate success and gives himself up to the exclusive service of Allah ﷻ and His Prophet ﷺ.

Through executing the different types of jihad, he saves himself and protects others from the evils of men and Satan, thereby establishing peace and justice for all. He perfects his inner self through continuous introspection. He strives for the success of other fellow human beings, which is more important for him in the court of Allah ﷻ than his energies, time, wealth, and even his worldly life. Thus, he becomes a true friend of humanity and the torchbearer of its success.

Through forgiveness and humility, he removes arrogance and pride. Through patience, he builds endurance. Through belief, trust, and confidence in Allah ﷻ, he achieves rectitude and uprightness. Through gratefulness, he becomes mindful of Allah's ﷻ bounties and of others' favors to him. Through controlling his anger, ill desires, and sexual urges, he saves himself from falling below the status of brutes. Through simplicity, he saves himself from competing with others and avoids the enslavement of society, thereby acquiring the true taste of life. Through fulfilling promises, abiding by contracts, and keeping trust, he earns respect and trustworthiness and becomes dignified.

Through fulfilling the rights of others, being just and removing injustices, standing along with the truthful ones, and condemning cruelty, oppression, tyranny, and those who practice such, he earns a higher status in society and becomes its savior. By being sympathetic, kind, helpful, merciful, affectionate, and respectful, he draws the love of people and becomes dear to them. Ultimately, by excelling in and committing good deeds, he becomes dearer and closer to Allah ﷻ.

When people look at this *momin* (believer), the delicately carved out sculpture, an embodiment of superior characteristics, they distinguish him from the other chunks of meat. They immediately become attracted to him, begin to imitate him, offer their loyalty to him, and wish to follow his example. He becomes their leader and begins to rule over their hearts, rather than their physical beings.

For a man to become a *momin* is his true purpose in life for which he was created. A *momin* is the vicegerent of Allah ﷻ on earth, as referred to in the holy Qur'an. He acquires Allah's ﷻ pleasure and is ultimately placed on the exalted station in the Hereafter. Through Islam, this is what Allah ﷻ wants us to become.

Now, you may astonishingly ask, do Muslims really do all of this? Well, what can I say here other than that this book is not about Muslims; it is about Islam? So after reading it, you can decide for yourself. I can only say that, through my personal experience, hundreds of millions of Muslims follow their religion of Islam to the best of their knowledge, belief, and ability. Allah ﷻ will only judge them according to their intent and capabilities. Of course, there are "black sheep" everywhere. Among Muslims, they are those who not only clearly violate Islamic principles and collide head-on with the commandments of the holy Qur'an, but also deface Islam and manipulate its true picture for personal and political reasons. Such hypocrites do this in the name of moderation, revivalism, fundamentalism, or this or that -ism.

The presence and behavior of these black sheep, hypocrites, *fāsiqs* (transgressors) and *fājirs* (sinners) at every level of society should not be a justification for others not to practice Islam or to reject it. To some extent, I can understand "Muslimophobia," because of some bad elements among self-proclaimed Muslims, but I am confident that there is no justification for "Islamophobia." Once the true understanding of Islam and its principles is acquired, only then can related matters be judged accordingly.

One unique aspect of Islam is that everyone will be held responsible and questioned on Judgment Day for their deeds and for any harm they may have caused. No one will be held responsible for anyone else or will be able to get away with blaming others for personal decisions and choices. May Allah ﷻ bless us all.

CHAPTER 10

Islam's Concept of the Hereafter

HROUGHOUT THE BOOK SO FAR, you have come across words like "Hereafter," "Day of Judgment," and "other-worldly," and you may have somewhat familiarized yourself with the concepts behind them. In this chapter, I will go into detail because these concepts are central to Islam. The period immediately after death, the Day of Judgment, the process of accountability, eternal life in Heaven or Hell, and everything beyond that are all part of the Hereafter.

According to Islam, when a person passes away from this world, he or she enters into the other world. The body stays here in one form or another, and Malak-ul-Maut (the Angel of Death) takes the *ruh* (soul) to *A'lam-e-Barzakh* (the transitory state, period/place).

Whether the body is buried or disposed of through other means, angels known as Munkir-Nakir bring the deceased back to life in *A'lam-e-Barzakh* and ask three questions related to beliefs. If the person answers all three questions correctly, the stay in this transitory period/place is made comfortable, while incorrect answers bring pain and suffering. One can only remember the right answers if he or she has lived accordingly and has put into practice the beliefs in question.

Whether the body is under ground or anywhere else on earth, regardless of its state, it remains connected to the soul in *A'lam-e-*

Barzakh. If the soul is at peace, the body is peaceful and feels pleasure; if the soul is in pain, the body feels the pain and suffers tremendously.

Death is the process of separating the soul from the body and is merely the mode of transportation for the soul to get to the Transitory State. The Transitory State lasts until Judgment Day. The human body grows on Earth, and after death it stays in the earth, in one state or another. The soul comes from *A'lam-e-Arwah* ("the world of spirits," where souls were kept since their creation), and on separation from the body the soul enters *A'lam-e-Barzakh.* The time of death is fixed, and Malak-ul-Maut (Angel of Death) is never late or ahead of schedule and is capable of being in many places at one time. The three questions of the grave are:

1) Who is your Lord?
2) What is your religion?
3) What did you say about this man? (pointing towards the
   Prophet Muhammad ﷺ). [Mishkat]

Whoever responds to the first two questions with "Allah ﷻ" and "Islam" and in response to the third question, recognizes the man shown as Prophet Muhammad ﷺ passes the test and is left peacefully. Whosoever fails to answer correctly is left to suffer in pain.

Every soul remains in *A'lam-e-Barzakh* until Judgment Day. When this Day arrives, Angel Israfil عليه السلام will blow into the *sūr* (trumpet), whereupon everyone alive will die and everything else will be "wrapped up." The holy Qur'an states:

> And (when) the trumpet is blown, they will die—what is in the skies and what is on land—except whom Allah wills. When blown into it again, so at that time, they will all be standing (and) staring. • [39:68]

Then, all will gather in the Mahshar Ground in the presence of the divine throne. All will be given their register of deeds to be weighed. Anyone's good deeds that weigh more than their bad deeds will be among the successful ones and will enter Paradise. If the bad deeds are heavier, he will be among the losers and will be thrown into Hell.

Having *iman* (faith) is the prerequisite for any good act to be considered a 'good deed' in Islam and to be rewarded in the Hereafter. Furthermore, *iman*, as explained in Islam, is in itself, the heaviest among all virtuous deeds, whereas *kufr* (infidelity) and *shirk* (polytheism) are the heaviest among all sinful deeds. In the life Hereafter, death will not come to anyone anymore. In fact, "death" itself will be put to death, and the concept of death will cease to exist. Thus, life in Heaven and Hell will be eternal and infinite. The holy Qur'an mentions the length of Judgment Day to be equal to 50,000 Earth years [70:4].

The belief in the Day of Judgment and in the concept of the Hereafter, including resurrection, is central to the Islamic belief system. The concept of the Hereafter and the accountability of deeds, as presented by Islam, make certain that spiritual and moral values are preserved and adhered to by its believers. The fear of painful consequences for criminal behavior brings crime down and reduces the likelihood of anyone resorting to crime. However, if there is the slight chance that a person could avoid punishment or imprisonment, a criminally minded person tends to commit crime. Since no one can escape from Allah 🕌 and accountability on Judgment Day, good Muslims remain vigilant against violating Allah's 🕌 commandments.

Man-made laws do not grant a society complete protection against crimes, simply because law enforcement authorities cannot absolutely keep a watchful eye on violators. Manmade laws are inherently weak and because of loopholes, they cannot always be enforced, resulting in proper justice not being served. Many inner and hidden crimes committed by people on a daily basis are beyond the scope of man made laws, let alone of man's enforcement and punishment. Sometimes, human rights' violators are so powerful that they cannot be brought to justice.

However, on Judgment Day, divine justice will be served, and just compensation will be granted to every victim of crime who was deprived of justice. Allah 🕌 is the best of all legislators, and no one can escape from His jurisdiction. His enforcement and His laws are comprehensive, and there are no loopholes in them. Therefore, no one can escape punishment for his or her crimes/sins. Allah is All-Powerful.

On Judgment Day, everyone's power will be taken away, and no one will be able to prevent Him from delivering proper punishment and due compensation. He is All-Knowledgeable and records every deed; thus, no proof of crime can be inadmissible in His court. Overall, justice will prevail, and whoever did not get or was brought to justice in this life will have it on Judgment Day.

> On the Day when each one will find, present in front, the goodness earned and the wrongdoings that were done, each one will wish that there were quite a distance between the wrongdoings earned and themselves, ... • [Qur'an 3:30]

Judgment Day is not only to hold people accountable for their deeds in this life, it is also payday for faithful people. Those who were on the right path, suppressed their ill desires for the sake of acquiring the Lord's pleasure, sacrificed their worldly wishes for the love of the Lord, truly served humanity as per the rules set forth by Allah ﷻ, performed all of their duties to the Lord and His creatures, and truly observed all of His commandments will be rewarded at this time.

The following are some verses of the holy Qur'an regarding the Day of Judgment and the Hereafter.

"So have you come to think that We created you just for nothing, and that you will not be returned towards Us?" • [23:115]

And do not invoke any deity with Allah. There is no deity except Him. All things will be erased except His being. The Command is His, and towards Him will you people be returned. • [28:88]

And those who brought faith and their progeny followed behind them with faith, so We joined them to their progeny, and We did not reduce anything from their deeds. Every soul that earned whatever, has full grasp of it. • [52:21]

Knowledge of what Allah ﷻ, our Creator, has revealed to us regarding accountability causes us to fear, which then makes us do what is right and proper, and this in turn brings us success and recognition. Thus, in this case, Islamic knowledge brings fear, fear brings right actions, and ultimately success is achieved. For example, many of us stop our cars at a red light because we fear the law, payment of fines, and points on our license. We fear because of the knowledge of accountability for our actions. Where law enforcement is weak, people do not observe red lights because there is nothing to fear. Certainly, those who stop at red lights and follow other rules because of respect for laws and the wish to protect others, are better citizens, and there is no shortage of them. For others, they truly need fear of accountability to make them law-abiding citizens.

Islam does a wonderful job of placing a great deterrent in the form of Judgment Day, in order to keep people on the right path. Unfortunately, many Muslims these days are not deterred and have brought much unrest among themselves and others. Muslims will also not escape Allah's ﷾ justice. Judgment Day will be the day of justice for all and not the day of favors, especially for those who have committed injustice to others. Allah ﷾ states in the holy Qur'an:

> O Faithful Ones! Keep fearing Allah and all are to see what they have sent forth for tomorrow, and fear Allah. Truly Allah is aware of every action you take. • [59:18]

> Has that time not come for them who brought faith that their hearts may yield for Allah for whatever the Truth was revealed to them. And be not like those who were given the Book before, and after much time passed upon them, their hearts became hardened, and many of them are disobedient • [57:16]

> (They) are in gardens. They will inquire. • of the sinners, • "What was it that took you to Hell?" • They answered, "We were not among the praying ones, • did not use to feed the needy, • and engaged in profane chat along with immoral jargon, • and we used to deny the Day of Judgment, • to the point death came upon us." • Now they will not benefit from the intercession of those who are to intercede. •
> [74:40-48]

Some people have difficulty believing that after becoming dust and scattered particles in the earth they will become alive again. They should not forget that Allah ﷾ created us the first time out of nothing; the second time around He will at least have our particles. Creating something for the first time is harder than making it again. He is our Lord, the All-Powerful, Who possesses unlimited power.

He can and will certainly bring us to life again and arrange for the Day of Judgment for justice and retribution. Allah ﷻ reveals:

> And he makes examples of Us and forgets his own creation, He asks, "Who will bring the bones to life when they are decomposed?" • Answer him, "He will give them life, Who brought them to life in the first place, and He is aware of all life— • Who created for you fire from the green tree, so now you kindle fires for yourself • —Does not the One Who created the heavens and the Earth have the power to create like (a human being again)? Why not; He is the absolute Creator, the All-Knowing. • Whenever He commands something to come into existence, all He says, "Be," and it is! • So glory to Him in Whose hand is the absolute right to do what He wills, and towards Him you people will be brought back. • [Qur'an 36:78-83]

Hundreds of verses of the holy Qur'an warn us to be serious and not overlook this important matter. Allah ﷻ did a great favor and showed kindness in warning us about Judgment Day. He is not cruel nor is He a tyrant. Thousands of signs and prophecies that are coming true prove that Doomsday is approaching. Everything that had a beginning must come to end. If everything were to just end without any purpose, this universal setting would be nothing more than a waste. Such a fine creation with no purpose and no end is absurd. Allah ﷻ does not just create something for no reason.

There is wisdom behind all that is kept "unseen," which is why there is great reward for believing in the unseen. At the time of death, nothing remains unseen—bringing faith at that moment will be useless and unacceptable. Additionally, admittance of truth on Judgment Day will not bear any fruit.

Heaven is the abode for believers, and Hell is for non-believers. This is the law of the Lord, Who is not unjust to anyone. He has nothing to lose or gain from it. He gives us every chance and equips us with every kind of tool and knowledge necessary to choose and make our decisions wisely. Now our fate is in our own hands. Injustice will not come to anyone. After all, each one of us is His creature, and He is our Lord.

CHAPTER 11

The Role and Importance of Intent in Islam

*I*NTENTIONS HAVE GREAT IMPORTANCE IN ISLAM, because, according to a very famous *hadīth*, "Actions are based on intention," meaning that acts are judged by Allah ﷻ on the basis of the intention with which they are executed. The action has secondary importance. Hence, the intention carries more weight than the act itself, and Allah ﷻ is precisely aware of everyone's intentions.

Many scholars of Islam confirm this *hadīth* and believe it to be half of Islam: whatever is in Islam, half of it is contained in this *hadīth*. Some even claim it to contain the entire philosophy of Islam, and call it *Ummul-Ahadīth* (The Mother of All *Hadīth*). [Bukhari] As far as my knowledge goes, no other religion can claim to have such a short statement comprising so much.

Intention is the first thought or set of thoughts that come to mind before one proceeds to act. For example, the idea to spread the knowledge of Islam and defend my religion came to me, so I began to write this book along with the intent to seek Allah's ﷻ pleasure. According to Islam, whatever is undertaken to seek the pleasure of the Lord is considered a part of worshiping Allah ﷻ and becomes a good deed. The ultimate goal of a *momin* (faithful Muslim) is to seek Allah's ﷻ pleasure through his or her every action. Thus, based on my genuine intention to please Allah ﷻ, I am hopeful that a reward for writing this book in the form of His pleasure will be granted to me.

If my intention were to earn fame and/or wealth through this book, I could not be eligible to earn His pleasure, because I did not intend to do so. I may earn fame and monetary benefits, but because of the love of material wealth and intending to acquire it, I do not deserve anything in the Hereafter, and this deed would not count as a good one and will be rejected by Allah ﷻ.

A famous example to explain this further is that of a Muslim who one day, out of simplicity but with good intent, inserted a few stakes in front of a *masjid* (mosque) for people to tie their horses, so they could pray peacefully and not worry about their animals. Instead, people began to trip over them. Although he should have thought about this possible harm, he receives rewards for his good intention. On the other hand, someone who did not like Muslims put stakes at another entrance with the intent to hurt them, and instead worshipers began to tie their animals to them, and no one was hurt. This person does not deserve any reward because of the ill intent, even though his action brought ease to the worshipers.

Anyone who intends to please the Lord in the few years of life he has would continue to please Him if he were allowed to live forever. Anyone who does not have those intentions would continue to live without pleasing the Lord as long as he or she lives. The rewards or punishments in the eternal life of the Hereafter reflect the kind of life we lived here on Earth. For example, as students, we learn for a semester or an entire year, but the exams that determine our fate last only a few hours, and determine success or failure.

This life is a testing ground for human beings. Every necessary instruction has been provided. If we intended to please the Lord within the few years of life given to us, we will pass the test. The rewards for good intentions during our just few years of life are eternal. If we fail to have good intentions, the loss is for eternity. It is the intent that is the deciding factor of our eternal fate. Of course, no one is going to be tested eternally to receive reward or punishment eternally.

Moreover, a millionaire who gives thousands in charity without intending to please Allah 🕮 does not earn any reward from Allah 🕮. On the other hand, a poor person giving few dollars to earn Allah's 🕮 pleasure receives abundant rewards because of his intention.

Humans are uniquely intelligent and can quite successfully fool their own kind. Very frequently and easily, they can hide the real motives of their filthy minds and their secret and selfish agendas. Through words and gestures, they know how to portray themselves convincingly and frame their message in such a way that they cannot be proven wrong. Like-minded people at once understand what their fellow means to say. We think such great orators and leaders work for our benefit and seem to be saviors, but only in the end, and only if we are lucky enough, we learn the truth of their inner intentions.

Intentions are deeply rooted in the mind, and only Allah 🕮 truly knows them. As such, even though one's intention is crucial in Islam, judging one is not permitted unless it becomes obvious. Muslims are only to pay attention to people's actions. They are to appreciate the good work, accept whatever appears to be good, and leave the matter of intent to Allah 🕮, the All-Knower. He will deal with peoples' intentions and properly reward or punish them as per His judgment. We just have to know that according to Islam, a good action becomes a good deed only when one performs it with the intent to seek Allah's 🕮 pleasure and when one executes it correctly to the best of one's knowledge and belief.

Islam demands its followers to have the pure intention of pleasing Allah 🕮 when performing every duty to the Lord and to fellow human beings. Since intentions occur inside the human mind, no one can instantly know; however, one can assess the intent after carefully studying the action, behavior, and outcome.

Islam's criterion is that a good action must be preceded with the intent to seek Allah's 🕮 pleasure for it to be included in the roster of good deeds. Similarly, many mistakes can be forgiven, if they were not intended to violate Allah's commandments. Had a human invented Islam, he would not have required the condition of intention, which he himself could not verify. However, since Allah ﷻ exists with all of His attributes, and since Islam is His guidance to humanity, this condition is absolutely essential for rewarding and punishing.

The demand of Islam for Muslims to have the intention of seeking the pleasure of Allah ﷻ is one of the most obvious proofs that Islam is a heavenly religion and that it was not proposed or invented by a human. There was no need for a personality like Muhammad ﷺ to introduce the concept that actions are based on the intent behind them. If Islam was his own creation, then for Muslims, to follow him and carry out his mission would have been sufficient, and there would be no need to demand the whole business of intention. However, the Prophet ﷺ came to connect human beings to their Allah ﷻ. Thus, it was necessary to emphasize this essential concept so that his followers could truly seek Allah's ﷻ pleasure and acquire ultimate success.

Some great benefits of intending to seek only Allah's ﷻ pleasure are that if we succeed in our endeavors (through our actions), we do not become arrogant or ungrateful, engage in illegitimate activities, or demand any reward from our fellow human beings because whatever we did was for Allah ﷻ and only to seek His pleasure. On the other hand, if for any reason we fail in our ambitions and struggles, we are not disheartened or depressed. Not being able to achieve that for which we strove, either because of our limited capabilities, because of unforeseen circumstances or perhaps because it was not a part of the Lord's master plan, He still rewards us because of our intention to seek His pleasure through our efforts. Allah ﷻ rewards for good intention and motives, even if the actions do not materialize.

Striving for and achieving our objectives are two separate things. Our duty is only to strive, whether we succeed or fail is left to our Lord.

CHAPTER 12

Free Will and Compulsion in Islam

*N*O CREATURE WAS GRANTED 'FREE WILL' by the Creator besides human beings and the jinn. Free will is a powerful tool, and to endow man with it clearly shows that there must be a special purpose attached to human life that is not the case with other creatures. Since no other creature besides humanity and the jinn has free will, this makes human beings far superior and controlling over other creatures. It is said that everything in the universe serves man in one way or another, and man's special purpose is to serve Allah ﷻ. Of course, the entire worshiping process is to serve Allah ﷻ, as discussed earlier.

According to many dictionaries, 'will' is defined simply as the power of making a choice or a decision or the mental faculty by which one deliberately chooses or decides on a course of action. Free will is defined as the freedom of humans to make choices that are not determined by prior causes or by divine intervention.

The fact that Allah ﷻ endowed man with free will is in itself sufficient proof that Allah ﷻ does not compel man to do anything. If humans were not granted free will, there would be neither any justification for testing them nor any need for Judgment Day to reward or to punish. By endowing them with free will and making choices available to them, Allah ﷻ is justified in testing them. It is on the basis of these test results that He apportions rewards or punishment.

One of the main purposes for Judgment Day is to assess how an individual utilized his power of free will. If there were even a minute interference to man's free will or if he were compelled in any way to follow a pre-ordained direction, then a 'just test' and 'just reward or punishment' could not be possible. Thus, there is no coercion, compulsion, or interference with human will.

Allah ﷻ conveyed His guidance to humanity through prophets and finally completed it in the form of Islam, through Muhammad ﷺ, His last prophet. Allah gives human beings the chance to choose between right and wrong via their free will and without any compulsion. Whoever wisely chooses to believe the ultimate truth, acquire ultimate success, earn the pleasure of the Almighty, recognize His prophets, become Muslim, submit and surrender his will to the will of Allah ﷻ, and wear the medal of servitude of the Almighty, benefits himself eternally.

The meaning of 'Islam' is to surrender and bow down, not to stones or trees, not to stars or the sun, not to animals or fire, but to the Almighty Allah ﷻ, the Creator of everything. We cannot see Allah ﷻ, witness His majesty, or directly observe His limitless power or any of His other qualities. Thus, it is difficult to surrender to Him unless we 'will' ourselves to do it through acts of beliefs and from the depths of our hearts. No compulsion or coercion can play an effective role in that process of surrendering.

Now, by saying, "There is no god but Allah, Muhammad is the Prophet of Allah," Muslims sign a contract with Allah ﷻ out of their own free will. Thus, by being under contract, they voluntarily surrender their free will and choices to conform to the pleasure of Allah ﷻ. There is no more selfish 'my way.' They now have to abide by all the rules of Islam, and if they do not, they suffer punishment for breaching this contract that they signed of their own accord. The rest of humanity still has free will as to whether or not to choose Islam, but according to Islam the wise choice will not be willfully to reject the call of prophets and ignore Allah's ﷻ guidance, resulting in ultimate sufferings. I think this is fair enough, and who can be fairer to us than our own Lord?

The kind of obedience that Allah ﷻ deserves and that which brings ultimate success cannot be achieved without embracing Islam out of one's own free will. If someone is forced into Islam by the sword, coercively, or through any other kind of compulsion, then true submission as required by Islam can never be achieved, and if there is some sort of submission, it cannot be permanent.

Unlike animals, human society needs moral values to survive. The kind of society Islam intends to build and the kind of moral values it advocates cannot come about through compulsion. For example, love, brotherhood, unity, piety, generosity, forgiveness, kindness, simplicity, cooperation, self-sacrifice, charity, chastity, and tolerance are all values that cannot be obtained through coercion. The fact of the matter is that coercion defeats the entire purpose of Islam.

Through the abuse of power and coercion, one cannot rule for a long time. It is only through love and compassion that the hearts of people can be conquered permanently. Any intelligent person will not imagine drawing any material benefit from anyone after his death, let alone centuries later. Thus, it was not for any personal reason that the Prophet ﷺ won the hearts of people through love. It was only so people could join him through their free will for the 'greater purpose.' Muhammad's ﷺ main mission was to connect humanity to Allah ﷻ. This could be achieved only through love. He did not use force or coercion, but he prevailed with the power of love and truth, and so did his true followers.

Islam does not intend simply to increase the number of its followers; it wants people to succeed here and in the Hereafter. The fact is that Islam does not need us, we need Islam. To bring everlasting change in the life of humans, acceptance from the heart and voluntary actions are required. Through coercion, one could only obtain verbal acceptance, but the major part of accepting and certifying by the heart, as required by Islam, cannot be achieved [Bukhari].

According to the Islamic teachings, Allah ﷻ disapproves of the actions of troublemakers and mischievous people. This clearly indicates that Allah ﷻ does not approve of coercion and commands, but He wants people to choose according to their will in reference to accepting Islam. Hundreds of verses in the holy Qur'an allow us clearly to deduce this message.

At the very beginning of the holy Qur'an, Muslims are directed to begin its recitation with:

"In the name of Allah, the Most Compassionate, the Most Merciful."

In another verse, Allah ﷻ says:

...We do not burden any soul more than it can bear... • [6:152]

According to two *ahadith* of the Prophet ﷺ:

Allah does not shower His kindness on anyone who is not kind to other people. [Bukhari]

The sign of a *momin* (true believer) is that he behaves well with his neighbors (both Muslim and non-Muslim). [Bukhari]

In another verse, Allah ﷻ commands:

...and show kindness to parents, and kindred, and orphans, and the needy, and the neighbor who is your relative, and the neighbor who is not your relative and the companion by your side and the wayfarer... • [4:36]

At another point in the Qur'an, Allah ﷻ describes a *momin*:

And the servants of the Lord, Most Compassionate, are those who walk on the earth humbly, and when the ignorant speak to them, they only say: "Peace be to you." • [25:63]

These verses and *ahadith* are but a few examples indicating clearly that kindness is the best virtue; to be kind is very much desirable in Islam. If an individual is kind, how could he be coercive? If one preaches kindness, then compulsion is out of the question. Allah's 🖋️ guidance is full of kindness; therefore, Islam is free from compulsion. The reality is that compulsion and coercion suppress free will. When Allah 🖋️ endowed us with free will, why would He suppress it?

One of the greatest commandments Allah 🖋️ reveals is:

> Call towards the way of your Lord with solid strategy and good counsel and debate with them in the most desirable manner... •
>
> [16:125]

Now, as Allah 🖋️ directs believers to utilize such a manner of calling people to His path, He certainly cannot compel us to coerce or impose His guidance on others.

In one very beautiful verse, Allah 🖋️ says:

> There is no compulsion in *deen* (way of life). Surely, true guidance now stands out clearly from error... • [2:256]

There is no compulsion in Islam. This means that if a person lives in an Islamic society/country and does not embrace Islam, he or she should not be compelled to do so.

THE ISSUE OF *IRTIDAD* IN ISLAM

*I*RTIDAD IS APOSTASY. A *MURTAD* IS AN APOSTATE; anyone who returns to *kufr* (infidelity) after being a Muslim. Many have heard about a heavy punishment for *irtidad*, which is in fact, true. There is a heavy punishment from Allah 🖋️ that He Himself brings on a *murtad*, both here and in the Hereafter. Of course, no one is compelled to enter into Islam, but once you are in, the story changes. By accepting Islam, a person recognizes Allah 🖋️, surrenders his will to the will of Allah 🖋️ and literally signs a contract to abide by His rules. Any violation of Islamic principles from thereon is a breach of that contract and is punishable by Allah 🖋️.

Now one can ask, since there is free will, how can anyone be punished for apostasy? There is no capital punishment for a *murtad*, because there is no compulsion in Islam. However, if a *murtad* denounces Islam publicly, purposely defames Islam, creates mischief, wages war against the Islamic state, and does not repent after repeated warnings, then he is due for capital punishment. Anyone purposely undermining and giving rise to instability and committing treasonous activities by waging war against the Islamic state is punishable through due process of law.

Man has free will, and when he enters into the fold of Islam, it is for his own good, and he benefits from it. On the same accord, if he decides to leave Islam out of his own free will, he chooses to become the ultimate loser according to the divine decree. Since there is no coercion in Islam, no one can be forced to embrace it, forced to stay in it, or forced out of it. One cannot even be punished if one decides to leave Islam. An ex-Muslim is not punished for *irtidad* but for treason if he goes so far as to commit treason.

There is no historical record showing that Prophet Muhammad ﷺ ever having executed anyone for *irtidad* (apostasy). However, a *hadīth* states that capital punishment applies to that *murtad* (apostate) who wages war against the Islamic state. [Bukhari] The issue/crime here is of treason against the state, not of becoming an apostate. Capital punishment for the crime of treason is not only a part of Islam, but is enforced all around the world, including the United States.

According to Islam, as people embrace it, they come to life, to home, and under the grace of the Almighty, but if and when they leave it, they become *murtad*, lifeless, and are withdrawn from the umbrella of peace and grace of Allah ﷻ. Islam is no different when it comes to bringing traitors to justice. Certainly, the road to repentance is always open to everyone until their last breath of life, and as far as Islam is concerned repentance is possible, up until the Angel of Death becomes clearly visible, whereupon the doors to repentance are closed shut.

WHAT IS THE PURPOSE OF FREE WILL?

$\mathcal{S}$OME MAY ASK, WHAT IS THE PURPOSE OF FREE WILL if we have to choose between Islam and suffering in the Hereafter? Since there is no way out, where is the freedom of choice? How is Islam free of coercion?

The freedom to choose means that we are free to choose any one of two paths: one is Allah's ﷻ path, which leads to Heaven; the other is not and leads to Hell. It is not possible to choose the path of *kufr* (infidelity) in this world and end up in Heaven in the other world. You cannot take half from one and half from the other. You have to take the whole package, whichever one you like. Allah ﷻ does not present the concept of Hell to make you choose Islam in this world. He simply shows us both paths and their respective destinations.

The mercy and kindness of Allah ﷻ are that He informs us of the two destinations, so that we may choose wisely. Allah ﷻ does not place hurdles even in the path of those who choose the path leading to Hell. Since we clearly know the two paths and their destinations, Allah ﷻ is justified in trying us according to what we choose through our own free will. Islam recognizes our decision-making ability and suggests that we make an informed decision.

Allah ﷻ has nothing to lose if all of us choose the right path and end up in Heaven or choose the wrong one and end up in Hell. It is we who win or lose.

FORGIVENESS AND TOLERANCE IN ISLAM

$\mathcal{H}$UMAN HISTORY HAS YET TO PRODUCE A PARALLEL to the concept of forgiveness and tolerance as defined and practiced in Islam. A few examples in support of this proposition are presented in the following.

After announcing his prophethood in Makkah and until his forced migration from there to Madinah, Muhammad ﷺ faced all kinds of sufferings and physical pains at the hands of disbelievers, most of whom were members of his own tribe. He never fought back, never raised arms against them, and never permitted his followers to retaliate. In the face of adversity, he and his companions held to a policy of forgiveness and tolerance. Even under such harsh conditions, he continued to deliver Allah's ﷻ guidance to humanity through patience, steadfastness, and absolute faith and determination.

Forgiveness and tolerance are among the great qualities professed and perfected by Islam and practiced by the holy Prophet ﷺ. He left indelible marks that attracted millions to Islam and, in a very short period, brought the East and the West under the umbrella of Islam. Among other things, the rapid growth of Islam was due to its basic teachings of tolerance and forgiveness.

Allah ﷻ reveals:

...And (O men) If you should forgive, it is nearest to piety... • [2:237]

Islam considers forgiveness and tolerance to be extremely desirable and laudable qualities. Allah ﷻ offers pardon to those who forgive and tolerate. The holy Qur'an commands:

...And let them forgive and overlook. Do you not love that Allah should forgive you?... • [24:22]

Despite continuous infliction of pain and hardship on the Prophet ﷺ and his followers, Allah ﷻ instructed them to:

Forgive and command what is good and stay aloof from the ignorant. • [Qur'an 7:199]

At another place, the Qur'an states:

And never can good and evil be equal. Remove what is to be removed through utmost good... • [41:34]

In the same manner, keeping grudges is strictly discouraged both in the holy Qur'an and the sunnah. Once, a companion of the Prophet ﷺ requested him to bring a curse upon the Makkans. Upon hearing this, the Prophet ﷺ, a man of tolerance, became filled with anger [Tirmidhi and Bukhari]. On another occasion, while preaching in the city of Tā'if, people threw stones at the Prophet ﷺ, whereupon an angel appeared and asked his permission to crush the city with the two bordering mountains. He replied, "I have come as the mercy to mankind and not as a wrath" [Tirmidhi and Bukhari].

He commanded his followers to create ease for people and not to put them in hardship, to make them happy and not hateful. He further stated:

> The one who is not kind, no kindness is brought upon him. [Bukhari]

The Prophet ﷺ also stated that

> If you are kind to people on Earth, Allah will be kind to you in the Hereafter. [Tirmidhi]

Once, the Prophet ﷺ stood up (in respect) as people passed by carrying a coffin. His companions informed him that the funeral was of a Jewish man. He replied, "Was he not a person?" meaning that he was a human, as we all are, and Allah ﷻ had created him just as he created us [Mishkat].

In reality, there are at least three types of commonality among all people. The first is that we are all slaves of Allah ﷻ. The second is that we are all descendents of Adam عليه السلام. The third is that we all, Muslims and non-Muslims, are part of the *ummah* (community) of Prophet Muhammad ﷺ. Here, the *ummah* means the community to whom a prophet is sent, whether they brought faith in him or not.

The beloved Prophet ﷺ always respected these relationships. In fact, even during battles, he prayed for his enemies [**Bukhari**].Has any general ever prayed in favor of the opposing army? This was nothing short of kindness from the merciful Prophet ﷺ. He never harmed, let alone killed anyone. He never even used foul language or became mad at people at his service. Once, in a battlefield while lining up his companions, he accidentally poked the chest of a companion with his staff. Immediately, he presented himself to the companion to allow him to avenge for this mistake. The Prophet ﷺ, with such an elaborate display of equality, justice, tolerance, and mercy, amazed the world and enlightened hearts and minds, permanently changing people's lives.

While migrating to Madinah from Makkah, his birthplace, the Prophet ﷺ, along with his most beloved companion, Abu-Bakr Siddīq ﷺ, was pursued by a non-believer named Surāqa bin Malik, who was promised a great reward for their capture. As he came close to them, his horse was miraculously buried knee-deep into the sand and could not move. He yelled out to the Prophet ﷺ for mercy and pardon. The Prophet of Mercy ﷺ forgave him. Moreover, he requested this forgiveness in writing to show to his people upon his return. Can such a show of mercy to one's staunchest enemy be duplicated?

Not only granting pardon, the Prophet ﷺ informed Surāqa that soon he would wear the gold bracelets worn at that time by the king of Persia. This prophecy came true just two decades later, when the second *khalīfa* (caliph) of Islam defeated the Persian Empire. The *khalīfa* took the gold bracelets from the king, put them on Surāqa's hand, and said, "Is this not of what the Prophet had informed you?"

When the Prophet ﷺ reached Madinah, he drew up The Madinah Constitution (Appendix I), which included all the tribes, including those of the Jewish faith. The following are some articles of that charter:

1. All parties to this agreement will have freedom of religion.
2. All may practice their religion without any hindrance.
3. Everyone's places of worship will be protected.
4. No one shall deceive, be unjust, or conspire against each other.

Every article of the charter expressed and clearly defined the basic philosophy of Islam and its principles of tolerance and mutual respect, as practiced and preached by the Prophet ﷺ. This newly formed setting was based on equality, justice, and freedom of religion and choice, with tolerance as its main element.

Even after his migration from Makkah to Madinah, the Makkan leaders/idolaters continued their efforts to undermine Islam and its followers. They conspired against Muslims and made secret alliances with tribes in Madinah and outside of it. Many battles took place between them and the Muslims in the first decade of the Prophet's ﷺ migration. Within this period, some tribes breached the treaties made with Muslims, and back in Makkah Muslims' houses and belongings were plundered.

Eventually, Muslims peacefully conquered Makkah and entered as victors into the city they had been forced to leave just a decade earlier. The Makkans feared a devastating backlash for their barbaric behavior towards innocent Muslim men, women and children, but instead the Prophet ﷺ granted general amnesty to all and pardoned everyone. The Prophet ﷺ said, "Today, all of you are free, and no charge is upon you" [Bukhari, Muslim, and Tirmidhi].

Among those freed was a woman named Hind, one of the staunchest enemies of the Prophet ﷺ. To avenge her father and brother, who were killed in the Battle of Badr, she had cut open the chest of the Prophet's beloved uncle, Ameer Hamza, and chewed his heart at the Battle of Uhud. The Prophet ﷺ forgave even her. Consequently, they all turned from being enemies of Islam to its protectors and loyal followers. No one before or since has duplicated this show of forgiveness and tolerance.

Commenting on the unparalleled tolerance and pure heart of Muhammad ﷺ, Stanley Lane Poole, a British orientalist and archeologist of the nineteenth century, wrote:

> But what is this? Is there no blood in the streets? Where are the bodies of thousands that have been butchered? Facts are hard things, and it is a fact that the day of Muhammad's greatest triumph over his enemies was also the day of his grandest victory over himself. He freely

forgave the Kureysh (Quraysh) all the years of sorrow and cruel scorn they had inflicted on him; he gave amnesty to the whole population of Makkah. Four criminals whom justice condemned made up Muhammad's proscription list; no house was robbed, no woman insulted. It was thus that Muhammad entered again his native city. Through all the annals of conquest, there is no triumphant entry like unto this one.

When Jerusalem was conquered by the second caliph Umar, he made an agreement with the conquered citizens of that city, clauses of which have not yet produced the parallel in history, that what kind of heartfelt generosity and tolerance they displayed with opponents and enemies. [quoted in introduction to Higgin's Apology for Mohammad, pp ixxi]

There are numerous opinions, commentaries, articles, and books by non-Muslim historians in recognition of such Islamic characteristics as forgiveness, generosity and tolerance. Unfortunately, however, some have dedicated their lifetime to creating misunderstandings about Islam and its teachings. One of the greatest misunderstandings of our time is that Islam was spread with the sword. Therefore, this issue must be addressed.

THE ROLE OF THE SWORD IN ISLAM

*P*UTTING IT SIMPLY, TO UTILIZE A SWORD, you need two things. Firstly, you have to possess a sword; secondly, you must know how to use it. The greater the purpose to be achieved through the sword, the more expertise you have to have. If you have a sword but lack swordsmanship and only know how to wave it in the air, you cannot achieve much with it.

As a general principle, anyone interested in pursuing a career in science must take, from the very beginning, every necessary course in the subject of science to reach their goal. Similarly, every field requires relevant studies and training for one to become an expert. However, this is the general rule, and there can be exceptions to it.

According to some, Muhammad ﷺ was "just an intelligent man" with many good qualities, but was not a prophet. For them, his prophethood cannot be verified through empirical means. For argument's sake, let us suppose that he was "just an intelligent man" and that through his intelligence and other qualities he invented Islam. Then, realistically, we will have to admit that he was not "just an intelligent man," but must have been "extraordinarily intelligent" because the system he developed, if he developed it, was such a great and fine system that "just an intelligent man" could not have developed it. Moreover, that extraordinarily intelligent man must have devised, well in advance, all the plans necessary to invent such a comprehensive religion.

If people's contention that Islam was spread by the sword is valid, then we have to suppose that Muhammad ﷺ must have known he would be utilizing a sword to spread that ideology. Therefore, he would certainly have thought of mastering an unparalleled skill in using the sword. Moreover, he must have trained himself to be a great swordsman and gathered many other swordsmen in advance, in order to achieve his purpose later on.

The problem is that we do not find anything to support the contention that the Prophet ﷺ or any of the early converts to Islam possessed any expertise or special training in swordsmanship. We also do not find any group that was trained well in advance that would join him later. Even if we assume that he did have special training or expertise in swordsmanship, then the question is, who or what prevented him from defending himself when, for example, Makkans threw filth, specifically camel intestines, on him while he was peacefully praying in front of the Ka'ba? Why did he not protect himself through his swordsmanship when children were led to throw stones at him in Ta'if? If he were a swordsman, why did he suffer all kinds of hardships at the hands of Makkans for thirteen continuous years and never retaliate with his sword? Why, even that night when all the chiefs of Makkah, through their representatives, raided his house in an attempt to take his life, did he not defend himself with his sword?

To make the long story short, he was a prophet from the Lord and did not invent Islam; instead, he delivered the message and guidance of the Lord to us. He never acquired any special training and never planned to use the sword. He did not come to fight but to teach the knowledge and wisdom of Islam and to warn about the assured events of the Hereafter. For this purpose, he did not need a sword because he could not have achieved by the sword what he was sent to achieve.

As far as his personal security and protection was concerned, the Lord Who sent him promised his protection. If swords never played any role, even in those early days of Islam when their use would have seemed to be necessary and justified to increase the number of followers, how could they be necessary at the climax of its success? However, even after emigrating from Makkah in order to practice Islam peacefully in Madinah, Muslims were not freed from the persecutions of the Quraysh. Soon, the situation became warlike, and the need to defend Muslims against the imminent threats to their lives and property increased. It was only then that the use of the sword was permitted. At this point, a role for the sword entered into Islam as a means of defense. It is to be remembered that even then it was not to promote or impose, but merely to protect, Islam. In the matter of propagation, Islam inherently contains enough qualities and benefits to attract people towards it; swords are not necessary and cannot play any role in the true propagation of Islam.

The first person, a woman, the first wife of the Prophet ﷺ, Khadija رضى الله عنها, embraced Islam as soon as the Prophet ﷺ declared his prophethood. She accepted Islam without the sword. The second Muslim, the first adult man to accept it, a successful businessman/merchant, embraced Islam under no coercion. Many other early converts to Makkah embraced Islam out of their free will and without a sword extended above their heads. As a matter of fact, swords were hanging over their heads threatening them if they did not leave Islam, but the firmly-rooted faith did not shake, and these new converts did not budge and stood firm in their commitment to Islam.

For example, when the fortieth Muslim and the second *khalīfa* of Islam, the famous Umar ibn al-Khattab ﷺ, a strong and brave man who was feared by many, surrendered his will to the will of Allah ﷻ in front of Muhammad ﷺ and embraced Islam, the sword was in his hands and he was in fact a great swordsman.

The famous general, Khalid bin Waleed ﷺ fought many battles against Islam, inflicted heavy injuries on Muslims, and was a great warrior and swordsman. It is thus obvious that even if a sword was used against him, it could not convert him to Islam. He embraced Islam through his own free will, laid his sword at the feet of the Prophet ﷺ and permanently surrendered himself to Islam. Through these two examples, we witness how swords were laid to rest before embracing Islam. During the lifetime of the Prophet ﷺ, the fear of the sword never converted anyone into being a Muslim; it was always the other way around. Swords were never used to propagate Islam, but were later needed to protect it.

Let us suppose that even if a sword were utilized, it could only acquire verbal submission, but could never obtain inner convictions, as its required in Islam. Swords may cause one to convert temporarily, but they cannot keep one in Islam permanently. If one does not convert from the heart, what is the sense of forcing him or her to accept Islam? Forceful acceptance brings no benefit to the individual or to anyone else. By the way, how many swords would you currently need, and how many people to hold them, to control and subjugate 1.6 billion Muslims throughout the world? Additionally, how many more swords would one need on a daily basis throughout the world for newcomers? Manufacturing swords would be a thriving business if this were the case.

A sword can slice a heart, but it cannot enlighten it. It can sever the head, but it cannot bend it voluntarily for daily prayers. It can separate one from this world, but it cannot bring any success in the other world. It can fill the heart with fear, but it cannot free it from the filth of this world. It can shut the eyes forever, but it cannot open them to see the truth. It can cause one to surrender everything else, but it cannot cause one to surrender his or her will. It can rob a person, but it cannot make him generous. It can make a person proud and arrogant, but it cannot make anybody humble and modest. It can exclude one from society, but it cannot make one caring and sharing.

Islam intends to kill the *kufr* (infidelity), not the *kafir* (one who commits infidelity). It wants to eradicate *shirk* (polytheism), not the *mushrik* (polytheist). It wants to suppress the evil inside of people, not the people themselves. It seeks to build societies, not turn them into graveyards. It wants humans to achieve the higher status, not eradicate people from the face of this earth. The portrayal of a Muslim holding a Qur'an in one hand and sword in the other is not only a misrepresentation of Islam, but it is purposely drawn to deceive and conceal the truth from people. The sword and Islam are not synonymous.

CHAPTER 13

Value of Life and Its Preservation in Islam

RECENT EVENTS AND THEIR COVERAGE BY THE MEDIA have left the impression that Muslims ignore the value of life. Because of their lack of knowledge, some believe that Islam does not attach any value to life or does not provide guidance for its preservation. In this chapter, I clarify these misconceptions and discuss the value of life and its preservation in Islam.

It is a matter of fact, as we will see, that Islam is such a kind and caring religion that not only does it give value to human life, but to animal life as well. Islam provides guidance for Muslims in all circumstances where the preservation of life is necessary. It protects human life from the embryonic state to the final moments of departure from this world. Islam not only takes into account the physical aspect of life, but its spiritual side as well.

Since it was for the very existence of human beings that Allah ﷻ created the earth and everything else and made all the arrangements for people's guidance to achieve their purpose during their lifetimes, why would He not command them to safeguard and preserve their lives? Why would He not attach any value to human life? If there were no value to life, then what is the sense of morality, values, rights, and duties? Also, the reason to protect life would be lost; hence, life would soon cease to exist if it were to lose its value.

Islam attaches great value to life and makes incumbent upon its followers the preservation of life at every cost. It not only commands people to live a harmless life on Earth, but even guides them to prepare for the same in the Hereafter. Human blood is not cheap to Islam. Islam promotes the philosophy of "live and let live" [Qur'an 4:29]. Without this principle, Islam cannot create an environment where it can achieve its ultimate goal. Islam punishes those who cause trouble to people's lives and who violate this basic principle of life. It was the miracle of Islam that this call was made to a society where the value and respect of life was non-existent, and within a very short period the value and respect for human life was fully established. In Islam, taking life without "just cause" is among the worst sins. The Prophet ﷺ declared:

(i) The greatest among the great sins is to associate someone with Allah ﷻ (*shirk*), murder, disobeying parents, and lying.

(ii) A believer stays within the vast boundaries of Islam, until he takes life without just cause, for blood is sacred.

(iii) On Judgment Day, Muslims will be accountable for their *salāh*, (obligatory prayers of worship) and the first thing decided will be the claims of spilling blood. [Mishkat]

He was not any ordinary man who reported this; he was the Lord's Prophet ﷺ, backed fully by Allah ﷻ and His commandments, Allah ﷻ instructs His servants:

...and do not cast yourselves with your own hands into destruction... • [Qur'an 2:195]

It is strictly prohibited to take any action that is harmful to oneself and that can bring destruction to human life. Islam does not allow taking even one's own life, let alone that of others. Islam wants us to live our life fully. Suicide is *harām* (strictly prohibited) in Islam and those who commit it are condemned to Hell eternally. Allah ﷻ states:

...and kill not yourselves. Verily, Allah is ever mercifully inclined towards you. • [Qur'an 4:29]

Life is not our own, it is entrusted to us by Allah ﷻ. On the Day of Judgment, we will be punished if we misuse it. Suicide is an extreme and clear sign of hopelessness. In Islam, even the slightest hopelessness is sinful, let alone suicide. A hopeless person is, in fact, denying the overall power of Allah ﷻ and loses faith in the fact that He is the All-Powerful and can change any situation at any time. Thus, we should try to protect and preserve life at every cost and never lose hope or faith. A true Muslim never becomes hopeless. When Muslims cannot take even their own life, how can they be justified in taking the life of others, except for 'just reasons' and through the due process of law? In the holy Qur'an, Allah ﷻ commands:

> And do not kill any person whose killing Allah has forbidden, except for justice... • [Qur'an 17:33]

Therefore, Islam strictly prohibits suicide, mercy killing, honor killing, euthanasia, or any unjustified killing. Islam also prohibits abortions, which many people feel does not constitute the killing of a human. In this regard, Allah ﷻ reveals:

> ...and do not kill your children out of the fear of poverty. We give sustenance to you as well as to them... • [Qur'an 6:151]

Often, the reason for abortions is the insufficiency of funds to support a child. Allah ﷻ, in order to preserve and safeguard life, even of the unborn, not only prohibited abortions, but assures that He Who provides for you will provide for them too [Qur'an 6:151]. Allah ﷻ guarantees sustenance; hence, there is no need to take the law into your own hands and have an abortion. When Islam does not permit the killing of an unborn out of the fear of poverty, how could it allow abortions in societies where food and other luxuries are taken for granted. Islam completely prohibits abortion. Clearly, preserving life is the wise decision and taking life is not, because the Lord reveals:

> That surely, We have created man in the best mold. • [Qur'an 95:4]

Allah ﷻ created this beautiful life, which is the most precious. It is by no means cheap and for anyone to destroy. He created life to preserve it, so humans could fully enjoy the bounties on Earth and prepare for eternal life in the Hereafter. This commandment could not be any simpler and all-encompassing. With regard to the value and respect Islam attaches to human life, Allah ﷻ states:

> …so whoever kills a human being neither to avenge for a murder (nor) for criminal disturbance in the land, so it is as if he has killed all mankind. And whoever saves from death any (human) life, it is as if he has kept alive all people… • [Qur'an 5:32]

No society or charter of law has ever placed such a high value on human life as the constitution of Islam, the holy Qur'an. There is a limit to how much humans can punish or reward someone for killing or saving lives, respectively. For example, if someone kills ten people, only one death sentence can be given to the killer, and the other nine victims can never be avenged. Similarly, rewards for noble acts and achievements are also limited. However, for the Almighty Lord, there is no limit. He can appropriately punish and reward as required for complete justice. How can Islam, which accords such a high value to life, allow for indiscriminate killing and not promote and reward life's preservation? The holy Qur'an states:

> And those who do not call upon with Allah other deities and do not kill such persons, who have been made sacred, except for justice, and do not commit adultery, and those who do this will face punishment; • whose punishment will be increased on Judgment Day and (they) will remain there humiliated, • but he who repents and embraces the faith and does good deeds, so they are those for whom Allah will convert their sins into good deeds. And Allah is the All-Forgiving, the All-Merciful. • [25:68-70]

Aside from forbidding indiscriminate/unjust killing and outlining severe punishments for murderers, in order to uphold the importance of life, Islam addresses the physical, mental, and spiritual issues of life as well. Islam intends for people to be physically and mentally fit in order to create an environment of peace and harmony. It wants to protect them from harm and to have them work their way through this world successfully.

Upon closely examining Islamic teachings and forms of worship, it becomes apparent that, in some way, every act done for the sake of Allah ﷻ benefits the human mind and body, both spiritually and physically. Dutifully performing such practices brings about the realization that human life is the most precious gift of the Lord Almighty. Subsequently, one begins to respect, honor, and protect human life from all harm.

Mental health and physical fitness are important for the well-being and preservation of life. Amazingly, in Islam, a healthy body and sound mind are achieved automatically through the regular and daily activities of worship. According to Islam, the time to live in this world is fixed by Allah ﷻ, and nobody dies before or after their time. However, one should strive to stay healthy until his or her last moments. Islam is highly demanding in matters of preserving and protecting human life. The holy Prophet ﷺ states:

> Humanity is not granted anything superior than forgiveness, health and wellness. [Nisa'i]

Guidelines regarding health were established by the Prophet ﷺ and when followed bring many physical and mental benefits. For example, many *ahadith* deal with the intake of food (i.e., when to eat, what to eat, and how to eat and drink), maintaining good hygiene (e.g., washing hands before and after eating, washing hands after using the bathroom, trimming nails, removing pubic hair, showering frequently, brushing teeth, etc.). Moreover, many *ahadith* talk about curing illnesses through proper medication and foods, living a routine life, waking up and going to sleep on time, eating on time, and having breakfast and dinner early. Maintaining a simple lifestyle for mental peace is in the *ahadīth* as well.

The following list further shows the importance Islam places on keeping the mind and body healthy and, at the same time, explains how to live according to Allah's 🕋 prescribed way as exemplified by the Prophet 🕌 himself.

- Islam prescribes eating only *halāl* (Islamically permissible) foods
- *Halāl* animals must be *zabīha* (slaughtered in the Islamic way, as stated in the Qur'an)
- Pork and all of its byproducts are *harām* (strictly forbidden)
- Alcoholic beverages are *harām*
- Beef is allowed, but not preferred
- To eat until one has a full stomach is not recommended
- Chew food as much as possible before swallowing
- Meats must be fully cooked and eaten with lots of gravy
- To drink water before/during eating, but not right after
- To talk while eating is not preferable
- To use the right hand to eat instead of utensils
- Even though it may seem strange to some, but slightly licking fingers that have come into contact with food is an important part of the food intake process; it has its peculiar benefits.
- To sit on the floor while eating is a *sunnah* of the Prophet 🕌
- To eat/drink while standing or walking is undesirable

The Prophet's 🕌 teachings on eating leave a true seeker of knowledge spellbound as to how and why the Prophet 🕌 would go into such minute detail. One of the main purposes of the Prophet 🕌 was to inform us about anything and everything that was either beneficial or harmful to live a comfortable and trouble-free life.

If the body and mind are at peace, one can proceed safely and easily to live life. Islam, the religion that addresses every bit of detail, surely intends to preserve life and asserts the highest value to it.

CHAPTER 14

Jihad: A Concept

efore explaining jihad, I request that you keep in mind that when Adam ﷺ descended to Earth, Allah ﷻ told him that His guidance would continue to come to mankind; whoever follows it, will be successful and will enter Paradise, and whoever does not, their abode will be Hell [2:38-39]. This clearly means that getting guidance to humanity was included in Allah's ﷻ greater plan.

Allah's ﷻ chosen prophets brought that guidance and spread it to their communities. Finally, Allah's ﷻ guidance was completed and perfected with Prophet Muhammad ﷺ. Since he was to be the final prophet and no other prophet was to come after him, the duty to advance this guidance to future generations became an obligation upon Muslims. With this, Allah's ﷻ promise to Adam ﷺ was fulfilled.

Moreover, like many other things, fighting, killing, and spilling blood, for one reason or another, is part of human nature. If these evil aspects of human nature are not controlled and regulated, it is not possible to bring peace and happiness to Earth. Therefore, since someone will always be looking to fight and kill, then not giving permission to fight back or to prepare to defend one's self, family, and property would be unjust. Oppressors and tyrants never let a single soul live in peace on Earth; in fact, they wish to bury them beneath it. When people are granted the permission to fight back, it must be accompanied with clear-cut and comprehensive rules to prevent the oppressed from becoming oppressors themselves, once they triumph over their oppressors. In contrast, if defense is not permitted, then consequently, not many people will be left alive. Therefore, it is natural and necessary to grant permission to defend oneself lawfully.

Muslims, as followers of Islam, are assigned the duty of jihad to spread the message of Islam. They are permitted to do *qital* (killing) to defend themselves, their land, property, and livelihood and to overcome those who hinder their struggle in the "prophetic" duty of spreading Islam, though of course only through religiously sanctioned means.

If the real concept of jihad and *qital* is not understood completely and properly, then other teachings and philosophies of Islam will seem contradictory to each other. Certainly, there cannot be contradictions in the guidance of the Lord. Once all other concepts of Islam are understood truly and correctly, the concept of jihad and *qital* can be comprehended easily.

Jihad, as per various dictionaries, is literally defined as struggle, strife, fighting, religious war, holy war (by Muslims), supreme effort, etc. However, jihad is a term that cannot be understood by any of its literal definitions or even what it literally means in Arabic. Jihad is a concept with many physical and spiritual aspects, temporary and everlasting effects, and worldly and otherworldly dimensions. Thus, on the basis of Islamic teachings, jihad should be more correctly referred to as "the striving of Muslims with utmost efforts in the way of Allah ﷻ by adhering to every rule and regulation related to it, with the intent of the greater good of Muslims and non-Muslims, and to achieve prominence for the *deen* (religion) of Allah ﷻ—*Deen-e-Islam.*" Therefore, every allowable struggle and difficulty Muslims undertake to spread the message of the Lord to humanity can be defined as jihad. [Qur'an 29:69]

Since *Deen-e-Islam* is the complete way of life covering every aspect of life, then Islam's various concepts, such as jihad, must include a whole lot as well. As per the above (most appropriate) definition, based on Qur'anic injunctions, the main purpose of jihad is to achieve prominence for the *deen* of Allah ﷻ. Now one might ask, "Is there one or several ways to achieve that prominence?" If there are several ways, as there should be, then there must also be several kinds of jihad. So now the question is, "Are there several kinds of jihad?"

Upon paying close attention to the commandments of Allah ﷻ and carefully analyzing the traditions of the Prophet ﷺ, we find that the main concern of jihad certainly is to achieve prominence for Islam and that jihad should continue to be a duty of Muslims until this goal is achieved. The Prophet ﷺ said, "…jihad will continue until the Last Day…" [Bukhari and Tirmidhi] Now, to achieve this prominence, let us suppose that there is only one way, which is to kill all disbelievers or convert them to Islam forcefully, even though this is impossible given the current setting of the world and in light of future expectations, but let us suppose this anyway. In this case, jihad will not continue to the Last Day, when the Prophet ﷺ has stated that it will. Therefore, contrary to the misconception of many, the intent and purpose of the institution of jihad is *not* to kill disbelievers or convert them to Islam forcefully. So clearly, there are many ways to achieve prominence for Islam; hence, there are many kinds of jihad.

Before proceeding, let me explain what is meant by "prominence for Islam." Allah ﷻ could have left Adam عليه السلام and his progeny alone, to spend their lives on Earth in any way they would like, without His guidance. In such a case, they certainly would have all gone astray. In fact, even with His guidance, many have gone astray; one can imagine what would happen without it. Allah ﷻ did not want this to happen. He wanted His 'Best of all Creatures' to succeed in the Hereafter. Thus, He informed Adam عليه السلام about sending guidance to humanity so, as a result, humanity, could have the choice to be successful.

If a religion is doubted, misunderstood, or fails to reach people, how can it ever be practiced for people to receive salvation? Allah ﷻ took it upon Himself to send His guidance through prophets and through their followers. Once the message of Islam has been successfully conveyed to all people, its true message, philosophy, and practices are understood, and Islam then is realized as the way of life revealed by Allah ﷻ for human salvation; this is thereby the prominence of Islam.

This is an important mission and necessary to be achieved. No doubt, this is quite a difficult course to travel for the betterment and success of humanity. Sometimes, it is difficult to get people to realize something, even when it is to their benefit. Certainly, this effort requires much physical, mental, financial, and spiritual struggle. Nevertheless, it can be done individually or collectively and whenever or wherever necessary. Every bit of effort is worth the cause because it can potentially result in the ultimate success for billions of people. That is why the entire concept of struggling in the way of Allah ﷻ, i.e., jihad, is established to seek prominence for Islam, so all people can have a chance to benefit from its guidance.

Let me clarify here that achieving prominence for Islam through jihad does not mean that everyone must convert to Islam. Of course, this would be excellent, but if this were what is meant by prominence for Islam, then why would Allah ﷻ have said:

> And if Allah so willed, He would have made you into one *ummah* (community)… • [Qur'an 16:93]

Since He Himself did not make us one *ummah*, forceful conversion cannot be the purpose of jihad. Allah ﷻ wants people to choose Islam willingly and not as a result of coercion. Prominence for Islam simply means that people are given a fair chance to become aware of Islam and to realize that Islam is the only true religion for people and that salvation is only possible through it. After this message has been conveyed to people, they are free to choose whether or not to embrace it. Whatever people choose, they will see the result of their choice.

The intent of a Muslim doing jihad must be to seek prominence for Islam, not for any personal goal. To achieve prominence for Islam, three things are necessary: preservation of Islam, protection of Muslims, and propagation of Islam. It is not possible to take the message of Islam to others and invite them into it without first preserving it and protecting Muslims. If Islam is not preserved in its original form and if Muslims are not well protected, how would it be possible to spread the message, make people realize that Islam is the true religion, and invite them to embrace it? Therefore, all of this is part of the greater goal of achieving prominence for Islam, and since jihad is the way to achieve it, there must be several kinds of jihad. Thus, the process of preserving, protecting, and preaching Islam will continue, and as said earlier, this is why and how jihad will continue until the Last Day.

Muslims have already surrendered their will to the will of Allah ﷻ. They did not make jihad incumbent upon themselves; it was Allah ﷻ Who commands Muslims to do jihad. This is Allah's ﷻ will, and Muslims have no choice but to follow Allah's ﷻ will and commandments. Based on Islamic teachings, Muslims are to participate in several kinds of jihad, of which the major categories are:

- "Jihad with One's Self," known as *Jihad bin Nafs*. As per the Prophet ﷺ, it is *Jihad al-Akbar*, i.e., "The Greater Jihad."

- "Jihad with Others." To the surprise of many, "Jihad with Others" is referred to as *Jihad al-Asghar*, i.e., "The Lesser Jihad."

Jihad bin Nafs means to struggle to purify one's base self. The base self attempts to focus on the material world and on illegitimate desires, taking a person away from the actual purpose of life: worshiping the Lord and completely surrendering to His will. *Jihad bin*

Nafs also includes *Jihad bish Shayta'n,* "Jihad against Satan," which is the inner struggle with the Devil, so he cannot misguide and lead you away from the *Sirāte Mustaqīm* (The Straight Path). "Jihad with One's Self" never ceases, even up until the last moments of life.

Jihad with Others is "The Lesser Jihad." It can be done with sword, pen, and wealth, and it is commonly referred to as *Jihad bis Saif, Jihad bil Qalam,* and *Jihad bil Maal,* respectively. These kinds of jihad can be exercised one at a time or simultaneously.

Jihad with pen and with wealth is usually associated with preserving and propagating Islam. Jihad with sword, supported by wealth, is utilized to protect and defend Muslims and their territory, and to remove any hindrance in the propagation of Islam. Jihad with sword is applicable only as a last resort, and only when the enemy has gone to extremes, and/or to protect the Muslim *ummah* and *dhimmis* (non-Muslims living under Islamic rule).

Before I go any further to explain jihad with sword, "armed jihad," which is the Lesser Jihad, I would like you to be fully acquainted with *Jihad bin Nafs* (Jihad with One's Self). This jihad is a prerequisite for all other kinds of jihad, and this is why it is called *Jihad al-Akbar* ("The Greater Jihad").

JIHAD BIN NAFS (JIHAD WITH ONE'S SELF)

JIHAD BIN NAFS MEANS TO STRUGGLE with one's *nafs* (base self). The human *nafs* is inherently attracted to this world and to worldly desires, while Islam intends to prepare its followers to be successful in the Hereafter, which means that believers must remove the love of this world from their hearts. This world and our temporary stay in it are not the end but the means to acquire ultimate success, which is the pleasure of Allah ﷻ. We must suppress anything and everything that hinders our struggle to that effect. The *nafs* is a powerful entity that independently and with Satan's support interferes in performing good deeds, in obeying the commandments of Allah ﷻ, and in seeking His pleasure.

Since jihad is carried out only for the pleasure of Allah ﷻ and for the greater good of the people, especially non-Muslims, qualities such as selflessness, sincerity, purity of intent, and obedience to every divine commandment are required of those participating in jihad. Since the *nafs* is always active against such human qualities, they are not easy to adopt without fighting against the base self. Hence, the *nafs* must be suppressed constantly, and this is what is meant by *Jihad bin Nafs*.

From the very beginning, in fact immediately after the Battle of Badr (the first and most important battle between the Muslims and the Makkans), the Prophet ﷺ established *Jihad bis Saif* (Jihad with the Sword), as "The Lesser Jihad" and *Jihad bin Nafs* as "The Greater Jihad." [Bukhari and Muslim] This important distinction should always be kept in mind.

Most of the time, people only discuss the Lesser Jihad and overlook the Greater Jihad. Tragically, some self-proclaimed Muslims kill people indiscriminately, wrongfully thinking that they are engaged in armed jihad when, in fact, they are not engaged in any Islamically sanctioned form of jihad. Because of the unlawful actions of some ignorant "followers," sometimes thousands of innocent men, women, and children pay the price. These murderers ignore the essential *Jihad bin Nafs* and stubbornly and wrongfully call their armed struggle "Islamic jihad," and many people even believe them out of their own ignorance about Islam. *Jihad bis Saif* without *Jihad bin Nafs* results in chaos and anarchy.

The superiority of *Jihad bin Nafs* over *Jihad bis Saif* can also be understood by the fact that no matter how much good a *mujāhid* (one who does jihad) brings to Islam and Muslims through his 'sword,' if his personal conduct and character are questionable and contradict Islamic teachings and philosophy, his good deed is rejected and does not count. In fact, he will be punished for his misconduct, and he will not be relieved of punishment simply because of his services to Islam [Zia-un-Nabi, Vol. 4, pg. 261-2]. Without successful jihad with one's self, a Muslim cannot truly perform armed jihad and achieve its true purpose. Therefore, jihad with one's self is the priority and is far more important than striving for prominence for Islam through arms.

If one cannot fight with his own base self for the pleasure of the Almighty, then how can he fight with others for the same reason? In such a case, his fight with others would be for personal sake/goals, but not for the sake of Allah ﷻ, and it would not be worthy of being called jihad. If he cannot defeat his own desires, which prevent him from becoming a better Muslim, how can he claim to have the right to convert anyone into Islam and to make vows to achieve prominence for Islam? If he cannot tame his own base self, how can he think of correcting others? If he cannot embark on the path to ultimate success, how can he call upon others to surrender their will to the will of Allah ﷻ? Regardless of the kind of jihad pursued, if the base self is not first successfully suppressed through *Jihad bin Nafs*, any other jihad will bear no fruit.

Narrated Abu Musa ﷺ:

> A man came to the Prophet ﷺ and asked, "A man fights for war booty, another fights for fame, and a third fights for showing off; which of them fights in Allah's cause?" The Prophet ﷺ said, "He who fights to achieve prominence for Islam, fights in Allah's cause."
>
> [Bukhari]

So it is important that before embarking on armed jihad, jihad with one's self must be practiced to avoid violating Islamic rules of war and peace and to avoid superseding the limits established by Islam. [Zia-un-Nabi, Vol. 4, pg. 365] Armed jihad must not be motivated by any personal reason or wish, including nationalism and geopolitical issues. Only then can that fight be Islamic jihad, holy war for peace, and struggle in the way of Allah ﷻ. Therefore, jihad with one's self, being the prerequisite, prepares Muslims to be fair, lawful, and aware of their religious obligations even during the craziness of war. Muslims conditioned through jihad with one's self maintain the true purpose of armed jihad, which is not to take away disbeliever's lives, but to struggle to bring Islam's message to people. [Zia-un-Nabi, Vol. 7, pgs. 572-3]

During the Battle of the Trench, an invincible warrior challenged Muslims to fight him. Ali ﷺ, the Prophet's ﷺ cousin and son-in-law, agreed to this challenge. During the fight, Ali ﷺ pinned his opponent to the ground. Certain of his death, the warrior spat on Ali's face. Instead of killing him out of rage, Ali ﷺ let him free, saying, "Had I killed you for personal rage, it would not have been for the sake of Allah." The honorable Ali's reaction and behavior could not have been possible without his successful jihad with self.

You may be wondering what the *nafs* is, that a Muslim is required to fight it first, in order to suppress and tame it. Within the human body, the *nafs* (base self) is like a king, and worldly wants and wishes are his soldiers. The *nafs* is blind, cannot distinguish between good and evil, and cannot see matters that cause death and destruction to the human soul. When the *nafs* invites man towards evil and subjugates him, it is in the state of *ammara*. A Muslim is commanded to disobey the *Nafs-e-Ammara*, to fight with it, suppress it, and take control of it. [Qur'an 12:53] Once this state of taming is achieved, Allah ﷺ blesses the *nafs* and enlightens it. At this point, its every negative feature become visible, and the believer recognizes the enemies of the soul and of the body, and it begins to clean and erase the vices, evil characteristics, and spiritual diseases. Once a believer cleanses his *nafs*, he decorates it with divine attributes and becomes worthy of being called the Best of all Creatures. This state of *nafs* is called *Nafs-e-Mutma'inna*, "the satisfied and the contented soul."

Jihad bin Nafs is necessary to convert *Nafs-e-Ammara* to *Nafs-e-Mutma'inna*, so that this structure of flesh and bones can develop from a brute to a human and can achieve the purpose for which he was created. Thus, certainly on the battlefield as well as elsewhere, Muslims maintain their humanity and are not reduced to barbaric beasts. This is why the Prophet ﷺ declared *Jihad bin Nafs* "The Greater Jihad." Islam intends to make man righteous before commanding him to fight in the battlefield. Islam recognizes that if the human mind is left unrestricted and independent of the fear of divine accountability, it brings great disaster. History is full of examples of those uncontrolled and independent monsters who brought irreversible harm to humanity.

When the thinking process is turned upside down and the power of reasoning becomes corrupted, wrong become right, and what is right becomes wrong. This is the worst state of the human mind and is the point of no return for righteousness and humanity. Jihad with one's self is the most effective tool against reaching this worst state. This is why jihad with one's self is the greater jihad. When one defeats the base self, it becomes easy to win others.

It is a very fine point and worth mentioning, that many modern-day Muslims ignorantly believe that they are actively engaged in some kind of legitimate jihad, whereas their sayings and actions clearly show that they have yet to overcome their *nafs*. As a result, instead of bringing prominence for Islam, their "struggle" has defamed it. They are wrong to call their actions Islamic. Another important point to note is that whenever jihad is mentioned in the holy Qur'an and *ahadith*, it is followed with the words *fi sabilillah*, "in the way of Allah ﷻ" or "for Allah's ﷻ sake," not for the sake of one's self.

JIHAD BIL QALAM (JIHAD WITH PEN/WRITING)

𝒯HE FIRST AND FOREMOST OBJECTIVE OF *JIHAD BIL QALAM* is to preserve and propagate Islam through literature. This kind of jihad is proof that fighting is not the only option and that *Jihad bis Saif* is not the only jihad or way to achieve prominence for Islam.

> So do not follow the infidels, but do jihad against them using (the logic) of this (Qur'an) with your utmost capacity. • [Qur'an 25:52]

Here too, Muslims are directed to present the logic and wisdom of the holy Qur'an, and using sword is not the priority. The application of the different kinds of jihad varies based on the circumstances at hand. As said earlier, it is important first to preserve Islam in its original form for later generations of Muslims, and before propagating it to others.

War between good and evil has existed since the history of mankind, and so it will continue until the end of time. This same war happened between Islam and its antithesis/enemies, and it will continue until the prominence of Islam is achieved. Thousands of Muslim scholars dedicated their entire lives in *Jihad bil Qalam* to preserve and explain Islam and its various philosophies. They provided answers to questions raised about Islam and its teachings, and current Muslim scholars continue to do so.

Through *Jihad bil Qalam*, Muslims interpreted, translated, and explained the wisdom and knowledge contained in the holy Qur'an and in the *ahadīth* of the Prophet ﷺ in every major language. The Prophet's ﷺ teachings and traditions have been preserved and explained in such unique ways that people have been awestruck. They extracted both spiritual and scientific knowledge, which helped to understand the message of Islam.

Jihad bil Qalam popularized Islam throughout the world, and many who were unaware of the religion of Islam understood and embraced it just by reading about it. Had Muslims not utilized this jihad, many people would have remained in the dark. There are no followers of any religion doing as much as Muslims did for Islam for preserving and propagating their religion throughout the world. The importance of *Jihad bil Qalam* over *Jihad bis Saif* can be understood through just one saying of the honorable Prophet ﷺ:

> The ink of the pen of a true scholar of Islam is holier than the blood of a martyr. [Tibrani]

If anyone still blames Islam for being violent or inciting violence, then that would be unjust. However, Muslims must keep on teaching until the moment arrives for the Lord to decide.

JIHAD BIL MAAL (JIHAD WITH WEALTH)

*J*IHAD BIL MAAL MEANS TO STRUGGLE with wealth. It is a fact that money is required for all projects undertaken. Muslims who provide their wealth to undertake other forms of jihad execute *Jihad bil Maal*. Of course, not everyone can do every kind of jihad; thus, different kinds of jihad enable all Muslims to participate as per their capacity and position. Wealth, like everything else, is given by Allah ﷻ. For true believers, spending their wealth in the way of Allah ﷻ and as per His commandments is not burdensome. In fact, Muslims merely spend what is given by Allah ﷻ in the way of Allah ﷻ and, in turn, receive rewards for free.

JIHAD BIS SAIF (JIHAD BY THE SWORD)

*A*S NOTED EARLIER, THE PURPOSE OF every kind of jihad is to seek prominence for Islam. The aim of jihad through the sword, i.e., armed jihad, is not to convert anyone to Islam forcefully or to kill someone if he refuses to become Muslim. Nor does this jihad mean to kill or be killed for forceful conversions. It means to protect Muslim's lives, their lands, their property, their interests, their livelihood, and their freedom to practice Islam. It is also to liberate people who call upon Muslims for help and to clear any hurdles from the way of preaching and propagating Islam. These are all part of the greater good/goal of seeking prominence for Islam.

Armed jihad was and never is aimed at common people, because they generally do not become obstacles to the propagation of Islam. It is always the governing authorities, the aristocrats and elites, and the rich and powerful people who resist, hinder, and prevent the Lord's message from getting to their people, so as not to give them a chance to embrace it. Armed jihad is directed towards those lords and tyrants who use their power, authority, and rule to resist the commandments and absolute authority of the Lord. In this way, such opponents of Islam do not do any service for their people; instead, they oppress them by preventing them from reaching the absolute reality.

In fact, armed jihad is in favor of the common man. It liberates from the tyranny of the few and connects people to the one true Lord. Because of a few selfish individuals and their supporters, millions of people should not be left to become ultimate losers. This is one of the main reasons Allah ﷻ instituted the obligation of jihad upon Muslims. Armed jihad is not as much in favor of Muslims as it is in favor of non-Muslims. It saves non-Muslims from everlasting harm and failure if they choose to embrace Islam. Nonetheless, through His loyal servants, Allah ﷻ fulfills His promise of getting the message across to all people.

Throughout history, there have existed, everywhere and in every system, people who resist change, either because they are satisfied with the status quo or because their personal motives and interests are involved, which they would like to see remain secured. Thus, even though change may be good for society, some people resist it. Where some see benefit in guiding people, there are others who find benefit in keeping them misguided. Therefore, they fight head-on to secure their interest. Some even resist change because they are proud of the system under which they are living.

When Allah ﷻ willed to get His message across through His prophets and through their respective followers, He made it incumbent upon them to fight in His cause for the betterment of all people. As with other nations before Muhammad's ﷺ, Allah ﷻ also made it compulsory on Muslims to do armed jihad in the way of Allah ﷻ in order to protect Islam, to provide shelter and security to all those under the umbrella of Islam, and to achieve prominence for Islam. In that regard, the holy Qur'an constantly reminds and warns its followers to avoid transgression and to abide by the rule of law in every aspect of their lives, especially in jihad; otherwise, their efforts will not be *fi sabilillah* (for the sake of Allah ﷻ), as it is required to be.

Since no more prophets were to come after Muhammad ﷺ, Muslims had to fulfill this obligation of preaching and protecting the cause of Islam. If this world were a peaceful place and if it were not in human nature to fight, fulfilling this obligation would be easy, and Muslims could have easily taken the divine message around. However, this was not and is not the case. Human beings fight over every small thing for which they can fight. The duty of carrying the message of the Lord was only attached to fighting if and when there became a need to fight to preach the message of Islam freely.

There have been times in the past when armed jihad was necessary, and it still is in some parts of the world where Muslims' life, property, and freedom are in danger and where their livelihood is being cut short. But overall, things have changed now, and in major parts of the world people have freedom of religion, freedom of choice, and the free flow of information about religion. So in my humble opinion, in those parts of the world, armed jihad is not needed, is contraindicated, and will not serve its purpose of removing hurdles from the path of propagating Islam. Still, if in the name of Islam or jihad, someone inflicts pain on people through any means, certainly, this behavior is un-Islamic and cannot be labeled *jihad*.

Once a person embraces Islam and embarks on the path to success, Allah ﷻ makes it incumbent upon him to strive for other's success, too. Allah 🕮 wants success for all of His slaves, and through jihad He makes it possible for all to be successful. He has designated great rewards for the *mujāhids* (those who do jihad) of Islam. Since Allah 🕮 put this duty upon him, since all the rules and regulations of jihad were also established by Him, and since the *mujāhid* is in the service of Allah 🕮, he must not allow his *nafs* to interfere and violate any rule thereof. If he does, then he is not a *mujāhid*; he can be called a terrorist, extremist, or whatever. To do true jihad with the sword, a *mujāhid* first needs to do *jihad* with his base self and take full control of it.

To elaborate further, *jihad* is an effort to eradicate sinfulness, impiety, mischief, and injustice and to employ righteous acts, not for any personal gain, but for the benefit of humanity (as mentioned in the *hadīth* quoted earlier). Jihad intends to solve the problems of people, to liberate them, to set them free from the bondage of people and society, and to uplift them from oppressive and depressive states. Most importantly, jihad results in connecting people to their Creator and shows them the true purposes of life.

Jihad's first and foremost purpose is not to kill or cause bloodshed, nor is it to acquire any worldly gain, including wealth, land, etc. It intends to invite people to the Lord. Once people receive the message of Islam and decide not to embrace it, Muslims are to leave them alone, because there is no coercion in accepting Islam [e.g., 2:256; 10:99; 15:2-3; 18:29; 42:48; and 50:45] If they do not accept Islam but choose to live under Muslim rule and protection, they have to pay *jizyah,* a fee/tax for the protection provided to them. These *dhimmis* (non-Muslims living under Muslim protection) are entitled to full rights as citizens, but unlike Muslims, they are exempted from giving *zakāh* (obligatory charity) and from serving in the military. With regards to *dhimmis,* the Prophet 🕮 directed Muslims to:

> Be mindful of the rights of *dhimmis*, because I will stand, on Judgment Day, as a plaintiff on their behalf for any injustice done to them. [Kanzul-Ammal]

The commandments underlined in the holy Qur'an and the teachings of the holy Prophet 🕌 clearly state that before the initiation of armed jihad, people must first be invited to accept Islam. Before going any further, I would like to present a few Qur'anic verses and *ahadith* in the next section to further correct prevalent misunderstandings and to present a clearer picture of jihad.

PERMISSION GRANTED TO FIGHT BACK

*A*FTER ABOUT FIFTEEN YEARS of pain and suffering from the time Muhammad 🕌 first declared his prophethood, Allah 🕌 finally permitted Muslims to fight back. Allah 🕌 revealed:

> The permission for war has been given to them against whom war is being waged, because they are oppressed. Without a doubt, Allah has the power to help them— • those who were driven from their homes unjustly, for that they used to say, "Our Sustainer is Allah…" • [Qur'an 22:39-40]

Through this holy verse, Muslims were granted the permission to fight back for the very first time. For almost fifteen years, the early Muslims suffered at the hands of the Makkans, who plundered their wealth and property and killed and drove their families out of Makkah. Even after migrating to surrounding areas and to the city of Madinah, the enemies of Islam did not leave them alone. The permission to defend Islam and Muslims was justified by every means, let alone that the Almighty granted it. Jihad against oppressive and tyrannical disbelievers guaranteed a peaceful future for Muslims and established Islam as a divine power against idolatry and polytheism. From the two verses quoted above, one can easily know the reason for the permission to fight back.

Although no one raised any objections when idol-worshipers and disbelievers inflicted pain and suffering on Muslims for 15 years, Allah 🕌, being the All-Knower, knew that once He granted permission to the believers to fight back against blatant persecution and once they then actually fought back against the injustice inflicted upon them, objections and condemnations would come from everywhere. Thus, Allah ﷻ further clarifies in the holy Qur'an:

> ...and had it not been for Allah to keep replacing some people by the means of others, so surely, sanctuaries would have been toppled, and Christian churches, and Jewish places of worship, and Muslim *masajid* (mosques), in which is invoked Allah's name greatly. And surely, Allah will help him who helps His *deen* (way of life; religion). Without a doubt, Allah is surely Powerful, Dominant. • [22:40]

This also indicates that this divine permission was not new, as it had been granted before to other nations that were sent a prophet. Thus, this permission was not a tool for transgression, but a means to prevent it. Another reason for jihad is given:

> And why would you not fight in the way of Allah and for the weak men, women, and children who supplicate, "O Sustainer, take us out from this community, whose inhabitants are oppressors, and make someone from Your mercy our supporter, and make someone from Your favor our helper." • [Qur'an 4:75]

This verse contains a clear message that jihad is to liberate people, especially the weak and oppressed men, women, and children, and that the commandment of jihad is in response to their call and prayer to the Lord, to uplift them from the oppression of tyrants. Obviously, in response to their call, Allah ﷻ would not descend to earth Himself, but would send His servants to answer the call of the oppressed. This is one just reason and purpose for jihad. Another important reason is given in the following verses. Allah ﷻ commands:

> And kill them until there is no more terrorism left and the *deen* (way of life; religion) of Allah becomes most prominent. Then if they refrain, so without a doubt, whatever they do, Allah is watchful over it. • And if they turn away—then know that without a doubt, Allah is your Master; how perfect a Master and how perfect a Helper. • [Qur'an 8:39-40]

In these verses and in some right before them, there are commandments that reveal the attitudes of the idolaters of Makkah and what appropriate actions were to be taken against them. This permission to kill by the Almighty is only given to remove evil and evildoers, and to establish Islam's prominence. It has no other purpose whatsoever. This permission must not be corrupted or misinterpreted to cause mischief and chaos. As soon as disbelievers stop, turn away, and refrain from causing mischief, Muslims are also to stop their fighting and to leave the matter to Allah ﷻ.

Another important verse regarding the killing of non-Muslims is worth quoting here in that many interpreters have misunderstood or misquoted it.

> Then, when the sacred months have passed, kill those idolaters wherever you come across them and capture them and imprison them and besiege them at every point of lookout, then if they seek repentance and begin to establish *salāh* (prayer of worship) and begin to give *zakāh* (obligatory charity), so get out of their way—certainly Allah is Forgiving, Merciful. • [Qur'an 9:5]

These verses are about the *mushrikin* (idolaters) of Makkah and not for any other disbeliever. The command in the above verse was eventually cancelled out by the following verse:

> And if they wish to make truce, then you are to accept the truce and have trust in Allah. Without a doubt, He is All-Hearing, All-Knowing. • [Qur'an 8:61]

Even as per Qur'an 9:5, killing them was not a necessity, if they enter Islam or if they simply seek refuge. This verse was specifically meant for them, and was intended to bring them to Islam, not just to kill them. This verse should not be taken out of context. In the following verse, there is clear indication of Islamic tolerance and absence of coercion. Allah ﷻ states:

And if some idolater seeks your refuge, so give him refuge until He hears the Words of Allah, then deliver him to his place. This is because these people are ignorant. • [Qur'an 9:6]

This means that he is not to be killed, even if he did not embrace Islam after hearing the message of truth. Muslims were to escort him safely to his destination and not kill him. What more can I say if one still believes that Islam is intolerant and permits indiscriminate blood-shed. While Islam is a religion of peace, it is not a religion of absolute pacifism, and that is an important distinction. Islam is not in favor of bloodshed, but it demands its followers to be courageous, not cowards.

Allah ﷻ reveals in the holy Qur'an:

Certainly Allah has bought from Muslims their souls and wealth for the price of Heaven, which is for them. They fight in the way of Allah, so they kill and are killed. On this, absolute promise has been made in the *Taurat* (Torah) and the *Injīl* (gospels) and the Qur'an. And whoever fulfilled the covenant with Allah, so be happy with your trade, which you made with Him—and this is the ultimate success. • [9:111]

Great rewards are for those who willingly perform great services to Islam. Certainly, it is not easy to kill or be killed. This verse reminds us that previous holy books (i.e., the Torah, Psalms and Bible) had verses of jihad similar to those now found in the holy Qur'an. Muslims have been commanded to do jihad against polytheists and disbelievers, as People of the Book (primarily Jews and Christians) were commanded before them. However, in the absence of oppression and persecution, jihad with the sword is not to be utilized.

There are many verses in the holy Qur'an regarding jihad, which if not properly understood and interpreted in the right context prevent jihad from being executed lawfully. Valid judgments cannot be formed on incomplete, improper, or distorted information. For further clarification, let me quote another verse to explain with whom Islam does not require jihad.

Allah does not forbid you—from those people who did not fight with you on account of religion, nor did they drive you out of your homes—from behaving well with them, and being just to them. Without a doubt, Allah likes those who are just. • Allah only forbids you—from those people who fought against you on account of religion, and drove you out of your homes, and helped in driving you out—from befriending them. Whoever befriends them is indeed the oppressor. • [Qur'an 60:8-9]

This clearly shows that with regard to those non-Muslims who are not enemies of Muslims, who do not wage war in matters of religion, and who have not thrown them out of their homes, one should be good to them and not wage war against them.

Many verses contain similar messages preventing Muslims from doing armed jihad against people who do not interfere in preaching Islam, do not make mischief and cause chaos, do not oppress people, and so on and so forth. Regardless of what religion or race they belong to or how opposing their religious beliefs are to Islam, Muslims should have no animosity against them, their lives, and their property. This is a divine and decisive decision. An important commandment regarding this is that "There is no compulsion in *deen* (way of life; religion); certainly, guidance has been separated from the evil path..." [Qur'an 2:256]. Whoever chooses to follow the divine guidance will see its fruit, and whoever chooses otherwise, their matter rests with Allah ﷻ.

Many verses of the Qur'an, in addition to the ones quoted above, clearly show that current misunderstandings about Islam and Muslims are false. Islam does not allow Muslims to kill indiscriminately, nor does it make them thirst for the blood of non-Muslims. The verses usually quoted to support the notion that Islam is a violent religion and teaches violence to its followers are simply ripped out of context in order to defame Islam and to misinform people. These commandments were revealed for specific times, i.e., during a battle in the battlefield. They were not meant to be taken out of context and used for other times and conditions. This is just like when a commander gives orders to his soldiers in the battlefield; such orders are not applicable beyond the battlefield.

There are also very clear teachings regarding this subject in the traditions of the Prophet ﷺ, which I present below.

> A companion of the Prophet ﷺ 'Abdullah bin Masud asked "O Prophet ﷺ, which act is most prominent?" He replied, "Performing *salāh* (prayers of worship) at its prescribed time." He then asked, "What is after that?" The Prophet ﷺ replied, "Serving parents." I asked, "Then what?" He replied, "Jihad in the way of Allah." I then stopped asking. [Bukhari]

> Someone asked the Prophet ﷺ, "O Prophet! Do I do jihad first or embrace Islam first?" The Prophet ﷺ said, "Embrace Islam first, then do jihad." So he embraced Islam, did jihad, and was martyred.
> [Bukhari]

> Someone asked the Prophet ﷺ, "Who is considered a soldier of Allah, one who fights to acquire wealth, fights to earn fame, or fights to prove his bravery?" The Prophet ﷺ replied, "The one who fights to achieve prominence for the righteous faith (Islam) is considered a fighter in the way of Allah." [Bukhari]

Preparing for a battle Prophet Muhammad ﷺ said, "I will hand over the banner to the person who shall conquer the fort." He called the honorable Ali ؑ, handed him the banner, and instructed him thusly, "We fight with them so that they may become Muslims like us. When you reach there, invite them to Islam, and explain their obligations towards Allah. So I swear to Allah, if even one person is found and accepts the right path through you, it is much better for you than acquiring one-hundred [red] camels." [Bukhari]

It is also narrated that if the merciful Prophet ﷺ reached the battleground at night, he would never attack the enemy and would wait until the morning. During a battle the Prophet ﷺ stated, "I, the Prophet of Allah, Muhammad, establish the tradition of loving for the sake of Allah and of having animosity only for the sake of Allah," (not for the sake of oneself) [Bukhari].

The exaltedness of his exemplary character and of Muslims was witnessed when they forgave their staunchest enemies on the day they conquered Makkah, without bloodshed. The Muslims had suffered for over fifteen years at the hands of the Makkans. Prophet Muhammad ﷺ always forgave people when they harmed him personally, but he punished them when they disrespected the holy commandments of Allah ﷻ. He spent his life in achieving prominence for Allah ﷻ and for Islam. He never allowed his personal needs, wishes, and priorities to interfere with his work for Allah ﷻ.

The struggle for peace is an integral part of life, and striving for good and condemning evil, supporting right and confronting wrong, fighting for justice and eliminating injustice, etc. should continue throughout life. It is also a fact of life that no civilized society prefers war, but it is also a universal truth that honorable and courageous nations fight headlong with enemies of peace and those who cause aggression. When enemies dare to challenge peaceful nations, that is not the time to show courtesy or decency, but to show power and bravery. It is the battlefield that decides who gets thrown into the cave of obscurity and who emerges to be the victorious leader.

Empirical evidence and history show that until nations are not confronted, they cannot progress and reach the point of perfection. Without defending themselves, they are never able to secure and promote their cause. Islam is blamed for being spread by the power of the sword, when clearly there is no truth in this argument. Yes, Muslims defended themselves with the sword and resorted to it when the enemy failed to recognize the universality of Islam and tried through every means to destroy the *deen* (religion; way of life) of the Almighty. Islam, as a religion, was never spread by the sword, but by the character of its followers in every corresponding era. As more people became Muslim, the message of Islam was then carried by them to every corner of the world; certainly, it was not done by the sword.

Many biased scholars relate the spread of Islam to wars and bloodshed. Certainly, waging war and spilling blood is in the nature of man, and human history is full of bloodshed. If it happened at the hands of a few so-called Muslims, it should not be attributed to Islam. Because of someone's biased opinion, we simply cannot disregard the work of thousands of Muslims saints, sufis, and righteous scholars, who dedicated their life for the peaceful propagation of Islam and never utilized a sword for it. A sincere study of how Islam spread throughout the world will remove the ever so repeated contention that Islam was spread through the sword.

In fact, the merciful Prophet ﷺ never killed a soul with his own hand. He did not lay waste human lives like bloody war-mongers did throughout human history. He fought wars only to the extent necessary and revived humanity from eternal sicknesses. He showed respect even to a dead body and made it unlawful to deface or mutilate it. After all, for him, a human being was a human being; there was no distinction between friends and foes in that regard.

The set of instructions given by the Honorable Abu Bakr ﷺ upon dispatching an army to Syria (632 C.E.) is worth mentioning here.

> There you will find monasteries with monks in seclusion. Beware that you do not confront them; nor kill women, children, and elderly; nor cut down the date trees or any other trees; nor destroy any structures/property. [Bukhari]

Anyone with oratory and writing skills can cleverly distort the meanings of the verses of the Qur'an and the teachings of the Prophet ﷺ in support of their hidden agendas. Some have distorted the true meaning of jihad and presented it in a way opposite to what it actually is. However, any wrong interpretation of jihad does not change the fact that one meaning of jihad is "holy war."

With regards to jihad, I personally do not agree with the word "holy," because these days, almost everything has been turned upside down, and anything can be labeled "holy," and at the same time not reflect any holiness; however, jihad by sword is an "Islamic war," a "holy" one in its true sense. As I have explained before, any Muslim who does not do jihad with his base self to overcome his inner evils should not partake in armed jihad to achieve prominence for Islam. In any case, one cannot cross any of the numerous strict limitations in doing armed jihad. If he does, then his war cannot be called "Islamic war."

In my opinion, these days jihad by the pen should be the priority, but of course only by those who practice jihad with one's self. After all, one of the commandments of the holy Qur'an is:

> Call towards the way of your Lord with solid strategy and good counsel and debate with them in the most desirable manner… •
>
> [16:125]

This can most easily be done through speech/writing/literature.

Let me summarize by saying that the purpose of armed jihad is not to kill non-Muslims or terrorize them. The overall purpose of jihad is to bring people closer to Islam, so they may voluntarily accept it, enter into the spiritual realm of Islam, and find the inner peace they are searching for elsewhere. Who else will do this besides Muslims?

DIFFERENCE BETWEEN JIHAD AND TERRORISM

THE MOST IMPORTANT distinction between jihad and terrorism is that only the *ameer* (leader) of an Islamic government can declare armed jihad. When declared by an authority, it is an official declaration of war, unlike terrorism. The declaration of war is not hidden from any relevant party. Also, the governing authority that declares jihad makes sure that the rules of jihad are adhered to and monitor any violation. Certainly, all of this is not true for terrorism and for terrorists.

To put it simply, through jihad, a *mujāhid* seeks the pleasure of the Lord. Through terrorism, a terrorist intends to grossly please himself and to achieve despicable personal and political agendas. Terrorism, in no way, shape, or form, has any place whatsoever in Islam.

When sending his cousin, Ali 🕮 to a battle, Prophet Muhammad 🕮 said that:

> ...you must first invite people to Islam...If at your invitation, even one person embraces Islam; this is better for you than the wealth of the entire world. [Bukhari]

There is no such invitation to Islam in terrorism and in terrorizing. Terrorists do not require anyone to surrender to Allah 🕮; they only seek to wipe people out of existence.

A *mujāhid* sells himself to Allah 🕮 and according to the Qur'an, "Allah has bought his life in return for Heaven..." [Qur'an 9:111]. There is no way he would jeopardize this reward by following his personal desires, violating divine rules, or breaking the covenant between him and Allah 🕮 at any cost. On the other hand, a terrorist, by definition, cannot be in a covenant with Allah, nor is he promised any reward for his actions, nor is he bound by any of His rules. He is ferociously and barbarically pursuing personal agendas that have nothing to do with Islam, its principles, or its mission. Terrorists satisfy their madness and insanity by upsetting the peace in society through violent acts of terrorism. Islam strongly condemns such acts.

By no means is terrorism a part of Islam, and in no way can jihad be defined as terrorism. Islam does not support or approve of any personal definition of jihad, nor can anyone just adopt any means of defending Islam and Muslims and label it as being jihad.

A Muslim can only be a *mujāhid* if his intentions, from the time of preparing for battle to striking his opponents, are purely for Islam and for the sake of Allah 🕮 alone. If he deviates even slightly from this intent, he automatically deserts his Islamic duty and is in violation of the principles of jihad. At this point, his actions are no longer *fi sabilillah* (for the sake of the Almighty).

Terrorism is a mischief and an insurgency against peace, whereas jihad seeks to prevent and eliminate mischief and injustice and their perpetrators. Allah ﷻ commands:

> And kill them until there is no more terrorism left and all that remains is the *deen* (way of life; religion) of Allah, but if they refrain, then certainly Allah is watchful of what they do. • [Qur'an 8:39]

This verse clearly shows that the command to fight is to eradicate terrorism. Once terrorists give up and there is no more terrorism left, jihad against them ceases. Certainly, killing is involved in both terrorism and counterterrorism, but there is a vast difference in these killings. For example, a surgeon cuts through the body of a patient and a cold-blooded terrorist cuts his victim's throat. Could both of these acts be regarded as the same, where one intends to save life and the other takes life? No. Such is the distinction between jihad and terrorism.

Allah ﷻ states in the holy Qur'an:

> …he who kills anyone except as punishment for murder or for terrorist acts on earth, it is as if he killed all people. And whoever saves one life from dying, it is as if he kept alive all people… • [5:32]

It is the philosophy behind the act of saving or killing that is worth noting here; saving life makes one superior, and killing makes one fall below humanity, worse than a beast and not worthy of any reward. Terrorism results in disappointment and in being deprived of Allah's mercy and kindness here and on Judgment Day [Qur'an 11:85], whereas jihad results in mercy, kindness, and blessings from Allah ﷻ.

Allah ﷻ reveals in the holy Qur'an:

> Certainly, those who brought faith and those who migrated and did jihad in the way of Allah, they should hope for Allah's mercy, and Allah is All-Forgiving, All-Compassionate. • [2:218]

The Prophet ﷺ stated:

Anyone who hangs around in a marketplace with weapons to terrorize people, tomorrow on Judgment Day, fear will overcome him, because Allah does not like to terrorize His creation for no reason. For him is a dreadful torment of the Hellfire. However, anyone who makes jihad will enjoy the bounties of Heaven. [Bukhari]

Terrorism is cruel, oppressive, tyrannical, and unjust, whereas jihad benefits the oppressed and is done to establish justice and to overcome tyranny and cruelty. The wisdom behind jihad is to help the oppressed, not to bring oppression.

Allah ﷻ reveals in the holy Qur'an:

And why would you not fight in the way of Allah and for the weak men, women and children who supplicate, "O Sustainer, take us out from this community, whose inhabitants are oppressors, and make someone from Your mercy our supporter, and make someone from Your favor our helper." • Those who have embraced faith, they fight in the way of Allah, and those who have denied, they fight in the way of Satan; so fight against the followers of Satan. Certainly, Satan's strategy is weak. • [4:75-76]

Jihad is devised to help weak men, women, and children who cannot defend themselves. It is to free the oppressed people and nations, to make them independent, to free them from injustices, and to connect them to their Lord. There is no way anyone can truly relate terrorism to jihad or call terrorism a part of jihad. The difference between jihad and terrorism is like the difference between liberty and tyranny. Conflating terrorism with jihad is absurd and is based on ignorance of the meaning of jihad in Islam.

Terrorism is based on hatred, arrogance, insolence, etc., whereas jihad is rooted in humbleness, submissiveness, and humility. Allah ﷻ wants to see a *mujāhid* (one who performs jihad) in the battlefield as a true servant of Allah ﷻ, far removed from arrogance, filled with humility, and devoid of any pretense. On the other hand, a terrorist appears as a ferocious beast filled with pride, overflowing with arrogance, intoxicated with power, sunk in malice, and indiscriminately ready to destroy and blow up anything and everything that comes in his way. Whereas, Allah ﷻ commands the faithful on their way for jihad:

> Do not become like those who came out of their homes bragging and showing off to people… • [Qur'an 8:47]

Terrorism is devoid of faith, whereas jihad is the sign of unshakeable faith. Claims of faith must pass through a decisive test to see how a claimant fares. Generally, one first registers for a test. Similarly, a *mujāhid* is first required to register as a Muslim and then prove his claim of unshakeable faith in Islam through a test—the test of jihad. On the contrary, a terrorist does not have any faith, nor does he believe in tests. He expects great rewards; yet, he fails to register himself as a Muslim. A terrorist does not believe in Allah ﷻ, he believes in his own judgment and because of faithlessness he does not fear Allah ﷻ, nor does he abide by His rules. A terrorist has no support of faith, and he bases his ideas on faithless ideologies of his own making. A *mujāhid* is well rooted in the heavenly religion, has a purpose worth achieving, and is supported by the mercy and blessings of the Lord Almighty.

Terrorism is unlawful, immoral, undisciplined, and destructive, whereas jihad is lawfully uniform, disciplined, constructive, codified, and regulated by heavenly laws, not by man-made laws. In the holy Qur'an, Allah ﷻ commands the *mujāhideen* (pl. of *mujāhid*):

> O you who brought faith! When you came out to fight and strike in the way of Allah, continuously carry on the process of verifying (with whom you are fighting, so no injustice is done)… • [4:94]

Allah ﷻ further instructs them that he who greets them with *salām* (the greeting of "peace") and says that I am Muslim, they must believe him, respect his words, and not kill him [Qur'an 4:94].

With this, it is quite evident how Islam instructs the *mujāhideen* to observe every rule of jihad and carefully carry out every act. Even if there is one percent truth in what someone says and the rest cannot be verified, then accept that, leave the rest to Allah ﷻ, and move along.

A terrorist is not bound by laws and is not instructed by anyone to care for others; his sole mission is to cause chaos. The more blood he spills, the happier he is. The more people he terrorizes, the more successful he thinks he is, and the more innocent lives he takes, the greater satisfaction he draws from his cowardly behavior. Now, does it make any sense or is it just to equate jihad with terrorism?

A companion of the Prophet 🕌 once asked, "What if a *kāfir* (a disbeliever) attacks me in battle and cuts off my arm. I am a believer, and when I attempt to attack him, he recites the *kalimah* and embraces Islam. What am I to do then?" The Prophet 🕌 replied, "You should withdraw your sword. If you strike him after he recites the *kalimah* (declaration of faith), it will show that you have used your sword to take revenge and not to achieve prominence for Islam—through *Jihad fi Sabīlillah* (jihad for the sake of Allah 🕌). You will become like him as he was before (a *kāfir*), and he will become like you (a Muslim), as you were before you used your sword." [Muslim]

I hope I have made clear the difference between jihad and terrorism. Let me reassure you that there are clear principles of jihad. The above example eliminates the foundation of the propaganda that "Islam allows killings and Muslims enjoy it." The purpose of a *mujāhid* in jihad is completely opposite to that of a terrorist in terrorism: a terrorist is a criminal and must be categorized as one, while a *mujāhid* belongs to a higher state of piety and abstinence.

ISLAM AND EXTREMISM

EXTREMISM IS DEFINED BY The American Heritage Dictionary of the English Language as, a tendency to go to extremes or a case of going to extremes; an extremist is one who advocates or resorts to measures beyond the norms. Other various dictionaries mention the meanings of extreme as including the highest or farthest possible, far from moderate or moderation, very severe, farthest limits. The opposite of extremism and extremist is moderation and moderate, respectively.

The following is an overview of those Islamic teachings from which you can understand the relation of extremism to Islam. However, here is not the place for me to provide an in-depth analysis.

Now, if Islam allows or advocates for measures beyond the norm, then extremism exists in Islam, but if Islam allows and advocates for moderation, then there is no place for extremism in it. There is not a single aspect of Islam that passes for extremism; its every teaching and practice is nothing but moderate and practical. Thus, not finding support for extremism, even in one place, confirms that there is no place for extremism in Islam.

Islam is a way of life completely covering every aspect of life, including death and beyond. It contains sub-systems that perfectly fit into the entire system. Islam's systems of belief, worship, preaching, morality, justice, charity, defense, governance, politics, economics, and so on and so forth are uniquely cohesive. Like the parts of a machine, if any of its sub-systems are out of place or fail to fit together, it cannot function properly and will break down as soon as it is put to work. Islam, as a system of life, has worked and is working for billions of people. This in itself is sufficient proof that all of its sub-systems are cohesive and fit the mainframe.

Now, through the Qur'an and *sunnah*, we will see if there are any extremes in Islam. I would like to remind you once again that Islam fits perfectly with human nature. None of its principles demand any extraordinary or unusual act that human nature will not allow without going into extremes. For example, the worshiping process is neatly in-sync with the requirements of the body and soul. Every Muslim who lives by the teachings of the Prophet ﷺ lives a good, balanced, and moderate life and at the same time assures Allah's ﷻ pleasure.

Even though the purpose of man's creation is to worship the Lord, Islam does not demand its followers to be busy 24/7 in acts of direct worship and not to allocate time for life's other necessities. When all

the other necessary chores of life are fulfilled according to Allah's ﷻ
rules and commandments, they become acts of indirect worship. In this
way, the life of a follower easily becomes a life of constant worship.
This may seem extraordinarily demanding and burdensome at first,
but hundreds of millions of Muslims do it with ease, and once this
becomes routine, life molds accordingly. Thus, Muslims enjoy and
draw physical and spiritual benefits out of life without becoming
extremists of any kind.

Islam is a moderate religion. All of its practices are well-balanced,
and everything that it requires of its followers makes them humble,
sincere, and modest.

SALĀH: The most important acts of direct worship are the five
daily *salāh* (obligatory prayers of worship). *Fajr Salāh,* the one before
sunrise, only requires two *rakāh* (a set of prescribed acts of recitation,
standing, bowing, kneeling, and prostrating), not counting *sunnah*
prayers, because people have other activities of life to take care of and
time is usually of the essence in the morning. It only takes about five
minutes to perform *Fajr Salāh.* On the other hand, *Isha Salāh,* the fifth
one, beginning approximately two hours after sunset, has seventeen
rakāh, counting *sunnah* prayers. By this time, all daily activities are
fulfilled; therefore, people have more free time, are relaxed, and can
easily spare twenty minutes or so to perform *Isha Salāh.* This shows
that people's daily activities of life were considered even when prescribing the daily prayers. In this is a clear sign of moderation.

SAUM: Fasting in the entire month of Ramadhān is compulsory,
but Allah certainly knows that many of his servants are old, weak, sick,
or are traveling, so they are relieved of this obligation and granted the
flexibility to make up for the missed fasts at a later time or in some
cases to feed the poor two meals for every day not spent fasting. Fasting
is easy to observe by adjusting one's daily routine without going out of
the way or towards any extreme. Where fasting may feel burdensome,
flexibility has been granted, such as in the case of the sick and weak.

ZAKĀH: The obligatory act of giving one-fortieth of your wealth annually is *only* for those Muslims who possess a certain amount of wealth. *Zakāh* is not obligatory on poor Muslims, who in most cases are its recipients.

HAJJ: The pilgrimage to Makkah has been made obligatory on Muslims only once in their lifetime, provided that they have all the means necessary to undertake the trip and its expenses. It is not incumbent upon Muslims who cannot afford to do it.

It is interesting to know that a companion of the Prophet ﷺ asked him, "Is Hajj compulsory every year?" When the Prophet did not reply, he asked two more times, and then the Prophet ﷺ said, "No." He then added, "Do not keep asking me about something until I tell you myself. Had I said 'yes' to your question, Hajj would have become compulsory every year." [Muslim] The Prophet's silence shows that Islam does not want to put its followers under any kind of hardship, let alone towards any extreme.

QUR'AN: It is a blessing to know how to recite the holy Qur'an in Arabic, but besides the necessity of reciting a few verses in Arabic in the daily *salāh*, studying the Qur'an only in Arabic is not mandatory. It would be difficult for non-Arab Muslims to know the Qur'an only in Arabic. However, the more it is recited in Arabic, the greater the benefits. Either way, the flexibility to study the holy Qur'an through translations is there.

In other areas too, Islam recognizes the natural scope and limits of humanity. For example, it does not make incumbent upon all of its followers to become scholars of Islam, preachers, or sufis and to live monastic lives or reach spiritual heights. A Muslim is only required to know as much as is necessary to enable him to perform his duties. Certainly, the more he knows and practices, the greater his status and rewards. No matter how or where you look in Islam, you will not find any extremes in it.

In the Opening Chapter and in over forty other places in the holy Qur'an, Islam is referred to as *Sirāte Mustaqīm*. In *Al Mawrid*, a modern Arabic-English Dictionary, *sirāt* is defined as the way, path, or road, and *mustaqīm* means straight, direct, correct, or right. Therefore, *Sirāte Mustaqīm* means "The Straight Path," and when something is referred to as being straight, it is also the shortest way. Even the slightest deviation from the straight path is no longer the shortest path.

(This life) **A** ◀━━━━━━ *Sirāte Mustaqīm* ━━━━━━▶ **B** (Ultimate Success)

Any deviation from *Sirāte Mustaqīm* is an extreme or a step towards extremism. Islam does not support any kind of extremism because any extreme step or act is a deviation and cannot bring ultimate success. Islam is the moderate way of life and so are its teachings and philosophies. Allah states in the holy Qur'an:

> And without a doubt, this is My Way, the straight one; so walk on it, and do not walk on any other way, that it may lead you away from the way of Allah... • [6:153]

> And those who act against the Prophet—after that the straight path became evident to them, and began to follow against the norms of the faithful ones—so We will leave them as they are and throw them into Hell, and what a terrible place of return it is. • [4:115]

> This is because they remained divided from Allah and from His Prophet. And those who remain divided from Allah, so without a doubt, Allah is strict in punishing. • [59:4]

Regarding moderation in spending money, Allah states:

> And do not keep your hand tied up to your neck nor open it completely, that you may have to sit regretfully and sadly. • [17:29]

When they spend, (they) are neither extravagant nor stingy but remained balanced in between. • [25:67]

...eat and drink, and do not be extravagant. Certainly, Allah does not like those who are extravagant. • [7:31]

Regarding moderation in obeying His rules, Allah ﷻ states:

O you who have brought faith! Do not make *harām* (prohibited) the pure things Allah made *halāl* (permissible) for you, and do not transgress. Verily, Allah does not like transgressors. • [5:87]

Regarding being moderate in walking and talking, Allah ﷻ states:

And be moderate in the way you walk, and keep your voice low. Certainly, the most hideous voice is undoubtedly the voice of a donkey. • [31:19]

Allah ﷻ is also moderate in burdening His slaves.

Allah does not give command to anyone except to his capacity... • [2:286]

...Allah intends ease for you and does not like hardship for you... • [2:185]

When performing *salāh* (obligatory prayers of worship), be moderate when reciting.

...and do not be loud in your *salāh*, nor murmur in it; and maintain the course in their middle. • [17:110]

When taking revenge, Muslims must not resort to extremes.

...so whoever did injustice to you, then you may retaliate likewise against him with as much injustice as he did to you, and fear Allah and be certain that undoubtedly Allah is with those who practice self-restraint. • [2:194]

During jihad, *mujāhideen* must never cross the limits.

And fight in the way of Allah against those who fight with you, and do not do any injustice (to them); undoubtedly, Allah does not like those who do injustice. • [2:190]

Being modest in character brings forth good.

So it is, indeed, due to Allah's mercy that you became soft-hearted for them, and if you were of ill-disposition and hard-hearted, then assuredly, they all would have dispersed from around you; so forgive them and seek salvation for them, and ask for their advice on relevant matters… • [3:159]

And good and evil cannot be equal; keep away what must be kept away, with utmost goodness… • [41:34]

When preaching Islam, be modest and do not go to extremes.

Call towards the way of your Lord with solid strategy and good counsel and debate with them in the most desirable manner… •
[16:125]

Regarding modesty, the Prophet 鷺 said:

Modesty is a part of faith, and the place of faith is in Paradise.
[Ahmad and Tirmidhi]

Modesty produces nothing but good. [Bukhari and Muslim]

The believer is simple and generous, but the profligate is deceitful and ignoble. [Ahmad, Tirmidhi, and Abu Dawud]

Zaid bin Talha reported Allah's Prophet 鷺 as saying:

Every religion has a character, and the character of Islam is modesty. [Malik]

Ibn Umar reported the Prophet 鷺 as saying:

Modesty and faith are both companions. When one is taken away, the other is taken, too. [Baihaqi]

Allah's Prophet 鷺 further stated:

Make things easy and convenient; do not make them harsh and difficult. Give cheers and glad tidings, and do not create hatred.
[Bukhari and Muslim]

The Prophet 鷺 said:

Two qualities that Allah 鷺 prefers and loves are mildness and toleration. [Muslim]

It is even more evident now, from the above-mentioned verses and *ahadīth* that Islam summons all of humanity to come towards modesty and refrain from every extreme act. It commands its followers to be moderate in all that they do. Muslims who remain modest and avoid extremism maintain a balanced life. Islam condemns extremism and is against all extremist behavior, attitudes, and tendencies. Islam is *Sirāte Mustaqīm,* the Straight Path that takes those who walk upon it directly to Allah ﷻ, not away from Him.

Currently, because of the extremist behavior of some Muslims, the entire *ummah* (Muslims community) is suffering, and many have become skeptical of Islam. In all honesty, extremists of all sorts have jeopardized world peace. Had Muslims truly replicated the character of the Prophet with regard to tolerance, forgiveness and modesty, and had some self-proclaimed Muslims not walked blindly on the path of/to extremism, they would have avoided disaster. A sincere study of Islam, on the one hand, can save the world from the extremism of some extremists and on the other hand, remove the false notion that Islam advocates extremism and its followers are extremists.

IS FUNDAMENTALISM A PART OF ISLAM OR NOT?

*F*UNDAMENTALISM ORIGINATES FROM AND RESULTS in extremism, and it cannot have any place in Islam. Whenever fundamentalism emerged, it was the result of ideological extremism/radicalism. When fundamentalism was attempted or brought into practice, it resulted in radical behavior, extremist actions, chaos in society, disruption of the status quo, and widespread insecurity. Fundamentalism, because of its inherent nature, never brought or can ever bring any good to society. As stated earlier, there is no place in Islam for any kind of extremism, whether it is extremism of the mind or of the body, theoretical or practical

Let me make it very clear that fundamentalism has nothing to do with Islam. What is referred to these days as 'Islamic fundamentalism' is nothing but a political approach for political ends. I also acknowledge that fundamentalism is a complex subject and cannot be covered in such a short space. While it is somewhat unfair to leave this subject incomplete and ambiguous, it is also the case that a truncated and hasty coverage will not suffice. Certainly, this can become a future task.

CHAPTER 15

Equality of Mankind in Islam

QUALITY IS AN ESSENTIAL ASPECT OF A CIVILIZED and moral society. Only the claim that its foundation is based on the principles of equality is insufficient to ground a civilized society; its system must practically reflect that the notion of equality is deep-seated in its philosophy and constitution. The daily practices of its citizens and government must also clearly show that they abide by the principles of equality. Moreover, if the laws laid down automatically enable the citizens to have access to basic rights, then this society is truly founded on the principles of equality. In such a society, one basic function of the government is to oversee the enforcement of equality and to remove hurdles, in order for its citizens to enjoy basic human rights.

According to Islam, Allah ﷻ is the highest authority, and true sovereignty only belongs to Him. Allah ﷻ is the Lawmaker, and Prophet Muhammad ﷺ delivered and explained His divine laws to humanity. After the Prophet ﷺ, the governing authority that is in charge of the affairs of the Muslim *ummah* is the implementing arm of the divine laws.

Anyone, individually or collectively, who fails to implement the divine laws and to fulfill the ordained responsibilities, or who infringes on human rights, is liable not only in this world, but will also be subject to severe punishments in the Hereafter. As noted earlier, Muslims are obligated to respects the rights of Allah ﷻ as well as the rights of people. It is also to be noted that if the rights of Allah ﷻ are violated for one reason or another, Allah ﷻ may forgive the violator, except for the unrepented sins of *shirk* (polytheism) and *kufr* (infidelity). However, it has been clearly ordained and made certain that anyone who violates people's rights will see no forgiveness from Allah ﷻ on Judgment Day, until and unless forgiveness is granted from the victim first.

Allah ﷻ, while describing Judgment Day, reveals in the Qur'an:

> When the sun is wrapped up. • And when the stars have fallen. • And when the mountains are set in motion • ... **And when the girl, buried alive, • is asked for what sin was she murdered?** • ... Thus, everyone will know what they have sent forth. • [81:1-3, 8-9, 14]

Judgment Day will not be an occasion to deliver the abrogated rights of people, but to make 'just compensation' to the victims. If the violators are unable to give 'just compensation,' which will most certainly be the case, they will have to suffer severe torment for their sins and crimes against humanity.

The strict rules regarding the establishing and delivering of basic human rights clearly indicates that the equality of mankind and preservation of human rights are embedded in every relevant commandment of Allah ﷻ. In this respect, no other system on earth can compete with Islam.

Whoever commits crimes against humanity, whether Muslim or not, will have to pay for those crimes. Some face punishments in this world through various means, and some will face it after death in *Alam-e-Barzakh* (the transitory state, period/place), but ultimately all of them—if not forgiven—will meet their ultimate punishment in the Hereafter.

After the Declarations of Faith, the entire foundation and the practical implementation of Islam are based on the principle of the equality of all humankind. Islam not only discusses this theoretically, but through comprehensive commandments that automatically deliver basic human rights it ensures equality and justice to all. Moreover, in this regard, Islam demands strict adherence from its followers. To address the entire concept of equality of humankind and every field and philosophy related to it, Allah ﷻ simply states in the Qur'an:

> O people! Without a doubt, We created all of you from one male and one female and made you into different branches and different tribes, so you may get to know one another. Certainly, the most honored of you, in the presence of Allah, is he who is most fearful of Allah. Certainly, Allah is the All-Knowing, the All-Aware. • [49:13]

In such a short verse, the Qur'an explains it all, while learned men have written volumes to shed light on the same issue. The truth that all people are the progeny of one male and one female (parents) clearly explains that there is no other species of man that could have created even the slightest inequality among the humans. Being sons and daughters of one man and one woman automatically establishes inherent equality among humans.

We can also easily infer from the common origin of man that no sane mother and father would create any inequality among their children, nor would they devise any principle to create social classes among them. Since Islam was the faith of our "parents" (Adam السَّلَامُ عَلَيْهِ and Hawwa), had all of their children followed Islam, we would have saved ourselves from inequalities that have given birth to numerous societal ills. We must believe firmly in the fact presented in this verse, that we all share the same mother and father, before embarking on eradicating inequalities and injustices.

This verse and many others of the holy Qur'an clearly show that equality is the main ingredient of a healthy society. Allah ﷻ wants to see us flourish on Earth, and so, right from the beginning, He embedded the principles of equality among men. Why then would Islam not designate proper and necessary rights and bring justice to all when it intends to bring peace, prosperity, and true happiness so humankind can work their way to ultimate success? How can Islam be unjust to humans and expect their willful submission? How can Allah ﷻ call Himself just and then do injustice to humans? How can the All-Knower, All-Powerful, Most Compassionate, and Most Merciful contradict Himself by not establishing the necessary means to bring equality and justice among men?

People do not have to wait long to see the display of equality in Islam. For example, as soon as one enters into the folds of Islam, he witnesses equality in the performance congregational of *salāh*, where there is no distinction between kings and slaves, rich and poor; all stand shoulder to shoulder to bow down to the Supreme Lord, Allah ﷻ. There are no reserved spaces, even for kings, governors, or dignitaries, in mosques for the performing of prayers in congregation. If a common person comes first, he occupies the space in the first row, and if a king comes late, he has to settle himself in subsequent rows or spaces. Throughout Islamic history, this has been a normal practice, and this is also one of the most practical examples of equality.

The verse quoted earlier addresses all human beings, not just Muslims. Whether they belong to one nation or another, it does not make anyone inferior or superior. The diversity among peoples is for the sake of them being able to recognize each other and nothing more. According to Islam, distinction among people cannot be based on color, ethnicity, wealth, or any other worldly or physical factors, but only on piety. However, even distinction based on piety does not earn anyone special privileges or rights; no special treatment can be formally granted or demanded. Of course, piety has a higher status in the sight of Allah ﷻ, and that is not earned easily. The pious must be respected and dignified as long as the principles of equality are not disturbed.

The greatest display of equality in Islam can be witnessed during the annual occasion of Hajj (the holy pilgrimage), when millions of Muslims gather in Makkah, Saudi Arabia, from all over the world. Here, Muslim males wear two sheets of white cloth, and Muslim women wear simple clothes. Dressed in this manner, they circumambulate the Ka'ba, glorifying their Lord and His Oneness, and expressing their submission to Him. This is the greatest show of equality in Islam. No distinction whatsoever of wealth or status, prejudice or bigotry, superiority or inferiority, or discrimination based on color or race is apparent there. Here we see nothing but the reign of equality and the proof that black and white, Easterner and Westerner, and rich and poor are all children of the same parents, slaves of the Almighty Allah ﷻ. The Hajj is a unique experience and a unique display of equality that no other gathering of people can duplicate.

The gathering during Hajj shows that although pilgrims are Americans, Chinese, Russians, Indians, Europeans, Africans, or Arabs, in fact the unity of their character, actions, and purpose is proof that the Muslim *ummah* (community) is not a group of different nations, but one nation in itself. As long as distinctions based on color, ethnicity, and language exist, true peace cannot prevail. Islam claims that the differentiation of human beings based on nationality, ethnicity, color, language, etc. is a human innovation and that such innovations have nothing to do with any heavenly decree.

The Prophet ﷺ stated:

> All human beings are equal. They are equal as the teeth of a comb. There is no distinction or preference for Arabs over non-Arabs or non-Arabs over Arabs; nor black over white or white over black. In the sight of Allah, preference is based only on piety and righteousness. [Last Sermon of the Prophet, Appendix II]

The Qur'an commands the believers:

> O faithful ones! Let not any man mock another man; it is very possible that he may be better than those who mock. And let not

women (mock) other women; it is possible that they may be better than those who mock. And do not insult your own, and do not give bad names to each other... • [49:11]

The Prophet 🕌 taught his followers that:

> Without a doubt, Allah does not look at your status, nor does He look at your body or wealth. Verily, He continuously watches your heart, so whoever is a good-hearted one, Allah is pleased with him. Without a doubt, you are the progeny of Adam. And among you, whoever is pious is liked by Allah. [Mujma-ay-Zawaid]

He further stated:

> That all creations are like the family of Allah; Allah loves most whoever loves most His creatures. [Sunan Behaqi & Mishkat Al-Masabih]

It is now evident that true equality among people exists in Islam and that Islam does not reserve special preference for anyone. The Qur'an and *sunnah* clearly spell out that in Islam there is no place for inequality, racism, favoritism, prejudice, discrimination, or bigotry. Such vices are man-made and adhered to for selfish reasons. Islam teaches the removal of evils from society, so that the world can become a replica of Heaven, thereby allowing people to work towards the real Heaven. Islam does not give rise to evil, but eradicates it.

As mentioned earlier, the basic duty of a Muslim is to fulfill his duties towards Allah 🕌 and towards his fellow man. Islam emphasizes duties over rights because when duties are properly executed, human rights and freedoms are automatically fulfilled.

Similarly, the basic duty of an Islamic government is to ensure—on the basis of Islamic principles—equality for all of its citizens and to remove any and all inequalities from society. Any governing authority unable to fulfill this basic duty must cease to exist or be replaced. Often, governments and its officials escape justice for crimes against humanity and are not held accountable. Let me remind that Allah 🕌 is the Sole-Owner of Judgment Day and that no one will escape from His sight and avoid deserved punishment. Therefore, there is more benefit in being just with people than there is in being oppressive.

Worldly laws provide limited accountability and often even that is escapable. Sometimes, it is difficult to differentiate between lawbreakers and lawmakers, and in the end the poor citizens suffer. Islam provides strict rules to bring justice and encourages people to fight for their rights and against injustice. Islam designates higher rewards for striving for justice; however, if a victim chooses to be patient or is unable to acquire justice, Allah ﷻ promises just compensation in this world and/or in the Hereafter.

According to a *hadīth* narrated by Abdullah ibn Amr:

> A true Muslim is one from whose hands and mouth other Muslims are safe. [Bukhari]

This infers that a true Muslim is one who fulfills the rights of Allah ﷻ as well as the rights of people.

In another *hadīth*, the Prophet ﷺ said:

> Allah does not bless a nation among which a weak man is not given his right. [Bukhari]

Equality is further exemplified by the rights Islam grants to all.

RIGHT TO LIFE

*T*HE RIGHT TO LIFE IS THE MOST IMPORTANT of all human rights. Islam guarantees this right from the state of fetus to the last breath of human life. It has made the life of a human – Muslim and non-Muslim – sacred. Indiscriminate bloodshed and killing of human beings are the worst crimes in Islam, for which the ultimate accountability is inescapable and quite painful. I have discussed this right in Chapter 13, "The Value of Life and Its Preservation in Islam."

RIGHT TO LIBERTY

*T*HE RIGHT TO LIBERTY, TO BE FREE, IS AN INALIENABLE natural right of man. When any right is referred to as a 'natural right,' it means that people are born with it; the simple fact of their existence gives them this natural right. Since Allah ﷻ is his Creator, it means that Allah 🕮 Himself gave people this natural right to liberty, and since Islam is the religion of Allah 🕮, it ensures that this natural

Societies can make every arrangement to set man free and not make him its slave, but who is stopping him from becoming a slave of society and, in almost all cases, a slave of his own self, a slave of his wants and desires?

right is not abrogated. It follows then, that we, as people, do not grant or allocate natural rights but are only to protect them. People should, as they have already done, make necessary arrangements to protect these human rights.

Islam is many steps ahead of human societies, because its divine values and commandments are ordained in such a way that man cannot even deprive himself of these rights, let alone abuse others' natural rights. Societies can make every arrangement to set man free and not make him its slave, but who is stopping him from becoming a slave of society and, in almost all cases, a slave of his own self, a slave of his wants and desires? Such societies may set man free by ensuring his right to be free, but who can prevent free people, out of their own choice, from becoming slaves to society and surrendering to it?

Islam, through its teachings, makes sure that man does not choose to become a slave of society. It also lays down rules so that society cannot take a shape where it leaves man with no choice but give up his right to be free. Through these arrangements, Islam sets man free from all kinds of slavery so that he can submit himself to Allah 🕮 and can submit his will to the will of Allah 🕮, because it is not possible to demand complete submission without first setting man totally free from all other bondage.

Man cannot simultaneously submit himself to himself, his society, and the Almighty; he must choose one. Anyone who totally and voluntarily submits his will to the Almighty can never become a slave of society or of himself, and he truly stays free from all other bondage. On the other hand, whoever voluntarily or involuntarily submits to society or to himself can never obtain true freedom, everlasting happiness, and ultimate success.

Islam first sets man free and then demands submission for his own good. Others also promise freedom, but end up resulting in all types of bondage in which man cannot achieve true success, here or in the Hereafter. How is this so? This is because, in the first case, He is Allah ﷻ, the Almighty and Our Creator,

> *By becoming a slave of the Supreme Being, man becomes superior to everything else, and nothing remains in the world to enslave him. When there is nothing to enslave him, man becomes truly liberated.*

Who sets us free and, after we submit to Him, keeps us in His bondage, in order to give us success in this life and in the Hereafter. He has all the power and knowledge to do so. In contrast, in the second case, the entity/system that promises freedom and success is weak and has no control over anything or, at the very least, what is beyond the visible.

Man ought not to submit to any weaker body/being, but he should submit to the Supreme Being, Who saves him from all types of humiliation, pain, and suffering, and Who brings him true peace, happiness, prosperity, and ultimate success. By becoming a slave of the Supreme Being, man becomes superior to everything else, and nothing remains in the world to enslave him. When there is nothing to enslave him, man becomes truly liberated.

The Islamic society was not created to enslave man, nor does man inadvertently become its slave; instead, by accepting the enslavement and bondage to Allah ﷻ, he truly begins to serve humanity. By having man in His bondage, Allah ﷻ does not draw personal benefits or services, but through this servitude man is set free from all bondage and truly acquires his right to liberty. Islam brings real freedom to man and sets him free.

RIGHT TO HAPPINESS / PURSUIT OF HAPPINESS

*I*SLAM FULLY RECOGNIZES THIS RIGHT OF MAN and helps him throughout his life to achieve it. As a prerequisite, to achieve

What is acquired can be lost, but what the Lord grants is permanent and never fades away. Pursuing happiness by way of material gains is a risky business, and, even if achieved, it is not permanent and can be lost at any time.

happiness or to embark in its pursuit, man must first know what happiness is, where it lies, and how to acquire it. If he does not know this, how can he acquire it? Any misconstrued meaning of happiness will cause all pursuit to go in vain and, because of the loss of time and energy, he may be unable to re-embark on the path to true happiness. Thus, coming to understand the concept of *true* happiness is crucial for its pursuit to be fruitful.

Man consists of a body and a soul and was created in such a way that he cannot taste true happiness by just fulfilling his physical and material needs; his spiritual needs must also be fulfilled. Only the Creator truly knows how man can acquire happiness, because He is the Creator of both man's body and soul, and only He knows their exact requirements. In the absence of His help, guidance, and direction, man on his own cannot achieve anything, let alone true happiness. Experience shows and millions of people can testify that even after having access to worldly wealth, satisfying physical or material needs and desires, and unlimited pursuits, true happiness has not been achieved, and the soul is still not in peace or at rest.

Happiness comes when an individual achieves his goals, acquires his needs, and fulfills his wishes. If his achievements fall short of his expectations—meaning that he does not acquire the pleasure he expected or that the luxury he attempted to attain did not bring any change or comfort in his life—then the happiness quickly fades away. Man is weak and does not have control over life's circumstances. Many times circumstances change by the time he achieves his goals, or the results turn out to be less than what was expected. Many other factors can become obstacles to happiness, and its pursuit can go to waste. A fruitful pursuit is that which results in permanent and everlasting happiness; it does not go away with the passage of time or a change in circumstances, and such happiness is worth pursuing. To pursue happiness that is not permanent or that fades away easily is a waste of time and effort.

True peace and happiness cannot be acquired, it can only be granted by the Lord Almighty. What is acquired can be lost, but what the Lord grants is permanent and never fades away. Pursuing happiness by way of material gains is a risky business, and, even if achieved, it is not permanent and can be lost at any time. On the other hand, pursuing happiness from the pleasure of the Almighty is a wise choice and the safest way to true happiness. When the Lord is pleased, peace of heart and true happiness are assured. The pursuit of true happiness in Islam, through pleasing Allah ﷻ, never goes in vain. Every believer has the right to acquire this happiness. Allah ﷻ clearly reveals in the holy Qur'an:

> It is He Who sent down tranquility in the hearts of Muslims so that they may advance in their beliefs in faith… • [48:4]

Allah ﷻ reaffirms that:

> All those who believed—and their hearts find contentment in the remembrance of Allah—without a doubt, in the remembrance of Allah, hearts find contentment. • All those people who believed and did righteous deeds, for them are glad tidings and a good end. •
>
> [13:28-29]

> Absolutely, Allah certainly became pleased with the Muslims when they were swearing allegiance to you under the tree, so He knew all that was in their hearts, then sent down tranquility upon them, and rewarded them with the acquisition of victory soon. • [48:18]

When true followers, servants, and slaves voluntarily fulfill their obligations to the Master and properly follow the rules and regulations He laid down, they attain a unique pleasure that is only felt by them and that cannot be described in words. Constantly observing religious obligations and constantly worshipping strengthen the spiritual connection to the Lord and result in wholesome satisfaction, peace of heart, and true happiness. This pursuit towards man's origin leaves no

Material bonds reduce the true and permanent pleasure of the soul and mind to mere animalistic, bodily, and temporary pleasures, which fade away very quickly and must be re-acquired soon.

vacuum in life because, as he eventually connects to his Master, the Source, his heart becomes fully content. The complete presence of his Master in his heart brings true and everlasting happiness, which instantly becomes a part of his body and soul and never separates from him ever again, even upon death when the body and soul separate,

because both are at peace. He thus acquires total happiness and the pursuit ceases.

In Islam, one does not have to do anything extraordinary to acquire happiness; just by practicing acts of direct and indirect worship, a follower not only fulfills the religious requirements, but he also auto- matically receives happiness, satisfaction, and unique pleasures. Islam does not prohibit going after the happiness of this world, nor is it against material pleasures, but it does make these things of secondary importance. A believer is commanded to attain higher pleasures, to seek higher status, and to free himself from any material bondage that reduces true happiness to artificial happiness. Artificial happiness hides one's actual state, which is full of sorrows. Material bonds reduce the true and permanent pleasure of the soul and mind to mere animalistic, bodily, and temporary pleasures, which fade away very quickly and must be re-acquired soon.

RIGHT TO RELIGION

*M*ANY THINK THAT ISLAM IS AN INTOLERANT RELIGION that refuses to co-exist with others' beliefs. I must tell you right now that this is not true, and I also expect that by now you must have realized this yourself. In fact, the well-documented history of Islam shows that it is by its very nature a tolerant religion.

Islam's focus is on quality, not quantity; compulsion, coercion, and forced conversion cannot bring quality. People who choose to embrace Islam only benefit themselves; Islam neither gains anything from anyone's conversion, nor does it lose anything by anyone's exit from it. There is no doubt that those who find great benefit in Islam truly become compassionate and wish for others to enjoy the same. Islam intends to give a true purpose to people's lives by bringing them (alive) under its umbrella, not by turning them into dead bodies through coercion and compulsion. It does not intend to increase its membership to be the biggest organization of human bodies; it intends to bring quality to peoples' lives.

Thus, it lays down the principle of freedom of religion and makes all the arrangements to protect and safeguard it. The very justification for not coercing people into Islam is evident in the following verses:

> There is no compulsion in *deen* (religion). Certainly, guidance is set apart from apostasy. So whoever rejects the Satan and believes Allah, then, surely, he has grasped a strong latch; for him there is no kind of defeat. And Allah is All-Hearing and All-Knowing. • [2:256]

> And if your Lord so wills, then all inhabitants of earth would bring faith, each and every one. So will you then force people to the point they become Muslim? And there is no one who can embrace faith without the will of Allah... • [10:99]

These verses clearly show that Islam is tolerant of others' beliefs and that Islam does not obligate Muslims to convert anyone into Islam via force. Further, Islam also prohibits disrespecting and insulting other people's deities.

> And do not speak ill of those (idols and false gods) that they call upon besides Allah... • [6:108]

Allah ﷻ directs Muslims to act in the following manner:

> Call towards the way of your Lord with solid strategy and good counsel, and debate with them in the most desirable manner... •
> [16:125]

And if they (non-Muslims) do not pay attention, say to them:

For you is your own way and for me is Allah's *deen* (religion; way of
life). • [109:6]

With the Lord's grace, everyday thousands of people find true
peace under the umbrella of Islam; there is no need for any
compulsion or coercion.

RIGHT TO PRIVACY

*T*HE IMPORTANCE OF PRIVACY and the effects of its violation
can only be truly understood by those whose privacy has been
violated. Everything deemed personal to us is our private matter, until
and unless we choose to share it with others. If personal information
is entrusted to someone and they have not been permitted to pass it
along or make it public, it must be guarded and kept confidential.
Privacy is an individual's right unless it is given up for one reason or
another, or unless it is surrendered at the demand of legitimate
governing authorities.

In America, I hear on an almost daily basis that the government
and social and business organizations adamantly ensure privacy and
inform their people/clients about guarding it. What a relief it is to
live in a society where the government guarantees and guards the
privacy of its citizens! Unfortunately, this is not the case in many
other countries.

To protect the dignity and well-being of individuals, Islam issued
heavy decrees some 1500 years ago to safeguard privacy and related
matters. The Lord Himself is the protector of our privacy, dignity
and well-being.

Allah ﷻ states in the holy Qur'an:

O Muslims! Do not enter into homes other than your own,
until you have taken permission and greet the residents with *'salam'*
(peace). This is better for you, if you think. Then, if you do not find
anyone there, so do not enter therein until permission is granted to

you. And if you are told to go back, so go back; this is more virtuous for you. And Allah knows whatever you do. • [24:27-28]

These verses certainly prohibit intrusion into people's privacy and safeguard their right to privacy. Each and every word of Allah ﷻ is deeply immersed in wisdom. Hence, all necessary and relevant rules and etiquettes can be formulated based on these foundational verses regarding privacy.

According to a *hadīth*, peeking into houses, looking into them from the outside, reading someone's letter/mail without permission, and erecting houses higher than your neighbor's houses with the intent to see into them are all strictly prohibited. Under Islamic laws of privacy, even if a victim knocks out the eye of an intruder, he will not be punished. [Tirmidhi] Even a blind person is not allowed to enter a house without the permission of its owner, because, even though he is unable to see anything, he can certainly hear private matters, which amounts to an invasion of privacy.

Furthermore, Muslims must get permission before entering their parent's home. Just look how specific this ruling is, in that it states that if a child/minor answers a person's call and gives permission to enter a home, that person should not enter it. Permission to enter is only valid if granted by an adult, preferably the owner. Moreover, one should not have hard feelings if on occasion permission is not granted.

In another *hadīth* it is stated that if a Muslim illegally searches through the property and/or life of a Muslim brother, then Allah ﷻ will seek into his private life on Judgment Day and disgrace him (as he did to his brother) [Muslim and Tirmidhi]. However, for lawful purposes and in certain emergencies, if the motive is not to invade privacy, entering into a house and searching through personal items without permission is allowed to the extent necessary.

Moreover, by also strictly prohibiting backbiting, Islam safeguards people's privacy (more on backbiting in Chapter 21, *Virtues and Vices*).

RIGHTS OF OTHERS

*U*NLIKE MANMADE SYSTEMS, ISLAM EXPLICITLY establishes the rights of others, including relatives, neighbors, and so on, that must be fulfilled by every individual and/or the society at large. By carefully examining and analyzing each right and the demands to fulfill it, one can clearly see the kind of caring and sharing society that Islam intends to build. Suffice it to say, Allah ﷻ reveals:

> They ask you as to what they should spend. Say, "Whatever you give to help parents, relatives, orphans, the wayfarer, and the needy is good, and whatever good you do, certainly Allah knows of it." •
>
> [Qur'an 2:215]

> So give to the relatives their right and to the needy and to the wayfarer. This is better for those who desire Allah's mercy, and such people are successful. • [Qur'an 30:38]

> And worship Allah, and do not make anyone His partner. And do good to parents and relatives, and (do good) to orphans, the needy, and your neighbors, whether they are near or unfamiliar to you, and to the companion by your side and to the wayfarer, and to those who are under your custody. Undoubtedly, Allah does not like he who brags and boasts... • [Qur'an 4:36]

Not just society as a whole, but every individual Muslim is required to fulfill the rights of others to the best of his ability and knowledge. Those who go out of their way and go beyond their means to bring peace and ease of life to others receive greater rewards and status from Allah ﷻ.

RIGHTS OF NEIGHBORS

*I*SLAM PLACES GREAT EMPHASIS ON THE RIGHTS OF neighbors. Regardless of their religious affiliation, neighbors have distinct rights, and Muslims are obligated to fulfill them.

The Prophet 🕌 stated that the rights of neighbors were so greatly stressed that he thought neighbors might also become heirs in inheritance. [Tirmidhi] The Prophet 🕌 explained that the inhabitants of the 70 houses around your house are your neighbors. With such brevity, what a network of cooperation the Prophet 🕌 established among the people. Such a great network of communal relationships is built not to promote conflict or to sow hate, but to increase cooperation and mutual love. Without involving any governing authority, building such an intricate web of cooperation and care among peoples is the specialty only of Islam.

Rich and developed societies, in which modern mechanisms are in place to deal to a certain extent with people's problems and emergencies, may not truly understand the need for neighborly cooperation. However, throughout human history, poor nations and communities have benefited from such Islamic principles of cooperation. Even today, in many parts of the world, if neighbors will not help each other to cope with problems of everyday life, it will bring hardship and misery to their society.

In times of both joy and sadness, neighbors can be helpful and beneficial to each other. During illness, emergency, economic hardship, death, and other tragedies, cooperation among neighbors results in immediate comfort and helps bring life back to normal. Even in times of celebration, the company of neighbors can bring greater happiness and love.

Sometimes, governmental authorities may not know of or may take longer to learn and respond to a situation, but in most cases neighbors can be there to respond and help immediately. On many occasions people become victims of bureaucracy, red tape, and other injustices such that, even if the government is able to help, it may never do so. Usually, neighbors know each other well, and nothing prevents them from helping in times of need. When neighbors respond in such times, favors are returned, and this continues to bring peace, happiness, and prosperity to all.

To sum up this section, let me quote two *ahadīth*:

When you prepare special foods, share with your neighbors (especially the poor ones). When you bring home fruits, share with your neighbors, and if by any chance you do not have enough to share, then at least do not throw its peelings outside your door so that the children of your poor neighbor may see them and become sad for not having the same. [Tirmidhi]

He whose neighbor sleeps with an empty stomach is not a believer. [Abu Dawud]

BROTHERHOOD IN ISLAM [QUR'AN 49:10]

A MUSLIM IS NOT A *MOMIN* (true believer) if he does not choose for other Muslims what he chooses for himself. Do not give to your brother what you would not take for yourself. Do not turn back your brother if you are able to help. To one who is kind to people on earth, Allah ﷻ will be kind on Judgment Day. The one who is not grateful for favors from his brother cannot be grateful to Allah ﷻ. Such teachings and commandments of the Qur'an and *sunnah* form the foundations for universal brotherhood in Islam. The following are the six duties a Muslim must fulfill towards another Muslim. [Bukhari]

(1) To greet each other with "*assalamu alaykum*" meaning, "peace be upon you," to which the reply is, "may peace be upon you too."

(2) To accept the invitation when invited for a feast.

(3) To show solicitude to him, when he expects it from you.

(4) To respond with *yarhamukullah* ("may Allah be kind to you") when hearing a Muslim say *alhamdūlillah* ("all praise be to Allah") after sneezing.

(5) To visit him when he is sick.

(6) To attend his funeral, pay last respects, and accompany the deceased to the cemetery.

When the persecutions by the Quraysh became unbearable, the Prophet 🕊 and his companions migrated to Madinah. The Muslims of Madinah, later called *Ansār* ("those who helped") extended themselves and divided in half everything they owned to give to the *Muhajirūn* (the migrants). This charitable act was unprecedented and has yet to be duplicated. Such unique brotherhood, as created by the Prophet 🕊, led the two separate peoples to become united forever under the banner of Islam. This could not have been possible without respect for human rights, equality, and justice.

JUSTICE IN ISLAM

*I*N A SOCIETY, EQUALITY CANNOT BE ACHIEVED without justice and the rule of law. Justice is such an integral need of human life that, to acquire it, people often willingly sacrifice their other rights.

The entire structure of Islam rests on justice. Allah 🕊 is Just, His prophets brought justice, and the Qur'an contains commandments of justice; hence, justice is a priority in Islam. Justice with oneself, justice in society, and justice for all are the basic teachings of Islam. In fact, the main purpose of Judgment Day is to bring justice to people and people to justice.

In the holy Qur'an, Allah 🕊 directs to do justice:

...and when you speak, say what is just, even if it is (in the case of) your relative... • [6:152]

O those who have brought faith! Stand firmly for justice for the sake of Allah, when testifying, even if it be upon yourselves or your parents and immediate relatives. Whether they are wealthy or poor, Allah is near both of them; thus, do not be led by lust that you stray from justice. And if you do not speak clearly or deny it altogether, so undoubtedly, whatever you do, Allah is aware of it. • [4:135]

O those who have brought faith! Establish yourself for Allah by being testifiers of justice. And let not the enmity of a people ever incite you to disregard justice. You do justice; it is very close to piety, and fear Allah. Certainly, whatever you do, Allah is aware of it. • [5:8]

Certainly, Allah commands you to give the trusts to their rightful owners. And when deciding among the people, decide with justice... • [4:58]

And do not consume each other's wealth unjustly, and do not take matters to court with the intent to illegally consume people's wealth, knowingly. • [2:188]

...and he who was slain unjustly, so We gave his kin the right, so he too must not exceed the limits in killing; that he has been helped. • [17:33]

As a final note on Islam's notion of justice, equality, and human rights, have a close look at the Prophet's ﷺ Last Sermon (Appendix II).

Finally, I would like to add here that it is a common practice of people to sow discord in order to divide man from man, making it easy to rule over them. This policy of "divide and rule" is and has been applied all over the world by powerful people and nations to subjugate others and thus extract all kinds of material benefits. Islam applies a different policy: it *unites people with love* and *rules over their hearts*, not for its own benefit, but for the greater good of humanity. This unity of people and their greater good are not possible without genuine equality and true justice.

Muslims who are in power and do not rule with justice will be held accountable on Judgment Day and cannot escape punishment for their injustices. Islam is not to blame for their abuse of power and un-Islamic behavior. Divine justice awaits everyone: Muslims and non-Muslims. It is said that the Day of Judgment will last fifty thousand years, which is plenty of time for justice to be served.

CHAPTER 16

Women in Islam: Status and Role

THE STATUS AND ROLE OF WOMEN IN ISLAM is inquired into more than any other matter. This is certainly a delicate subject. I request the reader to pay close attention, and proceed with an open-mind.

Islamic rules and regulations were given 1400 years ago and they had to define comprehensively and provide for every aspect of life. The laws and principles had to take into consideration people's psyche and habits, environment and circumstances, qualities and short-comings, nature and choices, needs and wishes, and natural urges and inner desires (good/bad) before prescribing to people a system of life. Had Islam not addressed even the smallest aspect or left anything unclear, it would not have qualified as the complete way of life. If there was a chance for something to happen, even once in a person's lifetime, Islam had to offer guidance for it.

The status and role of women in society are important issues for which Islam has provided all related rules, rights and guidance. In fact, in many ways, Islam is the only religion to do so. Not only in theory, Islam practically uplifted women's status nearly 1400 years ago, and for the first time in human history she felt her true being.

When the holy Qur'an mentions someone or something, it carries great importance. Given this, we can imagine how important the role, status, rights, and duties of women are that an entire chapter in the holy Qur'an is dedicated to women, namely *Sura an-Nisa'* (The Woman). It is the fourth chapter and the third longest in the Qur'an.

The general idea among non-Muslims and even among some modern Muslims is that in Islam women are not equal to men and are treated as second-class citizens. This idea is wrong, and it is based on misconceptions and, to some extent, ignorance. The holy Qur'an clearly states that there is *no* distinction among people, except on the basis of their piety [Qur'an 49:13]. The more pious a man or woman is, the more distinct and praiseworthy he or she is in the sight of Allah ﷻ.

Both men and women are creatures of Allah ﷻ and were created for the same purpose: to worship Him, specifically through the role(s) assigned to them. How then can one be treated differently than the other? Both men and women are slaves of Allah ﷻ, not slaves of each other. They both have to play distinct and essential roles in society as prescribed by the Lord. These roles are assigned according to their capacity and capability, and they are reflective of their physical, psychological, and biological makeup. To assign us the proper role befitting our nature, who else is a better judge than our Lord, Who created us, and who else knows our qualities better than our Lord?

If we demand more than what is assigned to us or perform less than what is required and necessary of us, then we are in clear violation of the oath we took, as His creatures, on the day He asked us, "Am I not your Lord?" whereupon, we all said "Yes..." [Qur'an 7:172]. It is also a violation of the contract we, as Muslims, made with Him on the day we willfully submitted to Him and agreed to obey Him and not to disobey Him. Both men and women ought to assume their roles as assigned by the Lord and perform them accordingly [Qur'an 16:91].

VERIFYING EQUALITY

*T*O VERIFY WHETHER EQUALITY EXISTS among women and men in Islam, one must first find out: Do women's basic rights differ from men's? Are they underprivileged or considered inferior beings? Are they treated differently as persons in acquiring justice, respect, and dignity, both in a household (as a mother, wife, sister, or daughter) and in society? Are they treated differently in receiving rewards and punishments and in achieving status and compensation? If the answer to such questions is yes, then women are not equal to men in Islam, and they are subject to limitations of their rights and freedoms to which men are not. If the answer is no, which is the case, then there certainly is equality between them. However, their roles and functions in life are different. These differences are necessary to keep society balanced and progressing in the right direction.

Allah ﷻ, through His divine wisdom, assigned some different functions and roles to women. The allocation of different roles to women does not make them inferior to men. If Muslim women think of themselves as inferior, it could be because of the lack of proper Islamic knowledge and understanding of their rights or because of social and cultural factors that have nothing to do with Islam. I strongly believe that Islam is not to blame for their situation.

Islam has done everything reasonably possible for women to live a happy life and enjoy the equality that Allah ﷻ granted them. Islam gives them the right to demand their rights whenever necessary, and it fully supports them. If, for one reason or another, they do not fight for their rights, Islam is not to be blamed. If some so-called Muslim societies' un-Islamic culture or customs suppress women and their rights, such behavior should not be referred to as Islamic.

I hold Muslim men entirely responsible for sometimes making women feel insecure, inferior, degraded, depressed, and weak. Muslim men who do not treat women with due respect and dignity are ignorant of Islamic teachings and principles regarding women's status, and they are not acting in an Islamic manner. They will not only pay for this unequal and unjust behavior in this world, but they will also be held accountable on Judgment Day. Ignorance is no excuse. I can guarantee, on the basis of Islamic knowledge and personal experience, that wherever men and women are fully aware of their rights and duties and abide by all the rules pertaining to their roles, they are enjoying a heavenly life on earth.

EQUALITY WITH MAN

*I*N THIS REGARD, ALLAH ﷻ REVEALED CLEAR VERSES to show how men and women are obligated to each other and must lawfully deliver their duties and uphold mutual rights.

Allah ﷻ states in the holy Qur'an:

Whoever does a righteous deed, man or woman, and they are a believer, so certainly, We will keep them alive in a state of righteous life and surely, We will give them their reward, befitting their best deeds. • [16:97]

O people! Without a doubt, We created all of you from one male and one female and made you into different branches and different tribes... • [49:13]

And this is from among His signs that He created for you pairs from within you, so you may find comfort in them. And created between you love and mercy. Undoubtedly, in this, indeed, are signs for those who think. • [30:21]

O people! Fear your Lord, Who created you from a single soul, and created from that soul its mate, and spread from both of them many men and women... • [4:1]

Through these verses and many others, we clearly see that there is no inequality between men and women. Both are equal in causing the spread of humankind on earth. Without partnering with women, men could not have done it alone. The terms 'mate' and 'pair' clearly define their inherent equality. The credit for populating the earth goes to them equally, although ultimate praise is for Allah 🕌.

EQUALITY IN RIGHTS

Allah 🕌 states in the holy Qur'an:

> ...and women, too, have rights (over men), as they (men) have rights over them (women) legally. But men have a degree (of advantage) over them. And Allah is powerful and wise... • [2:228]

That "men have a degree (of advantage) over them" simply refers to the physical advantages that men have due to their physique. It also refers to the fact that men are saddled with the responsibility and duty to bear the financial burden of their families and to provide the essentials of life, making men the natural overseer of the family's internal and external matters. However, if the wife is working outside the home and contributing to the family income, then both share this "degree (of advantage), and women receive greater reward for sharing his responsibilities.

In any group or organization, there is always a single person (i.e., leader, CEO, president) who is appointed the head, regardless of the size and scope of that entity. This makes him/her superior in terms of leadership over every other member of the organization. Similarly, there is nothing wrong in that Allah 🕌 grants man a "degree (of advantage)" along with added responsibilities and duties. This does not make women inferior by any means.

However, to make sure that man will not abuse his "degree (of advantage)" and abrogate the rights of women, Allah 🕌 first stated that "Women, too, have rights," meaning that these rights are not to be violated. The verse ends with "Allah is powerful and wise," which can be taken to signify that even though man was granted a "degree (of advantage)," Allah 🕌 is still dominant. If man abuses his powers, Allah 🕌 will punish him. Furthermore, when Allah 🕌 refers to

Himself as "wise," He means that superiority is not given to men to rule over women and make her inferior, but Allah 𐎓 very wisely designated specific powers and duties to men and women for their own benefit, for the benefit of their family, and ultimately for the greater good of society.

WOMEN ARE NOT INFERIOR TO MEN

*T*HE FOLLOWING VERSES FROM THE HOLY QUR'AN illustrate the status of women at the time when the holy Qur'an was revealed. Allah 𐎓 states:

> When anyone among them is given the good news of a daughter, so all day his face darkens, and he is full of angst. • He hides himself in shame from his community, on account of the unpleasantness of this good news. Should he keep her in disgrace or bury her alive in the ground? Look, how terribly do they judge! • [Qur'an 16:58-59]

Up until the time of the Prophet 𐎓, burying daughters alive in their infancy was a common practice of some Arab tribes. Islam put a complete end to this practice. Not too long ago, in India, when husbands died, their widow was required to be burned alive along with the husband's corpse. This was a Hindu ritual known as *sati,* which was only outlawed in 1829.

In Islam, a female, whether a newborn or a widow, is not in any way a disgrace either to an individual Muslim man or to Muslim society at large. She is a being independent of men and is not at the disposal of men or society. She cannot be buried alive or burned by the side of her deceased husband. In fact, Islam permits her to remarry, so that she and her children may live under the protection of a legitimate husband/father figure.

In the verse quoted above, Allah 𐎓 means that a woman is not an inferior being such that, at her birth, one is to become sad and grieve. These days, some people even pay large sums of money to know if the unborn fetus is a male or female, and the news of a male child often brings great joy. After learning of the gender, many unwillingly agree to give birth to females, and many even resort to abortion. If Muslims are saddened at the news of a baby girl, this is not because of Islam, it is because of their ignorance of Islam.

According to a Prophet's *hadīth*, daughters are a mercy from Allah ﷻ [Abu Dawud]. In another *hadīth*, it is said that when a father gets two of his daughters married successfully, Heaven is guaranteed for him [Muslim]. The Prophet ﷺ further stated that the best charity is to care for the daughter who was returned to you (divorced/widowed) and has no means of earning a living [Mishkat]. On the other hand, there will be severe punishment for those who bury their daughters alive. A similar consequence will be for those who consider a female child a burden, are disgraced by them, and fail to treat them as equal to their male children. Allah ﷻ reveals the horror of Judgment Day:

> And when the oceans are provoked, • when the souls are reunited, • **when the girl buried alive is asked** • **for what sin was she murdered,** • when the registers of deeds are laid open, • when the sky is stripped of its skin, • and when Hell is set ablaze • and Heaven is brought near, • then everyone will come to know what it has sent forth. • [Qur'an 81:6-14]

This is a serious matter. Islam concretely establishes that women are not inferior to men. Furthermore, the verse quoted below clearly shows the true status of women in the role of a wife. Allah ﷻ states:

> ...they (women) are your garment, and you (men) are their garment... • [Qur'an 2:187]

Much can be written to explain this simple statement regarding the relationship of men and women. The example of men and women being garments for each other says a lot about morality, trust, and security. Garments are worn to adorn and enhance a person's personality. They beautify one's appearance and looks. They hide deficiencies and deformities of the physical body. When worn properly, they cover the necessary and private parts of the body modestly. They reflect one's personality, state of mind, inner thoughts, sense, norms, and occasions. They send off expressions of whatever is meant by them. They protect from the elements and bring respect, dignity, etc.

Now suppose that a woman is inferior to a man. In such a case, how can she become his garment, and similarly how can a man become a garment to someone inferior to him? It is only when both are equal that they can become garments to each other and provide all the benefits mentioned above. This small portion of a verse of the holy Qur'an explains it all.

EQUALITY IN REWARD

*I*T WOULD CLEARLY BE UNFAIR if two people who were assigned the same task were rewarded differently. This inequality cannot be the case when Allah ﷻ is the One to assign the task and to designate the reward for it. Even though it is easier for women to earn rewards, they are rewarded equally to men. Allah ﷻ states:

> And whoever performs righteous deeds, whether man or woman, provided that he/she is a believer, they will enter Heaven, and they shall not be wronged even a bit. • [Qur'an 4:124]

> For men is the portion of what they earned and for women is the portion of what they earned. And beg Allah for His bounties. Undoubtedly, Allah is the knower of everything that exists. • [Qur'an 4:32]

Allah ﷻ further states:

> ...I do not discard the work of any laborer from among you, man or woman; all are from each other. Thus, whoever migrated and were exiled from their homes and were persecuted in My way, and they fought and were martyred, I shall certainly erase their sins from them and shall certainly admit them into the Heavens, beneath which are flowing streams. (This is) a reward from Allah, and with Allah alone is the excellence of reward. • [Qur'an 3:195]

Undoubtedly, men and women who give charity and those who give a loan to Allah, it will be doubled for them, and for them is a dignified reward. • [Qur'an 57:18]

Without a doubt, Muslim men and Muslim women and faithful men and faithful women and devout men and devout women and truthful men and truthful women and obedient men and obedient women and fearful men and fearful women and charitable men and charitable women and men who fast and women who fast and men who guard their private parts and women who guard them and men who greatly remember Allah and women who remember (Him); Allah has prepared for them forgiveness and a grand reward. • [Qur'an 33:35]

If women were inferior to men, the rewards for their deeds would be lower than the rewards for men doing the same deeds. However, this is not the case. The way Allah ﷻ equally addresses men and women and promises to reward them equally clearly shows that they are not inferior.

EQUALITY IN INHERITANCE

𝒯HE ALL-KNOWER AND ALL-WISE ALLAH ﷻ knew that the distribution of wealth and property would become a big issue, so He clearly outlined its equitable distribution, according to both men and women's needs and share of responsibilities. Thus, Allah ﷻ states in the holy Qur'an regarding inheritance:

For men there is a share in what their parents and relatives leave behind, and for women there is a share in what their parents and relatives leave behind. Whether more or less, it is a portion designated. • [4:7]

Prior to Islam, women had no share in inheritance; in fact, in many cases, she herself was part of the property to be inherited. Islam gave her a status in society and elevated her being a number of times over. Regarding inheritance, some argue that since her share is less than that of a man, i.e., typically half that of a male standing in the same degree of relationship to the deceased, this makes her inferior. The holy Prophet 鸞 did not set the percentages; it was the Lord Himself, the All-Knower and All-Wise, Who knows the wisdom behind His allocation of inheritance.

Scholars of Islam understood that since men have more responsibilities and duties to fulfill, they need a greater share of the wealth, whereas women have little to no financial responsibilities, and so less will suffice for them. For example, in Islam, the man has all the financial responsibilities of maintaining a family, any unmarried women that are his next of kin, including the woman who may be inheriting alongside of him, etc. In contrast, the woman is free of all such responsibilities; her money and inheritance are strictly hers, and she is under no compulsion or pressure to use her financial resources to support the family. Thus, while the man's inheritance is really an inheritance by his family, the woman's inheritance is strictly her own. Seen from this perspective, it might even be argued that the woman's strictly personal inheritance is actually larger than that of the man's.

PROTECTION OF WOMEN AND THEIR DIGNITY

*I*T IS IMPORTANT TO HAVE IN PLACE protective measures for women to safeguard their dignity and chastity, especially if they have no one else to stand up for them. Allah 鸞 clearly outlines severe punishments for those who mistreat women and behave unfairly with them. Allah 鸞 reveals in the holy Qur'an:

Undoubtedly, those who defame chaste, innocent women are cursed here and in the Hereafter, and for them is a mighty torment on the Day when their tongues, their hands, and their feet will testify against them for what they used to do. • [24:23-24]

And those who inflict pain on faithful men and faithful women for no reason; then certainly, they took upon themselves the burden of slandering and of manifest sin. • [33:58]

Historically, divorced/widowed women were considered disgraced beings in their communities, and many times ex-husbands and other relatives prevented or hindered them from remarrying. Islam removed such obstacles by permitting women to remarry and by commanding others to let them do so. In this way, women are able to maintain their honor and dignity. Allah ﷻ states in the holy Qur'an:

> And when you have divorced women, and when they have completed the prescribed waiting period, then do not prevent them from remarrying a husband of their choosing, when they have mutually agreed to this, legally... • [2:232]

> And those among you who die and leave behind wives, then they must wait four months and ten days (before they remarry). And upon completion of their prescribed waiting period, there is no blame on you for what they have decided for themselves, as per the law. And Allah is fully aware of what you do. • [2:234]

> And there is no blame on you, in that you discreetly convey to such women a message for engagement or if you have concealed the wish to marry in your heart (so to tell them later)... • [2:235]

Women have the right to seek separation from their husbands and can initiate divorce if and when they can no longer live with their husband. At times of divorce, some husbands try to take back whatever they have given to their wives and may bring forth different kinds of hardships. In this regard, Allah ﷻ states:

> O you who have brought faith! It is not permitted for you to become inheritors of women forcefully, and do not stop them with the intent to take something from the dowry that you had given them, except upon their manifest fornication... • [Qur'an 4:19]

WOMEN'S DIFFERENT ROLES IN LIFE

*W*OMEN, REGARDLESS OF THEIR RELIGIOUS or other affiliations, have four major roles to play in life: mothers, wives, sisters, and daughters. Women, as mothers, are respected throughout the world, and every society attaches a near holy status to her. Islam grants women the highest place in society in their role as mothers. With regards to her children, the status of a mother is exalted three times over the status of a father. No matter how much a mother is served, it is said that no child can ever be grateful enough for even the one day of pain she endured while giving birth and in caring for her child during infancy and thereafter. [Bukhari and Muslim]

The holy Qur'an mentions clearly:

> And your Lord commands to you the decision to not worship except Him and to treat your parents well. If in your life they reach old age, whether one of them or both, do not moan and groan at them, and do not rebuff them, but speak to them in kind words. And extend your arm mercifully for them, and keep supplicating, "O Sustainer, be kind to both of them, as they raised me in my childhood." • [17:23-24]

According to many *ahadith*, the Prophet ﷺ directed Muslims to serve their parents well and to not let them become a burden on society. Muslims are to shoulder the responsibility of caring for their parents themselves, as their parents did for them when they were young. A widely known *hadith* states that "Heaven is at the mother's feet," [Tirmidhi] meaning that by serving one's mother well (and of course the father, too), Muslims can easily acquire Heaven.

As a sister, a woman is not neglected in Islamic culture. If she is the eldest among the siblings, she takes the place next to her mother and draws the same respect. She is honored with even more respect if the mother is no longer living, as she takes the mother's place. Generally, she is kind to all of her siblings, and they in turn love her, pay her their utmost respect, and help her when she is in need. Even the sister's children naturally become dearer to their aunts and uncles and vice versa. In the absence of the father, a brother takes his place and is obligated to look after the well-being of his sister(s).

As mentioned earlier, while some misguided people may feel down at the news of the birth of a daughter, this is not the case in most Muslim families. Even if such feelings appear, they fade away quickly, and daughters become dearer to the parents and to the family. Daughters are always helpful to mothers in carrying out house chores and bring warmth to fathers. Commonly, love in abundance comes from daughters to parents, fathers especially. A Muslim father is awarded a place in Heaven if he successfully gets two of his daughters married.

It is incumbent on parents to educate their children in the best Islamic spirit. It is much more important for parents fully to train their daughters to perform well in their married and future life. Since a daughter has to leave the house of her parents when she gets married, she becomes beloved to everyone. She returns the same love and care for everyone in her family and brings the same love to her in-laws. Relatives come to offer all kinds of help to those needy parents whose daughter is to be married. Islam does not neglect or ignore a woman at any stage of her life. She is the center of every Muslim household.

WIFE – THE PARTNER OF MAN IN LIFE

*T*HE MOST IMPORTANT ROLE OF WOMEN IN SOCIETY, as well as in Islam, is that of a wife. It is in this role that most of the questions about her status, treatment, rights, and duties arise. It is here that women may be mistreated and suppressed by husbands who are violating Islamic rules out of their own ignorance, and it is here that some Muslim women may feel insecure and unhappy because of the non-Islamic behavior of their husbands. However, it is usually the case that in a Muslim marriage the wife can and does bring abundant happiness by becoming the queen and ruling over the heart of her husband, the king of the family. This is where she creates Heaven on Earth for herself and her family.

Most Islamic rules regarding women are for their status and role as wives. Islam defines and protects their being, status, rights, dignity, chastity, well-being, welfare, and so on and so forth. Islam establishes and clarifies the:

- *Rights and duties of wives* – so no one can insert personal injunctions to override the Lord's justice for women and thus mistreat them;
- *Rights and duties of husbands* – so they may not cross the limits set forth by the Lord and His beloved Prophet ﷺ;
- *Firm and equitable rules of marriage* – so in this sacred bond, men and women may live together as husband and wife and become partners to each other in managing the affairs of their family and fulfilling the other purposes of marriage;
- *Firm injunctions regarding divorce* – so if and when the time comes to discontinue the contract of marriage, they may do so peacefully and equitably within the limits of the law.

Moreover, Islam does not leave a woman in a vacuum in case, for example, her husband dies, whereupon it establishes guidelines for her to remarry if she chooses to do so. Islam even explains how and for how long she is to nurse her children. [2:233] The rewards for carrying out their duties and the punishments for neglecting rights are firmly in place for both husbands and wives.

The family is the most important unit of a society. If that unit is happy and peaceful, the whole society becomes peaceful, happy, and thus prosperous. How can a family be happy? It is only possible if each family member performs for the family's greater good.

In a family, the wife is usually in charge of the 'home ministry' and the husband of the 'foreign affairs,' so to say. Wives are usually relieved of matters outside of the home. The earning of income, hard labor for making ends meet, and all other matters pertaining to life outside of the home are not her concern; the husband is responsible for them. Similarly, a husband is relieved of the daily matters inside the home. Taking care of children by maintaining their good hygiene, proper clothing, preparing food, and the well-being of the family, etc. are not directly on his shoulders, but belong to the department of his life partner, his wife. Whatever husbands provide, wives utilize with utmost care, knowing that their husbands have worked very hard to earn it. Nonetheless, husband and wife work together hand in hand for the greater good of the family, to educate and practically train their children to become better persons, good Muslims, and loyal citizens.

A husband must provide respect, dignity, security, shelter, and appropriate provisions of life to his wife [The Prophet's Last Sermon, Appendix II]. During the absence of her husband, the wife is required to protect her chastity, her dignity, and her family's property [Tirmidhi]. Usually, when wives feel inferior or are mistreated by husbands, feelings of love and partnership fade away, and distance and insecurity take over. Thus, both husband and wife must build trust and loyalty to each other, for each other's sake and for Allah's ﷻ pleasure. If a husband and wife are not equal partners for one reason or another, or if both do not perform their part well, the household becomes disrupted, and eventually the family life is destroyed. By admonishing the Prophet's ﷺ wives, Allah ﷻ sends a message to Muslim wives and states:

> O Prophet! Say to your wives: "If it is the life of the world and its adornment that you seek, then come! I shall make a provision for you and release you honorably. • And if you seek Allah and His Prophet and the Abode of the Hereafter, then undoubtedly, Allah has prepared for the righteous wives among you, a great reward." • [33:28-29]

In Islam, a wife's proper place is usually in the home. However, for the greater good of the family, to help her husband, to share the burden of the household, or for other chores of the family life, or to pursue an appropriate occupation or profession, she is allowed to come outside, provided that she guards her chastity, respect, and dignity. After all, she is the partner of man in life.

There should be no question about the roles designated to men and women, because they have been established by Allah ﷻ Himself for the greater good. Men and women are to play their roles on this stage of life and will be judged on their performance. If people keep questioning their roles, they will never be able to perform them, let alone perform them well.

Women are required by Allah ﷻ to cover their body and to wear *hijāb* (head covering) when in public. If one pays close attention and sincerely explores the consequences of immodesty and obscenity, one will reach the conclusion that eventually, in one way or another, immodesty and obscenity brings disastrous results to society and irreversible damage to the dignity of men and women.

HIJĀB

*H*IJĀB IS TO VEIL, SCREEN, OR COVER and is the Arabic word used to refer to a woman's scarf. It literally means "a barrier." In Islam, relationships between Muslim men and women are of two kinds: they are either *mahram* or non-*mahram* to each other. The necessity of *hijāb* depends upon these two categories. In order to understand when *hijāb* becomes necessary, it is important to understand the meaning of *mahram* and non-*mahram*. According to Islamic law:

- *Mahram* – any male and female who cannot marry each other, such as parents and grandparents to their children and grand-children; aunts/uncles to their nieces/nephews, and biological brothers and sisters to each other. They are all *mahram*.

- Non-*mahram* – any male and female eligible to marry each other, at any point in their lives. For example, a sister-in-law is a non-*mahram* to her brother-in-law, because they are eligible to marry each other at the time of death/divorce from her husband.

Hijāb is necessary between non-*mahram* individuals, whereas *hijāb* is not necessary between *mahram* individuals. Old people, who are no longer able to marry, may choose to remove *hijāb*. In order to fulfill the requirements of *hijāb*, a Muslim female (generally between the ages of 12 and 45), must make every effort to cover herself from head to toe, leaving her face uncovered. She must never expose her body to a non-*mahram* and must dress modestly even among *mahram*. Through *hijāb*, Allah ﷻ protects a female from the evils of men, jinn, Satan, and the elements. However, the more she covers herself and protects her chastity, the more her status in piety increases.

Moreover, *hijāb* does not mean to cover only the head, while the rest of the body remains somewhat exposed to gazes; this is, in fact, a mockery of *hijāb*. Covering the head and dressing modestly, so that the body and its curves are not visible, is the complete exemplification of *hijāb*. *Hijāb* and lowering of gazes is not only for women, but men are also required to dress modestly and to lower their gaze in the presence of women. The main purpose of *hijāb* is to make both Muslim men and women pious, chaste, and modest. Allah ﷻ states to Prophet Muhammad ﷺ:

> Command your followers to keep their gazes lowered and to guard their private parts; this is purer for them. Undoubtedly, Allah is fully aware of whatever they do. • [Qur'an 24:30]

> And command the faithful women that they keep their gazes lowered, and guard their private parts, so as not to display their adornments, except for what is self-apparent. And (they should) draw their head-coverings over their bosoms and not make visible their adornments, except to their husbands... • [Qur'an 24:31]

> O Prophet! Say to your wives and daughters and the believing women that they keep their shawls hung over their bodies. This is the easiest way for them to be recognized (as respectable women) and not bothered (by strange men)... • [Qur'an 33:59]

Whatever Allah ﷻ has prescribed for men and women, including *hijāb*, is beneficial for them and to the society as a whole. Often, people fail to comprehend the everlasting benefits in obeying Allah ﷻ, fail to pursue the true purpose of life, and are attracted to temporary pleasures. Pleasures that come from power, wealth, fame, and sexual acts may surpass all other worldly pleasures. However, Allah ﷻ wants people to control their ill desires and acquire His pleasure. Real winners are those who control their wants and desires, and real losers are those who are controlled by them.

Among all worldly pleasures, the greatest may be the sexual pleasure, which is something that an individual must control and restrict before embarking on the path of righteousness, the destination of which is eternal life in Heaven. Not everyone struggles for power and fame, and intelligent people know the limits of pleasure gained from wealth and fame, but almost everyone, in one way or another, is striving to acquire as much sexual pleasure as possible. Moreover, the current state of human societies has made it extremely difficult to control sexual desires. This has led to many ills in society and has greatly contributed towards erasing sacred religious sentiments and fear of accountability.

Today, when the most sacred is no longer sacred, when the most private is no longer private, when the most personal is no longer personal, when there is not much difference left in what is mine and yours, and when everything is sacrificed in the name of freedom, sex, and other worldly pleasures, how can piety—or, at least, embarking on its path—be achieved? Whoever is courageous enough to overcome worldly and bodily pleasures and receive the pleasures of the Lord will emerge as a winner, is worthy of being called a 'gentleman,' deserves to acquire ultimate success, and proves himself to be the 'Best of all Creatures.' In that regard, let me assure you that people need not completely suppress their natural desires, but rather they need to control them. They do not need to erase them altogether, but limit them.

Islam does not only guides us to solve our problems, but uproots them. If we do not let them sprout in the first place, there will be no need to weed whack them, and only then can we utilize our energies towards more productive and worthy causes. Attacking problems at their very root means that we do not have to deal with them later. To achieve this same end, Islam requires women to wear *hijāb* and to dress modestly.

The *hijāb* and modest dress are not to make women inferior, but to protect them. It is not to discriminate against them, but to make them sacred. It is not to humiliate them, but to make them honorable. It is not to take away their liberty or freedom, but to safeguard them from predators. It is not to make them worthless, but to make them precious. It is not to subjugate them, but to elevate their status. It is not to place hardship on them, but to uplift their morale. It is not to make them weak, but to make them stronger in their being. It is not to make them fragile, but to make them unbreakable. It is not to insult them, but to dignify them. It is not to control them, but to enable them to control the ill desires of wicked men. It is not to degrade them, but to make them valuable. It is not to make them the property of man, but to liberate them to safeguard their own chastity and being, so no one can even think for a moment about acquiring them as property. It is not to take away any of their rights, but to secure their right to privacy, so no perverted and lustful gaze can penetrate their most private and personal being. It is not to snatch away something they own, but to let them keep what is actually theirs. Finally, *hijāb* is not to denigrate them, but allocates to them a higher status and unique respect, and prevents others from making them mere toys of pleasure. If there is nothing to look at, no one pays attention.

By commanding women to cover and safeguard their privacy and chastity, Islam not only does them a great favor, it saves men from all those sins and troubles that result from seeing immodestly dressed women. *Hijāb* saves society from great harm and from becoming immoral in a world where indiscriminate sexual relationships are the norms of the day and where people become mere objects of sex and slaves to sexual desires. Islam is not in favor of this kind of society; it intends to build a society where sexual endeavors are controlled and do not become the aim.

Hijāb is required for both men and women. Women must cover their body and hair properly, and men must lower their eyes, dress modestly, and avoid situations where there is the slightest chance of becoming sinful and committing 'fornication of the eyes.' [Mishkat] *Hijāb* discourages men from gazing at women who are modestly dressed. Unfortunately, these days, some women are using *hijāb* for different purposes; by adding fashion to it, instead of repelling men's gaze they attract it. Instead of keeping *hijāb* sacred, they made it profane. In Islam, the status of women is truly elevated, and Allah ﷻ guides both men and women to keep it that way. There are severe punishments from Allah ﷻ in one form or another for causing this status to become profane and impure. That which is precious is not to be displayed in public; it is to be kept private.

Even when performing *salāh*, which includes bowing and bending, it is preferable that a woman perform her *salāh* in a private room where even a *mahram* (including her husband) may not see her. Islam wants to protect her and her chastity at every moment of her life, so even a wrongful gaze could not penetrate her self.

Generally, when a woman dies, even her husband is not permitted to touch her body because touching it may remind him of the private moments they had together. Islam protects her dignity even at a time when she herself could not. Women and their bodies are so honorable and precious to Islam that it made all sorts of rules to maintain their dignity. No other religion or system protects women's honor, chastity, and dignity to such an extent. This clearly denotes that women are not inferior or a lower being in Islam. However, if women do not guard their own honor and chastity, and they display what they should keep to themselves, the results are devastating, both to themselves and society. In that case, who else could be blamed, but herself.

Keep in mind that there are degrees of flexibility in the application of Islamic rules according to different circumstances and the society in which a Muslim lives. Muslims should make themselves aware of Islamic rules and regulations and the flexibilities provided therein to adhere to them properly.

MARRIAGE: A SACRED INSTITUTION

*T*O SIMPLY STATE THAT MARRIAGE IS A SACRED INSTITUTION would be insufficient. Thus, to understand its sacredness, it is necessary to understand fully the wisdom behind it, and this requires paying greater attention to the entire notion of marriage.

As per the biological system devised by Allah ﷻ to spread mankind on earth, people are born into this world through sexual intercourse between a man and a woman, with the exception of the miraculous birth of Hawwa عليها السلام and Isa الـعليـه and, of course, the creation of the first man, Adam الـعليـه. Not only are humans born through sexual intercourse, but Allah ﷻ has prescribed, through marriage, a system where they are born into a "family," where one is called the mother, the other is called the father, and their offspring are called their children. One day, these children become parents, and the cycle of procreation continues.

Marriage does not take place only to fulfill the sexual needs of a man and woman, it makes them husband and wife, and at the birth of a child, father and mother. As a result, through marriage, a family is created, which later results in the greater human society. Man can be born out of wedlock and without the arrangement of marriage, and while this too increases the population of mankind, it does not create a "family." If this were the case in general, I do not know what kind of society we would be living in.

Among animals, there is no need for someone to be a father, mother, or child, because the needs of every animal are naturally fulfilled one way or another, and there is no need to create any type of bond, such as, for example, that of marriage. The purpose of the temporary sexual union between animals is only to procreate. They are not required to establish a family or a society because, in almost all cases, they are relatively independent from the time of birth to death, unlike humans.

Humans need help from the very beginning, and in one form or another, they are in need of help up until the last day of their lives. That help is provided through the family and later also by society. In a family, the parents are responsible for raising the child. If in case we do not know who the mother is, who the father is, or to whom the child belongs, then on whose shoulders are we going to place the responsibility of raising him/her? In this case, children get help from society, but if they do not, as is the case in many poor societies/communities, their growth and well-being will be hampered.

If, for example, after giving birth, the mother runs away, then we may never know who the father is. However, the mother of the child is generally known, at least at the time of birth, but society still has to rely on her to know who the father is, and to enter his name on the child's birth certificate. If any man comfortably accepts being the father, then even if the mother used to see many men before becoming pregnant, most societies will have no problem accepting him as the father. However, if no man accepts the child to be his, then on whom does the burden of fatherhood lie: on society, or on the mother alone, who will have to provide in place of the father, too?

From the very beginning, the system of marriage was instituted to avoid many of the problems we face today. Since marriage saves people from great problems and binds them to each other in the best manner possible, it has always been considered a sacred bond. Marriage gives a woman the role of wife, and certainly the performance of her role as a wife varies from one society to another.

Islamic regulations regarding marriage allocate many rights to and duties for women. Hence, with Islam, she is no longer merely an object of sexual pleasure and is no longer a silent victim of man's tyranny and oppression. She is a dignified being with full rights afforded to her person. She cannot be bought or sold, buried alive, burnt, or become an object to be inherited when her husband dies. Through Islamic liberty and equality, she can fight for her rights and seek justice for herself.

Sexual intercourse between men and women who are not married to each other is in Islam not only one of the greatest sins, but it carries severe penalties. Through marriage and by prohibiting intimate relationships out of wedlock, Islam creates a strong bond and mutual trust between a man and woman. They are able to fulfill their natural urges in a respectful and dignified manner and to acquire the true pleasure of family life. Muslim couples enjoy a good, private partnership and share life's responsibilities, respect in society, and honorable parenting, while simultaneously increasing the human population through legitimate procreation.

To have a happy marital life and to establish a peaceful and prosperous family, a man and woman must be married to each other through their own choice. If a society is to be based on necessary freedoms and is to be free from all types of coercions, its basic unit, the family, must be free from coercion and unnecessary suppression. Both the husband and wife must love, care, cooperate, protect, comfort, understand each other, and fulfill each other's rights and duties. This cannot be achieved if they have not come close to each other (married) through personal choice and consent, and without any reservation or pressure.

However, even after marriage by choice and consent, if pressure, suppression, and coercion occur later on, the relationship between a husband and wife will become fragile and cannot progress smoothly. Islam lays down all the necessary rules and regulations to form the union between man and woman, and it simultaneously provides cures for problems that may arise later in that union. Islam wants to see both men and women live happily and without being oppressed or coerced, in order that under all circumstances, in a union or out of a union, they can work to please their Lord and for the life Hereafter.

RIGHT TO CHOOSE LIFE PARTNER

*T*HERE IS A COMMON MISCONCEPTION that in Islam women are forced into marriage, having no right to choose their husband. It is true that marriages are sometimes arranged through parents, guardians, or other elders, but in Islam, a woman's consent is absolutely necessary. An "arranged marriage" simply means that the arrangements of marriage are made by the elders and not by the bride herself.

Since dating and courtship between men and women are not allowed in Islam, in order to keep the sanctity of marriage intact, all arrangements regarding the procedures of marriage often go through elders. If a woman was forced into marriage in violation of Islam , the Islamic courts can nullify it at her petition. All relevant members are directed to consider every matter, including the concurrence of women in advance, to avoid a later breakup, since separation and divorce are most undesirable to Allah ﷻ. Usually the proposal of marriage is initiated by the man through his elders to the elders of the woman. Her family has the right to reject or accept after consulting with her.

Marriage is not a simple matter; it requires many concrete decisions. Usually, young people do not have the experience of life that is required in the decision-making process. Therefore, they need the experience and consultation of their parents/elders. Especially, the bride's family must provide their experience in the field and assist her in making the decision. They often take extra care in this delicate matter, because the life and well-being of their daughter/sister is of great concern, and because they wish her to be successful and happy in her marriage life. Mutual consent and consensus are necessary, and her full consent is a must, because it is her life that is on the line.

Unfortunately, there is no shortage of forced marriages in some so-called "Muslim" societies, which are not only oppressive to women, but are un-Islamic and based on ignorance of Islamic principles. However, it is also true that many marriages, though forced, turn out to be successful, because couples make compromises and sacrifices for the greater good of their family to live together happily. Since it is customary for males to propose marriage and because he is responsible for the overall well being of the family, it is highly recommended that he be lenient, soft, and kind to his wife and children. Further, he must practice utmost tolerance.

The holy Prophet ﷺ said:

A divorcée or a widow must not be married until he/she is consulted, and a virgin (must not be married), until her permission is sought. [Bukhari]

A woman who has been previously married, has more right to her person than her guardian. And a virgin should also be consulted, and (sometimes) her silence implies her consent. [Muslim]

Khaula bint Huzam petitioned the holy Prophet ﷺ that her father married her to a person whom she did not like; the Prophet ﷺ revoked her marriage for her [Nisa'i]. Abdullah bin Abbas ﷺ reported that a woman came to the holy Prophet ﷺ and said, "My father has married me to a person whom I do not like," and, the holy Prophet ﷺ authorized that woman to either keep or revoke the marriage.

[Mishkat]

A young woman once came to the holy Prophet ﷺ and said, "My father has married me to my cousin, whom I do not like." Thereupon, the holy Prophet ﷺ gave her permission to adhere to or to revoke the marriage contract. Hearing this, the woman heaved a sigh of relief and said, "I have already given my consent to what my father has done, but what I want to impress upon women is that a father has no right to give the hand of his grown daughter without her consent." [Nisa'ī]

Many cases of this sort came to the honorable court of the holy Prophet ﷺ, where newlywed women showed their disgust with marriages that had been forced on them without their consent. The Prophet ﷺ either revoked the marriage himself or gave authority to the petitioning women to cancel the marriage contract. This clearly shows that Muslim women reserve the right to select their husband.

As per the holy Qur'an:

> ...when they have completed the prescribed waiting period, then you are not to prevent them from remarrying a husband of their choosing, when they have mutually agreed to it legally... • [2:232]

POLYGAMY IN ISLAM

$\mathcal{P}$OLYGAMY IS THE PRACTICE OF HAVING MORE THAN ONE wife at a time. In Islam, a man is allowed to have more than one wife—in fact, up to four wives—at a time. Why, and under what circumstances is this allowed?

Before Islam, men gave themselves the right to marry an indefinite number of women, and they typically did not do justice to any of them. Islam limited the number of wives to four and restricted men to marrying no more than this number. However, a man is only allowed to do so when he is able to do justice to them and treat them equally. The practice of polygamy in Islam has been well-publicized negatively by non-Muslims simply to defame the religion of Islam. I reiterate here that Islam did not raise the number of wives from one to four, but limited it from an unlimited number to only up to four.

Even though men are allowed to marry four women at a time, it is highly discouraged, and it is strongly recommended to have only one. Some Islamic rules were established for extraordinary, unusual, and special circumstances. The permission to allow up to four wives is one such rule, and only a handful of men throughout the Muslim *ummah* (community), choose to practice polygamy. However, because of what this rule entails, many men are discouraged from marrying two, three, or four women at a time. Keep in mind that the Muslim world extends across the globe; Arabs, who make up less than fifteen percent of the entire Muslim population and among whom polygamy is occasionally practiced, are not the only Muslims. Many times, Arabs have the means and can fulfill the necessities required by Islamic law to practice polygamy. Furthermore, polygamy has also always been an aspect of their culture. With regards to the permission to have more than one wife, Allah ﷻ states in the holy Qur'an:

> And if you are afraid that you will not be able to do justice among the (female) orphans, so bring into marriage who you like from among the women, two, three, or four. Then if you are afraid that you will not be able to deal equitably, so have only one wife… • [4:3]

When studying this issue, one must remember that this is not a divine commandment that <u>must</u> be followed, but it is permitted if need be and only if the condition of equitably dealing with multiple wives is fulfilled. If there were a commandment obligating men to be polygamous, it would be unreasonable, unnecessary, and unnatural. Likewise, if it were strictly forbidden under all circumstances, this too would be unnatural.

Islam is a religion fit for human nature, and it provides solutions and guidance under all circumstances and for every need. However, keep in mind that this special dispensation for men to be polygamous is conditional and is not without limitations, obligations, and responsibilities. The commandment clearly states that the number of wives should never exceed four at a time. If the husband cannot physically and financially support and fulfill his duties towards all of his wives, or if he is unable to act justly and to provide equal treatment to them, then he is not permitted to have more than one wife. This is evident from the verse mentioned above. Furthermore, Allah ﷻ states:

> And it is impossible that you do full justice among the wives, even though you are eager to; so do not lean over completely to one side, and leave the other hanging. And if you compromise and act piously, so certainly, Allah is Forgiving, Merciful. • [Qur'an 4:129]

This also shows that even though permission to have more than one wife is granted, it is highly discouraged, and Allah ﷻ implies that a man will not be able to do justice to all of his wives if he marries more than one.

The following are some scenarios in which a man can justifiably use the permission to have more than one wife, provided, first and foremost, that he is financially and otherwise capable. Moreover, it is preferable for the husband to consult his wife/wives before marrying another woman.

(a) A man loves his wife who happens to be barren, and he wants to have children. What is a solution if he does not want to divorce his barren wife, but still wants to have children of his own? In this case, a feasible solution is to marry a second wife who may bear children.

(b) A man is no longer attracted to his wife because of her attitude, personality, looks, etc. However, the matter is not grave enough for him to divorce her, because if he does, she may come under financial difficulty and possibly be separated from the children.

In this case, the feasible solution is to have another wife without leaving the first one.

(c) A man is sexually strong, and his intimate needs and desires are not satisfied through his only wife. Would it be a good idea for him to have un-Islamic, illegitimate relationships with other women, leading him to grave sinful behavior? No. In this case, he may marry another woman and fulfill his intimate needs within the boundaries of Islamic law, simultaneously providing for the needs of one more woman.

(d) In the rare, but possible, situation in which a woman has to choose between being a respectable wife of a husband who has other wives and who is willing to provide her protection, *or* becoming just a toy and object of sex of one or several men with no protection for herself, I think a dignified and chaste woman would choose the former. However, if Islam had not permitted men to have more than one wife, what choice would she have? In light of this, Islam provides women with safety and security, and it permits men to take such women under their protection as wives.

(e) In some societies, the ratio of females to males is out of balance, with there being far more females than males. Furthermore, countries at war lose and have lost a considerable portion of their male population, thereby increasing the ratio of women to men. Certainly, many women, in this case, are left without husbands and other male family members. This increases the chances for them to become victims of injustices or to spend their lives alone and abandoned. This, in turn, leads to women's health issues, increased medical expenses, depression, other psychological complications, and various ills in society. By permitting men to marry more than one woman and shoulder her responsibilities, Islam eradicates many of these potential problems.

(f) Would it be easier for a wife and children to accept their husband/father's legitimate and respected second wife, or his hidden, illegitimate, and disgraceful affair with another woman, who may also have her own affairs with other men? I guess if there is a just and legitimate need for a husband/father, the dignified alternative is to have a second wife.

There are millions of people who face the preceding situations. By permitting men to have more than one wife, Islam provides a feasible solution.

Overall, it is to be remembered that this permission to marry up to four wives at a time is granted by the All-Knowing Lord, Who knows all of our needs and the solutions to our problems. Islam does not compel men to practice polygamy, which is why only a handful of Muslim men practice it. The overwhelming majority of men are happily monogamous. The conditional permission for men to practice a limited polygamy is special and for unique circumstances, and it is not without increased duties and tough responsibilities for the husband.

To simply know and talk about polygamy does not automatically mean that someone is promoting it or personally likes the idea. However, only an unbiased study can show its wisdom and benefits to society. Anyway, I have presented this matter as Islam presents it. On a personal note, I am happily married and satisfied with one wife for over thirty years' duration. One good wife can create a heavenly household, while more than one… I do not know how those men do it. I would rather stick to the easy way and have only one wife.

CORRECTING MISBEHAVIOR

*T*HERE IS A VERSE IN THE HOLY QUR'AN concerning the treatment of wives about which even many informed people are confused. It is discussed ignorantly, and some even use it to defame

Islam. I would prefer not to deal with this issue, but if I do not explain it here, readers may think that I am purposely avoiding it.

However, before beginning this discussion, let me remind you once again that every Islamic law and teaching is inspired by Allah 🕌 and the Prophet 🕌, through Allah's consent. Not a single aspect of life has been left unexplained by Islam. The following verse was revealed as a solution to frequent problems between husbands and wives. If Allah 🕌 did not prescribe a solution, who else could have? Allah's 🕌 commandments and resolutions are full of wisdom, because He is the All-Knower, the All-Wise.

Allah 🕌 reveals in the holy Qur'an:

> Men are leaders over women, because Allah elevated among them one over another, and because men spend their wealth; thus, chaste wives are loyal behind (their) backs and guardians of which Allah has taken into (His) protection. And those of whom you fear being depraved, so make them understand, and leave them alone in their beds, and hit them. Then, if they become loyal to you, do not seek ways to accuse them. Certainly, Allah is Most Supreme. • [4:34]

In the kind of family system Islam creates, the role assigned to women does not require her, but does allow her, to be the breadwinner; typically, her role is to be at home and to care for the household. Men are to earn and provide for the needs of the family. Since men spend their money to raise the family and run the necessary affairs, they are the heads of the family. Not allocating appropriate power to husbands makes them weak and unable to run their family properly. Since husbands are responsible for providing for their wives' needs, livelihood, and comfort and for acting justly with them, in return wives are required to be virtuous, obedient, and chaste during their husband's absence. This is a fair demand. Islam makes sure that both husband and wife play their roles accordingly to run the family. Knowing that some men and women will not do so, Allah 🕌 reveals in this verse how, lawfully and conditionally, to attempt to correct the misbehavior of wives. Keep in mind that he who is not just, has no right to correct others.

As a first step, Allah ﷻ guides husbands to admonish properly their wives for disobedience. Certainly, for intelligent, sincere, and good wives, this is sufficient. If her disobedience gets out of hand, then as a second step, penalize her by leaving her alone and not sleeping with her. This usually resolves the matter. If she still does not understand, refuses to correct herself, and continues her flagrant misbehavior, which may mean that she does not realize the severity of the problem, then Islam gives her husband the permission to hit her lightly, but not cross the limits. This permission from Allah ﷻ is, as a last resort, to protect the marriage and prevent a break-up of the family through separation and divorce. However, this permission is not without strict restrictions and regulations.

Now, after these three steps of admonishment, if the least bit of dignity and care for the family is left, she will correct herself and save her family and husband from the agony of divorce. Allah ﷻ also says in the same verse that, if they begin to understand, they are not to be bothered anymore. If they do not do so, then, in later verses, Allah ﷻ directs both parties to seek mediation, and if this too does not work, then comes separation and divorce.

However permitted, divorce is most undesirable to Allah ﷻ. Allah ﷻ guides people to somehow save the marital relationship, even if it means slightly hitting the wife. Hitting, in this case, is the lesser evil, and divorce and disrupting children's lives are the greater evil. There is no doubt that hitting is uncivilized, but to avoid complete disaster, it is prescribed only as a last resort for betterment. The Prophet's *ahadīth* sets limits to this act.

> Hitting cannot and should not amount to brutality, breaking of bones or causing blood to spill, (i.e., it should not amount to beating, in any sense of the word). [Tirmidhi]

...do not strike her on the face... [Abu Dawud]

The specific Arabic word, *dharaba* in 4:34 clearly means "to hit." Even though there are numerous other meanings of this Arabic word, ranging from "slapping" to "beating," none of the other meanings besides "to hit" explains the purpose of the verse and nor would any other meaning fit into the overall philosophy of Islam. Instead, they will end up contradicting numerous undisputed relevant *ahadīth*.

The intent is carefully to correct her in private, so that her dignity is maintained. Once the husband beats her, which is likely to become known to the public, she loses her dignity. Even if she corrects herself after being beaten, she has already lost her dignity, and this is undesirable to Islam. By "hitting," if the problem is solved, her dignity remains preserved. The verse also clearly mentions that if she corrects herself, a husband is not to find ways to humiliate and oppress her. Therefore, "beating" is not allowed and slightly "hitting" is permitted only to indicate that the problem is getting out of hand. Moreover, "hitting" is permitted provided the husband's behavior towards his family is in line with Islamic teachings.

An educated, sincere, intelligent, and sensible woman would ask: how could Islam allow a husband to hit his wife? To this, Islam would in turn inquire: are all wives educated, loyal, sincere, chaste, and sensible? In families in which both are educated, sincere, and loyal, the situation does not reach the point where hitting is ever needed. Nevertheless, divine guidance must be available even if something were to occur rarely. Hitting is a last resort to save the household and the relationship of those very women who are unable, for one reason or another, to choose right from wrong and foresee disasters for themselves and their family. Hitting is allowed as a cure, not as a tool or justification to abuse.

A careful study shows that Islam is not against women and gives her full rights. Furthermore, there is no place for domestic violence in

Islam. If a husband abuses his position of leadership in the family, violates his wife's rights, and carries out a reign of brutality, then this matter should not be taken lightly, since the wife has the full right to secure her being and dignity.

I must conclude this chapter by mentioning two of the most highly elevated women, praised by Allah ﷻ Himself, showing that women in Islam are not oppressed or treated as second-class citizens.

> And when the angels said, "O Maryam, certainly Allah has chosen you and purified you well, and in your distinctiveness elected you among the women of the world. • O Maryam, be reverential to your Lord, and prostrate continuously and do *ruku* (bowing in worship) with the ones who do *ruku*." • [Qur'an 3:42-43]

> And Allah provided an ideal example in the woman of Pharaoh; when she supplicated, "O Sustainer! Make for me by You a house in Heaven and save me from Pharaoh and his misconduct and save me from the oppressors. • And Maryam, the daughter of Imran, who remained chaste; so We blew into her from Our Self a *soul*, and she testified to the words of her Lord and of His Books, and became among the obedient ones. • [Qur'an 66:11-12]

CHAPTER 17

Importance of Knowledge / Education in Islam

K NOWLEDGE IS THE KEY TO SUCCESS, and Islamic know-ledge is the key to ultimate success. Knowledge instills superiority, confidence, and satisfaction. It brings faith and gives a sense of direction. It opens up new avenues in life and establishes new faculties for human progress. It enables us to explore outer space and to discover our inner self. It is knowledge that causes us to know our purpose, our beginning, and our end. It is knowledge that can connect us to our Creator and free us from all other enslave-ments. It is knowledge that, if utilized properly, helps us to become worthy of being the best of all creatures. Overall, "knowledge is to light as ignorance is to darkness." The importance of knowledge was established from the very beginning and with the creation of the first human being:

> And when your Sustainer stated for the angels, "Certainly, I am to make a vicegerent on earth," they began saying, "Will You make in it those who will create mischief in it and will commit bloodshed, when in fact we speak Your Holiness with Your praise and keep glorifying You." (Allah) stated, "Certainly, I know what

you do not know." • And (He) taught Adam all the names, each and every; then (He) presented them to the angels. Then (He) stated, "Tell me all of their names if you are truthful!" • They began saying, "Holiness is Yours; we do not have any knowledge except of whatever You have taught us. Certainly, only You are All-Knowing, All-Wise." • (Allah) said, "O Adam, do tell them all of their names." So when they were told all of their names; (Allah) said, "Did I not tell you that without a doubt, only I know the mysteries of the heavens and Earth, and (I) know whatever you reveal and whatever you conceal." • And when We commanded for the angels to prostrate before Adam, they all prostrated, except Iblīs. He refused and became proud, and (he) became of the disbelievers. • [2:30-34]

The first thing Allah ﷻ bestowed on Adam السلام عليه, His vicegerent, was knowledge, and it was knowledge that gave Adam السلام عليه (humans) superiority over the angels, earning him the higher status. Allah ﷻ taught Adam السلام عليه the names of all things, and the one who is taught the names of things automatically learns their qualities and functions, as well. Knowledge, man's initial asset with which he began to live life, was given to him even before his arrival on Earth. Man's first teacher was Allah ﷻ. Imagine how important knowledge is, that Allah ﷻ Himself taught it to mankind. The first revealed verses of the holy Qur'an reveal the same basic message:

> Read in the name of your Lord, Who created. • He created man from a clot of blood. • Read! And your Lord is Most Merciful, • Who taught by the pen, • taught man whatever he knew not. •
> [96:1-5]

The revelation of the holy Qur'an to Prophet Muhammad ﷺ commenced with these verses, which testify to the importance of knowledge and education in Islam. The basic knowledge, from which humans later developed their know-how of life and expanded their knowledge, came from the Lord. It would have taken many thousands of years more to be where we are today had this basic knowledge not been there.

The merciful Allah • taught the Quran; • created this man • and informed him thoroughly. • The sun and moon are according to a measure, • and vines and shrubs and trees are fallen into prostration, • and heavens He raised and He indeed set the scale • and do not go under or over when weighing; • and establish weighing with justice and do not lessen the weight. • And He kept the earth for the creatures, • in which there is fruit and sheathed dates and grains of husks and scented flowers. • So, O Jinns and Men! How many of your Lord's bounties will you deny. • [Qur'an 55:1-13]

Knowledge and wisdom are so important to guide mankind and for one to be completely guided that Allah bestowed knowledge and wisdom to all of His prophets, who in turn conveyed it to wise men. In the beautiful story of Yusuf (Joseph) الَّسَلام عليه, Allah سبحانه وتعالى states:

When he reached his full maturity, so We gave him wisdom and knowledge, and in this way We reward the upright servants. • [12:22]

This shows the importance of knowledge that it was bestowed on Yusuf عليه السلام as a reward. See how Allah سبحانه وتعالى praised His Prophet Yaqūb (Jacob) عليه السلام in the holy Qur'an:

…and without a doubt, he was a man of knowledge, which We taught him, but most people act ignorantly. • [Qur'an 12:68]

While interpreting the dreams of two prisoners, Yusuf عليه السلام said:

…this is because my Lord has taught me… • [Qur'an 12:37]

Through knowledge, Allah سبحانه وتعالى exalts His true servants:

…We elevate the ranks of whomever We want, and over every knowledgeable person, there is a more knowledgeable One… •
[Qur'an 12:76]

When informing Yahya (John the Baptist) عليه السلام, son of Zakarya (Zachariah) عليه السلام, Allah سبحانه وتعالى said:

"O Yahya! Hold onto the Book strongly." And We had given him wisdom, ever since childhood. • [Qur'an 19:12]

When Ibrahīm (Abraham) عليه السلام tried to convince his uncle to follow the right way and refrain from idol-worship, he, referring to his knowledge, said:

O Uncle! Without a doubt, a part of that knowledge has come to me, which did not come to you; so keep following me; I will take you to the Right Path. • [19:43]

Regarding Prophet Lut (Lot) ﷽, Allah ﷻ stated:

And We gave to Lut, prophecy and knowledge… • [Qur'an 21:74]

Allah ﷻ stated the same regarding Sulayman (Solomon) ﷽, Musa (Moses) ﷽, and Yusuf ﷽:

And when he reached full maturity and youthful prime, We gave him wisdom and knowledge. And this is how We reward upright servants. • [Qur'an 28:14]

Knowledge and wisdom are the highest bounties; nothing is equal to them. Whoever is endowed with them is truly exalted and honored. Allah ﷻ states:

He gives wisdom to whomever He wills, and whoever is given wisdom, certainly he is given a great treasure. • [Qur'an 2:269]

For us to have a deeper understanding of the importance of true knowledge and in that in which it results in, Allah ﷻ reveals:

And people, beasts and cattle are of various colors. In this way, only the knowledgeable people among His servants fear Allah … • [Qur'an 35:28]

One of the greatest purposes of Allah's bestowing knowledge is:

And so they may know who has been given knowledge that undoubtedly, this indeed is truth from their Lord. So they may believe it, and so their hearts may become affectionate to it. And certainly, Allah will indeed grant the way to those who have believed, towards the Right Path. • [Qur'an 22:54]

And those who are given knowledge are observing that what has been revealed to you from your Lord is the truth, and it guides to the way of the Exalted, the Praiseworthy. • [Qur'an 34:6]

The greatest purpose of prophets was to bring knowledge and wisdom to their people, educate them about their purpose and tell them how they should behave in life. This too was the purpose of Muhammad 鸞, the last prophet. Allah 鸞 states:

> It is He, Who sent among the unlettered a Prophet from among them, who recites unto them His Verses and purifies them and teaches them the book and wisdom and without a doubt, these people before were in manifest apostasy. • [Qur'an 62:2]

Even though the human race has achieved so much in such a short period of its existence, its overall knowledge is still quite limited. People have no choice, but to continue to strive for more knowledge to the point where they completely understand their purpose. To show the limits of our knowledge, Allah 鸞 states in the holy Qur'an:

> And they ask you about the spirit. Reply to them, "The spirit is by the command of my Lord, and you were not given from knowledge except a bit." • [17:85]

> Those people know the earthly life's apparent condition, and regarding the Hereafter all those people are negligent. • Did they not think in their hearts that Allah did not create the heavens and Earth and whatever is in between them but accurately and for a fixed period, and certainly many people are deniers of meeting with their Lord. • Did they not travel on the Earth to see how was the consequence of those before them, who were much stronger than them and broke ground, and had inhabited it more than they inhabit it. And their prophets brought to them signs; so it was not Allah to oppress them, but, yes, they oppressed themselves. • [30:7-9]

> So did they not look what is in front and behind them, Heaven and Earth. If we would like to, we could bury them in earth or drop upon them a piece from the heavens. Certainly, there is indeed a sign in it for every person who pays attention. • [34:9]

> And those people said that there is nothing except this worldly life of ours, that we live and die and nothing perishes us, but time. And they know nothing about this; they only go about following suppositions. • [45:24]

> And they have no knowledge at all of this. They do follow nothing but imagination. And certainly apprehension and assumption

is not a bit useful in place of truth. • So, turn away from him who turns away from Our remembrance and wishes only for worldly life. • This is the extent of their knowledge… • [53:28-30]

By presenting to you the verses above, I hope I have brought you to a better understanding of the importance of knowledge in Islam.

ACQUISITION OF KNOWLEDGE

*K*NOWLEDGE IS SUCH A REMARKABLE and desirable power that Allah ﷻ instructed His prophets to strive and supplicate for it.

…and pray, "O Sustainer! Give me more knowledge." • [20:114]

In Islam, acquisition of knowledge is a form of indirect worship. Acquiring, furthering, and strengthening knowledge is so significant and beneficial that even Prophet Musa عليه السلام, upon discovering that there was a servant of Allah ﷻ named Khidr عليه السلام who possessed divine knowledge, immediately set out to learn from him.

Musa said to him, "Can I accompany you, so you may teach me that which you have been taught so well?" • [Qur'an 18:66]

Moreover, countless *ahadīth* establish the value of the acquisition of knowledge. The Prophet ﷺ stated:

Scholars are the successors of prophets [Bukhari].

For the one who embarks on the path to acquire knowledge, Allah makes easy for him the path to Heaven. Moreover, angels lay their wings under the feet of a seeker of knowledge, and all creatures supplicate for his success and salvation. A righteous scholar is superior over a devout worshipper, as the full moon is over the stars. [Mishkat]

Studying or acquiring the knowledge of the religion of Islam, even for a few moments in the night, is a lot better than worshipping all night long [Mishkat].

A single jurist is heavier upon Satan (to mislead) than a thousand devout worshippers [Bukhari].

Anyway, there is so much reward for acquiring knowledge and educating oneself and others that nothing equals it. The teachers and seekers of knowledge are exalted in this world and will be crowned accordingly in the Hereafter.

ISLAM AND SECULAR EDUCATION

*I*SLAM IS THE COMPLETE WAY OF LIFE that does not ignore or fail to cover any aspect of worldly life.

As Muslims acquire knowledge of Islam and become scholars of the Qur'an, *sunnah*, Islamic jurisprudence (*fiqh*), and other faculties, they not only become religious scholars, but at the same time they also become well equipped with the knowledge needed for worldly affairs. They become philosophers, psychologists, sociologists, politicians, economists, etc. Islamic knowledge gives them an understanding of law, governmental affairs, systems of justice, financial and social systems, the welfare of society, conflict resolution and peace management, warfare and foreign policy, human rights and duties, ethics, character building, and all the other necessities of life and society.

A fair study of Muslims' contributions in the field of the sciences and in other fields will show—as you will be amazed to know—that such contributors were not just experts in secular fields, but they were insightful scholars of Islam, too. It was and still is the knowledge revealed in the holy Qur'an and in the teachings of the Prophet Muhammad ﷺ that gave Muslims the knowledge to advance humanity intellectually to the point it is at today. Given the limitations of space available to me, I cannot go into more detail to explain their achievements. However, there are fields of knowledge to which Muslims, for one reason or another, did not contribute much. This does not mean that they were not capable of doing so or that Islam is against contributing to such fields of knowledge.

Islam is not against modernization or the advancement of science and technology. In fact, Islam laid down, in theory, the foundations of all sciences and gave legal and religious flexibilities to promote and advocate for innovations for the betterment of humanity. Islam supports any innovation or development that provides ease and relieves human suffering. These efforts earn abundant rewards in one form or another. "And without a doubt, towards your Lord is the final destination" [Qur'an 53:42].

Islam is against those actions and inventions that only bring short-term happiness, that overall do not serve humanity, and that result in long-term pain and misery. Generally, Islam does not hinder any field of knowledge, science, and technology that brings happiness and prosperity. If these days non-Muslims are succeeding in science and technology and are creating great innovations, they are well accepted in Islam. It seems to me that Allah ﷻ is also not ignoring their hard work and is rewarding them in this life. Keep in mind that, as per Islam, if those who advance the cause of humanity are also blessed with faith in Allah ﷻ, then their reward will extend to the Hereafter, whereby eternal peace and happiness is ensured.

Allah ﷻ invites *all* people to pay attention, think, ponder, and search and explore His Message, His world, and His universe. This makes it easy for us to reach the ultimate truth. Since this invitation results in our benefit, all related efforts become aligned with Islam. Islam does not hinder any thinker, explorer, or scientist in this process.

Allah ﷻ states in the holy Qur'an:

Truly, in the creation of heavens and Earth, in the alternation of night and day, in the sailing of ships on sea carrying that which benefits people, in the water which is sent down by Allah from the sky, through which the earth is given life after its death, in scattered animals of all kinds on [it], and the differing movements of clouds and winds bound in between the sky and earth—in all of this, certainly, are signs for those people who utilize intellect. • [2:164]

Certainly, it is Allah Who splits open the seeds and pits. He takes out the living from the dead and is the One to take out the dead from the living. This is your Allah, so where are you falling on your face. • He bursts forth the dawn and made night the time of peace, and the sun and moon to calculate time. This is fixed by the All-Conquering, All-Knowing. • And it is He, Who made for you stars to navigate in the darkness of land and water. We have explained the signs for those who have knowledge. • [6:95-97]

And it is He Who rains down water from the sky; then We produced from it all kinds of plants, then bring forth from it greenery, from which We take out seeds over seeds. And from date palms buds, clusters of dates hang within easy reach, and there are gardens of grapes, olives, and pomegranates, in some ways similar and in some dissimilar. You people see a fruit when it yields and as it ripens. Certainly, there are signs in this for those who believe. • [6:99]

And it is He, Who spread the earth, and created on it mountains and streams; and created from all kinds of fruits in pairs, two by two, and He covers the day with night. Therein, indeed, are signs for those who think and ponder. • [13:3]

Have they not looked towards the birds, that they are balanced in the air space; they are not held, but by Allah. Certainly, there are signs in this for those who come to believe. • [16:79]

Holiness is His, Who created in pairs all those things that the Earth produces, as well as these people themselves and other things that they do not know. • [36:36]

Finally, We will indeed show them Our signs everywhere and within themselves, until it becomes evident to them that without a doubt, this is truth. Is it not enough that your Lord, without a doubt, is witness of everything? • Remember that those people are in doubt about meeting with their Lord. Remember that He encompasses everything. • [41:53-54]

Without a doubt, these sacred verses clearly tell us about Allah's signs and His invitation to us to explore the earth, the universe, and ourselves. Without advancements in science and technology, how could this be achieved? How can Allah, on the one hand, invite humanity to search and explore and, on the other hand, restrict them through His own religion, Islam? From the holy Qur'an, we come to believe that any effort intended to reject Allah ﷻ as the Creator will go in vain, and any human progress that intends to prove His existence will be fruitful and ultimately beneficial. Whatever the case may be, Allah ﷻ does not hinder any action of man.

If you pay close attention to verse 41:53, you will see how Allah ﷻ informs us, and as we explore our inner self and outer surroundings, we discover systems within systems and worlds within worlds. With this, is it not clear that the holy Qur'an was not written by a man but is divinely revealed? Allah ﷻ says, "I will continue to show my signs," and He is doing as promised, to make us recognize and embrace the truth, the ultimate truth.

Even though all of our observations and explorations are proving the existence of the Supreme Being and that the entire universe is His work of art, very few of us believe in Him. Whether we intentionally try to disprove or discover our Creator, one thing is certain: the more we search, the more the results of our efforts show, confirm, and prove the existence of a Supreme Being [Qur'an 29:69].

In my view, in light of knowledge and wisdom, science and technology, intellect and experience and with His signs, we should utilize our energies to explore and understand the Creator's purpose in creating us, instead of proving/disproving the existence of the Creator Himself. Once our purpose becomes known, we can easily pinpoint our role in this arena of life, which will lead us to solve the problems of humanity.

Islam does not and no one else should suppress, discard, or reject any effort of any sort directed towards uncovering the truth. Through advancements in science and technology and through mutual cooperation, we can reach the ultimate reality, no matter which path we, individually or collectively, take to get there, provided we are sincere in getting there. Since the ultimate reality is one, every avenue must lead to it. Some can take the route of philosophy, and some can utilize the tools of biology, psychology, anthropology, archeology, etc. to get to this reality. Some can choose to explore space or look deep down in the oceans. Some can meditate or do bird watching. Some can learn the behavior of animals and of humans. All will reach the same conclusion: there is a Supreme Being, the Creator, the Almighty Lord.

The power of the Almighty becomes evident when human researchers in the likes of philosophers, scientists, and others fail or come to a screeching halt. When Darwin fails to explain the origin of humans, when Freud is unable to lay out the vastness of the human mind, when Rousseau can no longer provide solutions to social problems, when Newton and Einstein realize their limitations, when experts of medicine cannot save patients from dying, when with all the powers we have we cannot stop natural disasters, when with all the equipment at our disposal we cannot precisely predict the future, and when we, with all our intellect, cannot solve our own problems—this is when we come to realize the power of the Almighty.

We all, at one point or another, in one way or another, come to submit to Him, but reward and success are only for those who submit willingly. We all have the right to investigate, search through knowledge, and observe with our intellect, but the one right we do not have is to make up beliefs about ultimate truths and realities, especially on the basis of incomplete or doubtful knowledge. Certainly, we ought not hinder anyone from investigating and searching for knowledge. We ought to spread the knowledge of truth and educate people in the best possible manner. This is why Islam places great importance on acquiring knowledge and education.

Since it is in the nature of clouds to float, of rivers to flow, of trees to turn green in the spring, of thunder to roar, of lights to shine and make visible, of darkness to hide, of fire to burn, and so on and so forth, and since it is in our nature to think and reason, discern and see, feel and act, question and speak, and choose, decide, differentiate, pursue and follow, we should and do have the right to question and to use our faculties to seek into and discover ultimate realities. Having faith without questioning it has greater reward in Islam, but if faith comes through investigation and contemplation, Islam says, "Let it be." Coming to faith through knowledge and understanding is far better than having no faith. Knowledge is important in Islam because it helps in bringing faith and strengthens the faithful ones.

CHAPTER 18

Punishments in Islam

𝓔VEN THOUGH THE ALMIGHTY LORD is Most Compassionate and Most Merciful, in order to do justice and to bring people to justice, He prescribed and outlined an equitable system of punishments. It is inherent in human nature to violate laws, to deviate from the right course, and to commit crimes and sins. If people do not suppress their own ill desires and refrain from inflicting pain on their own souls and on others, a system of deterrence must be put in place to protect rights, persons, and property and to keep societies peaceful and secure.

Allah ﷻ established two systems of punishments. One is for this world, and the other is for the Hereafter. In the way this life and its pleasures are temporary, so are the punishments given herein. However, punishments given in the Hereafter are eternal and more painful. A careful study of Islam shows that its systems of punishments are based on justice, because Allah ﷻ is All-Just and All-Wise.

Allah ﷻ reveals:

> And the misfortune that befalls you, it is because of what your hands earned, while He forgives much more. • [Qur'an 42:30]

In this world, soft-hearted and compassionate people are not scarce. They grieve when tragedy strikes and when people fall victim to natural disasters or sickness. Such people may never take part in inflicting pain on anyone, but they, too, would approve of severing an ailing body part in order to save a life. They would also further agree that not removing the diseased or rotten part might result in losing the entire body.

Criminals are the rotten part of a civilized society. If they are not separated through various means, the entire society is negatively affected and may eventually be destroyed. To save a society, its criminal elements must be disciplined and punished appropriately. If a society becomes lenient with criminals or does not enforce punishments for crimes and violations, its law abiding citizens cannot live in peace and progress in the right direction.

No one denies the fact that criminals must be punished, but when it comes to legislating appropriate punishment for a given crime, different opinions come to the fore, especially in the matter of capital punishments. However, if punishments are not properly designed and carried out, the entire purpose of punishment can be lost. Thus, a society must decide what an appropriate punishment for a given criminal act should be. Before deciding on punishments, we have to consider the severity of the crime, which leads us to determine which crimes are severe and which are not.

In Islam, Muslims do not formulate laws; they just follow and enforce them. The lawgiver is Allah ﷻ. He truly knows our needs, the proper solutions to our problems, our pains and sufferings and their causes and the cure for our society's ills. He knows the severity of crimes and their consequences for victims and for society as a whole. Therefore, He is the best judge in legislating laws and appropriating punishments.

In a civilized society, an individual's life and property are among the most important things to be protected. Laws are made to secure them from the barbarity of criminals. Laws deter people from taking a person's life and property and punish them when they do. Good people always abide by laws under normal circumstances, but penalties and punishments prevent them from resorting to crime even under extreme circumstances. Peoples' lives and property are not safe where laws are weak or the justice system is not enforced. In such a society, anarchy is the business of the day.

CAPITAL PUNISHMENTS

*I*SLAM, EVEN WITH ALL THE KINDNESS and forgiveness embedded in it, lays down a system of capital punishments for capital crimes. Islam instills tolerance and patience in Muslims and at the same time requires them to enforce Islamic laws fully and to bring criminals to justice, especially when they abrogate the rights of others' life and property. Islam, to keep Islamic society headed in the right direction, commands its followers to be lawfully kind to both victims and criminals. Being kind to victims means bringing justice to them, and being kind to criminals means bringing them to justice. When criminals are punished appropriately, they refrain from committing more crimes and, most importantly, can thereby avoid the torment of Hell. If Muslims fail to punish criminals, they are and will be held liable by Allah ﷻ for not being just to victims.

Since laws and punishments deter people from committing crime, Islam establishes the method of enforcing punishment in public to achieve true and everlasting deterrence against crime. When a criminal is punished in public, the thousands of onlookers learn firsthand the consequences of crimes and as a result are deterred without any extra effort or expense.

Many times, those who commit crimes are not aware of the consequences of criminal actions to themselves and to others. The application of punishment in public leads people to think many times over before committing any criminal act. In my view, not thinking of the consequences before committing an act is one of the greatest factors that leads to crime. Upon realizing and visualizing themselves being punished in public, many choose otherwise and save themselves and others from harm, expense, and other burdens. In my opinion, in societies where crime rates are high, youngsters should be given tours of prisons and correctional facilities. This may help lower crime and prevent them from becoming criminals.

In the verses mentioned below, the severity of crimes is clear from the punishments decreed by the Lord. A careful study of such crimes and their impact on individuals and society will show that Allah's 🕋 decreed punishments are not cruel or inappropriate, but clearly just, viable, and beneficial. Certainly, our Lord cannot be unjust to any of His beings, including criminals, but justice must be brought to victims and their dependents, in order to maintain order in society.

MURDER

O Muslims! It has been obligated upon you to avenge in the case of murder of innocent people: a freed man for a freed man and a slave for a slave, and a woman for a woman. Yes, for whom some forgiveness is granted from his brother, so demand blood money nicely and it is to be paid gladly. This relief of punishment is from your Lord, and it is mercy... • [Qur'an 2:178]

And there is life for you in avenging for murder O people of reason! So, fear from now on. • [Qur'an 2:179]

And he who intentionally killed a believer, so his punishment is Hell; in it he will remain for a long period. On him is Allah's wrath, and Allah sent a curse on him and has set aside for him severe torment. • [Qur'an 4:93]

And We prescribed onto them in this (Torah), that certainly, life for a life, eye for an eye, and nose for a nose, and ear for an ear, and tooth for a tooth, and for all wounds, a just reprisal... • [Qur'an 5:45]

The consequences of an unjust murder are truly felt only by the victim's dependents. The unjust murder of a man takes a beloved husband from a wife, who may now have no supporter and caretaker. It takes away a father who is like an umbrella of peace, security, and happiness for his children and takes away their education, protection, independence, and well-being. They lose everything after his death. It takes a breadwinner from a family. It takes a son from parents, leaving them helpless. It takes a father-like brother from orphaned siblings. Losing someone brings chaos to the family and disrupts all aspects of life. If capital punishments are not enforced and unjust murders, rapes, and violent acts are not checked with capital punishments, progress will be disturbed and societies undermined.

Certainly, Allah ﷻ knows that people have emotions, which may play a part in doing justice. Therefore, Allah ﷻ did not give them the right to decide punishments for capital crimes, because however fair they try to be, they may still not be able to satisfactorily punish the guilty and bring justice to victims. However, Allah's ﷻ prescriptions of justice are fair and equitable, whether we like them or not or feel that they are unreasonable. There is great wisdom in such punishments. Besides punishing the guilty, in the case of a murder, Allah ﷻ gives full right and choice only to the victim's family to forgive the murderer, in exchange for *diyat*, a monetary compensation [Qur'an 4:92].

THEFT

> And the male and female thief, cut off their hands, in revenge for the misdeeds they demonstrated, and as punishment from Allah, and Allah is All-Conquering, All-Wise. • [Qur'an 5:38]

For the crime of stealing, Allah ﷻ commands the justice authorities, after due process and consideration of mitigating circum- stances, to amputate the hand of a thief. Through this prescribed punishment, Allah ﷻ shows the importance of safeguarding people's property and wealth. For example, a father/mother has saved for his/her children's education and marriage, their own retirement needs, or for any other livelihood, and someone comes along and steals everything. Such criminals should not get away with light punishments. Thus, amputation of a hand is quite appropriate and necessary, as well as being a one hundred percent failsafe measure of deterrence against theft.

In modern societies, the cost of securing money and property runs into billions of dollars, and the burden of this is passed onto the people to bear. The Islamic law of amputating a hand for theft through legal procedures is currently enforced in Saudi Arabia, where if you forget or leave your valuables, you can usually find them without any hassle and without theft having taken place. The Saudi government and local businesses, as per my knowledge, barely have any security measures in place against theft, nor do they spend huge sums of money to secure their valuables. Theft in Saudi Arabia is almost non-existent.

FORNICATION AND ADULTERY

And do not go near fornication/adultery, without a doubt, this is shamelessness and an evil way. • [Qur'an 17:32]

The fornicator female and the fornicator male, so hit each one of them with 100 lashes. And let not come to you the slightest pity on them in regards to Allah's Law, if you believe in Allah and the Last Day. And remain present at the time of their punishment, a group of Muslims. • [Qur'an 24:2]

Adultery, fornication and other related crimes and sins may not be considered unlawful in today's modern societies, and no punishment is usually set aside for them, but in Islam these acts are very sinful and their punishments must be served.

If an unmarried man or woman either admits to the crime of fornication or is found guilty based on the testimony of four (4) sane male adult Muslims, the punishment is one hundred (100) lashes, as outlined in the verse. For the crime of adultery, for both men and women, as per the *sunnah* of the Prophet ﷺ and his companions, the punishment is *rajm* (stoning to death).

Before analyzing the severity of punishment for this sinful act, we must first fully know the severity of adultery to understand the punishments prescribed for it in Islam. Suffice it to say, that this sexual act is a slap in the face of the sacred institution of marriage. It is shameful for a married couple, because they break the same covenant by which they came together in the first place. It severs the bond of trust between a husband and wife, brings disaster to their family, and damages relationships with children. It leaves children hopeless, undignified, and often parentless. They become mentally distressed or run away shamefully, thereby shattering the family unit. It is disgraceful to and disregards the religion of which one claims to be a follower. Adultery destroys the respect of a person among friends, colleagues, and family members. Overall, it is enough that Allah سبحانه وتعالى made it unlawful because it is shameless, immoral, and the evil way.

Committing fornication/adultery brings about disease, depression, mistrust, financial burden, insecurity, and irresponsibility, and it often leads to criminal behavior. It burdens society with abortions, increased medical expenses, birth control and health issues, single parenting, and the birth of illegitimate children, who may grow up undisciplined and immoral. It not only causes pain and grief to people here, but its consequences reach into the Hereafter, in the form of punishment.

Extramarital affairs and other immoral sins are acts that completely disregard Allah's سبحانه وتعالى commandments, and adulterous sinners are in clear contempt of Allah's سبحانه وتعالى existence and His commandments. Allah سبحانه وتعالى reserves the right to be feared, but committing such acts shows that one ignores and has become negligent of His wrath and justice. Besides other attributes of Allah سبحانه وتعالى, He is All-Aware, All-Hearing, and All-Knowing, but by committing such sins the sinner completely disregards these attributes. Allah has absolute power over everything: His temporary silence and postponement of punishment do not mean that we are not going to be held liable for our actions or that He does not exist. People cannot escape Allah's power of justice and enforcement of punishments, and this is exactly what people forget and why they fall into sin.

When people engage in sinful acts, Allah deems it a declaration of war against Him [Qur'an 2:278-9]. Certainly, no one can defeat Allah; therefore, it is quite foolish and dangerous to engage in such immoral acts. He will undoubtedly bring forth destruction and severe torment. Islam not only prohibits such immoral acts, but it also gives solutions to control and suppress them. Abstinence and self-restraint are the best alternative. For a few moments of pleasure, it is not wise to permanently displease Allah; it is just not worth it. I hope my reader has grasped the severity of this sinful act and the justification for its severe punishment in Islam.

ALCOHOL

The consumption of alcohol is specifically prohibited in the holy Qur'an. Lashing as the punishment for consuming alcohol was established by the *sunnah*; the number of lashes (80) was established through *ijma* (scholarly consensus). [Tirmidhi and Abu Dawud] There is not a single mature person who is unaware of the disastrous consequences of alcohol consumption. One simple commandment saved billions from drinking—see how beautifully Islam describes and declares alcohol and other destructive acts *harām* (prohibited) for its followers.

> O those who brought faith! Alcohol and gambling and idols and divining are in fact impure, works of Satan, so protect (yourself) from them, to acquire success... • [Qur'an 5:90]

They ask you about alcohol and gambling. Say, "Although in both there is great sin, and benefits for ordinary people; but their sin is far greater than their benefits... • [Qur'an 2:219]

Satan just wants to bring enmity among you and envy through alcohol and gambling, and to prevent you from the remembrance of Allah and from *salāh*. So will you now refrain? • [Qur'an 5:91]

Islam realistically admits some benefits of alcohol, as revealed in the Qur'an, but its harms clearly outweigh its benefits. People who sell alcohol earn their living through it, and those who drink it may often be found to have enhanced carnal desires. Its major harms include, but are not limited to, humiliation, impairment of judgment and vision, temporary physical handicaps, heart and other health complications, and a waste of money for pleasures that end soon. People who rely on drinking for peace and solace never find it, but find themselves under worse stress, depression, and other physical and psychological problems.

On many occasions people who drink and drive bring disaster to their lives and to others, and under its influence they end up committing unforgettable and heinous crimes. Alcohol is one of the major causes of accidents and deaths in almost every civilized society where drinking is the business of the day. Even though every society realizes the harms of drinking, they find themselves quite handicapped to do away with alcohol completely. So the Lord took it upon Himself to prohibit alcohol, saving hundreds of millions of Muslims from its harms.

When Islamic laws and punishments for crimes/sins are enforced, Islam is not the one to benefit, rather, people enjoy a good, healthy and peaceful life. Islam brings benefits and true peace in this world and everlasting success in the Hereafter. These days, some Muslims are colliding head-on with Islamic principles and prohibitions and meeting with harmful consequences. Allah ﷻ is just to everyone, and doing justice to all is one of His qualities. Some of His prescribed punishments may initially seem to be cruel and severe, but all of His punishments are quite just, proper, and based on the severity of crimes/sins.

FALSE ACCUSATION

And those who accuse chaste women and did not bring four witnesses, then strike them with 80 lashes, and do not accept their testimony ever. And they themselves are disobedient. • [Qur'an 24:4]

By specifically including in the Qur'an the punishment for falsely accusing a woman of committing adultery, Allah ﷻ shows the severity of this sin. Initially, it may not seem to be a big sin/crime, but in Islam it is such a huge crime that such a severe punishment has been prescribed for it by Allah ﷻ. Women's chastity is sacred in the sight of Allah ﷻ, and anyone who falsely tries to defame a chaste woman receives 80 lashes and the displeasure of the Almighty ﷻ. Though this punishment may seem cruel, it is a sufficient deterrence and thus makes it easy for women to defend themselves.

CHAPTER 19

Concept of State and Governance in Islam

STATE AND THE SYSTEM OF GOVERNMENT IN ISLAM are not goals in themselves, but a means to achieving a higher end. To be clear, the holy Qur'an and *sunnah* do not specifically propose any governing entity, such as state, nation-state, kingdom, or empire, and they do not provide an organized structure or type of government: democracy, monarchy, dictatorship, republic, etc. You might ask, "Since Islam addresses every issue and since it is the complete way of life, why did Allah ﷻ or the Prophet ﷺ not specify a form of government or political structure for the Muslim *ummah*?"

To answer this question in its entirety and to the satisfaction of some, I would have to go into many details, which would take me away from the subject matter of this book. However, I do not want to leave this question unanswered, so I will try to be as brief as possible. I ask the reader to bear with me and to utilize the knowledge gained so far to understand this matter.

As stated earlier, Allah ﷻ sent the first humans, Adam عليه السلام and Hawwa عليها السلام to Earth to live here temporarily. They and their future progeny (humanity) were to be the inhabitants of this Earth, where they were to multiply, so all the souls that are to come to Earth can live and work to achieve their ultimate goal, which is preparing for the Hereafter. We were and still are the inhabitants of this Earth. We were and still are the same creatures and members of the creation of Allah ﷻ, called humans. We had and still have the same purpose. To this end, guidance was the only thing we needed, both theoretical and practical, which we were to receive through the prophets.

Certainly, there was no need for anything else, let alone divisions or classifications based on color, ethnicity, nationality, etc. These man-made classifications have not and will not play any role whatsoever in preparing for the Hereafter. However, Islam categorizes people into three groups: 1) believers, 2) non-believers, and 3) hypocrites.

As I have said earlier, once I am dead, I am truly a no-body—rather a dead body. For example, there is no such thing as a "black" dead body or a "white" one. All dead bodies are to be disposed of, one way or another, regardless of their color, race, or religion. These classifications do not serve our purpose on earth or anywhere else, and for Allah ﷻ these distinctions have no meaning. Near Allah ﷻ, there is either the Muslim *ummah* (community) or those who do not belong to it. Even within the Muslim *ummah*, there are no different "nations," but all are members of one *ummah*. This is the universality of Islam, in which there is no distinction between black and white, American and Chinese, or Arabs and non-Arabs – all are Muslim.

Since the Qur'an and *sunnah* are sufficient to rule over Muslims, Allah ﷻ and the Prophet ﷺ did not specify any governing structure for Muslims to live under. At the time, for Islam, this was least impor-tant. However, the Qur'an and *sunnah* contains sufficient guidance on which basis Muslims can and actually did establish a just governing system, and Islam has perfected all the necessary components required to run such a system.

The wisdom behind not establishing a governing structure was to allow Muslims to choose for themselves whatever they deemed necessary, just and proper. So, as soon as the time arose at the passing of the Prophet 🕌, Muslims elected a *khalīfa* (caliph/leader). Thus, the natural and equitable process of selection/election took place among the Muslims, and a leader was chosen to lead the Muslim *ummah*. In this way, from the very beginning, even when there was no sign of any governing structure or its need, this democratic principle of choosing the form of government by the people was embedded in the Islamic system. This election established the process of choosing a leader, namely the caliph, and established a governing structure, called *khilāfat* (caliphate), by the vote/consent of righteous Muslims.

The holy Qur'an did not establish a political state, and neither did the Prophet 🕌. When the Prophet 🕌 arrived in Madinah and drew treaties with the local tribes for people to coexist peacefully and to advance the religion of Islam, he neither mentioned any political entity of Islam, nor did he mention himself as any kind of political leader of Muslims. Rather, he only described himself as the Prophet of the Lord. Even when he wrote letters inviting kings and rulers of neighboring empires to Islam, he never mentioned any Islamic political entity or any status in it for himself, except as Prophet of Allah [Appendix III].

The Prophet 🕌 was right in not choosing any political titles for himself, such as governor or king, because his status as a prophet was certainly above all. He also did not set any geographical boundary for Islam, which is usually necessary to establish an autonomous state.

Since Islam was to be for the whole world and for all people to come, both the Qur'an and *sunnah* called it the Muslim *ummah*, an entity that could comprise from a few to billions of people, without any boundaries. Both the Qur'an and *sunnah* taught and trained Muslims how to run the affairs of the *ummah*, e.g., how to become leaders, serve the people, establish rules of law, do justice, enforce punishments, deduce new laws from the Qur'an and *sunnah*, propagate Islam, serve minorities, establish financial and social systems, manage foreign affairs, defend and protect, form treaties, strengthen the *ummah*, establish consensus, assign and utilize power, follow leaders and form oppositions, and so on. Everything was taught by the holy Qur'an and exemplified by the Prophet ﷺ.

The main purpose of a Muslim's life is to worship Allah ﷻ, by fulfilling all of His rights and the rights of people. As Muslims fulfill their duties to Allah ﷻ and to people in light of the Qur'an and *sunnah*, Islam leaves them independent to choose or form any political or governing structure they deem fit and necessary for their situation, provided that its foundations are based on the following:

- Allah ﷻ is the All-Sovereign.
- The Qur'an and *sunnah* are the supreme law of the land.
- Governors are servants of the people and must never abuse their authority. Both the government, and those governed must observe Islamic *sharia* law.
- Justice must be served equitably; no one is above the law. In matters of justice, no distinction is to be made between the rich and the poor, officials and the public, and so on.
- A leader must fulfill all the requirements necessary to serve and represent Muslims, and he must possess good moral character and all the virtues laid down by Islam.
- Affairs of the *ummah* are to be carried out with the consultation of a *shura* (an advisory board).
- Above all, the rights of Allah ﷻ and the rights of the people (both Muslim and non-Muslim) must be fulfilled and observed.
- Muslims have the right, power and duty to remove unjust and unrighteous leaders, but they are required to follow them unconditionally as long as they act in accordance with Islamic *sharia*.

SYSTEMS OF GOVERNANCE

THEOCRACY

The ideal Islamic government cannot be referred to as theocratic, because even though it is governed by religious rules/commandments, the enforcers do not claim to be divinely guided. They cannot claim this because it would amount to blasphemy. Moreover, there is no religious hierarchy in Islam. In an Islamic government, Muslim officials can only enforce the laws outlined in and deduced from the Qur'an and *sunnah*, and in no way are they above them. No individual or group has any right or authority to rule over people in the name of Islam without actually observing Islamic principles. Allah 🕮 and the Prophet 🕮 rule, all else follow. No kind of obedience or loyalty can be sought or designated that violates Allah's 🕮 commandments.

CHURCH AND STATE

An Islamic government is fundamentally different from a secular one, where religion does not play a role or determine a direction in running the affairs of state. A secular government keeps itself away from following any religion or supernatural guidance. The church or religious institutions take charge of religious aspects of human life, and the states steer the secular aspects.

When and how this idea of separation of church and state was introduced or put into place is a subject I leave for historians. I can only guess that this separation between church and state was because the church was not playing its part properly and had abused the trust people put into it, *or* it was not interested in solving peoples' problems and had become political/authoritative, *or* it was no longer interested in public affairs, *or* the ideology it represented became irrelevant and incapable of uplifting human suffering, *or* because it was too sacred to be involved in matters of state, *or* finally, perhaps because it had become an obstacle to the state and its goals, and there was no choice but to separate it. Under any one or all of these circumstances, this separation has proved to be a wise decision, because history shows that it bore fruit.

As I mentioned earlier, in Islam, there is no part of life that can be defined as secular. Islam is not just a religion, and it does not only deal with otherworldly matters; it is the complete way of life and provides complete guidance for every facet of the life of this world and of the following one. As Muslims practice Islam completely, and as Islamic governments enforce Islamic law, nothing remains to be called secular.

Islamic rules apply whether in a mosque or anywhere else in the world. Hence, no visible or invisible wall can be erected between "mosque and state." In fact, the entire world is a mosque for Muslims [Bukhari and Muslim], meaning Islamic rules always apply everywhere. Muslims are always bound by some Islamic rule, wherever they go and whatever they do. There are no contradictory sets of rules for different places or occasions. In Islam, there is no such thing as, "business is business" and "a cup of tea is a cup of tea"; there is no such thing as "everything is allowed in love and war." Strict adherence to law is necessary for all Muslims, at all times, whether alone or in public.

An *imam* (prayer leader) of a mosque and a governor of a Muslim state are not above the law, and neither have or can produce separate guiding rules for themselves. There is only one set of rules, Islamic law (*sharia*), and it is for both of them to follow. In the case of a violation of any Islamic law, a state that is following Islamic principles can interfere in the affairs of a mosque, and a mosque that is following Islamic principles can interfere in the affairs of the state. Both of these institutions are governed under the greater umbrella of Islam and serve the need of individuals and of the society. Hence, there cannot be and there is no separation of "church" and "state" in Islam.

One of the qualities of Islam is that it does not permit the violation of any of its principles, no matter how minute it is, for any conceived greater good; the end result is always with Allah. There are also no contradictions in Islam that cause clashes among its principles. Islam does not allow its followers to achieve their goals by "all means." There is no excuse for any willful violation, even in the name of any greater good. If this affects someone's ambitions, he or she has to change his or her course, not the Islamic rules; Islamic principles must be upheld.

AUTHORITARIAN

Since Islam requires strict and complete adherence to Islamic law, does it propose authoritarianism? No. Authoritarianism means the rule of a person or a group. There is no such system of rule in Islam. The sovereignty and authority is of the Lord and of His rules. Since it is in the nature of power to corrupt, an authoritarian regime is bound to be corrupt and unjust. Allah ﷻ is All-Powerful, but He is not unjust. When Allah ﷻ Himself is not unjust, how can He allow authoritarianism, where many injustices occur?

MONARCHY

Monarchy also does not qualify as the kind of government Islam would have proposed because it is not formed by the consent of the people. A monarch is the absolute owner of his kingdom and maintains complete sovereignty over his subjects. He is much more likely to abuse his uncontested power, since the people have no say in a monarchy and are just subjected to his authoritarian rule. Moreover, authority is usually handed down from the king to his son, whether he is capable or not. Islam does not permit such a system, because this goes directly against its foundational principles, in which Allah ﷻ is the Sovereign and people are subject to His rules only.

DEMOCRACY

In the sense that a democratic government is established, replaced, and run by the people, and considering the other benefits it entails, democracy is the only system of governance that comes close to what Islam would have wanted or proposed. In fact, the caliphate system of governance as founded by the early Muslims is the closest to a democratic form of government. However, unlike democracy, in Islam people do not have the right or power to change the basic laws, principles of life, and economic, social, and judicial systems, because all of these things were pre-ordained by Allah ﷻ and His Prophet ﷺ. This means that no interest group can mold the policies of the state or tilt it towards one side or another for the benefit of one over the other. In fact, there is no need for interest groups in Islam. It is the duty of the government to fulfill all the needs of the people of all segments of society fairly and equitably, without any favoritism or elitism.

Islam would not have favored the contemporary nation-state setting, because this does not form one Muslim *ummah*, but different nations. In a nation-state setting, the identity of a person is based on his birthplace; however, in Islam, being a Muslim is in itself a sufficient identity. In Islam, everyone is part of the Muslim *ummah* and not part of different nationalities. In nation-states, interaction among people is limited due to geographical boundaries, border control, and other political/economic reasons. In the contemporary setting of nation-states, Muslim brotherhood diffuses. Instead of being a Muslim brother first, people are Pakistani, Bangladeshi, Egyptian, Moroccan, and so on and so forth. Nevertheless, if it was not for the occasion of Hajj, where Muslim unity, equality, and brotherhood are clearly displayed, sentiments of nationalism would have otherwise abolished Muslim brotherhood completely.

Since Muslims, for one reason or another, have come very far in establishing these nation-states, there is neither the need to nor would it be possible to abolish this nation-state system and create a unified geo-political unit for the entire *ummah*. It will suffice for Muslim nation-states to adopt democratically and truly the Islamic system to reap the benefits of Islamic principles and lifestyle.

By carefully analyzing the commandments of Allah ﷻ and related *ahadith* of the Prophet ﷺ, we can easily draw a clear picture and a true blueprint of an Islamic government. It would look exactly like the system of governance put in place by the companions of the Prophet

🕮 on his passing, which was truly Islamic and inclusive of democratic principles. For someone who would like to have a term for this system of governance, I would humbly propose "Islamicracy," where:

- Allah 🕮, the Omnipotent, is the All-Sovereign. All authority lies with Him, and He holds absolute power.
- Allah's 🕮 commandments and the Prophet's 🕮 teachings are the guiding posts in executing governmental affairs.
- The "in-charge" of the government, as chosen by the people, directly or indirectly through their representatives, acts as the vicegerent of the Prophet 🕮, and with the authority vested in him by Islamic law (*sharia*).

  ➢ This "in-charge," the vicegerent or any other appropriate title given to him, is not a "ruler" but serves the Muslim *ummah*. He does not hold any special rights, privileges, or immunity of any sort, and he is not above the law.

  ➢ There should be no term limit, but he can be removed as soon as he acts contrary to Islamic rules or becomes incompetent.

  ➢ He must carry on the day-to-day business of the state by consulting with the *shura* (Islamic Council), a body of dignitaries chosen by him and/or elected by the people.

  ➢ He must be physically fit, mentally sound, and full of wisdom and knowledge, and he must uphold good moral character and be pious, kind, selfless, and just. He must also bear other Islamic virtues and be free from all vices.

- The purpose of an Islamic state is to establish/enforce Islamic principles, collect and properly distribute the prescribed obligatory charity (*zakāh*), protect the life, rights, and property of its people, both Muslims and non-Muslims, defend the state, deliver justice fairly and equitably, fulfill people's basic needs, etc.

Overall, the basic and the most important duty of the Islamic state is to establish and assist in establishing *amar bil ma'ruf* (enjoining good) and *nahī anil munkar* (forbidding evil). From the following Qur'anic verses and *ahadīth*, a clearer picture evolves.

Those people, as we fortified them in the land, they established prayer (*salāh*) and kept giving obligatory charity (*zakāh*) and kept commanding to enjoin good and to forbid evil. And up to Allah is the outcome of all deeds. • [Qura'n 22:41]

You are better among all those nations that appeared for people, that you enjoin good and forbid evil and believe in Allah… • [3:110]

…mutually keep helping one another in good and in piety. And do not help in sin and in cruelty, and fear Allah… • [5:2]

These abodes of the Hereafter We make for those who do not wish to be superior on Earth and cause mischief. And safe outcome is for the fearful ones. • [28:83]

And those who have accepted their Lord and established the prayer (*salāh*); and their practice is to consult among each other… • [42:38]

…and (O Prophet!)…consult with them in matters… • [3:159]

…and (say), "I have been commanded to keep doing justice between you people…" • [42:15]

Do you not know that certainly Allah has control over the Heavens and Earth and that no one can save or protect you apart from Him. • [2:107]

…and the command is His… • [28:70]

…the command is Allah's alone… • [6:57]

…say, "Control is indeed absolutely of Allah"… • [3:154]

…indeed, it is Allah's command, prior to and after… • [30:4]

…certainly, Allah commands whatever He wills. • [5:1]

…is Allah not the Greatest Lord of all lords? • [95:8]

Say, "O Allah, The Owner of all kingdoms!—You give authority to whomever You will and seize it from whomever You will. And (You) dignify whomever You will and defame whomever You will. Indeed, in Your control is all goodness; certainly, You have power over what You will. • [3:26]

...certainly, the earth belongs to Allah; makes owner whomever He wills from among His slaves... • [7:128]

...these are limits (set by) Allah, so do not cross them; and those who cross the limits (set by) Allah, they indeed are the oppressors. • [2:229]

...and those who did not judge according to this that Allah revealed, so indeed they are unbelievers. • [5:44]

...and those who did not judge according to this that Allah revealed, so indeed they are wrongdoers. • [5:45]

...and those who did not judge according to this, that Allah revealed, so indeed they are rebellious. • [5:47]

O you who brought faith! Obey Allah, and obey the Prophet and the leaders among you. Then if you fall into dispute about something, submit it to Allah and the Prophet... • [4:59]

And do not follow the orders of those who are extravagant, • who cause chaos on earth and do not rectify. • [26:151-152]

...whenever you judge among people, so judge with justice... • [4:58]

...and you people, keep fulfilling promises. Certainly, questions will be asked about promises (on the Day of Judgment). • [17:34]

...so as long as they remain steadfast on that (agreement) for you, you too remain steadfast for them. Certainly, Allah holds dear the pious ones. • [9:7]

...with those disbelievers with whom you made a truce, then they did not fall short and did not incite anyone against you, so fulfill the truce until its term. Certainly, Allah likes the pious ones. • [9:4]

And if you fear any nation's breach of trust, so throw the truce towards them equally. Certainly, Allah does not like traitors. • [8:58]

And if those people wished to make peace, so you accept the truce, and have trust in Allah. Certainly, He indeed is All-Hearing, All-Knowledgeable. • And if they want to deceive you, so without a doubt, for you Allah is sufficient. • [8:61-62]

Allah does not stop you from those who did not fight with you about the religion of Islam and did not throw you out of your homes, that you keep good relations with them and be just to them. Certainly, Allah likes those who are just. • [60:8]

...so whoever oppressed you, so you too oppress them in the same manner he oppressed you. And fear Allah, and believe that Allah is certainly with the fearful ones... • [2:194]

And if you punish for the crime, so do it equal to the crime as done to you. And if you practice patience, so without a doubt, this is better for those who are patient. • [16:126]

Prophet Muhammad 🕌 said:

The nations that have gone before you were destroyed because they punished criminals from the lower class according to the law and pardoned those from the upper class. I swear to that Being, in Whose hands is my soul, that even if Fatima, the daughter of Muhammad, had stolen, I would have cut her hands. [Bukhari]

Any ruler, who is in charge of the matters of any community of Muslims, if he dies in the condition that he used to deceive and betray their trust, so Allah will forbid Heaven for him. [Bukhari and Muslim]

Any governor who takes control of any department of a Muslim government, then does not fulfill his duties wholeheartedly and does not work with sincerity, he definitely will not enter Paradise with Muslims. [Bukhari and Muslim]

It is obligatory for a Muslim to listen to and be obedient to his ruler, whether he likes or dislikes his rule, until he is commanded to perform a sinful act; and when commanded to commit sin, then there is no listening and following. [Bukhari and Muslim]

The following is a famous *hadīth* of the Prophet 🕌:

There is no following in the disobedience of Allah; following is only in good. [Muslim]

This means that if the person in charge of Muslims' affairs becomes disobedient to Allah's 🕌 rules and commandments, then following him is not required. Obedience is required only in performing righteous and good deeds.

If we closely study the era of *Khilāfat-e-Rashidūn,* the first four righteous caliphs, we can learn what kind of political entity and system of governance Islam wants to establish and in what it resulted.

The Honorable Abu Bakr Siddīq ﷺ, the closest companion of the Prophet ﷺ, was elected to become the first caliph, immediately after the passing of the Prophet ﷺ. He addressed the Muslim *ummah* as follows:

> Obey me as long as I am in the obedience of Allah and of His Prophet, and when I cease to obey them, there is no obedience from you to me. [Bukhari and Muslim]

On another occasion, the first caliph said:

> The one who has been made in charge will be heavily accounted for and will be greatly in danger of punishment on the Day of Judgment, because he is more likely to cause harm to people. The one who oppresses his people betrays Allah ﷺ. [Bukhari]

The second caliph, the Honorable Umar bin al-Khattab ﷺ, in Madinah at the time, said:

> I fear that even if a lamb is wasted far away at the bank of River Farat (Euphrates), Allah ﷺ will hold me accountable for it.
>
> [Abu Dawud and Muslim]

On another occasion, he said:

> There is no *khalīfa* without consultation (of *shura*). [Kanzul Ammal]

The fourth caliph, the Honorable Ali ﷺ, once said:

> While in the obedience of Allah, whatever command I give you, it is incumbent upon you to obey and follow, regardless of your like or dislike of it; and if I decree something upon you in Allah's disobedience, so there is no obligation of obedience for anyone.
>
> [Kanzul Ammal]

Once, Umar ﷺ, the caliph, was passing by an old woman in a faraway place and heard her cursing the caliph because her needs were not fulfilled and she was in pain and was helpless. He stopped and asked her, "What if the caliph has no knowledge of your situation?"

She replied, "Then he has no right to be a caliph of the Muslim *ummah.*" [Kanzul Ammal]

These were the standards set by the teachings of Islam and the practice of early Muslims in order to form a political entity and run its affairs. We do not find such an example in our time. This does not mean that there are weaknesses in Islam, but it is rather unfortunate for Muslims as they have failed to live up to and replicate such examples.

It is to be noted that Islam is not dependent on an Islamic government. It is good for Muslims to have an Islamic system of governance and live in an Islamic state, and certainly, it will help them. Nevertheless, Muslims are surviving and can survive without jeopardizing their beliefs and religious practices in the absence of an Islamic government.

In Islam, to become a true Muslim is the priority. If there are obstacles for one reason or another in the performance of religious duties in one place, Islam allocates great rewards for migrating to places where there is greater religious freedom. If migration is not possible and suffering and oppression are being faced, then the accountability for religious obligations rests with Allah ﷻ. Muslims are still required to hold onto their beliefs and practice as much as humanly possible. Certainly, there are flexibilities in Islam for Muslims living in non-Muslim countries. However, there are no excuses or justifications for not observing the required practices under any circumstance.

THE ECONOMIC SYSTEM IN ISLAM

THE MAIN PURPOSE of the Islamic model for an economic system is to remove financial hardship and bring economic independence and prosperity fairly and equitably to all people. Setting up such a model must not contradict other Islamic principles and must make people happy and peaceful, in order that they can work towards their ultimate goal.

Islam is not against earning and accumulating wealth, but it sets boundaries on how to do it, without creating any hidden or obvious harm to others. Islam does not want some to reap all the profits and economic advantages and others to be always at a loss. Islam does not approve of a financial system or arrangement where some go to sleep peacefully, without being in fear of any loss, and others can never achieve financial independence. From the following Qur'anic verses and *ahadith*, we can easily comprehend the Islamic economic system:

Allah 🕮 states:

And seek into the wealth given to you by Allah, the abode of the Hereafter, and do not be unmindful of your worldly share, and do favors as Allah sent favor onto you. And do not wish to cause chaos in society. Certainly, Allah does not like those who create chaos. •
[28:77]

And, certainly indeed, We have fortified you on Earth and produced for you the sustenance of life in it. You people are least grateful. • [7:10]

Then, when *salah* (obligatory prayers of worship) is completed, so disperse on Earth and seek Allah's bounties, and remember Allah much, that you may be successful. • [62:10]

...trade is made permissible by Allah and interest is made prohibited... • [2:275]

Those who consume interest will not stand on Doomsday, except as stands he who is horrified by the touch of a demon. This is so because they used to say, "Trade is indeed just like interest"... •
[2:275]

Allah wipes out interest (earnings) and increases charities, and Allah does not like any ungrateful sinner. • [2:276]

Hence, if you do not do this, then prepare to fight Allah and His Prophet, and if you surrender, then for you is your actual principal... • [2:279]

Prophet Muhammad 🕮 said:

The honest and trustworthy tradesmen will be with the prophets, the truthful ones, and martyrs. [Tirmidhi]

There is no better food to be eaten than that earned by the work of one's own hands. [Bukhari]

Making honest and permissible earnings is the obligation second to the obligation of *salāh*. [Abu Dawud and Nisa'i]

He further stated:

The body nourished with prohibited earnings is most deserving to be in the Hellfire. The one who brings sellable items to the market to sell earns great rewards, and the one who hoards is like an apostate. [Bukhari]

The one who brings items of trade in the market (to sell) gets provisions, and the one who hoards is damned. [Kitabul-Bayya]

The Prophet ﷺ also strongly prohibited the charging of interest on loans and spelt out severe punishment for those dealing in usury.

The focus of the Islamic economic system is not on money and wealth, but on the welfare of individuals and the society as a whole. Its aim is to develop a humanistic society, not a materialistic one. In Islam, accumulation of wealth is not the end but a means to bring peace, overall prosperity, and a sound environment for all to work toward the ultimate success. The motive of economic activities is not to multiply profits many times over but to increase production of goods, thereby fulfilling people's needs and expanding the economy.

As does everything else, wealth too belongs to Allah ﷻ. He gives it to whoever He wills. Allah ﷻ reveals:

...and if you have fear of becoming poor, Allah will soon enrich you with His blessings, if Allah wills... • [Qur'an 9:28]

Wealth is given as a trust to people, and they are required to use it as Allah ﷻ prescribed. On Judgment Day, anyone entrusted with wealth will be heavily accountable for how it was used.

LOVE OF WEALTH — Often, love of wealth makes man selfish, thus causing social and economic chaos for many. The gap between the poor and the rich becomes wider, and at last the rich become masters and the poor become their slaves. The holy Prophet ﷺ has regarded the love of wealth as the vilest of all human evils. To this day, many crimes trace their roots to the love and want of wealth.

Allah ﷻ further reveals:

> Believe in what Allah and His Prophet say, and spend from that wealth of which He made you a trustee. So those people who brought faith from among you and spent in charity, for them is great reward. • [Qur'an 57:7]

> And be aware that your wealth, your children, is indeed a trial. And certainly, with Allah is great reward. • [Qur'an 8:28]

Clearly, wealth in Islam is not only to live a comfortable life but, through its proper use, to attain the pleasure of Allah ﷻ.

TRADES AND PROFESSIONS — In Islam, all trades, professions, skills, services, and earnings must be *halāl* (permissible) in nature. A Muslim worker and businessperson must refrain from all *harām* (prohibited) dealings/activities, such as lying, deceiving, hiding facts or faults, bribery, stealing, unreasonable profit-making, taking advantage of the needy, gambling, lottery, and all other dealings with pork, alcohol, illicit drugs, and other harmful products. Consuming money earned from *harām* commerce is like filling the stomach with Hellfire [Qurtabi]. Under no circumstance is *harām* commerce allowed in the Islamic economic model or for a Muslim.

It is not only beneficial, but also incumbent on every Muslim to acquire the knowledge of *harām* (prohibited) and *halāl* (permissible), especially for those who are involved in trade or business.

- **Hoarding** is prohibited in Islam. To make a profit by creating artificial shortages of basic commodities in order to raise their prices and to take advantage of people's situations is one of the greatest sins, leads to Hell, and is completely prohibited.

- **Forward-trading** and trading based on speculation is another form of *harām* (forbidden) business dealing and profit-making. Here, trade occurs in the absence of commodities and out of the physical marketplaces. This type of dealing can be harmful to both the seller and the buyer. Moreover, one is unable to inspect the goods being bought or sold.

- **Smuggling** of goods is a form of treason, which hinders the fulfillments of the needs of the countrymen, creates shortages of products, raises prices, and reduces the custom duty revenues of the government that are to be utilized for the public's benefits.

- **Interest** is completely prohibited. This is the most important and unique feature of the Islamic economy and financial system. In dealing with interest, both the payer and the recipient (or bookkeeper/witness) are engaged in war with Allah ﷻ and His Prophet and will become inhabitants of Hell. [2:279] As noted earlier, Allah ﷻ wipes out interest (earnings) and promotes trade.

The outcome of *riba* (usury, interest) is that the rich become richer and the poor become poorer. For earning interest, no hard work, labor, and effort are involved on the part of the ultimate lender, the investor, while the end-user, the debtor, is exploited. In most cases, even after working hard, the debtor is never able to recover fully from the burden of interest.

Since Allah ﷻ is the Lord, Who brings blessings and prosperity, disobeying His commandments, specifically regarding *riba*, never brings any blessings, prosperity, happiness, security, contentment, or everlasting stability in society. [30:39] The Islamic economy is trade-based, not interest-based. There are flexibilities regarding *riba* for Muslims living in non-Muslim countries, the details of which cannot be discussed here, because of limitations of space.

Zakāh (obligatory charity), combined with other charities, provides a strong economic impetus and stimulus for Muslim societies. Millions of Muslims give *zakāh* annually to deserving people, which helps to eradicate the accumulation of wealth in a few hands. It provides for the circulation of wealth, reduces the number of poor people, and closes the gap between the haves and the have-nots. *Zakāh* has been previously dealt with in greater detail in Chapter 9.

SOCIAL WELFARE — A sound economic system has within it, a social welfare system to bring sustenance to the poor and needy people. A social welfare system is naturally embedded in Islam. Instead of placing this obligation on a government, it makes it incumbent upon Muslim men to support their family, upon children to support their parents, upon brothers to support their sisters, upon the rich to support the poor through *zakāh* and other charities, and so on and so forth. This also contributes to economic prosperity and prevents poverty and suffering to a great extent.

Furthermore, the Prophet's ﷺ saying, "Seek knowledge from the cradle to the grave," is a key for social well-being, that brought revolutionary change. Additionally, he said, "O Allah! I seek Your protection from such knowledge that brings no benefit to people" [Nisai]. An economic crisis occurs when spending is dictated not by needs but by wants and whims. By prohibiting extravagant spending, Islam saves from possible economic disaster, and made useful reform leading to a welfare economy.

SIMPLICITY

*I*T IS AMAZING that a minor concept like simplicity can have as great an impact on an individual's life and the society as a whole as it has. Unfortunately, many people do not recognize even the slightest importance of this virtue.

In Islam, simplicity is a virtue that contributes heavily in bringing economic prosperity, happiness, and contentment. This worldly life, as explained in Islam, is like a rest area on the journey to our destination. We are simply making a stop in this world, and it is not our permanent abode, so we ought to make this stay as simple as possible, sparing more time to prepare for the Hereafter. Simplicity makes this task much easier.

In Islam, a simplistic lifestyle does not mean removing luxuries of life; it means being modest in everything we do and being real rather than superficial. In fact, simplicity brings true luxury to life and saves us from the countless mental worries and physical hardships that normally accompany the pursuit of luxurious lifestyles. Even if we are successful in acquiring that for which we wish and work, in reality these things only bring temporary and artificial fame, respect, pleasure, and enjoyment, all of which fade away with the passage of time and completely end on our departure from this world.

A simple lifestyle saves wealth that can be used, for example, towards philanthropic purposes that not only bring true happiness but also genuine respect and true love from society, as well as the blessings of the Hereafter. Moreover, others may replicate these examples, thereby leading to happiness and prosperity throughout the society. The everlasting satisfaction, good name, undiminishing fame, and never-fading respect generated by such behavior could not be acquired through lavish lifestyles or through the abundance of the luxuries of life. Such luxuries and lavish lifestyles of people are infamous for bringing much pain and suffering in private and public life. Islam, through its teachings, replaces these often invisible pains and sufferings and brings true luxury and liberation.

MISERLINESS — Greed, and being stingy are not allowed in Islam. Such attitudes prevent the circulation of wealth and resources. Islam advocates spending for oneself, for family, and in the name of Allah ﷻ, but at the same time strictly discourages waste and extravagant spending. In spending too, as in every other matter, Islam teaches Muslims to be modest. Modesty, just like simplicity, is a positive approach towards economic well-being.

INHERITANCE — To avoid confusion and conflict, Allah ﷻ Himself prescribed the just and equitable distribution of inheritance. The laws of inheritance certainly indicate that Allah ﷻ does not want wealth to remain concentrated in a few hands. Islam, through the laws of inheritance, teaches the importance of the distribution of wealth so that it makes its way back into society. A Muslim does not have the right to leave all of his/her wealth to just anyone of his/her liking, except one-third (1/3) of it, the remainder (2/3) will be distributed to relatives such as children, parents, spouse, siblings, etc., as allocated by Allah ﷻ.

CONSERVATION — Conserving natural and essential resources is highly encouraged in Islam. It affects the economy in many positive ways and makes it possible for the masses to acquire their needs. Having in abundance does not justify waste. The following are some examples that fall under conservation. Even if you are by a river, you are not allowed to waste water. Food is the last thing to throw away or leave to spoil. Allah's ﷻ mercy and blessings are lifted from homes where food, water, and other essentials are wasted.

HUNTING AND CULTIVATION — Hunting for food is allowed, but hunting for fun/sport is not. The hunted animal must be consumed; otherwise killing it is a sin. Arable lands must be cultivated for agricultural purposes. If left unused while people suffer from hunger or poverty, then not cultivating it yourself or not allowing your brother or poor neighbors to cultivate it, falls under sin and oppression. If one cannot cultivate it, he should give it to someone who can. Subsidizing farms to keep prices high or to limit supply is a punishable sin in Islam.

EMPLOYMENT AND BUSINESS — Working to earn a livelihood for oneself and the family is part of indirect worship for a Muslim. Receiving unemployment benefits, public assistance, and begging without any justifiable reason are among the undignified things. Private ownership of business and property, as well as free trade, is not only allowed in Islam, but it is highly encouraged, provided Islamic principles are strictly adhered to. This provides an opportunity for everyone to work hard and efficiently, to earn a living, and when possible to save wealth for the well-being of oneself and others. Islam supports private ownership of business and property because it is far more beneficial for economic growth.

In conclusion, the foundation Islam provides for an economic system has the unique qualities of diminishing social classes, minimizing and eradicating poverty, eliminating unnecessary competition, removing physical and mental sufferings, and bringing true happiness and prosperity. Unfortunately, for many reasons a complete, practical example based on the Islamic economic model does not exist today; nevertheless, many small communities and individual Muslim families and businesses are flourishing by applying Islamic economic principles. Not too long ago, when righteous Muslims held the reigns of the Muslim *ummah* (community), the Islamic economic enterprise worked wonders for everyone, but those golden days are history. The fact is that this is a world of actions; what one sows is what one reaps. Here, Allah ﷻ does not let anyone's efforts go fruitless, but, as per Islam, eternal rewards are only for the righteous ones.

CHAPTER 20

Tasawwuf in Islam

ASAWWUF IS COMMONLY translated as "Sufism," "mysticism," or "Islamic spirituality." Many non-Muslims are unaware of *tasawwuf*, and those who may have some knowledge of it may not know its inner realities and concepts. The aim of *tasawwuf* is the realization of the Almighty by remaining within the boundaries set forth by Him. Sufis seek nearness to Allah ﷻ and do everything in their control to elevate their soul and to achieve the highest station, where the self and its awareness no longer exists, thereby witnessing the existence of the Lord Almighty and nothing else.

Some understand a Sufi to be one who attempts to purify the inner and outer self because, in order to become a true slave of Allah ﷻ and to achieve nearness to Him, purification of both is required in Islam. To many, a Sufi is one who simply puts on a coarse woolen garb, known as a *suf*, and separates himself from this world.

Even though *tasawwuf* is the inner doctrine of Islam and the seeker in it embarks on a journey to achieve a higher state, he is not exempt from or allowed to violate Islamic law. The one who claims to be on the path of Islamic mysticism but does not follow the commandments of Islam (Islamic *sharia*) is nothing but a liar. He deceives himself and others. As I have said earlier, Islam does not allow violation of any of its principles for any reason, no matter how great the goal may seem. In this way, *tasawwuf* is entirely different from non-Islamic forms of mysticism. As per the holy Qur'an, a part of the Prophet's ﷺ duty was to purify his disciples. It is this purification that is sought in Islamic Sufism. Allah ﷻ states:

> Certainly, Allah conferred a great favor on Muslims when He raised a prophet from among them, who recites to them the revelations of Allah and purifies them, and instructs them in the Qur'an and *sunnah*, whereas before, they were in manifest error. •
>
> [Qur'an 3:164]

This is where Sufis find the basis for the path of *tasawwuf*: to purify and to be purified.

Tasawwuf is best described by the example of a fruit. What is inside the shell/peel is essential and the point of focus. Whether or not the outer is desirable, it must be accepted if we are to reach the desired part. The outer part of the fruit is necessary to protect the inner. We must first be acquainted with the outer before reaching the inner. If, by looking at the outer, we come to deny the real fruit inside, then this would be sheer ignorance, and we will fail to extract any benefit from it. However undesirable the outer may seem, Sufis must accept it and pass through it to reach their point of destination: the inner.

Similarly, Islam has its two aspects: *sharia* (Islamic law) concerns the outer and *tariqa* (the spiritual path to Allah ﷻ) concerns the inner. If *sharia* is rejected, ignored, or not followed, no one can ever understand or follow *tariqa*. Similarly, those Muslims and others who reject or defy *tasawwuf* can never acquire the inner beauty of Islam. A Sufi's purpose is to acquire the inner aspect, the soul of Islam, and therefore he thoroughly fulfills every requirement of *sharia*. *Sharia* purifies the body, and *tarīqa* purifies the soul/heart upon which Allah's ﷻ resplendence is reflected.

Allah's Prophet ﷺ exclaims, "Die before your death." [Tirmidhi] By this, he means that you need to kill your 'self' before physical death comes to you, i.e., to kill every part of your 'self' that prevents you from acquiring closeness to Allah ﷻ and that brings impurities to the inner heart of hearts. [Qur'an 87:14-15] This purification process is *tasawwuf*, and when the higher state of spirituality is achieved, the Lord addresses the purified soul:

> O contented soul! • Return towards your Lord, happy, pleased. • So, join My servants, • and enter into Heaven. • [Qur'an 89:27-30]

This is the fruit of continuous *dhikr* (remembrance of the Lord). A Sufi never loses his focus on Allah ﷻ. He visualizes his Master through each of His creations, thereby making Him the occupant of his heart. As noted in the Qur'an, "His throne gave room to the Heavens and to the Earth..." [Qur'an 2:255]; then how can there be anything that can encompass Allah ﷻ? No. It is said that nothing but the heart of a believer can. Once a believer keeps his heart empty of worldly desires and successfully purifies it from all filthy passions and animal instincts, he makes his heart ready for it to become Allah's ﷻ abode. As Allah's ﷻ presence is felt, he becomes absolutely content. He never wants to lose the pleasure drawn from it, and when his actual death comes to him, it is in fact the liberation of his soul from this worldly state of incarceration to the everlasting life of nearness to Allah ﷻ. It is at this point that Allah ﷻ addresses him:

> O contented soul! • Return towards your Lord, happy, pleased. • So, join My servants, • and enter into Heaven. • [Qur'an 89:27-30]

A soul comes to this world in a pure form and is held captive in the human body for a temporary, but fixed period. The situation of the soul in a body is like a bird in a cage. The soul can take three different forms, as mentioned in the holy Qur'an:

- *Nafs al-Ammara* – that which commands one to commit evil.
- *Nafs al-Lawwama* – that which self-criticizes and commands one to struggle to do good and to refrain from evil.
- *Nafs al-Mutmainna* – that which is contented and at peace; it is this form that is addressed in the aforementioned verse.

A Sufi continuously struggles with his soul, i.e., *Jihad bin Nafs*, to reach the state of peace. He does this through continuous remembrance of Allah ﷻ, which never lets him deviate from the righteous path, disobey the Lord, and lose sight of His bounties. He constantly remains fearful, mindful of His presence, and steadfast in fulfilling the obligations to his Master. He always keeps material filth away from his heart for the sake of Allah's ﷻ pleasure.

> …Be mindful that with Allah's remembrance, hearts do find contentment. • [Qur'an 13:28]

According to Sufis, anyone who lives his life without paying any consideration to the inner meaning of Islam is just satisfied with the outer beauty of Islam and never gets to see the inner beauty; whereas Sufis use the outer to get to the inner and truly understand Islam. Hence, when Sufis recite the *kalimah*, i.e., "There is no god but Allah," they are not only saying it, but they are also consciously denying the existence of every "thing," thus embracing the true Lord Allah ﷻ. They, in fact, witness the ultimate truth because, as they inhale the inner meaning of the *kalimah*, the voice of truth comes out of their heart, which says, "There is nothing but Allah ﷻ."

The Prophet ﷺ instructed his disciples to perform *salāh* (obligatory prayers of worship), as if they were consciously seeing Allah ﷻ. If not, then they should know that Allah ﷻ is certainly watching them

[Mishkat]. People can only see Sufis perform *salāh*, the greatest obligation of Islam. They only see them bend, bow, and prostrate, but these devout saints, while performing *salāh*, are in the presence of Allah ﷻ , the center of their worship, for Whom worship is. It is this state of worship that is the spirituality of Islam, not just bending and bowing and not knowing what it is all about. The purpose is not physical movement of the body but the spiritual engagement of the heart and mind.

If and when Sufis give *zakāh* (obligatory charity), they not only give money to the poor but actually withdraw from their hearts the love of money. When it comes to giving wealth in charity, they do not give 2.5% as is required in *zakāh*; instead, they do the opposite and give 97.5%, keeping only 2.5%. By this, they relieve themselves from the burden and temptations that money brings, making themselves constantly available for the service and slavery of the true Lord.

When Sufis perform Hajj, they not only circumambulate the Ka'ba, but enjoy the company of their Master, by saying from the heart:

> *Labbaik, allahumma labbaik. Labbaika; la shareeka laka, labbaik.*
> *Innal-Hamdah, wan nematah laka wal-Mulk, la shareeka lak.*

> Here I am, O Allah; here I am. Here I am. You have no partners; here I am. For You is all praise, and (from You are all) bounties, and sovereignty (is Yours). You have no partner.

This is when they physically separate themselves from this world. By covering their body in just two plain sheets of cloth, they fully present themselves to the Lord, and spiritually speaking, they cease to exist.

In these and other ways, Sufis not only live their lives according to Islamic law (*sharia*), but they also fully abide by its inner doctrine. This is what it means to enter into Islam completely, as required:

O faithful ones! Enter into Islam completely, and do not follow in the footsteps of Shaytān (Satan). Certainly, he is for you a manifest enemy. • [Qur'an 2:208]

The Prophet 🕌 stated:

This world, for a believer, is a prison. [Za'd al-Mua'd]

And he also stated:

Death, for a believer, is a gift. [Za'd al-Mua'd]

In a prison, inmates are not free to do whatever they like. They must follow the rules strictly. For them, freedom is a gift. A true believer lives in this world strictly by the rules of the Master, and through the gift of death he is finally liberated to enjoy the life of the Hereafter. This is what Islamic mysticism or *tasawwuf* is all about.

CHAPTER 21

Virtues and Vices

EVERY CIVILIZATION HAS SOME system of morality by which it lives. Due to a variety of interpretations of virtues and vices, I feel it is necessary to bring your attention to their unique definitions from the Qur'an and *sunnah*.

TO ENJOIN GOOD AND FORBID EVIL

THIS UNIQUE ACT IS NOT ONLY A GREAT VIRTUE in Islam, but it is an important duty for Muslims. In fact, the Muslim *ummah* (community) is awarded the status of "the best of all *ummahs* that appeared for mankind." Islam does not only require Muslims to be good and to avoid evil, but it also obligates them to enjoin good and forbid evil to the best of their ability.

In Islam, one has no right to advocate for what one does not practice oneself. The struggle to enjoin good and forbid evil is a form of jihad. It is rewarded immensely, because it saves the doer and others from deviating and from ultimate failure in the Hereafter. This is the best favor one can do for oneself and others, and there are three ways one can or should practice this virtue.

- If anyone sees any wrong or evil taking place, he/she must step in and try to stop it physically.

- If one is not able to prevent a wrong or evil physically, due to lack of physical strength or because it is not feasible to utilize power, then one must voice one's opposition against that injustice.

- If the situation does not allow either of the above two options, then one must, at the very least, consider what took place as wrong in his heart and distance himself from it.

Islam, overall and especially through this virtue/duty, intends to bring good and eradicate evil. Whatever good a Muslim leaves behind in this life, its rewards continue to multiply as others practice it and draw benefit from it. Similarly, whatever evil is left behind, he/she receives its share, too.

Unfortunately, to a great extent these days, many so-called Muslims are responsible for the ills, injustices, and other sinful activities that take place in their societies, because they have either ignored this virtue or have performed it improperly. Muslims living in non-Muslim countries can at least spread this virtue within their own communities, but if sins are being committed all around them, then they are only responsible for saving their individual family. If worst comes to worst, the option to move out is always available.

IKHLĀS

IKHLĀS LITERALLY MEANS SINCERITY/PURITY. However, *ikhlās* in Islamic practices means performing an act with the pure intent of pleasing Allah ﷻ. As mentioned earlier, any action performed solely for the sake of Allah's ﷻ pleasure becomes a part of worship. *Ikhlās* is required in everything that is to be undertaken and in order to get appropriate rewards.

Muslims who do good things with the intent to show off, earn titles or fame. If they do good things with the intent to gain any other material benefit, they are far from *ikhlās*. Their hard work with such impure intention(s) receives no reward from Allah ﷻ, because Allah's ﷻ pleasure was not their sole intent. Muslims know and believe that ultimately their return is to Allah ﷻ; therefore, their hearts must be free from any purpose other than to please their Creator. Clearly, it can be said that *ikhlās* is the backbone of earning the pleasure of Allah ﷻ. However, be mindful that Muslims have no right to judge anyone's intention, since it is only Allah ﷻ Who truly knows a person's *ikhlās*.

SIDQ

S *IDQ* MEANS HONESTY, VERACITY, AND TRUTHFULNESS. In Islam, *sidq* is one of the greatest virtues. Muslims who reach the highest level of *sidq* are granted the title of *sādiq*, i.e., truthful and trustworthy. In Islam, to be a Muslim is to be honest and truthful under all circumstances. Allah ﷻ is the truth and wants His slaves to be and be with the truthful ones (*sadiqūn*).

It is said that lying makes the heart become deficient and unable to reflect and observe divine attributes. Man is created to be the vice-gerent of Allah ﷻ on Earth, so he must be able to reflect His attri-butes, and this cannot be possible without being *sādiq*. Muslims must speak truthfully, uphold truths, be alongside truth, and be honest in their actions and intentions when fulfilling commitments. Honesty and veracity are integral parts of a Muslim's life. In fact, it is through *sidq* that Muslims reach the state of being a *momin* (devout believer), and honesty and veracity are synonymous with *iman* (belief). Muslims who are not *sādiq* cannot be trusted. It is shameful for a Muslim not to practice *sidq*. Prior to declaring his prophethood, Muhammad ﷺ was known by the virtue of *sidq* among the Quraysh tribe of Makkah, who called him '*Sādiq*' and '*Ameen*' (i.e., trustworthy).

TAWAKKUL

T *AWAKKUL* IS TO TRUST, DEPEND, AND RELY ON. Muslims are to depend only on Allah ﷻ and faithfully trust Him, as He is sufficient for them. The virtue of *tawakkul* is extremely essential in the sight of Allah ﷻ. Whoever faithfully trusts and relies on Him Allah ﷻ will never let down and will always fulfill his needs. When the faithful put their trust in Allah ﷻ, it shows that they believe Him to be where they need Him.

Being faithful and trusting and relying on Allah do not mean that Muslims become immobile and do not utilize the resources provided to them. In fact, it means to do their best, but not to put complete trust on their resources and efforts. They should believe in their heart of hearts that their efforts can fail but that Allah's ﷻ power and will cannot. For example, people hire good, experienced lawyers and put their trust in them, but the chances of losing are still real. However, the more expertise a lawyer has, the more peaceful and confident the client is. With their faith in Allah ﷻ, Muslims become completely peaceful and certainly know that they cannot be defeated. With Allah ﷻ, success is absolutely guaranteed, because He is the All-Powerful.

Allah ﷻ wants all of His true slaves to trust Him. *Tawakkul* does not mean that one should not strive to achieve goals or that one becomes imprudent, or careless or that one puts oneself in danger or goes against the routines of life. *Tawakkul* means to trust Allah ﷻ and, when things go beyond one's reach, to maintain one's trust in Him and be content with whatever the outcome is. Muslims must trust Allah ﷻ before and after they undertake anything. Many times resources are limited, and the objectives are great; in this situation, Muslims should not back away, but they should proceed confidently with complete faith in Allah ﷻ. Allah ﷻ never lets down those who rely on Him. *Tawakkul* is not only a great virtue for Muslims; it is also a great tool for acquiring success.

HUMILITY

HUMANS ARE NOTHING when compared to Allah's ﷻ awesome power of creation and of absolute control. He created us, and we are powerless against His will. We are inherently weak. We seem powerful; yet, in reality, we actually have no control over anything. On our own, we cannot even scratch our back or lift both of our legs together to stay afloat in midair. We are in need of Allah's ﷻ assistance every moment of our lives and beyond. Allah ﷻ wants us to display humility and to admit our nothingness before His vast power. Allah ﷻ does not want us to be proud and arrogant because we own nothing, not even the power of motion within us; He owns everything.

The virtue of humility can be seen when Muslims perform the obligatory prayer (*salāh*). Here, they physically bow and, prostrate (putting their forehead on the ground), and spiritually their hearts bow and prostrate in front of Allah ﷻ, accepting His greatness and their weakness. The quality of humility brings forth compassion, friendship, and closeness among humans. In contrast, pride and arrogance divide people and may make one hate someone who may be honorable in the sight of Allah ﷻ. Humility is one of the basic teachings of the Qur'an and one which the Prophet Muhammad ﷺ exemplified through his actions.

LOVE

*L*OVE IS THE CENTRAL VIRTUE in Islam. In fact, it is the mother of all virtuous deeds. It brings many benefits to individuals and to society, and carries abundant rewards from the Lord Almighty. Brotherhood, tolerance, forgiveness, respect, benevolence, gratefulness, sacrifice, loyalty, charity, friendship, hospitality, sympathy, etc. are all born out of love. Whoever's heart is devoid of love lacks these virtues. Since all of these virtues carry considerable weight in the Roster of Deeds and are included in the broader concept of worship in Islam, one can easily grasp the importance and status of love in Islam.

In Islam, (allowable) love of things must come after the love of Allah ﷻ and of His beloved prophets, especially Muhammad ﷺ. It is the love of Allah ﷻ and the Prophet ﷺ that makes it easy for Muslims to abide by divine rules and to become true believers. When true and selfless love of people pays off, then certainly the love of the Almighty pays off as well. The slaves who love Allah ﷻ truly receive His love in return, and what reward can be greater than this for them. The true love of our Benefactor makes our salvation easy and guaranteed. Anyway, regardless of what He has already given us or the expectation of future rewards, He deserves to be loved, and we should be grateful to Him under all circumstances.

FEAR AND HOPE

𝓕EAR AND HOPE ARE TWO IMPORTANT virtues in Islam. Hope is understandable, but how can fear be a virtue? Since preparing for the Afterlife is a purpose of life, anything that helps to bring success in the Hereafter becomes a virtue. In this context, fear means to fear Allah ﷻ, Judgment Day, and punishment, and the greatest of all fears is the fear of displeasing Allah ﷻ. The fear of being accountable for sinful actions keeps a Muslim on the righteous path. Thus, fearing Allah ﷻ becomes a virtue that results in success.

Hope is generally known to be an important virtue in every society. Allah ﷻ does not like those who lose hope. A good Muslim never loses hope. Fear and hope are two virtues that are usually explained together. For example, faith is like a bird with two wings. The wings of faith are fear and hope. In order for a bird to fly straight, both of its wings must remain balanced. Likewise, for someone to remain faithful, fear of accountability and hope of salvation must remain active and balanced. On the one hand, absence of the fear of accountability and excessive hope of salvation prevent one from fulfilling the required obligations. On the other hand, unreasonable and excessive fear and complete absence of hope have the same outcome. A slight deviation changes the course, and any imbalance can bring one down and gradually lead to destruction. Maintaining balance between fear and hope on the path of righteousness helps Muslims towards a happy ending.

PATIENCE AND PERSEVERANCE

*N*O ONE CAN CLAIM THAT LIFE is smooth or free of worries. On many occasions in everyone's life, things will not go the way one wants or likes. To Muslims, Islam compensates greatly for patience and perseverance. Allah 🕮 puts his slaves to test through hardship and unfavorable events and circumstances. Whoever remains steadfast, does not lose faith, and does not become impatient or gives up, comes out victorious. Even if they do not get their legitimate wishes fulfilled here, full reward awaits them in the Hereafter.

Sometimes in life, the good a person does doesn't do him any good, and so people lose faith. Certainly, this is difficult, but the final outcome of patience and perseverance is always good and satisfying. For Muslims, it brings Allah's 🕮 pleasure and, of course, success in the Hereafter.

CORRECTING THE BASE SELF

*A*LL OF US ARE TRAVELERS and are simply passing through this world to reach the Hereafter. Our stay here is short, and the love for this world deceives and prevents us from thinking about our actual purpose in it. Our base self is inclined towards material wants and desires, has evil tendencies, and is poisonous and ever ready to misguide and mislead us, to deviate from our path. It is, in fact, a tool of Satan.

Islam requires Muslims to be always vigilant against the deception of our base self and to avoid becoming enslaved to it. Islam gives Muslims the proper tools to keep the self in check and in control.

304 WOULD YOU LIKE TO KNOW SOMETHING ABOUT ISLAM?

Muslims fight Shaytān and try to defeat and tame the *Nafs-e-Ammara*, the base self. Muslims must win this war against these great enemies to be successful in this world and in the Hereafter. This struggle is also what is meant by *Jihad bin Nafs*, as discussed earlier.

BEARING DEATH IN MIND

*W*HO COULD CONSIDER THAT EVEN REMEMBERING death is a virtue? Islam does because the result of remembering death and its effects on life is virtuous. Since the time of death is unknown, Muslims are directed to remember death at all times. This gives them a chance to focus on doing good deeds because no one wants to be caught dead in sin. Life is uncertain, but death is certain. Constantly remembering their eventual departure from this world reminds Muslims that one day they will meet their Lord. Thus, they become steadfast in living a pious life, which helps them in fulfilling the purpose of life. There are many benefits for keeping death in mind.

GRATITUDE

*O*FTEN, FAVORS CANNOT BE returned in the same manner they are received. At a minimum, a favor is returned through being grateful. Islam teaches that if a person cannot be grateful to those who do favors, he cannot be grateful to the Lord [Muslim]. However small a favor may be, it requires appreciation because Allah ﷻ does not like ungrateful and arrogant people. [Qur'an 40:76 and Muslim]

Allah ﷻ blessed His creations with so many favors that He deserves to be appreciated more than anyone else. Simple verbal appreciation is insufficient. The simplest form of gratefulness is when a believer utilizes a bounty in the manner Allah ﷻ prescribed. For example, when government officials are given cars for official use, they are not to be used for personal business; this would amount to unlawful use of government property, which is a crime. Similarly, Allah's ﷻ

bounties are His property; any unlawful use of them is sinful and truly unappreciative. Ingratitude is as great a vice as gratitude is a virtue in Islam.

FULFILLMENT OF PROMISES

*A*LLAH 🕮 REVEALS MANY VERSES pertaining to the importance of fulfilling promises. In about 6,600 verses, the holy Qur'an comprehensively reveals the knowledge and wisdom of everything people need to know to acquire salvation in the Hereafter. Every verse is important and underlines valuable information. The importance of fulfilling promises can be summarized by the following verses of the Qur'an. Allah 🕮 says:

...and (you) fulfill My covenant, that I may fulfill your covenant... • [Qur'an 2:40]

Without a doubt, the faithful ones became successful...and they are mindful of their trusts and covenants. • [Qur'an 23:1, 8]

...and keep fulfilling your covenant; certainly, covenants will be asked about. • [Qur'an 17:34]

Fulfilling promises and abiding by covenants are virtues that all the prophets of Allah 🕮 professed and practiced. The Qur'an further states:

...without a doubt, he (Ismaīl) was true to his promises and was a prophet, giver of news of the unseen. • [19:54]

Throughout his life, Prophet Muhammad 🕮 kept his promises and never abandoned his covenants. An example of this was when a Byzantine emperor, having inquired about him ever breaking a promise, received a resounding NO in response. [Bukhari] Whenever the Prophet 🕮 gave his word, he always fulfilled it, even if it meant incurring a loss for him or his followers. [Treaty of Hudaibiyah]

In Islam, overlooking promises amounts to hypocrisy and is sinful. Today, many of us can easily get away from reneging on promises, but

Muslims know for certain that Allah ﷻ is All-Hearing and All-Knowing. Islam makes the virtue of fulfilling promises and trusts incumbent upon Muslims. Historically, this virtue has impacted Muslims conscience in many ways. Fulfillment of promises or lack thereof will be examined on Judgment Day. It is certainly an important part of faith and a virtue among many great virtues.

SIMPLICITY

THE VIRTUE OF BEING SIMPLE and leading a simple lifestyle saves people from many inexplicable troubles in life. Simplicity protects one from becoming a slave of wants, wishes, and of society. A simple Islamic lifestyle shows that the abode of this life is temporary and the real life is that of the Hereafter.

Simplicity results in fewer needs and easy fulfillment of those needs, thereby saving valuable time and resources for other virtuous purposes. The Companions of the Prophet ﷺ sacrificed everything for the cause of Islam and were always prepared to do anything at his slightest gesture. Muhammad ﷺ could have lived his life more extravagantly than any king ever lived, but he chose utmost simplicity in food, shelter, clothing, and other aspects of life. He even rode on inexpensive animals when exquisite horses and camels were brought to him. This is exactly how his Companions lived, even though they ruled over half of the Earth and possessed unlimited power and prestige. Unfortunately, such examples are no longer found, even among Muslims.

CLEANLINESS

IN A *HADĪTH* OF THE PROPHET ﷺ, it is stated that cleanliness is half of faith, meaning that whoever maintains cleanliness fulfills half of the requirements of Islam. Physical and spiritual cleanliness plays an important role in Muslim character building, through which better interactions among people can take place. The closer people are to each other, the stronger the human community is. Thus, it becomes easier to achieve the common goals of peace, prosperity, and happiness.

The idea of cleanliness of the body, heart, and mind was pretty much established by Islam. For example, it is the Prophet's ﷺ *sunnah* to wash hands before and after eating. Today, every society is well aware that good hygiene helps develop attractive characteristics and personality. In Islam, cleanliness of the heart means to have the heart empty of arrogance, envy, greed, hatred, jealousy, prejudice, revenge, pretense/hypocrisy, enmity, and other vices. The heart of a *momin* (devout believer) is an abode of the Lord. Cleanliness enlightens the heart and the inner self, while adorning the physical appearance. This is why [it] is regarded as one half of Islam.

The list of virtues in Islam is quite long. What I have chosen to write about here are some of the important ones. The following are important vices that also need to be explained in order to show why Islam considers them evil and why they are to be avoided at all costs.

EXCESSIVE/USELESS TALK (GOSSIP)

*A*CCORDING TO A *HADĪTH*, "Because of the tongue (its misuse) many will be tossed into the Hellfire" [Bukhari]. A famous scholar and philosopher, *Imam* Ghazali رحمة الله عليه, stated, "Excessive talking causes the heart to die, losing its ability to receive divine manifestations" [Kimiya-e-Sa'adat]. Controlling the tongue and limiting its use are important in Islam. Needless and unnecessary talk is highly discouraged. Running one's mouth all the time brings harm to oneself and others, causes irreversible damage, and prevents admission into Heaven.

Muslims must say only good things, refrain from harmful conversations, and try to remain quiet most of the time. It is commonly known that loose talk and gossip destroy many relationships and usually cause long lasting family feuds, to say the least. Among vices, this one is perhaps the most harmful. Lying, backbiting, pointless quarreling, and mocking are just some of the results of useless talk.

LYING

*I*SLAM CONSIDERS LYING TO BE one of the great vices, as do others, too. According to the Prophet Muhammad ﷺ, lying is sinful and is unbefitting of a Muslim's character [Bukhari]. Faith and lying cannot be together in the heart of a devout believer. Like many other vices, lying makes the heart sick. Even when joking around, lying is discouraged. Lying is the mother of all vices. Islam condemns liars and their lies, and Islam declares that a liar's testimony cannot be accepted in a court of law [Qur'an 24:2]. Islam prohibits lying in every sense of the word and promotes the speaking of the truth.

BACKBITING

Allah ﷻ states:

O faithful ones! Save yourselves from assuming much. Without a doubt, some assumptions are sinful, and do not nit-pick, and do not backbite each other. Would any among you like to eat the flesh of your dead brother? • [Qur'an 49:12]

Here, backbiting is equated with eating the flesh of your dead brother, which is and should be an abhorrent act. According to Prophet Muhammad ﷺ, backbiting is worse than the sin of adultery [Bukhari & Muslim]. Backbiting is saying something bad behind someone's back that, if they were to hear it in person, they would not like it and would have their feelings hurt. Jokingly or angrily making fun of someone's height, weight, physical features, or level of intelligence, whether verbally, through gestures, or through rolling one's eyes, falls under backbiting. It is sinful and can cause irreparable damage.

Islam wants its followers to protect each other's dignity. However, Islam permits Muslims to share harmful information about someone in order to warn and protect people. Instead of looking for and finding fault in others, Islam commands Muslims to seek out their personal faults, correct them, and ask for forgiveness. One possible reason why we look for faults in others is that we believe ourselves to be free of fault, even though this belief, in itself, is a great fault for which we must seek immediate remedy. The only acceptable repentance for Muslims for the sin of backbiting is to seek forgiveness from the person slandered and then ask forgiveness from Allah ﷻ.

ANGER

*M*OST FORMS OF ANGER ARE PROHIBITED IN ISLAM. Anger is like a ball of fire from which one should usually stay as far away as possible. As per a *hadīth*:

> Knocking out a wrestler does not make a person strong. Strength is when a person knocks out his anger at the time of rage. [Tibrani]

Just as a bitter liquid destroys the sweetness of honey, anger destroys faith [Kanzul Ammal]. Anger gives birth to foul language, hatred, and jealousy, and it infringes on privacy, defames, and is the cause of many other sins. Generally during fits of anger, people say things that truly hurt the feelings of others, which is completely against the spirit and morality of Islam.

However, Islam permits anger at injustices and when encountering sin or sinful behavior and environments. Anger is to be tamed or kept in check through inner control, and it is only to be unleashed to correct wrongs within the limits of Islamic law. Bravery is when one controls his anger, not when anger controls him.

As per another *hadīth*:

> In the sight of Allah, the best thing for Muslims to swallow is anger. [Abu Dawūd]

Allah 🕮 greatly rewards people who control their anger and who forgive those who caused it, especially in the case of subordinates and employees. Allah 🕮 brings peace to the heart, strengthens the faith of such Muslims, and elevates their status.

ARROGANCE/PRIDE

*I*T WAS DUE TO ARROGANCE AND PRIDE that the enmity of Satan took hold against man. At the creation of the first man, Adam 🕮, Allah 🕮 commanded angels to prostrate before him. Iblīs/ Satan, a jinn who lived among the angels, refused to prostrate because of his arrogance and pride. When Allah 🕮 inquired about his refusal, Satan replied, "I am better than Adam. You created me with fire and Adam with earthly soil/dust; therefore, I am superior." Arrogance/pride is among the qualities most disliked by Allah 🕮.

There is no need to describe how this single most harmful vice caused the greatest harm to humans throughout history, and it is still the overwhelming factor in bloodshed. Millions of innocent men, women, and children have been killed in the name of a superiority complex of one form or another. This crime was initiated by Satan and has from then on been carried out by humans. Historically, the world has witnessed many despotic pharaohs and dictators, at every turn and corner, who were filled with arrogance and pride.

The Almighty Lord made us human, but many of us turned into junior "satans." If we refuse even to realize that we are arrogant or proud, how can we correct or extinguish this vice from within us? The spirit of every Islamic teaching intends to keep us away from pride, hatred, arrogance, superiority complexes, anger, prejudice, enmity, and so on and so forth.

JEALOUSY AND MALICE

*U*SUALLY, UNGRATEFUL PEOPLE ARE JEALOUS, become malicious towards other people, and wish them harm and loss. This vice is the worst disease of the heart and is explicitly prohibited in Islam. Jealous people are always unhappy with Allah's ﷻ distribution of wealth and bounties and are ungrateful for His blessings. Jealousy does more harm to those who are jealous than to their victims. The Prophet ﷺ said, "Jealousy eats up good deeds like fire eats up wood" [Abu Dawud]. Jealousy must be fully cured before one can become a devout believer. Certainly, the most foolish of all fools is the fool who harms himself.

BUKHL (STINGINESS)

*S*PENDING LAVISHLY AND WASTEFULNESS are not permitted in Islam, and *bukhl*, i.e., being cheap and stingy, is one of the fatal diseases of the heart. Allah ﷻ states in the holy Qur'an:

> And let those not think who become stingy in what Allah has given them by His grace that [it] is better for them; instead, [it] is harmful to them. Very soon, on Judgment Day, what their greed held back will be shackled to them. And Allah, indeed, is the Owner of the heavens and Earth, and Allah is quite aware of what you do. • [3:180]

Prophet Muhammad ﷺ said:

> Save yourself from stinginess because it has destroyed previous nations." [Abu Dawud, Nisa'i]

It is not worthy of a Muslim to be a miser and end up in Hell. Stinginess is the direct result of the love of material wealth that diminishes the love of Allah ﷻ. When a miser departs from this world, his heart is filled with love of the material wealth that is certainly left behind him, but he does not have even a shred of love for Allah ﷻ, which is necessary for him to be saved in the Hereafter.

While alive, he never wishes to meet Allah 🕮, and prefers to stay with his wealth forever, but this wish certainly does not and has not come true for anyone.

By being cheap, people may be able to accumulate material wealth, but at the same time they pile up a lot of painful retribution for themselves and for others who may follow their lead. They become mindless of the true purpose of life and forget their inevitable appointment with Allah 🕮. For Muslims, this is death in itself. Furthermore, accumulating needless wealth leads to a sinful lifestyle, which then makes it even more difficult to practice faith, patience, and abstinence from sins. This goes against the basic philosophy of Islam.

The more the heart is filled with the love of material wealth, the more painful death becomes. Usually, a stingy person's departure is full of sorrow, grief, and regret. Muslims who refrain from stinginess are not extravagant; they spend moderately and happily, and they do not have love for material wealth, but reserve their love for Allah 🕮. They depart from this world peacefully. Their death becomes easy on them, because meeting Allah 🕮 is dearer to them than anything else. The faithful willingly leave behind what belongs to this world and take from it what is useful for the Hereafter. Saving through stinginess and purposely living a lifestyle of the needy does not make a miser a wise person.

LOVE FOR NAME AND FAME

Allah 🕮 states:

> The bounties of the Hereafter are for those who do not desire name, fame, or worldly prestige. • [Qur'an 28:83]

The Prophet Muhammad 🕮 stated:

> A wolf in a herd of sheep cannot do as much harm as the love of wealth, name, and fame can do to the faith of a believer. [Tirmidhi]

It is to be remembered that love of name and fame is an inner sickness. It gives birth to hypocrisy, enmity, and malice. A true believer does not wish or act to earn a name, but if he becomes known, he remains humble. The wish to become famous and to acquire prestige in this world, which will be left behind, is a foolish desire. The name and status granted by the Lord is permanent, and no one can take it away–not even death. Allah-given titles and prestige ensure honor and success in this world and the Hereafter.

Intelligent and wise are those who do not wish to be famous in this world but wish, instead, to be crowned in the Hereafter. One should learn a lesson from the thousands of earthly-crowned people who are buried beneath the earth and did not utilize their power and status to earn the fame of the Hereafter—wise they were not.

SUPERIORITY COMPLEX

SUPERIORITY COMPLEX FALLS in the category of pride. The only difference is that in pride the self considers itself greater than others, and in a superiority complex the self claims to be perfect and superior in its own mind. As a result, the person suffering from a superiority complex takes the Lord's bounties for granted and as his or her natural right, and he is never thankful to the Lord. He is ignorant of the fact that the One Who gives can also take away. Needless to say, the world has witnessed this fact time and again. That is why, for a creature, superiority is a complex, not a reality. The real superiority is for the Creator and not for His creatures.

RIYA (TO SHOW OFF)

RIYA LITERALLY MEANS TO SHOW OFF. In Islam, it technically means to perform an act to show off to people either to deceive them or to earn praise and fame. *Riya* is the opposite of *ikhlās* (sincerity/

to act only to please Allah ﷻ). It is necessary for a Muslim to perform an act with *ikhlās*, and not to let *riya* enter it. *Riya* is like *shirk* (polytheism, making partners with Allah ﷻ), because with *riya* the act is performed for someone or something other than Allah ﷻ [Qur'an 107:5-6]. It is like placing someone other than the Lord in His place.

The Prophet ﷺ stated:

> Any act that has the slightest *riya* will be unacceptable in the court of Allah. [Bukhari and Tirmidhi]

How can one see if a person acts with *riya*, when only Allah ﷻ knows what he has in his heart? Of course, we have no right to nor can we correctly judge someone's intention; however, it is not difficult to see *riya* in an act. It is easily seen through analyzing the overall character/behavior of a person. We have no right to label anyone pretentious, but we can at least save ourselves from following his or her lead.

An everyday practice of some is to dress like pious people but to have no piety in their hearts, to worship like true slaves but have no intent to please Allah ﷻ, to talk, walk, and eat like Sufis but do not know the meaning of *tasawwuf* (Islamic spirituality/mysticism), to perform good and noble acts only when among people but when alone be careless of the duties prescribed by the Lord, to spend wealth in society and not seek Allah's ﷻ pleasure and instead seek public praise. Such people are filled with *riya*; they fool themselves and others, and accumulate fire in the Hereafter.

HYPOCRISY

*T*HREE KINDS OF PEOPLE are mentioned in the Qur'an: believers, disbelievers, and hypocrites [Qur'an 2:3-10]. Technically, hypocrites are those who *claim* to be believers, but in reality do not have faith in Allah ﷻ and the Last Day, as believers do. In fact, they are disbelievers, and in many cases the worst kind of people. Hypocrites are addressed as traitors who attempt to deceive Allah ﷻ and Muslims [Qur'an 2:9].

Allah ﷻ states:

They do not deceive anyone except themselves, and they do not realize it. • [Qur'an 2:9]

Munāfiqeen (hypocrites) pretend to be Muslim, but they never truly enter Islam [Qur'an 2:8]. They do not submit to the will of the Lord, and they follow their own agendas. Instead of being loyal to Islam, they defame it. They sit in the company of believers but conspire against them [Qur'an 2:14]. They overtly say what Muslims say, but they discreetly mock the ideology and beliefs of Islam. They interpret the Qur'an in their own style and are never sincere with its guidance. Even though they recite the cardinal articles of Islam and perform the obligatory prayers of worship, it is just lip service and physical exercise. The deepest level of Hell is reserved especially for them. Allah ﷻ states:

In their hearts is a disease, so Allah lets them progress in their disease, and for them is torment, a painful one, for they spoke lies. • [Qur'an 2:10]

They are not easily recognizable among Muslims because they look and act like believing Muslims. Among their many characteristics, one is that they do not practice what they preach. [Qur'an 9:67-68] A true believer's heart never becomes attracted to them, and they cannot hide their true face for long. Anyway, hypocrites and their hypocrisy have no place in Islam. They are condemned in the holy Qur'an [2:11-16], and true Muslims have been made aware of their treachery.

It is not possible or necessary to list and explain every vice of the base self. However, the ones mentioned above have been emphasized in the holy Qur'an and in the *ahadīth* with which Muslims should become familiar. The purpose of explaining them in such detail is to enhance the knowledge of people wanting to learn about Islam.

CHAPTER 22

Islamic Highlights

*B*Y NOW, YOU HAVE LEARNED MUCH ABOUT ISLAM, as its major concepts and practices have been covered in detail. Here, I would like to bring my non-Muslim fellows' attention to some common but unique practices of Muslims, so that they can comfortably interact and participate, if need be, with Muslim friends, clients, colleagues, and neighbors.

SUPPLICATION

Whenever Muslims begin to do anything, they recite:

BISMILLA HIR-RAHMA NIR-RAHIM

("In the name of Allah, the Most Compassionate, the Most Merciful")

When Muslims begin any activity "in the name of Allah 🕮," they inherently refrain from committing sinful acts. Not a single real Muslim has the audacity to commit a wrongdoing by initiating it with the name of Allah 🕮. Reciting this sacred verse [Qur'an 27:30] brings abundant blessings and makes work safe, sound, and smooth. Another benefit of this is that Muslims are constantly in communication with the Lord Almighty.

SALUTATIONS

Muslims use proper salutations whenever writing or saying the holy name of Allah 🕮, His prophets, and His beloved saints. Doing this shows their importance and our reverence and affection for them. Such personalities are not to be called on as we do to others among us. Some common salutations appear in the beginning of the book.

UTMOST RESPECT FOR THE HOLY QUR'AN

The holy Qur'an is not a regular book. It is the word of Allah ﷻ that contains divine laws and principles. Muslims handle the holy Qur'an with utmost respect and keep it safely and securely. A lot has been written about the holy Qur'an in Chapter 6.

GREETING WITH *"ASSALĀMU ALAYKUM"*

Whenever Muslims see, meet, or hear the voice of another Muslim (over the phone), or send regards through others, the proper greeting of *assalāmu alaykum* ("peace be upon you") is exchanged. In short, it is called '*salām*.' The proper reply to it is, *wa alaykum assalām* (and upon you be peace). Greeting with *salām* is a *sunnah*, but its response is mandatory for every Muslim. [Qur'an 4:86] It is, in fact, a supplication made to Allah ﷻ on behalf of another Muslim. Whoever greets with *salām* first receives more blessings than those who reply to it. *Salām* increases love and respect among Muslims.

Certainly, when Muslims supplicate for peace for each other, how can any animosity remain between them? The natural power of *salām* is such that Muslims begin to love one another even if they did not know each other and were meeting for the very first time. *Salām* is not limited to the morning, afternoon, or evening. It is the best greeting and the most proper way of beginning a conversation at any time.

USE OF RIGHT HAND

In Islam, the right hand has preference over the left hand. It is a *sunnah* of the Prophet ﷺ to use the right hand when eating, giving and receiving. Some people write with their left hand. There is nothing wrong with it; however, following the *sunnah* brings a lot of blessings. Allah ﷻ knows our adaptive nature, and He is All-Forgiving.

SNEEZING

Upon sneezing, Muslims say *alhamdūlillah* ("all praise be to Allah") and those who hear it should reply by saying *yarhamukullah* (blessings of Allah be upon you). When Allah entered the spirit into the body of Adam عليه السلام, he became alive, and upon sneezing said, "*Alhamdūlillah*," to which the angels replied, "*Yarhamukullah*." [**Abu Dawud**] Scientific research reveals that the human heart skips a beat as one sneezes. By saying *alhamdūlillah*, Muslims praise the Lord, accepting that only He controls life and sustains it. Our life and death is for and because of Allah ﷻ, and a proper thanks for the precious gift of life is to praise Him.

TAHĀRA (CLEANLINESS)

A state of *tahāra* (purity/cleanliness) is of great importance to Muslims. They must always keep their body and soul pure from dirt, filth, and sin. Islam teaches Muslims how to do this. Spiritual *tahāra* is acquired through Islam's various obligatory practices, such as *salāh* (obligatory prayers of worship), fasting, *zakāh* (obligatory charity), and Hajj. Such mindfulness of Allah's ﷻ commandments has the spiritual power to wash out all kinds of impurities from the heart. Physical *tahāra* is possible through the use of water, such as after urinating or defecating. Muslims are to properly wash their private parts with water and not use paper products, except under extreme circumstances. As exemplified by the Prophet ﷺ, Muslims must wash their hands before and after eating. The following are included in the process of acquiring *tahāra*/cleanliness [Bahar-e-Shariat]:

- Muslim men and women must shave the hair surrounding their private parts and their armpits. The hair must not grow to be more than the size of a grain of rice (one-half of an inch).
- Nails must be trimmed regularly. Moustaches should never grow long enough to dip into liquids when drinking.

- Muslims should not smell bad. They should use non-alcoholic perfumes (*itar*) to remove bad odor and especially when performing obligatory prayers in congregation.
- Women are not allowed to use blades to shave. Hair removing creams or any other method (besides metal blades) is allowed.

GHUSL (BATHING/SHOWERING)

Ghusl is the bathing/showering prescribed in Islam. *Ghusl* is required immediately after the ejaculation of sperm and the completion of the menstrual period. *Ghusl* is so important that it should not be delayed once it becomes necessary, and Muslims are not to do anything without first acquiring *tahāra* (cleanliness).

HALĀL AND *HARĀM*

Muslims must know what has been made *halāl* (permitted) and *harām* (prohibited), so they can bring into use *halāl* and avoid *harām*. Whatever has not been made prohibited, it is either permitted or *makrūh* (permitted under certain conditions, but generally disapproved of). Muslims do not have the right to make things prohibited or permitted on their own accord, because Allah ﷻ and His Prophet ﷺ have already completely distinguished between what is prohibited and what is permitted.

For example, Muslims can only eat those animals that are permitted; however, the animal must first be slaughtered by way of a special procedure called *zabīha* (cutting the neck halfway while invoking Allah's ﷻ name and then allowing the blood to drain thoroughly). Pork, alcoholic beverages, extramarital affairs, obscenity, prostitution, cursing, nudity, shamelessness, and gambling are strictly prohibited, as is stealing, cheating, and deceiving.

Sins of this nature carry severe punishments in this life, and if not sincerely and properly repented for, its penalties extend to the Hereafter. Engaging yourself and others in watching videos containing nudity, reading pornographic literature, and the use of alcohol, drugs, and other intoxicants are strictly prohibited. As a note of caution, when Muslims are engaged in sinful acts, their *iman* (faith) is taken out of them and remains suspended until the act is over [Mishkat]. True Muslims do not and should not take these prohibitions lightly, and they must refrain from all prohibited behavior.

NIKAH (MARRIAGE)

Nikah is a *sunnah* of the Prophet ﷺ. It is the only legitimate way for a man and a woman to become lawful husband and wife. It is a binding contract between husband and wife that, at the least, makes them *halāl* to each other. It is only through this contract that they can begin to conceive children and begin a legitimate family unit.

MARRIAGE BETWEEN FIRST COUSINS

In the United States and the West, it is uncommon for first cousins to marry each other. The holy Qur'an clearly explains who one is not allowed to marry, and first cousins are not included in this list. A large percentage of Muslims marry their first cousins. In fact, it is recommended and desirable in Islam to choose a life partner from among close relatives. [Bukhari]

TALĀQ

Talāq is commonly known as "divorce." It is an unpleasant event and completely undesirable in Islam. It should only be resorted to under extreme circumstances. *Talāq* nullifies the relationship between a husband and wife that was established through *nikah*. Among other things, *talāq* is very much despised by Allah ﷻ. Whenever it occurs, it is said to shake the foundations of the earth and sky.

NAMING GOOD NAMES

Muslim parents look for good, meaningful names for their children. Names directly influence the personality of children [Qur'an 49:11]. This is why parents often choose names of spiritual personalities or names that are meaningful. In any event, one must always choose names that help one's child to become morally good.

NAMES FOR NEW MUSLIMS: When someone embraces Islam, he/she enters into a state of divine tranquility, and as his/her knowledge increases he/she begins to embark on the journey to ultimate success, which is Allah's ﷻ pleasure. The first step on this sacred journey often begins by enlisting with a Muslim name, especially those that invoke Allah's ﷻ attributes. Whichever name is chosen to be recognized by in this life is the name by which one will be called upon on Judgment Day. Thus, it is better to choose a name that shows affiliation with Islam, although this is not a requirement.

MUSLIM CHARACTER

True Muslims are known for their outstanding character and behavior, which are modeled on the Prophet ﷺ's example. Islam commands Muslims to be respectful and to show hospitality, especially to parents, relatives, and neighbors. They must avoid hard feelings and sincerely accept and apologize for their mistakes, and they must keep their hearts free of hate and envy. Islam teaches that one should be respectful to elders, fair to equals, and compassionate to juniors. Mentors and teachers should always receive respectful behavior from their Muslim students.

Strangers, wayfarers, and the poverty-stricken are to be cared for, as are family members. Allah ﷻ loves those who rush to assist others in need, whether or not they ask for assistance. When it comes to helping others, Muslims do not hesitate, think twice, or do cost/benefit analysis. Muslims wholeheartedly remember that Allah ﷻ knows best one's inner thoughts and intention(s). The Prophet ﷺ said, "Be truthful, even if it hurts you." [Abu Dawud]

RESTROOMS/BATHROOMS

Muslims are not allowed to urinate standing up. [Tirmidhi] They are to be extremely careful when urinating and make sure that urine does not come into contact with their body or clothes. This is necessary to maintain *tahāra* (cleanliness). It is recommended to not spend more than the time needed in restrooms, to be silent while there, and definitely not take any (religious) literature into bathrooms.

MUSLIM ATTIRE

Islam does not outline any specific attire for Muslims, but it clearly requires both men and women to dress modestly and cover their body as required. How women are to dress is discussed in Chapter 16. Muslim men must at least cover waist down, up to just below their knees (naval to knees). In *salāh* (obligatory prayer), men must dress modestly, except in extreme circumstances. It is the *sunnah* of the Prophet 🕌 to cover the head (topi, kufi, etc.). Even though keeping a beard is not mandatory, it is most desirable and a *sunnah* of the Prophet 🕌. For *imams* (leaders of congregational prayer) and other religious figures, keeping a beard is a normal practice. Some scholars do not object to wearing a tie, and suggest wearing loose clothing as it provides ease in performing *salāh*. Any degree of nakedness is highly discouraged, sinful, and forbidden. Purposely intending to look like a member of the opposite sex, either through clothing, putting on make-up, hairstyles and/or physical behavior is sinful and strictly forbidden. As per Islam, clothing reflect one's personality and piety, and it affects one's dignity and respect in society; Muslims are to be mindful of this.

NAKEDNESS

Visiting public baths and swimming pools where people's private parts are fully or somewhat exposed is sinful. Exposing one's private parts intentionally is strictly discouraged and prohibited. On a separate note, Muslim patients and doctors must practice as much modesty as medically possible during physical check-ups. Whatever Muslims are not allowed to look at, they are not allowed to see on television or through any other means.

CIRCUMCISION

Islam commands all Muslim male children to be circumcised. This is a *sunnah* of Prophet Ibrahim ﷺ. Today, science has come to recognize the many benefits of circumcision. An adult male convert to Islam should do the circumcision by himself, or with the help of his wife, because they are not allowed to expose their private parts to anyone else for circumcision. However, Islamic *sharia* gives him the option to remain without being circumcised.

AQIQA

Aqiqa is the sacrificing of an animal at the birth of a child. As per the sunnah of the Prophet ﷺ, it is usually celebrated on the seventh day of the child's birth, and it is done out of thankfulness to Allah ﷺ for His grace. The meat of the animal(s) is distributed among relatives and poor people, and consumed by the family as well.

SADAQA (CHARITY)

Sadaqa is a form of charity, above the obligatory charity of *zakāh*, that Muslims are encouraged to give in the way of Allah ﷺ. Muslims who feel they may have committed some wrong or who believe that Allah ﷺ has been displeased give *sadaqa* (as repentance) to deserving Muslims to please Allah ﷺ.

Allah ﷺ shows His displeasure with Muslims – because of their sinful behavior – by inflicting upon them pain. Also by this, Allah ﷺ purifies them and saves them from eternal punishment. Muslims, in response to such pain, sickness, and misery give money and other valuables as *sadaqa* in order to be relieved of their situation.

The basic concept of giving money to the poor and in the way of Allah 🕌 is that the more Muslims give, the more purified they become. The more pure they become, the less problems and troubles they come across in life. Certainly, in this way, they become closer to ultimate success. However, whatever amount of money is spent, it cannot equal the success of the Hereafter.

SADAQA-E-JĀRIAH (PERPETUAL CHARITY) – *Sadaqa-e-jāriah* is any good thing or person a Muslim leaves behind in the way of Allah 🕌. For example, a good offspring, social service, funds for welfare purposes, Islamic literature, or anything to benefit mankind is *sadaqa-e-jāriah*. *Sadqa-e-jāriah* guarantees perpetual reward even posthumously. For those who have performed *sadaqa-e-jāriah*, their Roster of Deeds continuously increases with rewarding deeds until Judgment Day.

JANĀZA/MUSLIM BURIAL

Islam requires the dead to be buried as soon as they pass away. Burning, cremating, embalming, or any other method currently used to dispose/preserve the dead body is absolutely prohibited in Islam.

A dead body is to be given *ghusl* (ritual washing) and then wrapped in unstitched sheets of white cotton. It is highly recommended that the closest relative(s) give *ghusl* because it brings many blessings to both. Private parts of the body must remain covered while washing. If the deceased is a female, no male, including the husband, father, brother, or son, is allowed to see her body. Only females are to participate in giving *ghusl* to a female body.

Once *ghusl* has been given, the *janāza salāh* (funeral prayer) must be offered in congregation before burial. Bodies are to be buried at a depth of about six to eight feet. Muslim burial procedures are very sacred and simple. Muslims visit their loved ones' graves and seek forgiveness for them from Allah 🕌 in their prayers. Moreover, Muslims should visit graveyards frequently to be mindful that one day they too will die.

Since the dead can hear, reciting the holy Qur'an by their side is highly recommended [Abu Dawud]. However, crying profusely and loudly is highly discouraged. Generally, the official period of mourning is three days, except for the widow, whose period of mourning is four months and ten days. The deceased have a right to be buried as soon as possible, and it is a duty of Muslims to accompany the *janāza* to its burial site and bury it with due rites. On hearing the news of death, Muslims say:

"INNA LILLAHĪ WA INNA ILAYHĪ RAJIŪN"

("From Allah we came, and to Allah is our return")

THE ISLAMIC CALENDAR

The Islamic calendar is a lunar calendar. There are 12 months in it, and each month is either 29 or 30 days long. The beginning of each month is based on sighting the new moon. Muslims are recommended to look for the new moon at the end of each month. Usually, Islamic authorities and organizations announce the moon-sighting and establish the beginning of a new month. The 12 months of the Islamic calendar are:

1) Muharram	5) Jumadi al-Awwal	9) Ramadhan
2) Safar	6) Jumadi ath-Thani	10) Shawwal
3) Rabi al-Awwal	7) Rajab	11) Dhul-Qada
4) Rabi ath-Thani	8) Shaban	12) Dhul-Hijjah

The first of Muharram marks the new Islamic year. *Āshura,* the tenth of Muharram, is a significant day in the history of mankind and when many important events took place:

1) Allah 🕌 accepted the repentance of Adam عَلَيْهِ السَّلَام.

2) Allah ﷻ saved Nuh (Noah) عليه السلام and his companions in the ark.

3) Allah ﷻ extinguished the fire in which Ibrahim عليه السلام was thrown by Namrud (Nimrod).

4) Allah ﷻ restored Ayyub (Job) عليه السلام to health from leprosy.

5) Allah ﷻ reunited Yusuf (Joseph) عليه السلام with his father Yaqub (Jacob) عليه السلام.

6) Allah ﷻ took Yunus (Jonah) عليه السلام out from the belly of the fish.

7) Allah ﷻ spoke to Musa (Moses) عليه السلام and gave him the 10 Commandments. In an earlier year on this same day, Musa عليه السلام parted the sea and delivered the Nation of Israel from captivity, and Allah ﷻ destroyed the pharaoh and his army.

8) Allah ﷻ forgave Dawūd (David) عليه السلام.

9) Allah ﷻ restored Sulayman (Solomon) عليه السلام to his throne.

10) Allah ﷻ raised Prophet Isa (Jesus) عليه السلام to the heavens.

11) The Prophet Muhammad's ﷺ grandson, *Imam* Husayn and his family, were martyred by the army of Yazīd.

12) It is reported that *Yaum-e-Qiyamah* (Doomsday) will occur on the tenth of Muharram as well [Mishkat].

The holy Prophet ﷺ, because of the sacredness of Āshura, fasted on this day, and many Muslims do the same, following in his example. The 27th night of Rajab is known as the night of *Isra wal-Mirāj*, when, on Allah's ﷻ invitation, the Prophet Muhammad ﷺ journeyed from Makkah to Jerusalem and then to Heaven. As per the *sunnah* of the Prophet ﷺ, Shaban was his favorite month, in which he fasted on the 15th day and made preparations for the coming month of Ramadhan.

Ramadhan is the most blessed month of Islam. It is in Ramadhan that Muslims fast for the entire month. On the 27th night of Ramadhan (*Lailatul Qadr* – Night of Power), the first five verses of the holy Qur'an were revealed, and Muslims celebrate this night by worshipping all night long.

Hajj begins on the eighth day of the twelfth month.

Three *eids* (celebrations) are celebrated by Muslims:

1) *Eid-e-Milād-un-Nabi* ﷺ – 12th of Rabi ul-Awwal – The celebration of the birth of Prophet Muhammad ﷺ.

2) *Eid-ul-Fitr* – First of Shawwal – The celebration marking the end of Ramadhan.

3) *Eid-ul-Adha* – 10th of Dhul Hijjah – When every able Muslim family offers animal sacrifice in remembering and replicating Prophet Ibrahīm's عليه السلام sacrifice of his son Ismail عليه السلام. Allah عزوجل accepted Prophet Ibrahīm's (Abraham) sacrifice and replaced Ismail (Ishmael) عليه السلام with a lamb. The meat of the sacrificed animal is distributed among the poor and enjoyed by family and friends.

CHAPTER 23

Questions about Islam

MANY PEOPLE ASK OR MAY ASK

and their Answers

*A*LTHOUGH I HAVE COVERED a substantial amount of material in this book, I have come across many other questions that need to be answered. As noted earlier, Islam is an ocean of knowledge, and even though I have covered a lot, this is still only *something* about Islam.

Though it may seem small at times, the world is a big place, in which all kinds of people exist. Some would just like to know something about Islam, while others want deeper knowledge, and some are even considering embracing Islam and need more satisfactory and complete answers. I have tried to meet the needs of all in this book; therefore, readers may skip some sections or bear with me throughout. Regardless, the information is interesting, and the knowledge of Islam will prove to be invaluable in one way or another.

FROM WHOM SHOULD WE LEARN ISLAM?

*T*HERE ARE THINGS IN LIFE of which a small amount of information will suffice, but there are also things for which complete information and understanding are required. Certainly, information about Islam is readily available everywhere, but such raw and scattered information has the tendency to be misunderstood and may be inaccurate. Islamic concepts, principles, practices, and inner wisdom require a deeper understanding to be comprehended fully.

This book may have helped in understanding Islam, but nothing replaces a person-to-person (face-to-face) discussion for full understanding. So, with whom should a seeker consult about Islam? Just as plumbers cannot and should not do an electrician's work and vice versa, only qualified Muslim scholars can and should preach Islam.

The basic requirement for teaching Islam is that a Muslim must have sufficient knowledge of it and must practice what he/she preaches [Qur'an 61:2-3]. Unqualified and non-practicing Muslims can mislead and, in my opinion, should never be consulted or believed. Arrogant statements such as, "I know a lot" or "I should teach whatever I know," do not fulfill the purpose and bring harm to oneself, others, and certainly to Islam. Allah ﷻ states:

> Call towards the way of your Lord with solid strategy and good counsel, and debate with them in the most desirable manner... •
> [Quran 16:125]

Certainly, not everyone has the wisdom or possesses the ability to debate articulately. A lot of knowledge and expertise is required, and a scholar must be equipped with qualities of teaching and be courteous. It is also incumbent upon a student to choose carefully the person from whom he is to learn Islam.

HOW MUCH ONE OUGHT TO KNOW TO BE A GOOD (PRACTICING) MUSLIM?

ONE MUST HOLD FAST TO THE basic beliefs under all circumstances, because this is the least requirement for success in the Hereafter. Those who wish to avoid any punishment in the Hereafter must punctually perform the basic obligatory duties (Chapter 9). I believe that what Islam requires of us in this short life is nothing compared to the eternal reward it offers. Those who wish to progress in piety, become elevated, acquire spiritual heights, and become nearer to Allah ﷻ, will have to work harder and dig deeper into Islam. However, Allah ﷻ does not require us to do more than that of which what we are capable.

CAN 'TRUTH' BE FOUND ONLY THROUGH RELIGION?

*G*ENERALLY, WE LEARN THROUGH OUR SENSES, but no matter how intelligent we are, if our senses cannot sense something, how can we learn through them? Even with our senses, on many occasions, it becomes difficult to comprehend general truths, so how can it be possible to know absolute truths without any extraordinary means? Religion and its spiritual wisdoms are those extraordinary means, but even with their assistance, it is not possible without the help of the Lord. Certainly, only the Lord can guide us to the absolute truths through His divine guidance.

The best way to know and understand the truth is through divine revelations inspired by the Lord to His prophets. Only a true understanding of the deeper wisdom of revelations can bring about unshakeable belief in the unseen. Those who have brought faith in the unseen are relieved of further exploration, but those who wish to see to believe, their wish will never come true, because "the unseen truths" are matters of the other world and are beyond reach.

Science is "human effort," and religion is "beyond human effort." Religion is far in advance of science; however, it can be said that science is on the right track, yet very far from reaching ultimate truths.

Allah ﷻ states:

Finally, We will indeed show them Our signs everywhere and within themselves, until it becomes evident to them that without a doubt, this is the truth. Is it not enough that your Lord, without a doubt, is a witness of everything? • Remember that those people are in doubt about meeting with their Lord. Remember that He encompasses everything. • [Qur'an 41:53-54]

Having faith means believing without seeing. When all truths will be revealed, then believing will be unacceptable and fruitless. Millions of followers of science, who did not come to believe in ultimate truths and realities, have lost their lives in the effort to witness ultimate truths. Only the Lord's way, i.e., the religious way, and the Islamic way leads to truths and ultimate truths.

CAN ONE LIVE IN AMERICA/THE WEST AND AT THE SAME TIME BE A GOOD MUSLIM?

*I*F ONE HAS TRULY READ this book and understood the Islamic concepts, worshipping processes, and duties described therein, I do not think it is difficult to understand how to be a good Muslim, as well as a good citizen of America or of European countries. Islam does not take away anyone's citizenship or nationality, and it does not require Muslims to live only in Islamic countries.

In fact, I believe that living in the West and being a good Muslim is more rewarding. If a Muslim lives in a place where he cannot even act in an un-Islamic fashion—even though there is no such place—then for what can he be rewarded? On the other hand, in a place where a Muslim is free to do whatever he wishes but instead controls his desires and fulfills his Islamic duties, he truly deserves more reward.

Muslim Americans are engaged in almost all facets of the American society. They are responsible for following their religion and at the same time for abiding by America's rules and regulations as citizens of the United States. Moreover, society has a duty to fulfill responsibilities towards its citizens of Islamic faith. Based on my personal experience, I am more than satisfied that American society is doing its job wonderfully for all of its citizens, including Muslims. As an individual, I am very much thankful for living in America.

Not a single country in the West is generally concerned with or prevents Muslims from performing their religious duties, nor does it force them to commit *harām* (what is Islamically prohibited). I have lived in America for the past 30 years or so, and no one has ever prevented me from praying, fasting, going to Hajj or giving *zakāh* (obligatory charity), nor has anyone ever interfered with my beliefs or required me to drink, dance, eat pork, or fool around. When someone converts to Islam, he/she is not fired from his/her job or discriminated against, and no one forces him/her to engage in un-Islamic activities. (Some isolated incidents are not worth mentioning here.)

However, if a weak or perverted Muslim brings himself to do *harām* (what is Islamically prohibited), justifies it as being due to peer pressure or in the name of advancement/modernity, and only occasionally becomes full of shame because he realizes he is Muslim, then America or the West should not be held responsible for his behavior. This kind of Muslim has no right to blame America or the Western lifestyle, but he should live life according to Islam and draw rewards. Sacrificing worldly desires in exchange for ultimate success is the motto of Islam, whether one resides in America, Europe, Makkah, or Madinah.

Allah ﷻ protects and helps sincere followers, but He does not help anyone who lives a hypocritical lifestyle. There is freedom of religion in America and Europe, but if Muslims encounter some difficulty here and there, for one reason or another, it is just a temporary thing. Once everyone properly comprehends Islam, I am confident that this will bring forth mutual understanding and happiness to all. On a general note, Muslims are rewarded for being patient and for persevering, and they should play their part in bringing about a better understanding of Islam by all means, specifically through their character.

IS THERE ANY FLEXIBILITY IN FOLLOWING ISLAMIC RULES?

*I*SLAM WOULD NOT BE FIT for human nature if it did not provide flexibilities for varying situations and circumstances. Since Islam contains guidance for all times and circumstances, it must provide the required flexibility to practice Islamic rules. It must also do the same if it is truly fit for human nature.

Let me assure you that Islam does provide flexibility for everyone and for all special circumstances and situations. The main purpose of Islam is not to subjugate humans through strict rules and practices, but to connect them to their Creator, so that may achieve piety on the basis of their ability and efforts. To achieve this goal, Islam demands, wherever necessary, strict adherence to the core rules of Islam and provides full flexibility where people have less ability and opportunity or are hindered in any way. An individual's circumstance and intent plays an important role in performing every act in his daily life. Allah ﷻ knows our abilities, circumstances, and the intentions behind all of our actions. We can fool others and ourselves, but not Allah ﷻ.

Where the majority of people are Muslims, it is relatively easy to practice and enforce Islamic duties/rules, because the society provides all the necessary arrangements. However, in other parts of the world, which can be referred to as non-Islamic, practicing Islam may not be as easy. There are numerous examples to understand the rigidity and flexibility in Islamic rules. Muslims should be aware of them, so they do not cross the limits or overburden themselves. Also, non-Muslims should be aware of the rigidity and flexibility in Islamic rules, if and when they decide to embrace Islam, so they may not regret this important decision later.

For example, the five daily *salāh* (obligatory prayers) must be performed; however, if one cannot stand because of weakness, sickness, or any other allowable reason, he is allowed to perform *salāh* sitting down. If even sitting is not possible, then performing *salāh* lying down and through the gestures of the eyes fulfills the requirement. Women are relieved from outside duties, but when it becomes necessary they can go outside. Fasting in Ramadhan is incumbent on all Muslims, but if one is traveling or is sick, he is allowed to miss fasting and perform it later. Hajj is incumbent once in a lifetime on every Muslim, as soon as one is able to perform it. If one's travel route is not safe, for example, due to war, then one can delay the Hajj until the route becomes safe. These are just a few examples out of many. During times of extreme circumstances, even what is prohibited becomes permissible, but only to the extent needed. [Qur'an 2:173]

WHY ARE ALCOHOL AND PORK PROHIBITED IN ISLAM?

I WOULD LIKE TO BE VERY FRANK HERE and say that regarding Allah's ﷻ commandments, Muslims are encouraged not to ask why. However, to enhance knowledge and understand the wisdom behind a commandment, there is nothing wrong in asking why.

Every rule, regulation, permission, or prohibition of Islam is to benefit humankind. The harms of eating pork and consuming alcohol greatly surpass their benefits. They stimulate sinful behavior and contribute towards many physical and spiritual diseases. Islam's inherent motive is to protect humanity from all harm, ill desires, and immoral behavior, so they may reach their purpose of creation. Thus, whatever contributes towards this end, Islam permits, and whatever works against this end, it prohibits.

Throughout the world, the effects of consuming alcohol are well known. There is no need to shed any more light on this topic. As far as eating pork is concerned, medical science is fully aware of its harmful effects on the human body. The spiritual, psychological, and behavioral harms of consuming pork are not visible to the naked eye but are a matter of fact, and a close study of human behavior will show that. Allah ﷻ has nothing to lose in what we drink or eat; however, when Islam addresses any issue, there must be a lot of meaning to it.

IF ISLAM IS SUCH A GREAT RELIGION, WHY ARE THERE SO MANY FACTIONS, AND WHICH ONE IS THE RIGHT ONE?

THERE IS NO QUESTION THAT ISLAM IS THE GREATEST RELIGION, because it is prescribed by Allah ﷻ, the Almighty Lord. It is also a fact that there are no different versions of Islam. The various divisions/denominations are not of Islam, but of Muslims. Islam is one, Muslims are many. Islam is not because of Muslims; Muslims are because of Islam. Islam cannot be divided; Muslims can and have been divided. Allah ﷻ gave power and free will to everyone to choose between good and evil, success and failure, etc. Allah ﷻ commands Muslims:

> And strongly grasp the rope of Allah, all of you, and do not be divided... • [Qur'an 3:103]

In a very famous *hadith*, Prophet Muhammad ﷺ stated:

> There were 72 factions in bani (children of) Israel, the family of Yaqub (Jacob), and in my *ummah* (community), there will be 73 factions, out of which only one will be the rightly guided, the vindicated one. The Companions inquired as to which one will that be? He replied, "The one that follows me and my Companions, the *Ahle-Sunnah wa Jama'a.*" [Muslim]

The Prophet ﷺ lived by the Qur'an, and his Companions lived by both the Qur'an and *sunnah*. Through the Companions' lives and efforts, the Qur'an and *sunnah* reached Muslims, and true Muslims have abided by them ever since. Anyone who deviates or carves out a separate path from the *Ahle-Sunnah* (people of the *sunnah*), he is responsible for his innovation, deviation, and separation. A close study of any deviated faction will show that it misinterprets one or more principle(s) of Islam, while the *Ahle-Sunnah wa Jama'a* does not, and abides by Islam completely and as laid down by the Qur'an and *sunnah*.

It is astonishing to know that regardless of how many factions and/or sub-factions there are, the fundamental beliefs of all Muslims are the same. ALL Muslims:

- Believe in *tawhīd* (Oneness of Allah)
- Believe in the finality of prophethood. No more prophets to come after Prophet Muhammad ﷺ
- Believe in the holy Qur'an as the word of Allah ﷻ
- Face the Ka'ba during *salāh* (obligatory prayers of worship)
- Fast in the month of Ramadhan
- Give charity to the poor and needy
- Perform the obligation of Hajj, if and when possible
- Believe in the coming of Judgment Day
- Believe in Heaven and Hell
- Believe in the eternal life of the Hereafter

The basic differences in each faction are *faroi*, of secondary and tertiary nature. Some factions are extreme, and some are unnecessarily liberal, while the true *Ahle Sunnah wa Jama'a* is moderate, as is required in Islam to be on the right path. Keep in mind that the true path can only be one, which in Islam is the *Sirāte Mustaqīm* (straight path). Whoever was on this path from their heart will become known on Judgment Day. Every Muslim must strive to understand and follow the righteous path. The majority of the Muslim *ummah* belongs to *Ahle Sunnah wa Jama'a*, which is the righteous path.

WHAT DOES ISLAM SAY ABOUT PREDESTINATION?

*I*F MAN, HIS ACTIONS, AND HIS FATE ARE PREDESTINED, then the question is, by whom? If predestination is by our Lord, then it can be asked, is our Lord Who first destined everything and then put us in the turmoil of life so unjust? If everything is predestined, then what is the sense of trying man and endowing him with free will? What is the sense of the coming of Judgment Day? He could rather have simply created us and right from there sent some to Paradise and the rest to Hell.

According to Islam, success and failure and our destination are not predestined. Allah ﷻ has not already made His decision about our fate, although He is aware of it, just as He has knowledge of everything else. Having knowledge does not mean He caused it to happen. There are so many things that He kept in His control to run the affairs of the universe, including humans, but at the same time He has given all the power necessary for humans to live their life on Earth and make decisions about their fate in the Hereafter.

Man does not control when, where, or how he will die, but he certainly controls whether to live a pious or perverted life. Allah ﷻ knows what we do or will do in the future, but He does not cause any of it. The notion of predestination is based either on arrogance or on ignorance. No one is predestined to Heaven or Hell. Islam does not approve of arrogance and condemns hopelessness.

DOES ISLAM GUARANTEE COMPLETE PEACE AND PROMISE A TROUBLE-FREE LIFE HERE?

*W*E COME TO THIS WORLD TO BE TESTED, and a testing ground is never trouble-free and can never be full of peace. How can people be tested for patience and steadfastness if life is completely trouble-free and peaceful? If life is empty of troubles, how are people to remember their Lord, pray to Him, or try to please Him? How can people help each other and earn the Lord's blessings if everyone is full of happiness and has no worries?

This world is not Heaven, but it does reflect some qualities of Hell, so we can learn and prepare to be saved from the Hellfire. If this life were trouble-free and peaceful, how could we have known the greater pain and misery of Hell? Islam guarantees inner peace, not absolute peace in this life. However, if we acquire the ultimate success, we are guaranteed both in the Hereafter. Islam does not promise a trouble-free life on Earth, but it trains its followers in how to cope successfully with life. It provides sufficient peace and happiness for us to work our way towards ultimate success.

If people want to acquire inner peace, they have to choose slavery to the Lord and relieve themselves from slavery to society and to the self. Regarding the solving of man's problems, a famous French philosopher, Jean Jacques Rousseau, suggests that man leave the state of society and go back to the state of nature. In my opinion, since this is not possible, it is not a solution. Man can no longer return to the state of nature. Is it possible to convert all thriving metropolises and trade centers to create a state of nature? No. Man has already come a long way, so for him this is not a solution.

The problem is not cities or the state of society; the problem is in man himself. As long as he chooses to be a slave to society, he will continue to encounter problems. It is only the slavery to the Lord, his true Master, through which he is relieved of the slavery to society, wants, lust, etc. By being the slave of the Master of all masters, he will be in peace wherever he lives. The true Master does not require man to leave the state of society to acquire peace and happiness; He provides him with what he needs within it. For a Muslim, absolute peace and a guarantee for a trouble-free life are not the goal. The goal is the pleasure of his Lord and Master.

WHAT ARE THE BENEFITS/REWARDS OF EMBRACING ISLAM?

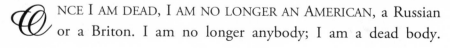 NCE I AM DEAD, I AM NO LONGER AN AMERICAN, a Russian or a Briton. I am no longer anybody; I am a dead body.

However, even at this point, it will still matter what faith I belonged to and/or practiced. My burial ceremonies will not take place according to my nationality but according to my religion. Once I am dead, all connections to this world are cut off, but the connection with my religion never severs. Even after burial, my faith will still matter.

As mentioned earlier, the stay in A'lam-e-Barzakh (the transitory state/period/place) is decided on the basis of faith and religious practices. According to Islam, salvation is not possible through any other religion; not being a Muslim means being the ultimate loser. The greatest reward for embracing Islam is that one is saved from becoming the ultimate loser. All previous sins are forgiven as one submits to the Lord's will and embarks on the journey of pleasing Him, not according to one's wishes, but as per His direction and guidance. A convert to Islam is one who returns home to where he belongs. Islam does not promise anything less, nor does a follower need anything more.

IF SOMEONE IS INTERESTED IN EMBRACING ISLAM, BUT FIRST WISHES TO SEE A MUSLIM COMPLETELY REFLECTIVE OF ISLAM, WHERE DOES ONE LOOK?

EVERY MUSLIM *SHOULD BE* A COMPLETE REFLECTION OF ISLAM and an embodiment of the virtues and values it presents. However, if this were the case, then people would not have difficulty in locating a *momin* (devout believer) near them. In fact, I would not even have written this book because you would have already known about Islam through those *momins*. Even though there is no shortage of true believers throughout the Muslim *ummah* (community), do you know of any near you? I cannot say. Even if you do find one, do you have enough time and patience to observe closely his character and lifestyle?

For true reflections of Islam, should someone look to high profile claimants to being Muslims, such as those kings and the royalty, those leaders and their supporters, those politicians and the interest groups behind them, those claimants of religious authority, those teachers and preachers, those scholars, and those half-Sufi and half-goofy in the Muslim world? I do not think so.

If you still truly insist and are willing to look elsewhere, then look beyond the media, and observe the tens of millions of performers of daily *salāh* (obligatory prayers of worship) in mosques throughout the world. Look among those thousands of sincere *imams*, teachers, and preachers who have dedicated their lives for the sake of Islam and not for material wealth, fame, or power. Look among the 1.6 billion ordinary Muslims who are not leaders, but who are slaves to their Lord. They always spread love among each other, are generous and content, follow Islam with utmost sincerity, and embody the virtues Islam promotes. They are the reflections of Islam. They do their best, and that is all Allah ﷻ requires of them. This is where your wish will come true. You may just have to go a long way to meet them, but I guarantee that you will not be disappointed.

In responding to the aforementioned question, I suggest you to study Islam deeply and not spend precious time looking for some practical reflections. It is your fate that is on the line, and about which you should be worried. I think the shortest route is to read about those Muslims who were true reflections of Islam.

DOES ISLAM TEACH HATE FOR NON-MUSLIMS, THEIR TEACHINGS, AND LIFESTYLE?

*I*SLAM IS THE GUIDANCE NOT JUST FOR MUSLIMS, but for all of humanity. It is from the Lord, Who is the Creator not only of Muslims but also of all humans. The Prophet Muhammad ﷺ was sent by the Lord for all of humanity, not just for Muslims. The holy Qur'an does not only command Muslims, but invites all of humanity, to a peaceful and righteous path and a successful end. How then can Islam teach hate?

With hate, one cannot move forward. With hate, one cannot bring any peace and happiness. With hate, one cannot show love and generosity and increase the numbers of followers. With hate, one cannot bring people closer to each other, guide them, and enlighten their hearts. With hate, one cannot make a man human and obtain true submission to his Lord.

There is nothing in Islam that even suggests hating others. However, Islam does teach hate for sinful behavior and oppression. It teaches one to hate lust, transgression, and every act that harms humanity. But even all of these "hates" are not for worldly or personal reasons, but have a higher reason: to be successful in the Hereafter. This entire book is written to clarify that none of Islam's teachings, principles, and duties teach hate of others or their beliefs. The readers can ultimately judge this for themselves.

SHOULD AMERICA FEAR ISLAM?

I F I SIMPLY SAY, "NO," YOU MAY ASK, "WHY NOT?" *Alhamdulillah* (all praise is due to Allah ﷻ), I have studied Islam deeply and have lived in the United States for more than a quarter of a century. I have not found anything in Islam that should make anyone fear it.

If this fear is because of some bad elements in the worldwide Muslim community, then I would ask the common question: "Which community on the face of the Earth is free from bad elements?" Then why only fear Islam? If this fear is because of the fact that Islam is the fastest growing religion, then I would say that this is a worldwide phenomenon and not limited to the United States. Moreover, many religions have previously flourished in the U.S. and brought no harm to its society; in fact, they contributed towards the American experience. Now, if it is Islam's turn, so be it. This society is organized, intelligent, educated, religiously oriented, patriotic, and understands good from bad; it will not let anyone bring any harm to it.

It is estimated that the total number of Muslims in the U.S. ranges from seven to nine million, including immigrants, first and second generation Muslims in America, and converts to Islam. Muslim immigrants come from all over the Muslim world. For decades or, by some accounts, centuries, Muslims have lived here peacefully and contributed significantly to the American society. They call America their home. They are law-abiding citizens, doctors, engineers, architects, businesspersons, teachers, social workers, and much more. They love and protect America and will continue to contribute towards the well-being of this great country. True Muslims never betray the land in which they live.

Of course, America has all the right to protect and strengthen itself, but one thing is certain: it does not have to fear Islam. A greater understanding of Islam and Muslims would help in eradicating many concerns and fears about Islam, if there truly are any. My message to fellow Americans is to learn about Islam, not to fear it.

WHY EMBRACE ISLAM WHEN ONE IS ALREADY DOING THE GOOD THAT ISLAM PROMOTES?

*M*Y HUMBLE TONE AND THE WAY I HAVE PRESENTED Islam should not lead anyone to think that my intent is to convert them. I presented the facts about Islam in the manner my personality and beliefs allowed me to do.

I confidently believe that there are good people in the world doing much good, just like many Muslims are. So then, why should they embrace Islam? I humbly say that I did not make the rules. It is the Lord's way, not my way or anybody else's. If the Lord wants to be pleased with humans only through Islam, what can I say? He is the Lord. My duty is to get the message across, plain and simple.

According to Islam, one can achieve all the success in this world by doing good of all kinds, but to achieve ultimate success in the Hereafter, one has to do a lot more: recognize Allah ﷻ, obey Allah ﷻ, and then work to please Him. People who do good deeds are rewarded for them only in this world, whereas Muslims exchange good deeds for eternal reward, in the form of Paradise and Allah's ﷻ pleasure. The Lord is merciful, but we have to recognize His lordship in the way He prescribed in order to receive His mercy. In Islam, Muslims properly recognize His lordship and then hope for His mercy.

CHAPTER 24

What Islam Says to Jews and Christians

ALLAH ﷻ REVEALS IN THE QUR'AN THE taking of an oath from every soul about His lordship and said that all creatures are His servants. This was the basic message all prophets brought, reminding humanity that all should worship the One and true Lord, Allah ﷻ. Allah ﷻ also gathered and took a special oath from the *arwah* (souls) of all the prophets-to-be that they would bring faith upon, help, and follow the last prophet, Muhammad ﷺ, if he appeared during their time. [Qur'an 3:81-2] They all agreed unconditionally.

Every prophet who came informed his nation about the eventual coming of Prophet Muhammad ﷺ. Allah ﷻ reveals in the Qur'an how past nations corrupted the teachings and holy books revealed to them. At the coming of Prophet Muhammad ﷺ, people who believed in Musa (Moses) عليه السلام and Isa (Jesus) عليه السلام, Jews and Christians respectively, rejected their respective prophet's calls by denying Prophet Muhammad ﷺ. However, many Jews and Christians recognized him and embraced Islam, fulfilling their prophet's teachings.

The teachings and commandments revealed to Prophets Musa ﷺ and Isa ﷺ guided Jews and Christians respectively. Those were the *sharia* of Musa ﷺ and the *sharia* of Isa ﷺ, for their respective times. Their rules and practices were applicable to the times in which they were enforced. Since not all times and conditions were the same, their revealed laws and teachings had to be different as well, but the basic beliefs of each *sharia* remained the same throughout.

As the teachings of Prophet Musa ﷺ and Prophet Isa ﷺ were corrupted by human intervention, some Jews and Christians who wanted to live by their original teachings sought refuge in seclusion and parted ways from their societies. They knew very well that the coming of the Last Prophet ﷺ would renew their commitment to Allah ﷻ and bring them comfort and eternal peace. [Qur'an 2:89]

In the holy Qur'an, Allah ﷻ reminds Jews and Christians about the teachings of Musa ﷺ and Isa ﷺ and commands that, if they are truthful to them, they must have faith in Prophet Muhammad ﷺ for ultimate success. [5:12] Many truthful Jews and Christians knew—through their respective books—the signs of Prophet Muhammad ﷺ, and so, at his coming, they embraced Islam. [Qur'an 61:6]

On the coming of Prophet Muhammad ﷺ, those Jews and Christians who had faith in him finally received the comfort and relief for which they had been waiting for so long. Allah ﷻ took away from them the burdensome commandments and practices that were present in their *sharias*, and established Islam as the religion for mankind. Now, salvation and ultimate success are only possible through Islam. [Qur'an 3:85]

To inform my fellow readers of the Jewish and Christian faith, I present a few of the many verses Allah ﷻ revealed in the holy Qur'an addressing them. In numerous places, they are addressed as the *Ahle-*

Kitāb (People of the Book), *Yahūdi* (Jews), *Nasrāni* (Christians), and *Bani Israel* (Nation of Israel), and *Āle-Yaqūb* (Family of Prophet Yaqūb (Jacob) ﷺ). Another title of Prophet Yaqūb was Israel.

Allah ﷻ reveals:

> And the past peoples were not, but one *ummah* (community/religion), then they began to differ. And had Allah not already determined one thing, so indeed it would be decided for them, in which they used to differ. • [Qur'an 10:19]

Allah ﷻ also informed us and affirmed that:

> Neither was Ibrahim (Abraham) a Yahūdi (Jew), nor a Nasrāni (Christian); but (he) was a believer of truth, a Muslim. And nor was he of the polytheists. • [Qur'an 3:67]

Prophet Ibrahim ﷺ was the forefather of many prophets and grandfather of Yaqūb (Jacob) ﷺ. Yaqūb ﷺ took an oath from his children, of which the holy Qur'an informs us:

> ...and Yaqūb said, "O children! Certainly, Allah chose for your benefit, the *deen* (religion; complete way of life). So do not, at all, die, but in the state that you are Muslim." • [Qur'an 2:132]

The holy Qur'an reveals the necessary history of Banī Isrāil and the prophets that came to them. Many *surahs* (chapters) of the holy Qur'an, e.g., al-Baqarah, Āle-Imran, al-Maida, an-Nisa, Banī Isrāil, Maryam, and others, contain detailed accounts of Jews and Christians, the piety and purity of the beloved Maryam (Mary) عليها السلام, and the miraculous birth and ascension of Isa (Jesus) ﷺ to the heavens. The holy Qur'an and the Prophet Muhammad ﷺ repeatedly invite the People of the Book (Jews and Christians) to embrace Islam. Allah ﷻ states:

> Say, "O People of the Book, come to that which is common between us and you, which is that we worship none except Allah and do not believe in anything to be His partner, and may any of us not make anyone their lord, leaving aside Allah. So if they turn their face, then you people say, "Bear witness that we all are Muslims." • [Qur'an 3:64]

Allah 🕮 commanded the Prophet 🕮:

> So whoever raise an objection concerning him (Isa/Jesus 🕮), now that the knowledge has reached you, then say, "So, come on now, let us call our sons and your sons, and our women and your women, and our own and your own, then let us imprecate and ask for Allah's curse upon the liars." [Qur'an 3:61]

But they never showed up. Allah 🕮 then asked them:

> O People of the Book! Why do you mix truth with falsehood, and conceal the truth deliberately? • O People of the Book! Why do you deny Allah's verses, even though you yourself are witnessing them? • [Qur'an 3:70-71]

But again, they never responded. Then Allah 🕮 said:

> ...and had the People of the Book brought faith, then definitely it would be better for them... • [Qur'an 3:110]

Nevertheless, the holy Qur'an recognizes:

> ...among them, some had brought faith, and many of their people are all disobedient. • [3:110]

> And certainly, there are some People of the Book that believe in Allah, and that which is revealed upon you, and that which is revealed upon them, humbly cowering in front of Allah; they do not take in return for Allah's verses a demeaning amount. They are those for whom there is reward with their Lord. Certainly, Allah is to take account soon. • [3:199]

The holy Qur'an further acknowledges:

> And if the People of the Book had brought faith and feared Allah, so We would have relieved them of their sins, and We would definitely admit them into gardens of bliss. • [5:65]

> And had they held to the Taurat (Torah) and to the Injil (gospel), and that which (Qur'an) was revealed towards him (Muhammad 🕮) from his Lord, so definitely they would eat from above their head and from below their feet... • [5:66]

Say that "O People of the Book! You are nothing, until you behold the Taurat (Torah) and Injīl (gospels), and that which (Qur'an) was revealed towards him (Muhammad ﷺ) from his Lord... • [5:68]

Allah's invitation in the holy Qur'an is still open for everyone:

Certainly, those (Muslims) who believe, along with Jews, and Sabians, and Christians—any comes to believe in Allah and the Last Day, and who does righteous deeds, there is no fear upon them, nor do they grieve. • [5:69]

We have also come to know from the holy Qur'an that on Judgment Day, Allah ﷻ will ask Isa عليه السلام:

And when Allah will say, "O Isa (Jesus) son of Maryam (Mary), did you tell people to make me and my mother deities, leaving aside Allah? He will say, "Glory be to Allah! I have no right to say that for which I have no right. If I had said that, certainly, You would have known it. You know whatever I have in my heart, and I do not know what is in Your knowledge. Certainly, You are the knower of all secrets. • I did not say to them, except of what You commanded me to say: 'Worship Allah, my Lord and your Sustainer.' I kept watching them, while I was among them. Then when you completed my duration of stay among them, then it was You Who remained the Overseer, and You are everyone's Guardian. • [5:116-117]

Because of their disbeliefs, Allah ﷻ states:

Certainly, they transgressed who said, "Masīh (Messiah) son of Maryam (Mary) is indeed Allah." And Masīh said, "O Banī Israīl, worship Allah, my Lord and your Sustainer." Certainly, he who does *shirk* (make partners) with Allah, so certainly Allah has prohibited Heaven for him, and his destination is Hell. And there is no helper for the oppressors. • Certainly, they transgress, who say Allah is 'a third of the three.' There is no deity, but one Deity. And if they do not repent for this nonsense, so definitely a tormenting punishment will reach those who committed this transgression. • So why do they not finally repent to Allah and ask forgiveness for that (*shirk*). And Allah is All-Forgiving, All-Merciful. • Masīh son of Maryam, is indeed a prophet. Certainly, before him passed many prophets. And his mother was truthful. Both used to eat food (like any mortal human). Look, how clearly we explain to them the Signs; then look how they have been deceived. • [5:72-75]

For more information about the People of the Book, one should further consult the holy Qur'an. It is not possible to include all of it here, so I have noted only some of the verses to show what Islam says about Jews and Christians. My intent here is neither to dishonor anyone nor to disrespect anyone's beliefs. My wish is that the Lord's words be known through any means, in order that whoever chooses to correct him or herself can have full knowledge of what Islam says about the People of the Book.

CHAPTER 25

What Others Have Said About Islam

*I*NSTEAD OF ASKING MY READERS to go through many books and check the history themselves about what others have said about Islam, so they may develop a better understanding of it, I have included many quotations from a variety of individuals in this chapter. I hope this will strengthen what I have said throughout the book. (All quotes are in chronological order.)

Simon Ockley (1678-9-August 1720) was a British Orientalist and was appointed Sir Thomas Adams Professor of Arabic at Cambridge University in 1711. He wrote in his book History of the Saracens:

> It is not the propagation but the permanency of his religion that deserves our wonder, the same pure and perfect impression which he engraved at Mecca and Medina is preserved after the revolutions of twelve centuries by the Indian, the African and the Turkish proselytes of the Koran....The Mahometans have uniformly withstood the temptation of reducing the object of their faith and devotion to a level with the senses and imagination of man. 'I believe in One God and Mahomet the Apostle of God' is the simple and invariable profession of Islam. The intellectual image of the Deity has never been degraded by any visible idol; the honors of the

prophet have never transgressed the measure of human virtue, and his living precepts have restrained the gratitude of his disciples within the bounds of reason and religion. [London, 1870, p. 54]

Canon Taylor, a distinguished historian and philologist, while reading a paper before the Church Congress at Walverhampton (UK) on 7 October 1887, stated that:

> It (Islam) replaced monkishness by manliness. It gives hope to the slave, brotherhood to mankind, and recognition of the fundamental facts of human nature.

Edward Montet, in his La Propaganda Chretienne et ses Adversaries Musulmans (translated as "Christian Propaganda and its Muslim Adversaries"), stated that:

> Islam is a religion that is essentially rationalistic in the widest sense of this term considered etymologically and historically. The definition of rationalism as a system that bases religious belief on principles furnished by the reason applies to it exactly... It cannot be denied that many doctrines and systems of theology and also many superstitions, from the worship of saints to the use of rosaries and amulets, have become grafted on the main trunk of Muslim creed. But in spite of the rich development, in every sense of the term, of the teachings of the prophet, the Quran has invariably kept its place as the fundamental starting point, and the dogma of unity of God has always been proclaimed therein with a grandeur, a majesty, an invariable purity and with a note of sure conviction, which it is hard to find surpassed outside the pale of Islam. This fidelity to the fundamental dogma of the religion, the elemental simplicity of the formula in which it is enunciated, the proof that it gains from the fervid conviction of the missionaries who propagate it, are so many causes to explain the success of Mohammedan missionary efforts. A creed so precise, so stripped of all theological complexities and consequently so accessible to the ordinary understanding might be expected to possess and does indeed possess a marvelous power of winning its way into the consciences of men.
>
> [Paris, 1890. Also in T.W. Arnold in The Preaching of Islam, London, 1913]

S.H. Leeder, a British author best known for his book Modern Sons of the Pharaohs (published in English in 1918), wrote in his book Veiled Mysteries of Egypt and the Religion of Islam:

> How, for instance, can any other appeal stand against that of the Moslem who, in approaching the pagan, says to him, however obscure or degraded he may be "embrace the faith, and you are at once equal and a brother." Islam knows "no colour line."
>
> [New York: Charles Scribners' Sons, 1913]

Sarojini Naidu, famously known as The Nightingale of India and the first Indian woman to become the President of the Indian National Congress in 1925, wrote:

> Sense of justice is one of the most wonderful ideals of Islam, because as I read in the Qur'an I find those dynamic principles of life, not mystic but practical ethics for the daily conduct of life suited to the whole world. [Lectures on "The Ideals of Islam", Speeches and Writings of Sorijini Naidi, Madras, 1918, p.167]

De Lacy O'Leary, a British clergyman, Arabist and Semitist wrote in his Islam at the Crossroads:

> History makes it clear however, that the legend of fanatical Muslims sweeping through the world and forcing Islam at the point of the sword upon conquered races is one of the most fantastically absurd myths that historians have ever repeated. [London, 1923, p.8]

Sir Hamilton Alexander Rosskeen Gibb (commonly referred to as H.A.R. Gibb), a Scottish Orientalist and distinguished professor at Harvard University, wrote in his book Whither Islam:

> But Islam has a still further service to render to the cause of humanity. It stands after all nearer to the real East than Europe does, and it possesses a magnificent tradition of inter-racial understanding and cooperation. No other society has such a record of success in uniting in an equality of status, of opportunity, and of endeavors so many and so various races of mankind...Islam has still the power to reconcile apparently irreconcilable elements of race and tradition. If ever the opposition of the great societies of East and West is to be replaced by cooperation, the mediation of Islam is an

indispensable condition. In its hands lies very largely the solution of the problem with which Europe is faced in its relation with East. If they unite, the hope of a peaceful issue is immeasurably enhanced. But if Europe, by rejecting the cooperation of Islam, throws it into the arms of its rivals, the issue can only be disastrous for both.

[London, 1932, p. 379]

Col. Donald S. Rockwell was a poet, critic and author, who gained the rank of colonel while participating in World War II, when the United States was fighting against Germany and Japan. In one of his books, i.e., Beyond the Brim and Bazaar of Dreams, he writes:

The simplicity of Islam, the powerful appeal and the compelling atmosphere of its mosques, the earnestness of its faithful adherents, the confidence inspiring realization of the millions throughout the world who answer the five daily calls to prayer – these factors attracted me from the first. But after I had determined to become a follower of Islam, I found many deeper reasons for confirming my decision. The mellow concept of life – fruit of the Prophet's combined course of action and contemplation – the wise counsel, the admonitions to charity and mercy, the broad humanitarianism, the pioneer declaration of woman's property rights – these and other factors of the teachings of the man of Mecca were to me among the most obvious evidence of a practical religion so tersely and so aptly epitomized in the cryptic words of Muhammad, "Trust in God and tie your camel". He gave us a religious system of normal action, not blind faith in the protection of an unseen force in spite of our own neglect, but confidence that if we do all things rightly and to the best of our ability, we may trust in what comes as the Will of God.

The universal brotherhood of Islam, regardless of race, politics, color or country, has been brought home to me most keenly many times in my life–and this is another feature which drew me towards the Faith. [Published by Islamic Review, 1935]

George Bernard Shaw, an Irish playwright, co-founder of the London School of Economics, and the only person to have been awarded both a Nobel Prize for Literature and an Oscar stated in his book The Genuine Islam:

I have always held the religion of Muhammad in high estimation because of its wonderful vitality. It is the only religion which appears to me to possess that assimilating capacity to the changing phase of existence which can make itself appeal to every age. I have studied him – the wonderful man and in my opinion far from being an anti-Christ, he must be called the Savior of Humanity. I believe that if a man like him were to assume the dictatorship of the modern world, he would succeed in solving its problems in a way that would bring it the much needed peace and happiness: I have prophesied about the faith of Muhammad that it would be acceptable to the Europe of tomorrow as it is beginning to be acceptable to the Europe of today. [Vol. 1, No. 8, 1936]

Arnold J. Toynbee, a British historian who authored a twelve-volume analysis of the rise and fall of civilizations titled A Study of History, wrote in his book Civilization on Trial that:

The extinction of race consciousness as between Muslims is one of the outstanding achievements of Islam and in the contemporary world there is, as it happens, a crying need for the propagation of this Islamic virtue. [New York, 1948, p. 205]

Arthur Stanley Tritton, a British historian and scholar of Islam, who was appointed Professor of Arabic at the School of Oriental and African Studies, University of London in 1938, and also spent some time teaching at Aligarh University, states in his book Islam:

The picture of the Muslim soldier advancing with a sword in one hand and the Qur'an in the other is quite false. [London, 1951, p. 21]

James A. Michener, (1907-1997) was an American author of more than 40 titles. Michener was known for the meticulous research he did for his work. In an article entitled, "Islam: The Misunderstood Religion," Michener writes:

No other religion in history spread so rapidly as Islam. The West has widely believed that this surge of religion was made possible by the sword. But no modern scholar accepts this idea, and the Quran is explicit in the support of the freedom of conscience.

[Reader's Digest, May 1955, p. 68-70]

John Alden Williams, an African American author, journalist and academic, wrote in his book Islam:

> Islam is much more than a formal religion: it is an integral way of life. In many ways it is a more determining factor in the experience of its followers than any other world religion. The Muslim ("One who submits") lives face to face with God at all times and will introduce no separation between his life and his religion, his politics and his faith. With its strong emphasis on the brotherhood of men cooperating to fulfill the will of God, Islam has become one of the most influential religions in the world today.
> [George Braziller, New York, 1962, inside dust cover]

William Montgomery Watt, a Scottish historian, Emeritus Professor in Arabic and Islamic Studies at the University of Edinburgh, and one of the foremost non-Muslim interpreters of Islam in the West, wrote in his book Islam and Christianity Today:

> I am not a Muslim in the usual sense, though I hope I am a "Muslim" as "one surrendered to God", but I believe that embedded in the Quran and other expressions of the Islamic vision are vast stores of divine truth from which I and other occidentals have still much to learn, and 'Islam is certainly a strong contender for the supplying of the basic framework of the one religion of the future.'
> [London, 1983, p.IX]

Jared Diamond, a world renowned UCLA sociologist and physiologist who won the Pulitzer Prize for his book, Guns, Germs, and Steel, states in it that:

> Medieval Islam was technologically advanced and open to innovation. It achieved far higher literacy rates than in contemporary Europe; it assimilated the legacy of classical Greek civilization to such a degree that many classical books are now known to us only through Arabic copies. It invented windmills, trigonometry, lateen sails and made major advances in metallurgy, mechanical and chemical engineering and irrigation methods. In the middle-ages the flow of technology was overwhelmingly from Islam to Europe rather from Europe to Islam. Only after the 1500's did the net direction of flow begin to reverse. [New York, 1997, p. 253]

Hillary Rodham Clinton, currently the 67th U.S. Secretary of State, serving under President Barack Obama, stated:

Islam is the fastest-growing religion in America, a guide and pillar of stability for many of our people...

[Los Angeles Times, May 31, 1996, p.3]

William Jefferson "Bill" Clinton, the 42nd President of the United States, said in an Iftar Reception at the White House in 1999:

And I thought it was particularly moving that the Imam read the passage from the Koran that said that Allah created nations and tribes that we might know one another, not that we might despise one another.

There's a wonderful passage in the Hebrew Torah, which warns people never to turn aside the stranger, for it is like turning aside the most high God. And the Christian Bible says that people should love their neighbor as themselves. But it's quite wonderful to say that Allah created the nations and tribes that they might know one another better, recognizing that people have to organize their thoughts and categorize their ideas, but that does not mean we should be divided one from another...

Let me say, also, that there is much that the world can learn from Islam. It is now practiced by one of every four people on Earth. Americans are learning more in our schools and universities. Indeed, I remember that our daughter took a course on Islamic history in high school and read large portions of the Koran, and came home at night and educated her parents about it, and later asked us questions about it...

I ask all of you to help with that, to share the wellsprings of your faith with those who are different, to help people understand the values and the humanity that we share in common, and the texture and fabric and fiber and core of the beliefs and practices of Islam...

The Koran also teaches, in addition, to the fact that we should do unto others as we wish to have done to us, and reject for others what we would reject for ourselves, but we should also make a commitment to live in peace...

George W. Bush, the 43rd President of the United States, organized, for the first time in American history an *iftar* (the evening meal that breaks the fast in Ramadhan) meal. This meal was attended by the ambassadors of Muslim countries and the heads of Muslim organizations. In his address, the president commended Islam and called for dialogue and understanding among different faiths:

> Ramadan is a time of fasting and prayer for the Muslim faithful. So tonight we are reminded of God's greatness and His commandments to live in peace and to help neighbors in need... All the world continues to benefit from this faith and its achievements. Ramadan and the upcoming holiday season are a good time for people of different faiths to learn more about each other. And the more we learn, the more we find that many commitments are broadly shared. We share a commitment to family, to protect and love our children. We share a belief in God's justice and man's moral responsibility. And we share the same hope for a future of peace. We have much in common and much to learn from one another.

Barack H. Obama II, the 44th and current President of the United States, stated when he spoke to the Muslim world from Cairo University (Cairo, Egypt) on June 4, 2009:

> America and Islam are not exclusive and need not be in competition. Instead, they overlap and share common principles of justice and progress, tolerance and the dignity of all human beings.

Conclusion

*A*S A READER, YOU HAVE COME a long way and have hope-fully acquired abundant knowledge of Islam. I am also hopeful that you achieved the purpose for which you read this book. In concluding this book, I realize that I have covered more than I initially intended under its title. My purpose was to clarify and explain as fully as I could every necessary concept of Islam, so, at least for now, my reader would not need to go anywhere else.

By now, you can easily comprehend the way of life Islam promotes and the expected behavior of its follower. On the one hand, there are Muslims who profess a strong faith that is evident in their daily lives, and, on the other hand, there are some who do not. With the proper knowledge of Islam, one can easily distinguish them and at the same time see for oneself whether one would like to join or just interact with the Muslim community and the *ummah* at large.

To sum it all up, it is necessary to distinguish between humans and two of their closest associate beings, angels and animals, and, secondly to know the magnetic and opposing pull and power of *aql* (the power to reason; intellect) and *nafs* (inner, base self).

Human beings are neither angels nor animals. However, they do possess both angelic and animalistic qualities. Humans consist of a body and soul and have physical and spiritual needs. They have a unique nature that is considerably different from angels and animals, and they enjoy a variety of different powers compared to them. They are capable of both good and bad actions, while angels and animals are not. They have been endowed with the will to surpass angels or fall below animals if they choose to do so.

Unlike angels and animals, humans are endowed with *aql* and *nafs*. *Aql* wishes man to be successful and *nafs* forces him to be its slave and fulfill its desires. *Aql* is modest and *nafs* extremist. *Aql* pushes towards good and pulls back from bad, and *nafs* does the opposite. The internal struggle and collision between the two causes man to commit good and evil acts, depending on which one takes over him.

Aql has qualities of water (cool, tranquil, satisfying, etc.), and *nafs* has qualities of fire (burning/destructive, corrosive, annihilating, etc.). They are both equally powerful, and whichever one subdues man reigns over him. The demands of *aql* seem dry and discontented, while *nafs'* propositions are entertaining and full of pleasures. *Aql* only promises a better tomorrow, while *nafs* looks for instant gratification. The physical pleasures of the world help *nafs* overcome *aql*, especially of those who lack any religious/spiritual support. Moreover, *nafs* is not alone; its greatest help comes from Iblīs (Satan), the greatest and oldest enemy of man. He helps *nafs* to defeat *aql*, so man ultimately loses and does not achieve his goal. This internal war continues until one becomes dominant over the other.

By sending the divine guidance in the various forms of Islam, through the prophets and by perfecting it through Muhammad ﷺ, His last prophet, Allah ﷻ assisted man's *aql* through Islam. Now, if man's *aql* does not surrender to his *nafs*, it will guide him to the path of Islam. If man sincerely hears and obeys the call of *aql* and controls the reins of his *nafs* to the required extent, he will be successful in the Hereafter. If and when man's *nafs* gets control of the reins of his *aql*, Satan wins, and man loses. This means one more man down the drain of Hell, so to speak.

In brief, this has been the basic philosophy of the teachings of all the prophets of Allah ﷻ sent for mankind's ultimate success. Allah ﷻ chose the name "Islam" because it best suits man's inherent nature and need. Islam means peace, and all over the world rich and poor, healthy and sick, young and old, black and white, powerful and weak, and religious and secular, to say the least, are looking for PEACE. Through utilizing Islam, we achieve true peace, defeat Shaytān (Satan) and please our Lord Allah 🕮 all at the same time. This is what Islam is all about, and this is what a Muslim tries to do throughout his life.

A WORD TO THE WISE

When an individual or a group does harm to a society, feelings of hate and the desire for revenge towards the inflictor(s) are most natural. Wise and just people place and should place the blame where it belongs and not generalize. When facts are known and the inflictor(s)/conspirator(s) are exposed, all unjust accusations, hatreds, confusions, and states of insecurity must be removed for societies to return to normalcy.

Based on my personal experience, Americans have the quality and desire to search for truths, and they realize them once they come across them. As long as the majority of the people of a nation continue to search for and realize truths, they will be able to uphold their good status in the worldwide family of nations.

Islam makes it clear to everyone, Muslims and non-Muslims, that it is not wise to walk on a path that leads to Hell while wishing to end up in Paradise. Islam obligates its followers to act according to its precepts. It is improper and unfair to wish to end up in Paradise simply by thinking oneself to be on the right path while not behaving properly. Islam says to all, "Be mindful that Judgment Day – through which we *all* must pass – is in between us and Heaven and Hell."

Islam does not require its followers to obtain its acceptance through imposition or through any means of coercion – mental or physical, social or political. The basic duty of a Muslim is to spread the knowledge of Islam in the best manner possible and to the extent of one's ability. This is precisely what I have tried to do here.

A REQUEST TO NON-MUSLIM PREACHERS

I request every non-Muslim preacher who preaches peace, love, and coexistence to study Islam closely and thoroughly. A better understanding of Islam by non-Muslims will bridge many gaps between them and the followers of Islam. Then, by working together, we can bring peace and happiness to all. I request them not to criticize any Islamic concept without first knowing the whole structure of Islam. Moreover, Islam should not be held responsible for the actions of some Muslims.

REQUEST FOR COMMENTS

As I said earlier, I consider this book to be a drop in the bucket of attempts to bring worldwide peace, happiness and greater under-standing of Islam. I request my readers to comment on my efforts. Even though I am somewhat aware of my weaknesses, I would like to read and hear about them from you. I thank you in advance.

May Allah ﷻ bless us all.

The Madinah Constitution (Charter)
622 C.E.

In the name of Allah, the Compassionate, the Merciful.

(1) This is a document from Muhammad the prophet (governing the relations) between the believers and Muslims of Quraysh and Yathrib, and those who followed them and joined them and labored with them.

(2) They are one community (*ummah*) to the exclusion of all men.

(3) The Quraysh emigrants according to their present custom shall pay the bloodwit within their number and shall redeem their prisoners with the kindness and justice common among believers.

(4-8) The B. 'Auf (the tribe of 'Auf) according to their present custom shall pay the bloodwit they paid in heatheism; every section shall redeem its prisoners with the kindness and justice common among believers. The B. Sa ida (the tribe of Saida), the B. 'l-Harith (the tribe of 'l-Harith), and the B. Jusham (the tribe of Jusham), and the B. al-Najjar (the tribe of al-Najjar) likewise.

(9-11) The B. 'Amr B. 'Auf, the B. al-Nabit and the B. al-'Aus likewise.

(12)(a) Believers shall not leave anyone destitute among them by not paying his redemption money or bloodwit in kindness. (b) A believer shall not take as an ally the freedman of another Muslim against him.

(13) The Allah-fearing believers shall be against the rebellious or him who seeks to spread injustice, sin, animosity, or corruption between believers; the hand of every man shall be against him even if he be a son of one of them.

(14) A believer shall not slay a believer for the sake of an unbeliever, nor shall he aid an unbeliever against a believer.

(15) Allah's protection is one; the least of them may give protection to a stranger on their behalf. Believers are friends one to the other to the exclusion of outsiders.

(16) To the Jew who follows us belongs help and equality. He shall not be wronged nor shall his enemies be aided.

(17) The peace of the believers is indivisible. No separate peace shall be made when believers are fighting in the way of Allah. Conditions must be fair and equitable to all.

(18) In every foray a rider must take another behind him.

(19) The believers must avenge the blood of one another shed in the way of Allah.

(20)(a) The Allah-fearing believers enjoy the best and most upright guidance. (b) No polytheist shall take the property of a person of Quraysh under his protection, nor shall he intervene against a believer.

(21) Whoever is convicted of killing a believer without good reason shall be subject to retaliation unless the next of kin is satisfied (with blood-money), and the believers shall be against him as one man, and they are bound to take action against him.

(22) It shall not be lawful for a believer who holds by what is in this document and believes in Allah and the Last Day to help an evil-doer or to shelter him. The curse of Allah and His anger on the Day of Resurrection will be upon him if he does, and neither repentance nor ransom will be received from him.

(23) Whenever you differ about a matter, it must be referred to Allah and to Muhammad.

(24) The Jews shall contribute to the cost of war so long as they are fighting alongside the believers.

(25) The Jews of the B. 'Auf are one community with the believers (the Jews have their religion and the Muslims have theirs), their freedmen and their persons, except those who behave unjustly and sinfully, for they hurt but themselves and their families.

(26-35) The same applies to the Jews of the B. al-Najjar, B. al-Harith, B. Sai ida, B. Jusham, B. al-Aus, B. Tha'laba, and the Jafna, a clan of the

Tha'laba and the B. al-Shutayba. Loyalty is a protection against treachery. The freedmen of Tha'laba are as themselves. The close friends of the Jews are as themselves.

(36) None of them shall go out to war save with the permission of Muhammad, but he shall not be prevented from taking revenge for a wound. He who slays a man without warning slays himself and his household, unless it be one who has wronged him, for Allah will accept that.

(37) The Jews must bear their expenses and the Muslims their expenses. Each must help the other against anyone who attacks the people of this document. They must seek mutual advice and consultation, and loyalty is a protection against treachery. A man is not liable for his ally's misdeeds. The wronged must be helped.

(38) The Jews must pay with the believers so long as war lasts.

(39) Yathrib (Madinah) shall be a sanctuary for the people of this document.

(40) A stranger under protection shall be as his host—doing no harm and committing no crime.

(41) A woman shall only be given protection with the consent of her family.

(42) If any dispute or controversy likely to cause trouble should arise it must be referred to Allah and to Muhammad, the Messenger of Allah. Allah accepts what is nearest to piety and goodness in this document.

(43) Quraysh and their helpers shall not be given protection.

(44) The contracting parties are bound to help one another against any attack on Yathrib.

(45) (a) If they are called to make peace and maintain it they must do so; and if they make a similar demand on the Muslims it must be carried out except in the case of a holy war.

(b) Every one shall have his portion from the side to which he belongs.

(46) The Jews of al-Aus, their freedmen and themselves have the same standing with the people of this document in purely loyalty from the people of this document. Loyalty is a protection against treachery. He who acquires aught acquires it for himself. Allah approves of this document.

(47) This deed will not protect the unjust and the sinner. The man who goes forth to fight and the man who stays at home in the city are safe unless he has been unjust and sinned. Allah is the protector of the good and Allah-fearing man and Muhammad is the Messenger of Allah.

This text, with minor editorial revisions, is taken from A. Guillaume, The Life of Muhammad — A Translation of Ishaq's Sirat Rasul Allah, Oxford University Press, Karachi, 1955; pp. 231-233. Numbering added.

Prophet Muhammad's Last Sermon

<u>Date delivered</u>: 632 C.E., 9th day of Dhul Hijjah, 10 A.H.
(after the migration to Madinah) in the 'Uranah Valley of
Mount Arafat.

After praising and thanking Allah ﷻ, he said:

O People, listen well to my words, for I do not know whether, after this year, I shall ever be amongst you again. Therefore listen to what I am saying to you very carefully, and TAKE THESE WORDS TO THOSE WHO COULD NOT BE PRESENT HERE TODAY.

O people, just as you regard this month, this day, this city as sacred, so regard the life and property of every Muslim as a sacred trust. Return the goods entrusted to you to their rightful owners. Treat others justly so that no one would be unjust to you. Remember that you will indeed meet your LORD, and that HE will indeed reckon your deeds. Allah has forbidden you to take usury *(riba)*, therefore all *riba* obligation shall henceforth be waived. Your capital, however, is yours to keep. You will neither inflict nor suffer inequity. Allah has judged that there shall be no *riba* and that all the *riba* due to 'Abbas ibn 'Abd al Muttalib shall henceforth be waived.

Every right arising out of homicide in pre-Islamic days is henceforth waived and the first such right that I waive is that arising from the murder of Rabi'ah ibn al-Harith ibn 'Abd al-Muttalib.

O men, the unbelievers indulge in tampering with the calendar in order to make permissible that which Allah forbade, and to forbid that which Allah has made permissible. With Allah the months are twelve in number. Four of them are sacred, three of these are successive and one occurs singly between the months of Jumada and Sha'ban. Beware of the devil, for the safety of your religion. He has lost all hope that he will ever be able to lead you astray in big things, so beware of following him in small things.

O people, it is true that you have certain rights over your women, but they also have rights over you. Remember that you have taken them as your wives only under Allah's trust and with His permission. If they abide by your right, then to them belongs the right to be fed and clothed in kindness. Treat your women well, and be kind to them, for they are your partners and committed helpers. It is your right that they do not make friends with anyone of whom you do not approve, as well as never to be unchaste.

O people, listen to me in earnest, worship Allah (The One Creator of the universe), perform your five daily prayers (*salāh*), fast during the month of Ramadan, and give your financial obligation (*zakāh*) of your wealth. Perform Hajj if you can afford to.

All mankind is from Adam and Eve; an Arab has no superiority over a non-Arab, nor does a non-Arab have any superiority over an Arab. Also, a white has no superiority over a black, nor does a black have any superiority over a white, except by piety and good action. Learn that every Muslim is a brother to every Muslim and that the Muslims constitute one brotherhood. Nothing shall be legitimate to a Muslim that belongs to a fellow Muslim unless it was given freely and willingly. Do not, therefore, do injustice to yourselves.

Remember, one day you will appear before Allah (The Creator) and you will answer for your deeds. So beware, do not stray from the path of righteousness after I am gone.

O people, NO PROPHET OR MESSENGER WILL COME AFTER ME AND NO NEW FAITH WILL BE BORN. Reason well, therefore, O people, and understand the words that I convey to you. I am leaving you with the Book of Allah (the QUR'AN) and my *SUNNAH*; if you follow them, you will never go astray.

All those who listen to me shall pass on my words to others and those to others again, and may the last ones understand my words better than those who listen to me directly. Be my witness, O Allah, that I have conveyed Your message to Your people.

APPENDIX III
——————————

Letters from the Prophet Muhammad ﷺ

In the Name of Allah, the Most Beneficent, the Most Merciful.

FROM MUHAMMAD, THE MESSENGER OF ALLAH
TO CHOSROES, KING OF PERSIA.

Peace be upon him who follows true guidance, believes in Allah and His Messenger and testifies that there is no god but Allah Alone with no associate, and that Muhammad is His slave and Messenger. I invite you to accept the religion of Allah. I am the Messenger of Allah sent to all people in order that I may infuse fear of Allah in every living person, and that the charge may be proved against those who reject the Truth. Accept Islam as your religion so that you may live in security, otherwise, you will be responsible for all the sins of the Magians."

'Abdullah bin Hudhafa As-Sahmi was chosen to carry the letter. This envoy carried it to the king of Bahrain but it is uncertain if the latter dispatched to Chosroes by one of his men or chose 'Abdullah himself.

The proud monarch was enraged by the style of the letter as the name of the Prophet had been put above his own name. He tore the letter into shreds and forthwith dictated a command to his viceroy in Yemen to send a couple of troopers to arrest the Prophet and bring him to his presence. The governor, Bazan by name, immediately sent two men to Madinah for the purpose. As soon as the men reached Madinah, the Prophet was informed by a Divine Revelation that Pervez, the emperor of Persia, had been murdered by his son. The Prophet disclosed to them the news and they were stunned. He added asking them to tell their new monarch that Islam would prevail every-where and outstrip the sovereignty of Chosroes himself. They hurried back to Bazan and communicated to him what they heard. Meanwhile, Sherweh, the new monarch sent a letter to Bazan confirming the news and bidding him to stop any procedures as regards the Prophet till further notice. Bazan, together with the Persians in Yemen, went into the folds of Islam, and gladly signified his adhesion to the Prophet.

[Fath Al-Bari 8/127,128]

Al-Bukhari gave a long narration of the contents of the letter sent by the Prophet to Hercules, King of the Byzantines:

In the Name of Allah, the Most Beneficent, the Most Merciful.

FROM MUHAMMAD, THE SLAVE OF ALLAH AND HIS MESSENGER TO HERCULES, KING OF THE BYZANTINES

Blessed are those who follow true guidance. I invite you to embrace Islam so that you may live in security. If you come within the fold of Islam, Allah will give you double reward, but in case you turn your back upon it, then the burden of the sins of all your people shall fall on your shoulders.

Say, "O People of the Book, come to that which is common between us and you, which is that we worship none except Allah and do not believe in anything to be His partner, and may any of us not make anyone their lord, leaving aside Allah. So if they turn their face, then you people say, "Bear witness that we all are Muslims." • [Qur'an 3:64]

The Muslim envoy, Dihyah bin Khalifah Al-Kalbi, was ordered to hand the letter over to king of Busra, who would in turn, send it to Caesar.

Incidentally, Abu Sufyan bin Harb, who by that time had not embraced Islam, was summoned to the court and Hercules asked him many questions about Muhammad and the religion which he preached. The testimony which this avowed enemy of the Prophet gave regarding the personal excellence of the Prophet's character and the good that Islam was doing the human race, left Hercules wonder-struck.

Glossary

A'MEEN—recited at the end of a prayer, for its fulfillment

AMEEN—trustworthy; a title granted to the Prophet ﷺ

AHADITH *(sing. hadīth)*—sayings of the Prophet ﷺ

AHLE SUNNAH WA JAMA'A—Muslims who believe in Islam as taught by the Prophet ﷺ. They hold fast to the *sunnah* of the Prophet and of the holy Companions.

AL-HIJRI—the year of the Islamic calendar that began with the migration of Prophet Muhammad ﷺ from Makkah to Madinah, on 12/13 September, 622 C.E.

ALHAMDULILLAH—Arabic for "All praise is due to Allah ﷻ"

ALIM—a knowledgeable Muslim; a scholar

ALLAH—the Almighty Creator, from Whom all power and energy is derived

AQEEDAH—basic beliefs and principles

ASAR—the time of day between *Zuhar* (noon) and *Maghrib* (sunset), and when *Asar Salāh* is performed

ASMA-E-HUSNA—99 Names of Allah representing His qualities and attributes.

AWLIYA-ALLAH—the friends of Allah ﷻ, with whom Allah ﷻ chose to share His secrets. They preserve Allah's secrets and carry out duties assigned to them.

AYAH *(pl. ayaat)*—a verse from the holy Qur'an

DEEN—the way of life; religion.

EID—Arabic for "festivity." There are two eids: Eid-ul-Fitr, a Muslim holiday that marks the end of Ramadan, and Eid-ul-Adha, the day of sacrificing animals in the name of Allah ﷻ to remember and honor the sacrifice of Prophet Ibrahim (Abraham) عليه السلام and his son, Ismail (Ishmael) عليه السلام.

FAJR—the time of day between dawn and sunrise; Fajr Salāh is performed within it

FĀJIR—sinner

FALAH—Arabic for 'ultimate success, happiness, and well-being'

FARDH—compulsory; actions that are incumbent upon a Muslim

FĀSIQ—transgressor

FATWA *(pl. fatawa)*—religious edict; injunction

FATIHA—the name of the 1st chapter of the holy Quran; invocation for the dead; The Opening

FITNA—mischief; to cause chaos; to disturb peace; to corrupt genuine teachings of Islam; to cause friction; to divide and to confuse

G

GHUSL—bathing/showering according to the rules set forth by the Prophet 鵜; to wash and clean after being in the state of impurity.

H

HADITH—sayings and traditions of the Prophet Muhammad 鵜.

HADITH-E-QUDSI—the sacred *hadīth*, they have a particularly important status because their meaning is entirely from Allah 鵜, while the wording is that of Prophet Muhammad 鵜.

HAFIZ—one who memorizes the entire Quran by heart

HAJJ—the holy pilgrimage to Makkah in the month of Dhul-Hijjah (the 12th month of the Islamic calendar); the 5th pillar of Islam; an obligation upon every able Muslim to fulfill, at least once in his or her lifetime.

HALĀL—that which is permissible; allowed

HANAFI—one of the four schools of thought of the Ahle-Sunnat wa Jama'a, as established by Imam Abu Hanīfa, one of the greatest Muslim scholars and jurists.

HARĀM—that which is forbidden; unlawful; restricted.

HIJRA—the emigration of the Prophet 鵜 from Makkah to Madinah

IBLĪS—proper name of Shaytān, the devil; open enemy of man as revealed to us by Allah 鵜 and from whom we should protect our self and others

IMAN—unshakeable faith; to believe in the Oneness of Allah through the teachings of the Prophet Muhammad 🕌 and to believe that the Prophet Muhammad 🕌 is the Final Prophet of Allah 🕌.

INSHA'ALLAH—"Allah willing"; recited by Muslims whenever something is to be undertaken in the future.

ISHA—the time between Maghrib and Fajr in which *Isha Salāh* is performed

ISLAM—means "submission," to surrender oneself to Allah 🕌. An adherent of Islam is a Muslim, meaning "one who submits (to Allah 🕌)."

ISRA WAL MI'RAJ—the night of ascension of the holy Prophet 🕌 to the heavens to physically meet with Allah 🕌 and see His divine dominion; the Prophet 🕌 received the gift of five daily *salāh* for his followers to perform and prepare for the Hereafter

J

JANĀZA—funeral procession of a Muslim

JIHAD—to struggle in the way of Allah 🕌 and for the sake of Allah 🕌 alone

JINN—a creation of Allah 🕌 made of fire; invisible to the human eye; of whom only a few are faithful, but the majority are evil

K

KA'BA—the House of Allah 🕌 (Makkah, Saudi Arabia)

KAFIR *(pl. kuffar)*—disbeliever; heretic; one who denies Allah 🕌, Muhammad 🕌 and Islam

KALIMAH—an Islamic creed

KHALĪFA—caliph; vicegerent; deputy; representative

KHATIMUN-NABIYYEEN—Seal of the Prophets; title of the Final Prophet of Allah, Muhammad 🕌

KUFR—infidelity; heresy; Allah 🕌 abhors this belief of man

KUN—'Be'; Allah's command that brings forth whatever Allah 🕌 wishes

L

LAUH-E-MAHFOOZ—the Sacred Tablet on which the destinies of the worlds are written.

M

MADINAH AL-MUNAWWARAH—the second holiest city of Islam, and the resting place of Prophet Muhammad 🕌.

MADRASSA—Islamic school; academy; institution for Islamic education

MAGHRIB—time of day between *Asar* and *Isha*; *Maghrib Salāh* is performed during this time

MAKKAH—city in Saudi Arabia; the first holiest city of Islam; established by the Honorable Prophet Ibrahim (Abraham) ﷺ

MALAK *(pl. Malaika)*—angel; creature Allah made with divine resplendence (nur)

MALAK-UL-MAUT—the Angel of Death

MASJID *(pl. masajid)*—place of worship for Muslims; Allah's ﷻ house

MASJID-E-NABWI—Masjid of the holy Prophet Muhammad ﷺ in Madinah

MASLAK—school of thought; beliefs

MOMIN *(pl. momineen)*—believer; faithful; one who has complete faith in Islam and practices it with strict punctuality

MUHAMMAD ﷺ—is the Prophet of Islam and the Final Messenger and Prophet of Allah ﷻ. The name Muhammad literally means, "One who is overwhelmingly praised"

MUHARRAM—the first month of the Islamic calendar

MUNĀFIQ—hypocrite

MURTAD—apostate

MUSHRIK—polytheist; idolater

N

NABI—prophet; one who is entrusted with divine secrets and discloses them whenever Allah ﷻ wants him to

NIJĀSAT—the state of impurity as described by *sharia* (Islamic law); dirt; filth

NUR—light

Q

QARI—reciter of the holy Quran

QASR—to cut short; people who travel a distance of 57.5 miles from their home may perform *qasr salāh* (a shortened form of *salāh*)

QAZA—to make up for missed *salāh*

QIBLA—direction in which Muslims turn in prayer, the holy Ka'ba.

QUR'AN—is the central religious text of Islam. The Qur'an is the book of divine guidance and direction for mankind, and the text (in the original Arabic) to be the final divine revelation of Allah ﷻ as revealed to Prophet Muhammad ﷺ

QURAYSH—the old, powerful tribe from Makkah.

R

RAHEEM—merciful; one of the 99 Names of Allah

RAHMAN—compassionate; one of the 99 Names of Allah

RASUL—Allah's messenger.

RASULLULLAH —the Messenger of Allah, Muhammad

RIVAYAT—tradition; narration(s).

RUH—soul; spirit; Allah's divine command, energy, power

S

SADIQ—truthful

SAFAR AL-MUZAFFAR—the 2nd month of the Islamic calendar

SAHABA—the holy Companions of *Rasullullah*

SAHIH—the authentic form of *hadīth*

SALĀH—the five daily and obligatory prayers

SAUM—to fast; the third pillar of Islam, without which faith is incomplete.

SHAFA'Ī—the school of thought established by *Imam* Shafa'ī

SHARIA—Islamic jurisprudence, law

SHAYTĀN—(see Iblīs)

SUNNAH—spiritual guide; what Prophet Muhammad actually said and did with regard to religion

SURAH—a chapter of the holy Qur'an, (there are a total of 114)

T

TAHĀRA—state of complete purity

TALĀQ—divorce; to separate

TARĪQA—spiritual path to Allah

TASAWWUF—mysticism, Sufism; the spiritual aspect of Islam

TAWHĪD—the Oneness of Allah

TAYAMMUM—to cleanse oneself with clean sand, rocks, etc. in the absence of water to make *wudu* (ablution).

U

UMMAH—believers of Islam; the faithful community of Muslims

W

WITR—the *Waajib* with *Salaat-ul-Isha*.

WUDU—ablution performed with water to begin an act of worship (i.e. salāh, recitation of the holy Quran, etc.)

ZAKAT—obligatory charity equal to 02.5% of one's accumulated wealth, as well as a certain percentage of one's agricultural produce

ZUHAR—the obligatory prayer due at noon